D1041790

"An engaging and entertaining account of three of the most colorful characters involved in the American Revolution. It is hard to believe that their story is true, but it is." —Gordon S. Wood, author of the Pulitzer Prize–winning *The Radicalism of the American Revolution*

"*Unlikely Allies* is an amazing story compellingly told. I kept turning the pages in eagerness to find out what would happen next. Conspiracies abounded, and hardly anyone was what he or she seemed. If the eighteenth century in Europe was an era of Enlightenment, it was also an Age of Deception. Yet thanks to Joel Paul's sympathetic portrayal, Silas Deane emerges as an unsung hero of the American Revolution." —Robert A. Gross, Bancroft Prize–winning author of *The Minutemen and Their World*

"Ever tire of worshipful accounts of the Founding Fathers' wisdom and fortitude? Then try this wonderful book about how an American businessman and two Frenchmen, a dramatist and a spy, came to their aid. A rollicking romp as well as a serious history, it reminds us of the role of duplicity, hypocrisy and corruption, and of human frailty and chance, in safeguarding the American Revolution." —William Taubman, Pulitzer Prize-winning author of *Khrushchev: The Man and His Era*

"Rollicking and surprising, this is history as it really happened—as it was made by all-too-human actors. *Unlikely Allies* is a lively read and an important counterpoint to Founder hagiography." —Evan Thomas, author of the bestselling *Sea of Thunder: Four Naval Commanders and the Last Sea War* and *John Paul Jones*

UNLIKELY ALLIES

HOW A MERCHANT,

A PLAYWRIGHT, AND A SPY

SAVED THE AMERICAN REVOLUTION

JOEL RICHARD PAUL

RIVERHEAD BOOKS

New York

RIVERHEAD BOOKS
Published by the Penguin Group
Penguin Group (USA) Inc.
375 Hudson Street, New York, New York 10014, USA
Penguin Group (Canada), 90 Eglinton Avenue East, Suite 700, Toronto, Ontario M4P 2Y3, Canada
(a division of Pearson Penguin Canada Inc.)
Penguin Books Ltd., 80 Strand, London WC2R 0RL, England
Penguin Group Ireland, 25 St. Stephen's Green, Dublin 2, Ireland (a division of Penguin Books Ltd.)
Penguin Group (Australia), 250 Camberwell Road, Camberwell, Victoria 3124, Australia
(a division of Pearson Australia Group Pty. Ltd.)
Penguin Books India Pvt. Ltd., 11 Community Centre, Panchsheel Park, New Delhi—110 017, India
Penguin Group (NZ), 67 Apollo Drive, Rosedale, North Shore 0632, New Zealand
(a division of Pearson New Zealand Ltd.)
Penguin Books (South Africa) (Pty.) Ltd., 24 Sturdee Avenue, Rosebank, Johannesburg 2196,
South Africa

Penguin Books Ltd., Registered Offices: 80 Strand, London WC2R 0RL, England

The publisher does not have any control over and does not assume any responsibility for author or third-party websites or their content.

First Riverhead hardcover edition: October 2009
First Riverhead trade paperback edition: November 2010
Riverhead trade paperback ISBN: 978-1-59448-487-2

The Library of Congress has catalogued the Riverhead hardcover edition as follows:

Paul, Joel R.
Unlikely allies : how a merchant, a playwright, and a spy saved the American Revolution /
Joel Richard Paul.
p.   cm.
Includes bibliographical references and index.
ISBN 978-1-59448-883-2
1. United States—History—Revolution, 1775–1783—Secret service.   2. United States—
History—Revolution, 1775–1783—Participation, French.   3. United States—Foreign
relations—1775–1783.   4. Deane, Silas, 1737–1789.   5. Beaumarchais, Pierre Augustin Caron de,
1732–1799.   6. Eon de Beaumont, Charles Geneviève Louis Auguste André Timothée d', 1728–
1810.   7. Arms transfers—United States—History—18th century.   8. Arms transfers—France—
History—18th century.   9. Saratoga Campaign, N.Y., 1777.   I. Title.
E279.P38   2009   2009034986
973.3'85—dc22

PRINTED IN THE UNITED STATES OF AMERICA

10   9   8   7   6   5   4   3   2   1

For Jane, John, Bertrand, and Micky

CONTENTS

Perhaps Chance is God's pseudonym, when He
does not wish to sign His name.

—THÉOPHILE GAUTIER

INTRODUCTION

In 1776, the lives of three extraordinary characters—a Connecticut merchant, a French playwright, and a cross-dressing French spy—collided to produce the Franco-American alliance. This is the story of how Silas Deane, Caron de Beaumarchais, and the Chevalier d'Eon saved the American Revolution.

They were unlikely allies and improbable heroes. Each rose to prominence at a young age by force of wit and energy, and each enjoyed wealth and social standing as a member of the elite. Deane, the son of a blacksmith, became a leading figure in Connecticut politics and an influential member of the Continental Congress. Beaumarchais, a French watchmaker and musician, achieved fame as the author of *The Barber of Seville*. D'Eon, a child prodigy whose public life belied a dark secret, was a decorated French soldier, diplomat, and spy. Each risked his career to pursue a grand design, abandoning the comfort of an insider to become a social outlaw. Though each suffered disgrace and poverty, they persevered with ingenuity and moxie.

Before Silas Deane became Congress's secret emissary to France, he was a merchant and shopkeeper who had lived his entire life in

Connecticut and could not speak a word of French. Benjamin Franklin chose Deane for this delicate diplomatic mission because he considered Deane such an unlikely choice that the British spies in France would never suspect him. Months before Franklin got there, Deane arrived in Paris on the eve of the Declaration of Independence. With little cash, few resources, and no friends or family, Deane improvised. He eluded would-be assassins who hounded him; managed the mercenaries, privateers, and saboteurs who sought to help him; and fought off American "patriots" who plotted to destroy him.

Deane succeeded with the aid of the comic writer Beaumarchais. Together they conspired to arm the Americans at a time when the Revolution's prospects seemed dim. Through their romantic misadventures and uncanny bad luck, they formed a friendship that became the foundation of the Franco-American alliance.

And none of this would have been possible without the leavening influence of the flamboyant Chevalier d'Eon. The chevalier's disguises, gender confusion, and eccentricity made him notorious. Voltaire once famously called the Chevalier d'Eon "A nice problem for history." And when he began blackmailing the French king, d'Eon became a problem that only Beaumarchais could resolve. In the end, d'Eon would unwittingly become the catalyst that persuaded Louis XVI to arm the Americans against the British.

Despite their prodigious intelligence, courage, and spunk, Deane, Beaumarchais, and d'Eon were vain, arrogant, impatient, and at times bad tempered. Their government careers were cut short because they flouted social convention and challenged authority. Beaumarchais once wrote, "If you are mediocre and you grovel, you shall succeed." By that measure, they were all prodigious failures.

This is not a conventional narrative of the American Revolution. The conventional story is that Ben Franklin was our first emissary to the court of Louis XVI and that through charm, cunning, and persistence Franklin obtained arms and forged an alliance with France. This is not that story. In fact, Franklin is really an accessory after the fact. Long before Franklin set foot in France, Deane had already formed the foundation of our alliance. Most histories of the American Revolution ignore Deane. If he is mentioned at all, he is usually described as a scoundrel who tried to enrich himself at public expense, a puppet of the British Crown, or a traitor who betrayed the Revolution's ideals. But Deane is the hero of this story. While he was accused of many crimes, none was ever proved. He gave his wealth, his honor, and his life to his country, and for his troubles he has been either reviled or forgotten, until now.

We are accustomed to reading about the great men who won our Independence. We know that the Revolution was also inspired by the ideals of the Enlightenment and realized by mass social movements. While it is true that great men, great ideas, and great movements all influence history, history is never so predetermined. We know from our lived experience the impact of random events, chance meetings, and peripheral characters. So too, the arc of history is often diverted from its intended trajectory. These three intertwined lives tell us much about the power of personality, the complexity of human motivation, and the accidental path of history.

SILAS DEANE
by William Johnston (1732–1772), ca. 1766
Photograph © Ruth Hanks
Reprinted with permission of the
Webb-Deane-Stevens Museum

ONE

THE MERCHANT

London, September 1789

H e certainly looked like a man of no importance. The old man wore a shabby cloth coat and tattered boots as if he had just left debtors' prison. His clothes hung loosely on his bony frame. Despite the man's destitute appearance Captain Davis helped him aboard the *Boston Packet* and showed him around the ship with great deference. Like other packets, the *Boston Packet* was primarily a mail ship that also carried goods and a few passengers on its regular route between Boston and London. But this ship was built for speed. With good weather it could make the trip to Boston in about four weeks.

On the morning of Tuesday, September 22, 1789, the ship set out from Gravesend, just south of London, its sails filling as it moved swiftly down the Thames. The old man stood on the quarterdeck, looking back toward London. A few minutes later he was talking with Captain Davis. He seemed animated, even excited, then suddenly he turned and stumbled into the captain's arms. There were shouts as he collapsed on the quarterdeck. He tried to speak, but his words were slurred and incoherent. He appeared to be out of breath. Captain Davis signaled some of his men to carry the passenger below.

They gently laid the old man down on a bed. He looked crazed and smelled bad. His eyes were unfocused and moved rapidly as if he saw things that were invisible. Despite the cool autumn weather he was sweating profusely. One of the hands watched over him as the ship proceeded out into the Strait of Dover, hugging the coastline as it rounded England. Another passenger, a Mr. Hopkins, knew the old man and waited anxiously by his side. Within minutes the old man became delirious. Soon, his breathing grew rapid and shallow. After an hour he lapsed into unconsciousness. By two o'clock that afternoon, Silas Deane was dead.

When men died aboard ship, burial at sea was customary. But instead Captain Davis brought the ship into the nearest port, Deal, a tiny village on the southeastern tip of England just a few miles north of Dover's white cliffs. One of the crew gathered up Deane's personal items. In his single bag, Deane had few personal papers, no jewelry, and very little clothing. Among his paltry belongings the hand discovered a gold snuffbox encrusted with diamonds surrounding a portrait of the French king Louis XVI. His eyes widened; it must have been worth at least a hundred guineas. Was the old man a thief?

Captain Davis disembarked at Deal with Mr. Hopkins and the body. Mr. Hopkins agreed to stay behind to arrange for a pauper's burial in an unmarked grave at St. George's churchyard. Mr. Hopkins offered to inform Deane's family in Connecticut, and the captain gave him Deane's belongings, including the jeweled snuffbox, to return to the family. Then the captain rejoined his ship and headed back to sea.

When news of Deane's death reached London, there was a flurry of colorful obituaries. One newspaper reported:

> Silas Deane, who died a few days since, at Deal in Kent, is one of the most remarkable instances of the versatility of fortune which have occurred perhaps within the present century.... [A]t an early period of the American war, he was selected by Congress as one of the representatives of America at the Court of France.... Having... been accused of embezzling large sums of money intrusted to his care for the purchase of arms and ammunition, Mr. Deane sought an asylum in this country, where his habits of life, at first economical, and afterwards penurious in the extreme, amply refuted the malevolence of his enemies.

The Gentleman's Magazine described Deane's demise with an ironic twist:

> Thus lived and died his Excellency Silas Deane, whose name is rendered immortal in the calendar of policy by having ruined himself and family, and deranged France and America with the charming words, *Liberty, Constitution* and *Rights.*

When Thomas Jefferson heard that Deane was on his way back to America, he wrote to James Madison in Virginia: "He is a wretched monument of the consequences of a departure from right."

No one had any reason to suspect that Deane had been murdered.

SILAS DEANE WAS born Christmas Eve 1737, in Ledyard, Connecticut, a sleepy farming town along the Mystic River, near the southern coast of the colony. His father, also named Silas, was a blacksmith who worked hard for little money. Everyone in Ledyard depended on him. The smithy was a noisy hub of activity. The elder Silas forged, repaired, and customized every form of metalwork— tools, pots, nails, spikes, ploughs, hoes, kitchen utensils, sleighs, and horseshoes. As the forge blasted heat and belched smoke, he pounded the hot metal into shape. Local children played around the shop with metal rings shaped from discarded scraps, listening to the incessant clang of hammers and marveling at the shower of sparks bursting into the smoky air. The blacksmith shop was filled with curiosities—betty lamps, tree chisels, and husking pegs. In the summer, farmers waited outside under the shade of an elm while their horses were shod, or their plows fixed. In the winter, customers crowded inside to warm themselves around the charcoal. Patrons drank, sang, and caroused. They traded stories and news of the Indian wars, crop conditions, and local politics.

The younger Silas was a precocious and intelligent child, inclined more toward reading than working with his father and brothers around the forge. As a middle son, he had no hope of inheriting his father's property. He learned to blend in and to adjust to the expectations of others. He was gregarious, with an easy smile and a ready laugh. His parents foresaw that he might have greater opportunities in life and prepared him for an education. It is not known whether Deane attended a locally funded grammar school, or whether he was tutored by his minister or a private schoolmaster. In any case, by the time he was seventeen, he could read and speak both Greek and Latin.

DEANE'S OPPORTUNITY to escape the smoky labors of the blacksmith's life came one autumn day in 1754. Deane and his father rode to New Haven, about fifty miles southwest of Ledyard, to seek admission for the boy to Yale College. To enroll at the college, he was examined by Yale's president, the Reverend Thomas Clap, and some of the faculty, who found the blacksmith's son able to "Read, Construe and Parce Tully, Virgil and the Greek Testament; and to Write True Latin in Prose and to understand the Rules of Prosodia, and Common Arithematic." The examiners were sufficiently impressed that they awarded Deane a full scholarship.

President Clap required all students to study Latin, Greek, and Hebrew, and to declaim in one of these languages every Friday before the assembled class. Students were expected to speak Latin even in daily conversation. Deane studied logic, rhetoric, geometry, geography, natural philosophy, astronomy, and metaphysics. He read Homer, Euclid, Livy, Horace, Cicero, Tacitus, Locke, and Newton.

PRESIDENT CLAP WAS a strict Congregationalist who required his faculty and students to adhere to religious orthodoxy in every aspect of the school. Deane's life at the small college was rigorous and austere. He lived with seventy or so other students in ascetic accommodations in Connecticut Hall. The same building also contained the college's faculty, library, and classrooms. Deane rose at six to say prayers before a light breakfast of a quarter-loaf of bread. He carried water and firewood to the upperclassmen's rooms before donning his gown and hat for classes, which ran until dinner at noon. At dinner, the students ate a small portion of meat disguised in a nondescript sauce and served with cold bread and warm beer. They had another three hours of lectures until afternoon prayers at four. For supper the students ate apple pie and drank more beer and continued studying until lights-out at nine sharp. The college forbade any cards, dice, or rowdiness. Most of the other young men at Yale were sons of preachers or prosperous farmers. Some came from families that had founded the Connecticut colony a century before. Deane lacked the social advantages of his classmates, but he was determined to become a gentleman and worked hard at his studies. Life around his father's forge had taught him how to tell a good story, and his warm personality and high spirits won him friends easily.

Deane's lively intellect quickly impressed his tutors. He excelled in all subjects, but was especially distinguished in Latin. At his graduation, in 1758, he won a fellowship to continue his studies at Yale toward a master's degree in theology, which he completed in 1760. Unlike many of his classmates, Deane chose not to pursue a career as a clergyman. Greek, Latin, and metaphysics all interested him, but "there should be a due Limit set to these Inquiries," as one of his textbooks counseled. "[A] Genius of active Curiosity may waste too many hours in the more abstruse Parts of these Subjects, which God and his Country demand to be apply'd to the Studies of the Law." Deane embraced this advice and decided to read for the bar.

While studying the law, Deane earned a living as a schoolteacher in Hartford, the bustling capital of the colony. Hartford was growing rapidly as a gateway to western New England. Sloops navigated up the Connecticut River, carrying cloth, spice, saltpeter, tea, molasses, sugar, wine, and slaves, and returned downstream laden with timber, barrel staves, horses, rum, apples, salted fish, pork, flour, corn, and rye, bound for markets in the West Indies and Europe. Rich merchants built large houses along the leafy bank of the Connecticut River, which wound magisterially through town. Deane had never seen so much wealth before. His training in theology had not extinguished a desire for material success. Walking along the river, Deane envied the fine houses of the "River Gods." The humble life of a schoolmaster could not satisfy his desire for greater wealth and social standing.

IN 1761, Deane entered the Connecticut bar and opened a law office in Wethersfield, a few miles downriver from Hartford. Wethersfield's prosperous merchants and farmers needed lawyers to settle
debts, transfer property, and draft wills, and there were few other
lawyers around. Deane's law office was centrally located, opposite
the commons, in a small wooden building. Just up the street from
his law office was a handsome white Congregational meetinghouse
recently completed and Joseph Webb's feed and dry goods store,
housed in a large whitewashed building.

Joseph Webb was one of Deane's first clients. He lived in the biggest and most stylish Georgian house on the town commons, di-
agonally across from the store and Deane's law office. Webb enjoyed
a monopoly in town. As Wethersfield grew, so did his dry goods
business. Now old and ailing, Webb retained Deane to draft his will,
and he died just months later. The will named Deane as executor of
the estate, and in that capacity, Deane became a frequent visitor to
Webb's widow, Mehitabel, who had inherited her husband's profitable business. Mehitabel was five years senior to Deane and looked
even older, with an angular face and severe features. At twenty-six,
Deane was a well-mannered gentleman of average build, boyishly
handsome with flashing dark eyes, auburn hair, a high forehead,
delicate features, and a strong chin. The widow Webb found Deane's
confident presence reassuring and welcomed his visits, which gradually increased in length. Despite her plain face, age, and a brood of
six children, Silas found much to admire in the rich widow.

WITHIN A YEAR OF Joseph's passing, Mehitabel was pregnant
with Deane's child, and they quickly married. Eight months later,

Mehitabel bore Deane a son, Jesse. Jesse, who would be Deane's only child, suffered from several diseases, including rickets, in his infancy, and, as a consequence, developed numerous infirmities throughout his life. His body was contorted and covered with ulcerations. His mind and speech were slow, and he remained dependent on his family throughout much of his life. Life in colonial New England was difficult enough for the able-bodied; a child who was physically and mentally disabled was considered a drain on society, and his disability was often viewed as divine retribution. Surely, a child who did not have the capacity to comprehend Scripture could not be redeemed.

Deane closed his modest law practice to devote himself to managing the Webb store. The dry goods business operated like a full-scale department store, but without a distribution network, reliable suppliers, or a medium of exchange. The store typically carried a huge assortment of whatever goods were obtainable at a given time. These might include glassware, pewter, furniture, tools, linen, wool, warming pans, baskets, sugar, tobacco, flour, horses, cattle, books, lumber, seeds, feed, lanterns, saddles, and wigs. Hard currency, such as gold or silver coins, was scarce, and the colonial economy largely depended upon barter. Deane's customers would often buy items on credit. All these transactions would be recorded in his account books. At a later time, customers settled their accounts by barter. A customer who bought fabric and saddles might pay off his account by exchanging a quantity of tobacco and pork. When someone died or left town, all the merchants would have to reconcile their accounts together—exchanging hats for feed and pigs for wool. It was a cumbersome way to do business that relied on the expectation that neighbors would honor their debts to other neighbors.

With Deane in charge of the Webb business, it grew quickly. He saw the opportunity to expand it by trading with the West Indies.

He purchased his own sloop for importing and exporting goods to the Caribbean. He also invested in marine insurance contracts, betting on the probability that a given vessel would be lost at sea. Soon Deane's success eclipsed Joseph Webb's, and he became one of the wealthiest men in Wethersfield.

AT HOME, his family of nine, plus five slaves, fit comfortably enough in their spacious home, but it still felt like Joseph Webb's house. Deane wanted a home of his own. He yearned for recognition for his business acumen. After all, he had not simply married wealth; he had expanded and diversified the business. Deane wanted the attention of the River Gods, whose houses he had once envied.

There was a lot adjacent to Webb's house, and on it Deane designed an even grander house. Unlike his neighbors' houses, which were nearly identical Georgian colonials, Deane's would be asymmetrical, in the style of a French colonial, with an above-ground basement, exterior stairs, and a large front porch. It had a grand entry hall with a ceiling higher than in any private home in Wethersfield, a sweeping staircase, and a fine parlor with a brownstone fireplace. The kitchen was especially large, with a capacious fireplace that could roast several pigs and turkeys at the same time, and a wide sink nearly large enough to bathe in. The adjoining dining room, with its elegantly painted floor, faced the old Webb house across the yard, which Deane kept for the three older children and some of the slaves Mehitabel had inherited. Upstairs was a large library. When the furniture was moved out and the carpets were rolled up, it could be used for dancing. There were cozy bedrooms for the master, the four youngest children, and a few of the house slaves.

Deane was a gracious host, and he filled his home with warmth and gaiety. Guests enjoyed an abundance of food and drink, lively music, and imported furniture. He developed expensive tastes and dressed fashionably. His reputation in this quiet Congregationalist town grew in proportion to his wealth. Probably, he attracted envy. Perhaps some of the townspeople questioned his extravagance, but none doubted that Deane could afford it.

MEHITABEL DIED OF CONSUMPTION only four years after they were married, leaving Deane with a booming business and seven young children, six not his own. By then he had assumed a leading role in the town government and church. Membership in the First Congregational Church was highly selective and the process for joining the congregation was both intensely emotional and probative. Deane was required to profess his conversion before the congregation and submit to cross-examination by the members who would have to judge if he were one of God's elect. It was not enough to state that you had accepted Christ or that you performed good acts. Deane was compelled to present convincing evidence that he was destined for the Kingdom of Heaven. Only a truly godly man, a "real saint," one who was "regenerated," would be accepted into the congregation and allowed to receive communion at the Lord's supper. Deane's admission into the congregation was both a sign of his own deeply held religious convictions and of the congregation's judgment of his character.

WITHIN A FEW MONTHS OF Mehitabel's death, Deane met another recent widow, Elizabeth Saltonstall. She was a shy, good-natured woman and the granddaughter of the colony's former royal governor, Gurdon Saltonstall. Her family was well established in

New England. Elizabeth was fascinated by this fashionable social upstart with his stylish home and his charming manner. Within the year, Elizabeth wed Silas. With this marriage Deane sealed his social position. He now possessed both wealth and a link to one of New England's most esteemed families. Deane marveled at all that Providence had bestowed upon him.

His commercial interests gradually drew him into politics. Merchants like Deane relied on Britain for nearly all of their manufactured products. They exported cheap raw materials like tobacco, timber, and cotton to Britain and imported more expensive products like guns, cloth, and saltpeter. The British had long regulated trade with its colonies through the Navigation Acts, but these acts were only loosely enforced, and the regulations benefited some American producers, while they burdened others. British customs officers often winked at American smuggling. The British recognized that so long as they did not interfere too much in the American colonies, the colonists would remain loyal subjects. This was the policy that Edmund Burke famously described as "salutary neglect."

All that began to change after Britain's victory in the French and Indian War, which ended in 1763. Having pushed France out of North America, Britain now imposed new restrictions on American trade in order to squeeze more profits out of its colonies. Britain prohibited merchants like Deane from purchasing imports of certain commodities, like tea, from any other country, and also required that certain exports, like tobacco, could only be shipped to Britain.

The other major irritant to American merchants was British taxation. Britain's victory over France had left Britain with a staggering war debt of about 137 million pounds (roughly $25 billion in today's money). The annual interest on this debt alone accounted for more than sixty percent of the British government's total annual budget. Moreover, after the war, the British decided to maintain a permanent military presence in North America. The North American commander-in-chief, Lord Jeffrey Amherst, told Parliament that he would need 10,000 troops to secure the colonies, and the annual cost of this standing army would exceed 300,000 pounds (roughly $56 million in today's money). British taxpayers were loath to pay higher taxes to protect the colonists thousands of miles across the ocean, and, quite naturally, the British expected colonists to contribute to their own security.

Parliament enacted a series of new tariffs and taxes on the Americans to increase revenues. First, the Sugar Act of 1764 imposed some new tariffs on sugar, coffee, wine, indigo, and textiles, while tightening customs enforcement to prevent smugglers from evading tariffs. The following year, Parliament adopted the Stamp Act, which taxed all printed materials and most paper. This was the first time Parliament had directly taxed Americans without the consent of the colonial assemblies. Colonists protested that Parliament did not have the authority to impose taxes on them without the consent of the colonial assemblies, and eventually Parliament repealed the Sugar Act and the Stamp Act, but it continued to insist it had the power to tax the colonies. Then, in 1767, Parliament adopted the Townshend Revenue Acts, which imposed tariffs on a range of products, including tea, glass, lead, paper, and paint.

In response to each of these measures, merchants, like Deane, throughout the colonies began organizing committees to protest British taxes and trade regulations. They signed nonimportation agreements pledging to boycott British goods. The nonimportation movement was the first widespread consumer boycott in history, and it was remarkably effective. As a result of the American boycott, the British government raised less than 21,000 pounds in revenue from the Townshend duties, but British businesses lost 700,000 pounds in exports to the American colonies. More importantly, the nonimportation movement united the colonies for the first time in opposition to Parliament, and it brought a new class of American merchants to political prominence.

Following the enactment of the Townshend duties, the citizens of Wethersfield gathered at the Congregational meetinghouse on the town commons on Christmas Day, 1769. It was the day after Deane's thirty-second birthday. As the largest merchant in the town, Deane stood up and urged his fellow townsmen to pass a resolution condemning British taxes as "unconstitutional, offensive, and tending to that total subversion of the liberties of his Majesty's subjects in America." By an overwhelming vote, the men of Wethersfield agreed. They resolved not to buy any goods from Great Britain until the British measures were repealed, and they appointed Deane to the local Committee of Correspondence to consult with neighboring towns on measures for the defense of their liberties. These Committees of Correspondence formed a resistance movement against oppressive British policies throughout the American colonies.

Sitting in the meetinghouse that day, Deane must have experienced an enormous rush of pride. He had become a well-respected leader in his community and an elected representative in a movement that had continental ambitions. The possibilities before him seemed intoxicating. As he prepared to enter colonial politics he surely must have recalled an essay he had written years earlier as a sophomore at Yale College. The essay won the Latin prize and was a great source of pride to him. The president of Yale was sufficiently impressed by it that he promised to preserve it in perpetuity in the Yale library. In his elegant script the young scholar began by quoting from one of Cato's Distichs: "*Nulli tacuisse nocet, nocet esse locutum.*"

("Silence harms no one; it is harmful, instead, to speak.") In a democracy Deane argued, men who are tempted to enter politics are fools and a danger to the commonwealth. The wise man should instead beware of "the deceits of the human heart." For this reason, "True safety lies in silence." As Deane now assumed a leadership role in Connecticut, his destiny would be an object lesson in the wisdom of this advice.

TWO

THE PLAYWRIGHT

Paris, 1767

The audience began booing before the curtain descended. Angry painted faces with hair stacked like wedding cakes, men and women—stuffed into heavy gold embroidery, silk, linen, ruffles, and lace—snarled like wild dogs. The play, which opened in Paris at the Comédie-Française on January 29, 1767, closed the same night. Despite a talented cast, the first performance of *Eugénie* was long, overwrought, and too controversial for the audience. One vicious critic hissed that the playwright, a young man named Pierre-Augustin Caron de Beaumarchais, "will never achieve anything, not even mediocrity."

That was untrue. Beaumarchais had already written one moderately successful comedy, a short sketch called *The Barber of Seville*. *Eugénie* was his first attempt at a serious full-length drama, and the criticism stung him deeply. He had labored for eight years on the script, and he had taken command of every detail of the performance, staging, and lighting. He had even designed and built new equipment for moving scenery. Still, the fact remained that his play was a flop, and at thirty-four, though he had done many things, he had not yet found his true calling.

Beaumarchais was a man blessed with many talents, but cursed with a restless mind that never found true contentment in any of his accomplishments. From an early age, Beaumarchais, born Pierre-Augustin de Caron, displayed a genius for music, but at thirteen Pierre-Augustin began working as an apprentice to his father, a modest watchmaker on the bustling rue Saint-Denis in Paris. Possessing a sharp mind and the discipline necessary for detailed work, Pierre-Augustin excelled as a watchmaker's apprentice. With his fine fingers, accustomed to playing viol, guitar, harp, and flute, he had extraordinary dexterity, which enabled him to work on very small watches. The same creative passion that inspired him musically, also sparked his inventiveness. He tinkered with watches, trying to find ways to improve the precision of timekeeping. One might expect that a serious young man obsessed with mastering music and learning the solitary craft of watchmaking would be awkward socially. To the contrary. People quickly took to the young man with his witty conversation, physical grace, and almost feminine beauty.

At the age of twenty-two, Pierre-Augustin Caron revolutionized timekeeping. He designed a radically new escapement—the device that regulates the movement of a clock. Before Caron, watches were spherical and awkward to strap onto a wrist. Caron's escapement kept time more accurately and made it possible for a watch to lie flat against the wrist. If he accomplished nothing else in his life, he would be remembered for the Caron escapement, which is still used today.

The young Caron proudly showed his design to the king's watchmaker, Jean André Lepaute. Lepaute was impressed enough to submit the design to the French Academy of Sciences as his own. Caron might never have learned that Lepaute had stolen his invention except that the design sparked so much interest that a Paris newspaper, the *Mercure de France*, reported that Lepaute had invented a new watch. As bold as he was ingenious, the twenty-two-year-old wrote to the Academy and to the *Mercure de France*, exposing Lepaute's fraud. The Royal Academy was persuaded by Caron and declared that Caron's escapement "is in watches the most perfect that has been produced, although it is the most difficult to execute." He won both the patent and considerable public acclaim for his genius. His bold move pushed Pierre-Augustin Caron onto the public stage for the first time.

Caron's defiance and brilliance also won him the attention of Louis XV. In 1754, he was invited to Versailles to meet the king, who was fascinated by the young man and commissioned a watch for himself and the tiniest watch possible for the dainty wrist of his powerful mistress, Madame de Pompadour. For her, Caron disguised her watch within a ring for her small finger. She was delighted. Soon, all of the king's ministers were ordering watches from Caron, who replaced the disgraced Lepaute as the king's watchmaker.

Now tall and slender with a handsome face and confident expression, Caron caught the attention of the court at Versailles. The young courtier had many social opportunities, but he hungered for wealth and fame. At that time, public offices in France were routinely bought and sold as personal property. He had an affair with the beautiful Madame Francquet, ten years his senior and the wife of the aged Comptroller of the Pantry. Madame Francquet persuaded her frail husband to retire and sell his office to Caron for a modest annuity. In reality, the comptroller's job was merely honorary; its only perk was that Caron had the right to promenade into the royal dining room behind the king's dinner—but it was a start for an ambitious young man. Two months after selling his office, Monsieur Francquet died of apoplexy, and Caron was thus freed from the obligation to make annual payments. Once the estate was settled in 1756, Francquet's grieving widow quickly married Caron. Caron now had servants, a carriage, a mansion in Paris, and another in the country. Caron was particularly taken with the large country house in Alsace called "Beaumarchais" (or "beautiful walk"). He thought that the name of his wife's house sounded more suitable to his new rank than Caron, so Pierre-Augustin Caron restyled himself Caron de Beaumarchais.

Madame Francquet, like Beaumarchais, was a gifted harpist. She encouraged him to redesign the pedals, an arrangement that remains in use on harps today. Beaumarchais organized recitals for his friends at his home, and his reputation as a musician grew. Madame Francquet's happiness was short-lived, however. The youthful Beaumarchais was unfaithful, and their marriage rapidly deteriorated. She died from typhoid fever in 1757, less than a year after marrying Beaumarchais. Her family immediately challenged Beaumarchais's right to inherit anything from his wife's estate. As Beaumarchais had failed to record the marriage contract in a timely manner, a long court battle determined that he was not entitled to any of her property. All he kept was the name Beaumarchais. Once again, he was a watchmaker.

Louis XV took pity on the recently widowed Beaumarchais. When he learned of Beaumarchais's musical talent, he invited Beaumarchais to tutor his four daughters, the princesses Louise, Adélaide, Victoire, and Sophie. Beaumarchais earned nothing as a tutor, but access to the royal family was a valuable commodity at the Court of Versailles.

In the spring of 1760 Beaumarchais was invited to visit Madame de Pompadour's glittering château d'Etoiles. There he was introduced by Pompadour's husband to Joseph Pâris-Duverney, one of the richest men in France, who had made a fortune selling arms in the war against Austria in the 1740s. Pâris-Duverney, at seventy-six, was a heavyset man with a double-chin and an upturned nose that veered sharply to the left. He had recently established L'Ecole Militaire to provide military training for the sons of impoverished nobility. Pâris-Duverney had repeatedly invited the king to visit the school, located near Hôtel Royal des Invalides, but Louis XV had little interest in this project. Pâris-Duverney, who could afford nearly anything, was completely frustrated in his efforts to get the king's attention. When Pâris-Duverney heard of Beaumarchais and his close relationship to the princesses, he set up this meeting. Pâris-Duverney was immediately enchanted by the young man with the dark, intelligent eyes. Pâris-Duverney offered Beaumarchais "his heart, his help and his credit, if he could succeed in doing what everybody has tried to do in vain for nine years." If Beaumarchais could arrange for Louis XV to visit the military academy, Pâris-Duverney would become his patron.

Beaumarchais invited the princesses to see the academy first, and they were delighted by the young officers in their handsome uniforms parading on the grounds. They rushed back to Versailles excitedly to tell their father that he really should see the academy for himself. The king agreed to pay a formal visit, and Pâris-Duverney was thrilled. From this small exchange an intense and intimate relationship blossomed between the twenty-seven-year-old music tutor and the seventy-six-year-old financier.

Pâris-Duverney, who was unmarried and childless, pursued the young man like a prize, buying him extravagant gifts and launching him in a number of ambitious business ventures. "I love you, my child," Pâris-Duverney gushed to Beaumarchais in a letter. "From now on I will treat you like my son. Only death will prevent me from my commitment to you." Pâris-Duverney gave him an annuity of 6,000 livres (about $46,000 today). He taught Beaumarchais the business of arms trading and gave him a percentage of his military contracts. He loaned Beaumarchais a considerable sum to purchase the offices of Secretary to the King, Lieutenant General of the Chase of the Tribunal, and Bailiwick of the Warren of the Louvre, responsible for enforcing hunting regulations on the king's property—all sinecures from which Beaumarchais derived a small income. Pâris-Duverney also helped Beaumarchais purchase a mansion at 26 rue de Condé, where Beaumarchais lived with his father and younger sister. Over the next decade Pâris-Duverney gave or lent Beaumarchais at least 800,000 livres (about $6 million today).

For his part, Beaumarchais offered the older man companionship, youth, and affection. For nearly a decade the two men were inseparable. Beaumarchais composed romantic songs for Pâris-Duverney and penned intimate letters. Their ambiguous correspondence suggests that Pâris-Duverney may have been more than a patron to the beautiful young inventor. Beaumarchais teased Pâris-Duverney affectionately, calling him "dear little girl": "How goes the dear little girl? It is a long time since we embraced. We are queer lovers. We dare not see each other because our parents frown at us; but we still love each other. Come now, my dear child. . . ."

Some biographers have suggested that this language was a quaint form of salutation, but it was hardly customary among men, even in its time; other biographers have insisted that Beaumarchais was writing to Pâris-Duverney in what they called their secret "oriental" code. Yet there was nothing "oriental" about the language, and why would two grown men have found it necessary to disguise the contents of their private letters? The plain language of their few surviving letters and the circumstances of their relationship suggest that theirs was not merely a "father-son relationship," as some biographers have described it. Whether or not their relationship was physical, there were at least homoerotic overtones, which would hardly have shocked anyone around Versailles. While sodomy was officially outlawed in France, same-sex relations were neither uncommon nor well hidden at the court, where courtiers winked at men with what they called the "Italian taste."

Pâris-Duverney introduced Beaumarchais to the world of politics and diplomacy. As a military veteran and an ardent nationalist, Pâris-Duverney believed passionately in the necessity of revenging France's defeat at the hands of the British in the Seven Years' War. He impressed upon Beaumarchais the historic conflict between these two powers and the rightful place of France as the Continent's dominant power. Only France could safeguard European society and check the power of Britain's navy, Pâris-Duverney argued. To do that, Pâris-Duverney believed France must first divide Britain's colonial empire, which was the source of its economic power. This strategic lesson was not lost on Beaumarchais.

While Pâris-Duverney tutored Beaumarchais in business and politics, he also encouraged Beaumarchais's playwriting. At first Beaumarchais showed little talent as a playwright, and his early plays were poorly received. One of his early works, *The Two Friends*, was about the moral relationship between two businessmen. It was probably based in part on Beaumarchais's partnership with Pâris-Duverney. The play was a failure. On a poster outside the theater advertising *The Two Friends* one wit scrawled: "By an author who has none." Nevertheless, Beaumarchais kept tinkering with theater in the same spirit of experimentation with which he had tinkered with watches and musical instruments. During a business trip on behalf of Pâris-Duverney to Madrid, Beaumarchais was inspired to write a play set in Spain—a farce about a clever barber who helps a young suitor to insinuate himself into a noble household as a music tutor, and it ends with some confusion about a marriage contract. *The Barber of Seville,* which eventually became one of his most successful plays, and inspired Rossini's classic opera, drew on his experience as a music tutor and entrepreneur.

BEAUMARCHAIS WAS DETERMINED to salvage *Eugénie* after the withering criticism it had received. He quickly revised the second and third acts and reopened the play two days after it had ignominiously closed. The response was vastly different—literally overnight. The critics now roared their approval and audiences flocked to it. *Eugénie* went on to shatter performance records at the Comédie-Française. Suddenly, Beaumarchais was the bright young talent of the Parisian stage. It made no sense to him, but he smiled at the fickleness of his audience. Beaumarchais's fortune often swung from disaster to triumph.

Beaumarchais lived much of his life onstage, and it was not merely his theatrical productions that were mounted as public spectacles. His inventions, music, writing, romances, legal problems, and political battles were public performances, part comedy and part drama. But the most fascinating plot Beaumarchais ever imagined was the one he enacted behind the scenes—the one story he never had the chance to write.

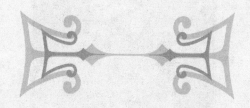

CHEVALIER D'EON, Captain of Dragoons
by J. B. Bradel, 1779
Reprinted with permission of the
Bibliothèque Nationale de France.

THREE

THE SPY

London, 1771

The crowd at Jonathan's coffeehouse in Change Alley was glad to be warm and dry on a Saturday in late March. No one minded the stench of pipe tobacco or the noise. For two pence a waiter brought you a "dish" of tea, coffee, or hot chocolate. You could trade political news, and you could conduct some business as well.

Jonathan's was located in a wood-framed building with small windows near the Royal Exchange and was one of London's most famous—some would say notorious—coffeehouses. In 1771, it was the hub of stock trading in Britain. The main room was up a narrow set of stairs on the second story. It was sparsely furnished, the floor was rough-hewn, and the walls were stained brown from generations of smoke. There were usually knots of well-dressed bankers, merchants, and stock traders, the latter known derisively as "stock jobbers," clustered around the few tea-stained tables. Most English gentlemen regarded these stock jobbers as gamblers whose wild speculation would lead to their financial ruin. Though the better classes snubbed these men, Jonathan's patrons would eventually form the London Stock Exchange. In addition to trading shares, the clientele at Jonathan's regularly bet on the occurrence of almost any event. There was always someone willing to scratch out a betting contract on whether the government would fall, or whether a famous person would die, or whether France would go to war.

On this particular Saturday the room grew unexpectedly quiet at the appearance of an extraordinary-looking stranger wearing the crisp dark green-and-crimson uniform of a captain of the French dragoons bedecked with military honors. It was the Chevalier d'Eon. That very week, articles had begun appearing in the *London Evening Post*, the *Public Advertiser*, and the *Gazetteer and New Daily Advertiser* about wagers as to whether or not the French diplomat and soldier was a woman in disguise. Hundreds of pounds sterling were being bet on this unlikely proposition.

The assembled stock jobbers—with their frilly Irish linen blouses, embroidered jackets with contrasting waistcoats bordered in gold and silver, three-cornered hats, and silk stockings in a dizzy array of purple, blue, white, and black stripes, specks, and patterns—were not accustomed to being confronted by a French military officer in their cozy coffeehouse. In a thick accent the chevalier demanded to know if a certain "money-broker" Mr. Bird were present. The chevalier had a handsome face with a prominent nose and a strong chin. His muscular body moved with a swagger. He appeared taller than he was in his knee-high boots. The chevalier's right hand rested on an ornate walking stick that he wielded like a weapon. When Bird meekly stood up, the French captain angrily accused him of initiating these "impudent" bets and warned Bird that he had better "beg his pardon." The banker fumbled for the right words to apologize. After all, he had done nothing wrong; English law permitted anyone to place a bet, even concerning the royal family. But d'Eon was in no mood for legalisms. He demanded satisfaction and challenged the whole roomful of incredulous stock jobbers to fight him. No one would dare to cross sticks with this accomplished swordsman. The terrified stock jobbers fell silent. They avoided his glare, looking down at the reflection in their shiny black high-heeled shoes. The point was made. No one doubted the chevalier's mettle. Yet, his intemperate outburst only underscored in everyone's mind that d'Eon was an unpredictable creature. And that may have been precisely the chevalier's intent.

ONE OF D'EON'S BIOGRAPHERS later wrote that he was "one of the strangest challenges that history has ever offered to fiction." The unusual circumstances of d'Eon's astonishing life continue to be a subject of scholarly inquiry and debate, and the chevalier's luminous writings have only obscured the truth and enlarged d'Eon's mystique.

Christened Charles-Geneviève-Louis-Auguste-André-Timothée d'Eon de Beaumont, he was born in 1728 in Tonnerre to a petty noble family with an ancient lineage of eccentric personalities. (Indeed, one of his twelfth-century ancestors had claimed to be the only son of God.) Tonnerre was a rural town with a population of a few thousand along the Armançon in Burgundy, more than a hundred miles east of Paris. D'Eon lived near the center of the small town in an impressive stone mansion built by a duke in the 1500s. D'Eon's father was the mayor of Tonnerre, and the rest of his paternal family was equally if not more distinguished.

From an early age, d'Eon was an accomplished student, athlete, and swordsman, and, much like Beaumarchais, he showed considerable musical talent and a keen wit. At thirteen, he entered the College of Mazarin in Paris, where he studied civil and canon law, graduating with distinction when he was twenty-one. Like his father and uncles, he became an attorney in the Paris courts and Secretary to the Intendant of Paris, who was the king's principal agent overseeing the city government. He harnessed his remarkable mind and warm personality to his ambition. By twenty-five, d'Eon had published serious works on finance and government that won him approval from the court at Versailles.

People often noticed d'Eon's exceptional appearance. In his twenties, his yellow hair fell softly around his face in perfect ringlets. He had a beautiful face with piercing blue eyes, high cheekbones, a delicate mouth, smooth skin, and a slender frame. On his left cheek was a small birthmark, a faint port stain under his ear that was easily covered by hair. Once, while serving in the French embassy in St. Petersburg, a Russian commented that he was so angelic-looking he might be mistaken for the baby Jesus. Affronted by this infantilizing remark, d'Eon nodded, "[T]hat's right, which is why I'm in a filthy manger." Even in his middle years, d'Eon maintained his remarkably androgynous appearance. Though his voice was soft and high, he was neither effeminate nor frail. He smoked, drank, and swore like any hardened soldier.

In 1755, at twenty-seven, d'Eon was invited by a family friend, the powerful Prince de Conti, Louis XV's cousin and close adviser, to join the king's elite network of about two-dozen secret agents known as "*le secret du roi.*" Louis XV created "the Secret" to expand French influence in Eastern and Central Europe without alarming France's suspicious ally, Austria. Louis XV selected his talented cousin to lead the Secret, and Conti recruited the young d'Eon for a secret mission to Russia.

In the War of the Austrian Succession, which lasted from 1740 to 1748, France and Prussia were allies against Britain, Russia, and

Austria. Since then, France had switched alliances to join with Austria in recapturing lands taken by Prussia. By 1755, France found itself without strong allies to check Britain's growing military power. Austria was weak, and Spain, France's traditional Bourbon ally, was preoccupied by its rivalry with Portugal. That left Russia as the greatest potential ally for France. But France and Russia were at that time rivals on the Continent and had not had diplomatic relations for fourteen years. Louis XV had sent several envoys to St. Petersburg to try to reestablish diplomatic relations, but Russia's chancellor, Count Bestuchef, hated France and would not allow them to meet the empress, Elizabeth I. Chancellor Bestuchef had even imprisoned France's most recent emissary. The Russian empress herself was believed to favor a rapprochement with France. Under these circumstances, Louis XV would have to find some other means to communicate with the empress secretly.

What happened next is a subject of historical speculation. According to d'Eon's version of the story, Louis XV and Prince de Conti secretly wrote to the Empress Elizabeth trying to establish a diplomatic connection, but the empress wanted some assurances that her letters would be kept secret. She suggested that Conti send her a discreet, young, educated Frenchwoman who could assist her in translating her French into a secret code that only Prince de Conti could read. Conti and the king selected d'Eon, whose intellect, courage, and androgyny made him uniquely suited to this intrigue.

According to d'Eon, Conti invited him to his lavish home at the Hôtel du Temple in Paris. There he was ushered into the bedchamber where the prince was propped up in bed. Conti asked d'Eon to put on a skirt "in the service of a great foreign princess who is rich and powerful and who is aware of your talents and how much I love you." He ordered d'Eon to go to Russia disguised as a female tutor for the empress. D'Eon protested, but the prince promised d'Eon that this service would guarantee d'Eon's professional future. Reluctantly, d'Eon agreed to go.

Some scholars doubt whether any of this actually occurred, since the archives of the French Foreign Ministry contain no evidence that d'Eon was sent to Russia disguised as a young Frenchwoman. It makes sense, however, that the French Foreign Ministry would have no record of d'Eon's service in Russia. Louis XV and Prince de Conti specifically kept the foreign ministry in the dark about the activities of the Secret. The king could not risk having anyone know that France had placed a secret agent in the court of the Russian empress. The British government had spies all over Paris, and if they discovered that France was seeking an alliance with Russia they would have reacted swiftly.

We have only fragments from which we can try to piece together the true story of d'Eon's life, and all of this evidence is contestable. A copy of a letter—possibly a forgery—from Louis XV to d'Eon dated 1763 reads: "You have served me as usefully in the garments of a woman as in those which you now wear." Similarly, the memoirs of the daughter of a French official in the foreign ministry mentions d'Eon's having penetrated the Russian court in the disguise of a young Frenchwoman. D'Eon's own correspondence to Louis XV refers to having worn dresses in the service of the king. And as early as 1771, d'Eon complained to the Comte de Broglie, who eventually replaced Prince de Conti as chief of the Secret, that "It is not my fault if the Court of Russia . . . has assured the English Court that I am a woman." If Louis XV and Broglie disagreed with d'Eon's recollections, their protests were not recorded. Perhaps the most intriguing evidence of d'Eon's secret mission is a portrait of the youthful d'Eon drawn by Louis XV's own portraitist, Maurice Quentin de la Tour. The drawing depicts d'Eon as a beautiful young woman with a rosy complexion, elegant pearl earrings, a fancy lace cap, and a neckline revealing ample breasts. Why would the king's portraitist have sketched d'Eon as a young woman, and for whom? Portraits of women were typically drawn or painted as an expression of affection between men and women. One possibility is that it was drawn for the Prince de Conti, who may himself have had romantic designs on the young d'Eon. While none of this evidence proves indisputably that d'Eon actually disguised himself as a woman while he was serving the king in Russia, it does suggest that in his youth d'Eon had appeared in women's clothing.

What is indisputable is that in the summer of 1756, Louis XV sent d'Eon and Sir Alexander (Mackenzie) Douglas, a Scotsman working as a spy for France, on a secret mission to Russia. Louis XV wanted to open up relations with Russia. The king knew that the English were seeking an alliance with Russia against France, and there was little time to spare. Sir Douglas posed as a British geologist examining mines in Russia for investors. When the British ambassador's spies reported that Douglas was a French agent, the British ambassador informed Chancellor Bestuchef. Terrified of being imprisoned, Douglas fled Russia, leaving the young d'Eon behind.

A few months later the Seven Years' War had erupted, and by then, Russia and France, once fierce rivals, were now allied against Prussia and England. What had happened in the intervening months to transform Franco-Russian relations? During this time, d'Eon was alone in St. Petersburg, and when Douglas returned to St. Petersburg as France's minister plenipotentiary in the spring of 1757, he was warmly received by the empress, and diplomatic relations with France were fully restored. Apparently, during the five-month hiatus, between Douglas's hasty departure and triumphant return, the twenty-seven-year-old d'Eon had smoothed relations between France and Russia behind the back of the suspicious Russian chancellor. It is unclear how d'Eon reached the empress and accomplished this rapprochement. D'Eon later wrote that whatever happened during his time alone in St. Petersburg was "secret, lengthy, and warrants a long chapter."

According to one version of d'Eon's story, he remained in Russia disguised as Sir Douglas's French niece, "Mademoiselle Lia de Beaumont." It may be that d'Eon invented this story years later, but it seems probable that d'Eon must have disguised himself to avoid arrest as a French spy. D'Eon later claimed that disguised as Mlle. Beaumont, he met the empress, who was delighted by the lovely French "girl" who spoke with such intelligence and wit. Empress Elizabeth retained Mlle. Beaumont in her retinue of ladies-in-waiting as a French tutor and secret envoy from Versailles. Once d'Eon had won the empress's confidence, he told Elizabeth that he was a man and that he was carrying a secret message from Louis XV. D'Eon produced a letter from the king, which d'Eon had secreted in the binding of a volume of Montesquieu's *De l'esprit des lois*. The empress, far from expressing outrage that she had been duped into permitting a Frenchman into her private circle, was amused by d'Eon's daring.

Unfortunately, there is little documentary proof to support this story apart from d'Eon's own writing, and, as we shall see, d'Eon sometimes constructed facts to serve his own purposes. While it is possible that d'Eon conducted these negotiations dressed as a man, it is hard to see how it would benefit him to invent the story of Mlle. Beaumont. In the absence of any conclusive evidence explaining how France reestablished diplomatic relations with Russia during this period, d'Eon's story is at least plausible.

Once the empress agreed to an alliance with France and Austria against Britain, d'Eon wanted to tell Louis XV himself. On his way to Versailles, his coach overturned, and he suffered a broken leg, but he was undeterred. When d'Eon arrived with the news of his diplomatic success, Louis XV was delighted, and the king rewarded d'Eon for his secret service with a commission as a captain in the elite Royal Dragoons. As Prince de Conti had predicted, d'Eon's star was rising rapidly, though Conti himself would soon fall out of Louis XV's favor.

IN 1761, d'Eon quit his diplomatic post in order to fight Britain during the Seven Years' War. D'Eon proved to be a fierce and intrepid warrior. He was wounded in the head and thigh and crushed when his horse fell on him at the battle of Ultrop; he risked his life saving a large store of cartridges under fire at Höxter; and he led a vastly outnumbered detachment of eighty dragoons in a charge on a Prussian battalion at Rhes and took them prisoner. He performed with remarkable valor and withstood overwhelming military attacks and life-threatening wounds fearlessly.

The king recalled d'Eon to Paris in 1762 with the intention of naming the thirty-three-year-old d'Eon ambassador to Russia. However, the recent death of Empress Elizabeth I meant it was not the right time to name a new ambassador. Instead, d'Eon was appointed as secretary to the ambassador to Britain, the Duc de Nivernais, to head the peace talks. D'Eon, who had made his diplomatic career negotiating the alliance with Russia against Britain, and his military career fighting the British, was now charged with negotiating the peace with Britain.

In the treaty negotiations with Britain, France had little bargaining power. Britain had crushed France in the Seven Years' War, and no French diplomat, however resourceful, could alter that brutal reality. The peace imposed by England was deeply humiliating to France. The British demanded that France destroy its harbor at Dunkirk in order to prevent France from attacking England in

the future. D'Eon had steadfastly rejected this demand and succeeded in winning this concession. Perhaps the greatest compliment
paid to d'Eon's diplomatic skill was that some English politicians
believed that the treaty d'Eon had negotiated was still too generous
to France and even charged that the French had bribed British
negotiators.

After the treaty was signed in 1763, d'Eon remained in London
as secretary to the ambassador. At the same time, without the ambassador's knowledge, d'Eon continued to be employed as a spy by
the Secret. Louis XV and Comte de Broglie, who was now the chief
of the Secret, were conspiring in an audacious and ill-considered
plot to invade England and repudiate the treaty, even before the ink
had dried. Louis XV wrote to d'Eon, instructing him that he must
"keep this affair strictly secret and that he never mention anything
of it to any living person, not even to my ministers." Even the foreign
minister knew nothing about the plan. D'Eon's job was to identify
possible landing sites for a French armada and forward the information to Broglie in code. D'Eon faithfully followed his orders, thereby
planning to destroy with one hand the treaty he had crafted with the
other. The invasion plan had not the slightest chance of success:
France was nearly insolvent and possessed only a remnant of its
navy, while Great Britain was a naval and economic superpower.
Fortunately for France, other events would intervene to prevent
Louis XV from launching his ludicrous invasion plan.

When d'Eon returned to Paris for instruction from Comte de
Broglie in March 1763, he was knighted "Chevalier" and for his efforts was awarded France's highest military honor, the *Croix de
Saint-Louis*. The king publicly awarded the cross for d'Eon's courage
as a captain of the dragoons in the Seven Years' War, but it was also
a private acknowledgment of d'Eon's secret service to the king in

Russia and England. D'Eon wore the cross proudly on his chest for the rest of his life, long after his king abandoned him.

That same year, the king named d'Eon his envoy to Britain with title of "Minister Plenipotentiary." Though the post was only temporary (pending the arrival of a new ambassador), the appointment was proof that d'Eon, at thirty-five, was a dazzling new star in France's diplomatic firmament. Within a few short months in London, d'Eon became a favorite of King George III and was a familiar guest in the homes of the most powerful men in Britain. (He was, in fact, so close to the royal family that one of his biographers made the extravagant claim that d'Eon had an affair with Queen Charlotte and fathered George IV!) He earned a colorful reputation among London's high society for his good looks and witty conversation.

Yet, d'Eon's diplomatic popularity came at a cost. The French Foreign Ministry balked at the astounding bills he presented to support his luxurious lifestyle and his extravagant gifts. He spent a small fortune on his wardrobe and furnishings and accumulated an impressive library of books in several languages. The chevalier was famous for lavishly entertaining celebrated and powerful men like Horace Walpole, David Hume, the Duke of Grafton, and Lords Hertford, March, Sandwich, and Villiers. D'Eon liked to present his friends with crates of the finest Burgundy that was grown near his birthplace in Tonnerre. In a single day d'Eon purchased 2,800 bottles of the best Burgundy, costing about 150 pounds (roughly $28,000 today). D'Eon imported so much wine that the British prime minister warned d'Eon that the British government might be compelled to impose tariffs on his wine imports—in contravention of the legal principle that diplomats are immune from paying tax on their personal property.

The French foreign minister, the Duc de Praslin, wrote to d'Eon several times during the summer of 1763, questioning his expenses and ordering him to economize. At that point, d'Eon claimed he was owed almost 90,000 livres, (nearly $700,000 today) by the French government and defended his expenses to Praslin, pointing out the high cost of living in London. "When I was secretary of embassy I went about plainly dressed in my uniform and cambric cuffs; now, much against my will, I must wear a few decent clothes and a little lace." D'Eon continued, "If the King's [financial] affairs are in a bad state, mine are going from bad to worse." His debts, he wrote, were distracting him from his duties and threatening his mental and physical health.

The tone of d'Eon's letters triggered a sharp reproach from Praslin. He warned d'Eon not to let the title of Minister Plenipotentiary go to his head. "If you are not yet satisfied, I shall be obliged to discontinue employing you, for fear of being unable to recompense your services adequately. . . . I hope that you will be more circumspect in your demands in the future, and more sparing in your use of other people's money."

If d'Eon had dropped the matter there, the history of Anglo-French relations and the fate of the American Revolution might have turned out very differently. But d'Eon could neither restrain his pride nor curb his expenses. His correspondence with Praslin grew increasingly antagonistic. D'Eon's reaction to a relatively minor question of reimbursements was uncharacteristic for the loyal soldier and the patient diplomat. He poured forth a torrent of intemperate letters. His friends cautioned him to be reasonable and tone down his rhetoric. But d'Eon seemed incapable of calming down. Clearly, the issue was no longer about his allowance. Some sort of psychological wall had been breached. D'Eon warned a friend who served as the chief clerk at the foreign ministry, "I will always go my own way, fate has determined that; the bomb must burst; the fuse is at the end of the wick."

HIS EXTRAVAGANCE QUICKLY depleted the allowance provided by the French government for the newly appointed ambassador to London, the Comte de Guerchy, who had not yet arrived. D'Eon had served with Lieutenant-General Comte de Guerchy during the Seven Years' War. Guerchy was as arrogant as he was talented. Once, on the battlefield, he had refused to carry out an order from the commanding officer and had left it to d'Eon instead. From this single incident d'Eon harbored a deep resentment toward the comte. D'Eon knew that the principal reason for Guerchy's promotion to the rank of ambassador over him was the result of Guerchy's close relationship to Madame de Pompadour, the king's mistress. Guerchy had ingratiated himself to Pompadour in the most servile manner—even to the point of carrying her slippers. Though Guerchy had distinguished himself by his military service, he had no qualifications or instincts to function as a diplomat. D'Eon viewed his appointment as an insult.

Praslin wrote to d'Eon that the budget could not support having both an ambassador and a minister plenipotentiary. As a result, when Ambassador Guerchy arrived in London in October, d'Eon would be demoted to his former title as secretary to the new ambassador. D'Eon's pride was deeply wounded. He had proven himself adept as a spy, a soldier, and a diplomat. He was a tough man when the king needed him to be a man, and he was a charming woman when the king needed him to be a woman.

The chevalier would not accept this demotion. To the Comte de Guerchy, who was still packing to leave France, d'Eon wrote pre-

sumptuously that "the chance which gave the title of minister plenipotentiary to a man who has negotiated successfully during the last
ten years was perhaps not one of the blindest." He then added this
pointed insult: "What has come to me by chance might come to
another by good luck." If there were any possibility that d'Eon might
have been able to serve as secretary to Guerchy, d'Eon was determined to destroy that: "A man, no matter who, can only form an
estimate of himself by comparison with one or many men," d'Eon
continued. "[E]xcept," he added, "in certain cases where men measure themselves by women." Was d'Eon implying that Guerchy was
less than a man, or was d'Eon slyly hinting about his secret service
to Louis XV? D'Eon's language was so inflammatory that Guerchy
might have suspected that d'Eon either was indulging too freely in
his beloved Burgundy, or he was going mad.

As d'Eon's angry rhetoric escalated, the king and Comte de Broglie, as chief of the Secret, became more concerned about d'Eon's
stability. They concluded that d'Eon's position in London threatened relations with Britain. Even if firing d'Eon meant the end of
the secret plan to invade England, the king could not risk the very
real chance that d'Eon would expose the whole operation and trig-
ger war with Britain before France was ready.

FOUR

BLACKMAIL

London, 1763–1771

The Comte de Guerchy arrived in London in early October 1763, and moved into the embassy, which was located in Monmouth House, on Soho Square, a few blocks from d'Eon's residence. Monmouth House was a grand columned mansion built in 1682 by Christopher Wren. Guerchy carried with him a letter from Praslin recalling d'Eon to Versailles, but when he presented it to d'Eon, the chevalier refused to leave London. He insisted that since the letter was not personally signed by Louis XV, it had no effect. He politely informed the British secretary of state that contrary to what the French ambassador was saying about him, he would remain as the minister plenipotentiary. Even more boldly, he continued to take his meals in Monmouth House at the ambassador's table. Not knowing how to respond to d'Eon's insolent behavior, Ambassador Guerchy shared meals with d'Eon in stony silence.

Louis XV had an embarrassing crisis to confront: two ministers in London, both claiming to speak for him, but neither speaking civilly to the other. Neither Ambassador Guerchy nor Foreign Minister Praslin knew what Louis XV and Broglie knew: d'Eon possessed certain incriminating letters that Louis XV had sent to him while he was the secretary to the ambassador in London, instructing d'Eon to scout out landing sites for a surprise attack by French troops on London. Now Louis XV was desperate to keep this correspondence secret. It clearly violated the letter and spirit of the treaty d'Eon had negotiated ending the Seven Years' War, promising peaceful relations with Britain. The publication of these documents would have given Britain grounds for war, and France could ill afford another crushing military defeat. Louis XV tried to silence d'Eon by ordering to have him arrested, kidnapped, or assassinated, but d'Eon survived every attempt by the king's agents. Conscious of the growing threat to his life, d'Eon felt pushed to his emotional limits.

IN MARCH 1764, d'Eon published in London a 200-page history in French of his dispute with the French government and his recall, including reprints of secret correspondence concerning his expenditures and his title. Never before had anyone published diplomatic correspondence. For the first time, the public could glimpse the inner workings of diplomacy. It was an overnight sensation. Within the week, 1,500 copies sold out—perhaps a record for a diplomatic history. Publication of secret government documents was considered criminal, and the book was instantly banned in France. D'Eon's papers depicted an embarrassing tale of petulant French officials threatening each other over expenditures and titles. At the same time, d'Eon portrayed himself as a popular hero taking on a corrupt and ineffectual bureaucratic elite.

Despite its popular success, the book's publication led to more problems for the chevalier. The British attorney-general charged d'Eon with criminal libel for defaming Ambassador Guerchy. The charges against d'Eon were serious, but they also generated more publicity and increased book sales. On the day the case was scheduled to be heard, d'Eon failed to appear in court, and Lord Chief Justice Mansfield issued a default judgment against him. When the police came to arrest him, d'Eon was not at home. According to one story, possibly apocryphal, the police were informed that he was in hiding at the home of a Mrs. Eddowes. When the police arrived there, they found only Mrs. Eddowes and two other women sitting quietly by the fire. It never occurred to the police that one of the women was d'Eon.

D'Eon responded to his guilty verdict by charging that Ambassador Guerchy had tried to poison him. D'Eon alleged that he had dropped in for dinner at the embassy one October evening. After dinner with Ambassador Guerchy and Lord Sandwich, he suddenly became tired and experienced a burning sensation in his stomach. As he hurried home from Monmouth House, some men at the front gate tried to hoist him into a waiting sedan chair, but he fought them off and stumbled home on foot instead. When he arrived home, the chevalier fell into bed and slept until noon the next day. D'Eon charged that Guerchy had tried to kidnap him and return him forcibly to France. One of Guerchy's assistants, Vergy, later admitted that Guerchy had offered him d'Eon's position as secretary to the ambassador if he would slip opium into d'Eon's wine, but Vergy had refused. To the embarrassment of the French and British governments, a grand jury at the Old Bailey found d'Eon's charges credible and indicted Ambassador Guerchy for attempted murder. However, the indictment was suspended by the prime minister on the grounds that because Guerchy was a diplomat, he was immune from the court's jurisdiction. Guerchy's butler, who was suspected of administering the poison, fled England. Though the case was never tried, the judgment against d'Eon for defaming Guerchy was voided.

FRIGHTENED FOR HIS LIFE, and having exhausted his credit, d'Eon now lived in constant fear of assassins and prepared to defend himself. "I have at home no fewer than eight Turkish sabres, four pairs of pistols and two Turkish rifles," he wrote, warning Louis XV not to pursue him. His paranoia was not unfounded. Louis XV had sent two dozen plainclothes police officers to London for the purpose of capturing the chevalier, and a French vessel waited off the coast of England to bring d'Eon home. Guerchy attempted to take advantage of d'Eon's growing anxiety by trying to convince the chevalier that his rooms were haunted. Each night ghostly noises emanated from d'Eon's fireplace. It was not the chevalier's imagination; the ambassador hired a chimney sweep to stand on the chevalier's roof and make eerie sounds. The chevalier was not spooked, but he was tired of the harassment. He decided to move into a flat on Golden Square, a tony neighborhood of handsome Georgian houses constructed around a square that was once a mass grave for thousands of plague victims. Though he loved his new rooms, he could not escape his ghosts. Fearing imminent arrest, d'Eon transformed his home into a fortress. He hired a contingent of loyal dragoons from his old company to stand guard inside his house. He hid the secret correspondence Louis wanted under the floorboards. He kept a glowing poker in the fireplace, ready to defend against an intruder, and left his lamps burning all night. He even placed explosives around his home, ready to be ignited if the French police somehow managed to break in. He would rather blow himself up than submit to his pursuers.

D'Eon was prepared to do anything to remain free, and he knew that he could not survive much longer in London without financial support. His creditors were demanding payment, while, at the same time, he was being offered substantial bribes from the opposition Whigs to provide secrets that would embarrass the French and the British Cabinet. By 1764, d'Eon was desperate enough to threaten to sell to the British his secret papers detailing Louis XV's plan to invade England. He wrote the king's secretary that if by Easter the king did not accede to his demands, he would be forced "into the arms of the King of England." The disclosure of the secret plans was sure to provoke a military response from Britain with disastrous consequences for France. D'Eon warned the Comte de Broglie that "[Y]ou will be determining the fate of the next war, of which I will certainly be its innocent author." He added that if that happened, "your grand projects, so glorious for the King and so advantageous for France, will turn against you."

The king and Broglie knew that d'Eon's threat was not idle. By now Louis XV was convinced that "d'Eon is mad and perhaps danger-ous," but he concluded that "there is nothing to be done with the mad except shut them up." The king decided to reconcile with d'Eon. First, Louis XV replaced Guerchy with a new French ambassador, Durand de Distroff, whom d'Eon knew and liked. The king also offered d'Eon an annual pension of 12,000 livres (about $92,000 today). (Even that much was nowhere near enough to cover d'Eon's extravagant life-style.) In exchange, d'Eon agreed to provide intelligence to the king concerning British politics. Ironically, d'Eon's notoriety had given him greater access to the opposition Whig members of Parliament and increased his value to Louis XV as a spy. Though d'Eon still re-tained most of the secret correspondence, he showed his good faith by giving the new French ambassador one of the most incriminating letters in which Louis XV instructed d'Eon on the plans for invading

England. For a few years, the matter of d'Eon seemed settled. Then something curious happened.

SOMETIME AROUND 1770 in the fashionable salons in London and Paris and in the corridors of Parliament and Versailles, people began to speculate about d'Eon's true gender. It is unclear where or how these rumors started. One story was that a Russian princess visiting London saw d'Eon dressed as a man and recognized him as Mlle. Lia de Beaumont; it was the birthmark under d'Eon's ear that the princess recalled. Even assuming that d'Eon had dressed as a woman in St. Petersburg, it would be hard to believe that the princess, who would have been very young at the time, could have remembered that birthmark. A second possibility is that d'Eon's rival, Guerchy, paid someone to write a libelous pamphlet that accused the chevalier of being an insane hermaphrodite. A third is that d'Eon started the rumors as a way to discourage the king from having him assassinated, kidnapped, or thrown in prison. Or perhaps under the emotional weight of his estrangement from the king, his enormous debts, and the continuing threats to his life, d'Eon had simply snapped.

In any event, word reached Paris by the spring or summer of 1770 that d'Eon was actually female. Louis XV, who could hardly be surprised any longer by the chevalier, wrote in October to one of his military officers that "d'Eon is a girl." The Marquise du Deffand wrote Horace Walpole from Paris that "I almost forgot to tell you that M. D'Eon is a woman." Rumors quickly flowed from the British upper classes to the commoners. A London paper reported "that a celebrated Chevalier (D'—n) has, within a few weeks past, been discovered to be of a different sex." Journalists and poets picked up their pens, some mocking and some praising d'Eon's beauty and

strength. Cartoonists sketched d'Eon boxing in her skirts. A flattering poem by d'Arnaud, titled "To a Mademoiselle Disguised As a
Man," appeared in the *Almanach des Muses* of 1771. A London newspaper reported that d'Eon had confided in his favorite footman that
he was a woman.

Though at first the stories seemed too fantastic to be true, they
captured the public's imagination. In London, where betting on everything was the rage, wagers were placed in popular coffeehouses
like Jonathan's and Lloyd's, as well as at fancy St. James gentlemen's
clubs such as Brooks's and White's, on the question of whether the
chevalier was a woman. Newspapers reported daily on the betting,
and by March, the odds were even as to whether d'Eon was female.
Reportedly, as much as 60,000 pounds (more than $11 million
today) was gambled on this question.

For unknown reasons, d'Eon did not respond publicly to the rumors, which had the effect of confirming the suspicion in the minds
of many. Perhaps he welcomed the publicity, or perhaps he found it
too much to answer. To Comte de Broglie, d'Eon wrote privately
denying these rumors, which d'Eon attributed to the absence of a
normal libido. D'Eon felt "mortified at being what nature has made
me, and that the natural lack of passion . . . which has prevented my
engaging in amorous intrigues," would cause people "to imagine, in
their innocence, that I am of the female sex."

When newspapers reported that d'Eon himself was wagering
large sums on the question of his gender, d'Eon finally had enough.
He was incensed by this outrageous libel. He might be a woman
pretending to be a man and a spy blackmailing a king, but he was
no swindler. D'Eon, armed with nothing but his captain's uniform
and a walking stick, appeared at Jonathan's, and at several other coffeehouses, to confront the stock jobbers who had laid down these
bets. He challenged anyone who doubted his manliness to a duel.

His appearance that day was a colorful display of male bravado, but it did nothing to quell the rumors. If anything, it only stirred up more interest in the story.

Was d'Eon really mad, or did he merely want Louis XV to think he was mad enough to publish the king's secret correspondence? A madman is always too dangerous to ignore—especially when he is in a position as sensitive as d'Eon's. If that were the chevalier's plan, it worked. At Versailles, Louis XV and his counselors worried that they would have to find some other way to neutralize the threat that the chevalier posed.

FIVE

FIGARO

Paris, January 1770–April 1775

The year 1770 began with Silas Deane, age thirty-two, emerging as a leading figure in the Connecticut Committee of Correspondence, and Beaumarchais, at thirty-eight, marrying his second wife, Geneviève-Madeleine Watebled. Geneviève had lost her husband only four months earlier, but she was already pregnant with Beaumarchais's child. A year younger than Beaumarchais, Geneviève was tall and shapely with a pretty face and long blond hair. She was as lovely and good-natured as she was rich. Her late husband had left her with an annuity that assured her an ample income for the rest of her life. Soon after their marriage she gave birth to a son, Pierre-Augustin-Eugènie, and they bought a grand estate on the outskirts of Paris in Pantin. Beaumarchais still maintained the mansion on the rue de Condé for his two sisters and father.

Beaumarchais had other reasons to be thankful as well. Since the success of *The Barber of Seville* and *Eugénie*, he had become a popular and critically acclaimed playwright. Although his latest play, *Two*

Friends, about the friendship between two business partners, was a flop, some people were already speaking of him in the same breath as his contemporary, Voltaire. While his artistic reputation blossomed, his business investments with his partner Pâris-Duverney were also growing handsomely. Pâris-Duverney had persuaded Beaumarchais that as France rebuilt its navy, there would be a great demand for timber. Taking advantage of Beaumarchais's connections in Versailles, they jointly formed a logging company that bought the exclusive rights to a lush 2,400-acre forest in the Loire valley. Their lumber business soon became highly profitable. It seemed that this was Beaumarchais's moment. All at once he held in his hand everything that one can aspire to—domestic bliss, fame, and fortune. And then in an instant it vanished.

Beaumarchais's enterprise sparked envy among Louis XV's idle courtiers and raised questions about the source of his newfound wealth. It was not merely Beaumarchais's money that ruffled them. The popularity of his plays, which he knew would be controversial, even revolutionary, irritated many aristocrats, who criticized this social upstart for daring to mock the nobility. Though some aristocrats, including Marie Antoinette, admired his pluck and laughed at his jokes, many others were offended by the liberties he took. Beaumarchais could not resist the temptation to poke fun at the powerful, and his wit often landed him in trouble. Once he joked that the king owed more livres than all the minutes since Christ had died. Louis XV was not amused by what he disdainfully referred to as this "clockmaker's arithmetic." Beaumarchais's enemies quietly bided their time until his fortune turned. They did not have long to wait.

Pâris-Duverney, now eighty-six, was ailing, and Beaumarchais worried that his friend might die soon. Up to this point, they had conducted their business based on trust. Their partnership was founded on their mutual affection, and they had no need for legal

documents or precise accounting. Now, however, with a wife and
child to consider, Beaumarchais worried that if Pâris-Duverney
died, he had no legal right to any of the property they had amassed
together. Beaumarchais knew that his friend and patron, who was
childless and unmarried, had reluctantly decided to leave all of
his wealth to his grandniece. Under French law, this meant that
Pâris-Duverney's estate would end up in the hands of her husband,
Alexandre-Joseph Falcoz, the Comte de La Blache. Beaumarchais
knew that La Blache lusted after Pâris-Duverney's money, and he
dreaded having to do business with the mean-spirited comte. La
Blache, in turn, viewed Beaumarchais as a rival for Pâris-Duverney's
wealth. The comte once exclaimed that he hated "Beaumarchais the
way a lover adores his mistress." Beaumarchais needed to settle his
accounts with Pâris-Duverney before the comte could get his hands
on Beaumarchais's money.

One spring day in 1770, Beaumarchais visited Pâris-Duverney's
palatial home in Paris to discuss the situation. To his surprise he was
turned away at the door. It was not like Pâris-Duverney to refuse to
see his beloved friend. He wrote to Pâris-Duverney, but received no
reply. For days he heard nothing from the man who had been devoted to him for a decade. Eventually he realized that La Blache had
moved into the mansion and had made Pâris-Duverney a prisoner
in his own home. After days of trying, Beaumarchais somehow managed to smuggle a letter to his old friend. In it, he acknowledged their
enduring relationship in an elliptical fashion and asked for his help:

> Read, my beauty, what I am sending you and give me your opinion
> about it. You know quite well that in an affair of this sort I can
> decide nothing without you.
>
> I am using our oriental style on account of the means by which
> I am having this jewel of a letter conveyed to you. Give me your

opinion, and give it quickly for time flies. Goodbye, my love, I embrace you as warmly as I love you. I don't send you any messages from the Beauty. Her own letter to you will be enough.

In another letter, Beaumarchais wrote cryptically:

I wish this may turn out to your mistress's good. Everything is for the best if she shares your opinion. To express my own would be unbecoming as I should be setting myself between the jealous lover and the well-guarded wife. I think success will be difficult.

If Pâris-Duverney were the "well-guarded wife," and his nephew La Blache the "jealous lover," was Beaumarchais the "mistress"? This confusion of gender roles seems characteristic of Beaumarchais's correspondence with Pâris-Duverney. Though some biographers have argued that Beaumarchais wrote this way to hide his business relationship to Pâris-Duverney, their business relationship was already well known. More likely, Beaumarchais was writing, as he often did, with affectionate whimsy. La Blache himself may have suspected that Beaumarchais had an improper relationship with his uncle. La Blache sent anonymous letters full of the "vilest insinuations" about both men. What were those "insinuations"? We do not know, but one possibility is that La Blache insinuated something about the intimate nature of their relationship in order to suggest that Beaumarchais had exercised undue influence over his aged uncle. Regretting the interference of his nephew, Pâris-Duverney wrote to Beaumarchais, "My friend, you are the finest passion of my soul. But I seem to be only your shameful passion."

Beaumarchais and Pâris-Duverney set up a secret meeting in March at which they agreed on a settlement of the business. Pâris-Duverney released Beaumarchais from any debts he owed him and signed a promissory note promising to pay Beaumarchais 15,000 livres (about $116,000 today). In addition, he agreed to lend him, interest free, another 75,000 livres (about $580,000) for eight years. The generous terms that Pâris-Duverney agreed to reflected his deep affection for Beaumarchais, but they also proved to be the cause of one of Beaumarchais's biggest disasters.

Three months later in July, 1770, Pâris-Duverney died. Beaumarchais felt an enormous loss. Over the prior decade Pâris-Duverney had opened so many doors for him; Beaumarchais could not have imagined the life he now enjoyed without Pâris-Duverney's support. Years later, in the sweet-scented garden of his Paris mansion, Beaumarchais erected a plaque to Pâris-Duverney's memory etched with the words, "*C'est par lui que je vaux, si je vaux quelque chose.*" ("It is thanks to him that I am worth something, if I am worth anything.")

Beaumarchais's grief for the loss of his dear friend and business partner was quickly eclipsed by other more urgent matters. Beaumarchais's wife gave birth in March, 1770, to a daughter, Aimable-Eugénie, who died days later. Soon after, Geneviéve was bedridden with a high fever and cough that continued through the fall. The doctors diagnosed it as tuberculosis. In November, Geneviéve, too, died. Still mourning the loss of Pâris-Duverney, Beaumarchais now had to cope with the twin loss of his wife and child. (Beaumarchais's other child, Augustin, also died less than two years later from fever.)

To add to his anguish, the court at Versailles showed him very little sympathy. Vicious rumors circulated that he had poisoned both of these rich widows—and possibly their husbands, as well—in order to abscond with their estates. In defense of Beaumarchais, Voltaire wrote that Beaumarchais was far "too droll" to murder his wife. In point of fact, since the income from his wife's annuity terminated at her death, Beaumarchais inherited none of it. His grief from the loss of his wife and son were sincere, and now, when he most needed his friend Pâris-Duverney, he had nowhere to turn.

With Pâris-Duverney gone, Beaumarchais's worst fears were realized: La Blache refused to pay the 15,000 livres that his uncle had promised to Beaumarchais from the settlement of their business. La Blache claimed that the document with Pâris-Duverney's signature was forged and that Beaumarchais had extorted money from his wife's uncle. In fact, he went even further and alleged that Beaumarchais now *owed* his uncle's estate nearly 140,000 livres (more than $1 million today). Infuriated, Beaumarchais sued him for the debt, and the comte retaliated by spreading wild stories to discredit Beaumarchais before the judges. La Blache alleged that "this vulgar person" had been disowned by his family "for theft and vice" and that Beaumarchais lived on the street before he married. He even accused Beaumarchais of murdering both of his wives. This was the beginning of Beaumarchais's problems with the law. He would later remark that La Blache was "the father of all my sorrows."

Despite the comte's lies, the trial court determined that the signature of Pâris-Duverney was legitimate and ordered the Comte de La Blache to pay Beaumarchais 15,000 livres, but the comte appealed the decision. Judge Advocate Goëzman was appointed to hear the appeal in 1773. Through a mutual friend Beaumarchais learned that the judge's wife could arrange an interview with Judge Goëzman to hear Beaumarchais's claim. Madame Goëzman bluntly admitted that "It would be impossible to live decently with what we get, but we know the art of plucking the fowl without making it cry out." If a party with a just and honest cause needed her husband's help, it would not offend her "delicacy to receive a present." The judge's wife demanded 2,400 livres (about $18,000 today) to set up a meeting. Beaumarchais borrowed the money to pay her fee, and spent barely fifteen minutes with the judge. Unfortunately, La Blache paid an even larger bribe, and the judge ultimately found in favor of the comte. The Paris Parlement, which functioned as a court of appeal, upheld the judgment against Beaumarchais. The Parlement ordered Beaumarchais to pay the comte 56,000 livres (about $430,000 today) plus interest and legal costs.

To make matters worse, Beaumarchais was already in jail for a separate incident in which he had insulted the Duc de Chaulnes with whose mistress Beaumarchais had an ill-timed affair. Beaumarchais had been allowed to leave the Paris jail at For-l'Evêque only long enough to have his appeal heard by the Paris Parlement. The quarrel with the Duc de Chaulnes made Beaumarchais an even less sympathetic figure in the eyes of the Court of Versailles. Beaumarchais was ruined. He had no way to satisfy the judgment against him. La Blache seized his home and furnishings at the rue de Condé and evicted Beaumarchais, his aged father, and two sisters. The family was forced to move back into his father's small house on the rue Saint-Denis, at the sign of the clock, where Beaumarchais had begun life. In three tumultuous years he had lost everything he had earned since he first appeared at Versailles two decades earlier. He would have been better off if he had remained a watchmaker. After the court's judgment against Beaumarchais, Madame Goëzman discreetly returned to Beaumarchais his bribe less 15 louis (360 livres or about $2,800 today) that she insisted she had paid to the judge's secretary to arrange the interview. Beaumarchais wrote her demanding she return the 15 louis: "The injustice should not be subsidized by the one who is suffering so cruelly."

In September 1773, Beaumarchais responded to Judge Goëzman's allegation with his most effective weapon: his prose. In a series of witty pamphlets he titled "Memorials," he blended caustic humor with a froth of rhetoric. Beaumarchais brilliantly skewered the judge, his wife, and associates. In the process he also laid bare the corruption of the French courts. The "Memorials" were an instant sensation, and Beaumarchais became a popular hero. On the street, Parisians joked that "The Parliament of Louis XV will fall for fifteen Louis," the amount of Beaumarchais's alleged bribe. Not only in France, but throughout Europe, people were talking about Beaumarchais's bold indictment of the French justice system. Even Voltaire exclaimed after reading Beaumarchais's pamphlet that "nothing has ever made a deeper impression on me."

But popular acclaim for Beaumarchais only enraged his detractors. Judge Goëzman, probably at the urging of Beaumarchais's enemies, accused Beaumarchais of attempted bribery. Beaumarchais countered that he had not offered a bribe; the judge's wife had demanded one. Now both Beaumarchais and the judge were charged with bribery.

After a bitter legal battle, during which Beaumarchais was released from jail, both Beaumarchais and Judge Goëzman were ultimately convicted of bribery and stripped of their official positions, titles, and state pensions. In effect, Beaumarchais was declared a nonperson. His controversial "Memorials" were burned in public by the state executioner, and he was warned not to make any public statements about the verdict or face corporal punishment. His punishment only served to magnify his popularity, but the more people rallied to him, the more he was perceived as a threat to the state. At the urging of the king's mistress, Madame du Barry, the government forbade performances of his newly revised comedy, *The Barber of Seville*. Though Beaumarchais felt vindicated in the court of public opinion, his friend Antoine de Sartine, chief of the Paris police, privately cautioned him that "It is not enough to be reprimanded, it is also necessary to be modest." Sartine advised Beaumarchais that he must leave Paris before the police were ordered to arrest him again for threatening the public order. Within seventy-two hours Beaumarchais fled north to Flanders under cover of night.

IN DEBT, indicted for bribery, convicted of fraud, publicly reprimanded, and barred from his title, pension, and offices, Beaumarchais desperately searched for a way to rehabilitate himself. Only Louis XV had the authority to restore Beaumarchais's legal status, but it seemed unlikely that the king would pardon a subject who had caused him so much trouble and offended so many courtiers and officials. Most of the courtiers who surrounded Louis XV had little use for this upstart and were, no doubt, glad to be rid of him. They were glad to see that Beaumarchais had finally gotten his just desserts.

Another man in Beaumarchais's position might have quietly disappeared from the scene, but Beaumarchais was not like other men. He was not shy about asking for the king's forgiveness. He felt he had nothing to lose. He wrote to the man whose access to the king was unequaled—Louis XV's valet, Jean-Benjamin de La Borde, whom he knew from his time at Versailles—and asked him to intercede on his behalf. La Borde spoke to the king. Remarkably, despite Beaumarchais's offenses, Louis was still fond of the precocious young man who had revolutionized timekeeping and tutored his daughters, though not enough to meet with Beaumarchais in any public place.

La Borde invited Beaumarchais to a secret meeting in March, 1774, at Versailles. The king did not want anyone to know that Beaumarchais was coming to the palace. Beaumarchais was directed to the marble court in the south wing. There he could slip unnoticed through an open window near La Borde's apartment on the ground floor. He was ushered into one of the king's wardrobe rooms and down a flight of stairs to a maze of damp basement rooms lit only by candlelight where the king's vestments were stored. They would not be seen or heard here as their voices echoed off the stone walls.

La Borde offered Beaumarchais a chance to redeem himself in the service of his sovereign. He told Beaumarchais that Louis XV was being blackmailed by a vicious pamphleteer, Charles Théveneau de Morande, the publisher of a popular rag in London filled with titillating gossip about the indiscretions at the French court. Morande was threatening to publish a pamphlet called "The Secret Memoirs of a Prostitute." He had sent a copy to the king's current mistress, Madame du Barry, thus leaving no doubt that she was the target of his attack. Louis would not allow Madame du Barry to be publicly humiliated by Morande, but his attempts to silence Morande had failed. Perhaps Beaumarchais, who had been such an effective advocate in his own defense, might be able to persuade Morande to abandon this project. If Beaumarchais could stop the publication, the king would restore Beaumarchais's rights and privileges. At a subsequent meeting in the king's private study, Louis XV gave Beaumarchais 20,000 livres (about $150,000 today) to buy Morande's silence.

Beaumarchais eagerly embraced the opportunity to impress the monarch. The romance of a secret mission on behalf of the king was irresistible to him. He left immediately for London, chartering a private boat to cross the channel from Flanders. Once in London he settled into a modest flat off High Holborn on Ploone Street under an assumed name—the Chevalier de Ronac. No one was supposed to know that the disgraced Beaumarchais was working for the king, but it did not require much imagination to recognize that "Ronac" was a simple anagram for his family name, Caron. Beaumarchais proved to be an able and charming negotiator, and he readily befriended Morande, who was happy to sell his work for the right price. Beaumarchais purchased all the copies of Morande's work. Under a darkening sky, he carted them by carriage to a spot near St. Pancras, where there was a deserted kiln once used to make lime. There he burned every copy of the offending text, the billowing smoke signaling that his mission was accomplished.

IN MAY 1774, Beaumarchais returned to France, confident that Louis XV would restore his title and civil rights and repay him the 12,000 livres (roughly $92,000 today) Beaumarchais had spent on his mission. But the king, stricken with smallpox, died just days after Beaumarchais arrived. Now Louis's twenty-year-old grandson, Louis XVI, ascended to the throne, determined to rid the court of his grandfather's flatterers and schemers. As one of Louis XV's secret agents, Beaumarchais was no longer welcome at Versailles. Beaumarchais's mission to safeguard Madame du Barry's reputation was hardly appreciated by the young king, who referred to his grandfather's mistress disdainfully as "the du Barry"—as if he were describing a social disease. Beaumarchais faced a deadline to appeal his criminal sentence, but the king refused to see him. If the king did not intervene on his behalf quickly, he would be thrown into prison.

A month later Beaumarchais wrote to Police Chief Sartine that an Italian named "Guillaume Angelucci" was preparing to publish "an outrageous libel" that would embarrass France and Spain and threatened to sabotage their alliance. Sartine recommended to Louis XVI that he appoint Beaumarchais as an intermediary to negotiate with Angelucci. Neither Sartine nor the king suspected that Beaumarchais had invented Angelucci and fabricated the libel himself. Having created a problem for the king, Beaumarchais agreed to negotiate with his fictional character for the destruction of this imaginary manuscript in exchange for the restoration of his civil rights and the dismissal of his prison sentence. Beaumarchais could justify this deception to himself as a way of compelling Louis XVI to honor his grandfather's promise to him.

Beaumarchais proceeded to London to meet with the imaginary Angelucci. He reported that he encountered numerous obstacles to stopping Angelucci's libel and was forced to pay about 30,000 livres (about $230,000 today) for 4,000 copies of the manuscript, which he claimed to destroy. To add drama to the story, Beaumarchais wrote that the scoundrel had fled England to the Continent with the intention of publishing his libel there. Beaumarchais chased his mythical villain across Holland through Germany to Vienna. Traveling by coach through Prussia in hot pursuit of his phantom, Beaumarchais went so far as to slash his face and chest with a razor to fake an attempt on his life by robbers.

When the crusading Beaumarchais reached Vienna, he rashly requested a private audience with Empress Maria Theresa, mother of the French queen, Marie Antoinette. Meeting the world's most powerful woman in her impressive country palace at Schönbrunn, he could not resist boasting to the empress about his romantic adventures chasing Angelucci. By now his story had become so embroidered that it aroused the empress's suspicions. She asked the Austrian chancellor, Wenzel Anton von Kaunitz, to investigate. Finding that some of Beaumarchais's facts were contradicted by his coachman, he ordered Beaumarchais arrested for fraud. Eventually, Marie Antoinette had to intervene to secure Beaumarchais's release.

Beaumarchais returned to France in disgrace. Whether anyone still believed his story about Angelucci is unclear, but Louis XVI had concluded that Beaumarchais was a "mad man," and the Court of Versailles regarded Beaumarchais as a clown. All his efforts to regain his stature had only gone to prove that he was a masterful and disingenuous schemer who could not be trusted. Once again, the king refused to restore Beaumarchais's title and status. He remained shut out of Versailles, but he did manage to have the king compensate him for the expenses he undertook in his pursuit of the imaginary Angelucci. This money allowed him to pay off the liens on his house on the rue de Condé.

Over the next months, Beaumarchais wrote to the king repeatedly pleading his case. He was answered with silence. Refusing to admit his own deceit, Beaumarchais complained that he had traveled over 1,800 leagues and stopped the publication of two libels for the king with no compensation. "To do this I have allowed my own affairs to go to rack and ruin. I have been tricked, robbed, assaulted, imprisoned, and my health is impaired." If only the king were satisfied with his services, "I shall be the most contented person in the world." Beaumarchais began to despair that he would ever overcome his legal disabilities.

In April 1775, Beaumarchais was invited to Versailles to meet with the foreign minister—the Comte de Vergennes—and others. Once again, a French king was being blackmailed. But this time it was real—and more than the reputation of the king's mistress was at stake.

Louis XVI had finally learned that his grandfather had had a secret network of spies working against France's nominal ally—and Marie Antoinette's homeland—Austria. To Louis XVI the network— *le secret du roi*—was symptomatic of the duplicity in which Louis XV indulged. Louis XVI ordered Vergennes, himself a conspirator in the Secret, to dismantle the organization, retire the spies, and destroy their correspondence immediately. Vergennes patiently explained to the young monarch that while most of the spies could be retired, there was the "special problem" of the Chevalier d'Eon, which was likely to require more delicacy.

The chevalier's prominence and mercurial temperament made him difficult to control. Although d'Eon was no longer minister plenipotentiary in London, he continued to receive a pension from the French government. D'Eon was once again threatening to publish some of Louis XV's secret correspondence, which would reveal that the French king had planned to invade London. The publication of these documents would risk war between England and France, and Louis XVI was not prepared to defend his country against the British. D'Eon was demanding a lump sum of 12,000 livres (about $90,000 today) from the king, and he wanted the government to pay off the staggering debts he had accumulated during his brief tenure as minister plenipotentiary under Louis XV. The chevalier owed about 320,000 livres (almost $2.5 million) mostly for the cost of entertaining and for his lavish gifts.

Louis XVI thought d'Eon's demands were "impertinent and ridiculous." Vergennes called d'Eon's letter "a new monument to madness from such a unique mind," but he knew that d'Eon was too dangerous to ignore. Vergennes suggested to the king that they send Beaumarchais to persuade d'Eon to surrender his correspondence. Initially, Beaumarchais must have seemed like an odd choice to Louis XVI. Beaumarchais was not known for his discretion, honesty, or reliability. True, he had succeeded in preventing Morande's blackmail, but Morande was a seedy swindler, while d'Eon was an elite officer and diplomat—a gentleman known for being a snob. Beaumarchais had offended many aristocrats like d'Eon, who would not have considered him their equal. Beaumarchais had a reputation as an adventurer, a troublemaker, and a fraud, who was recently convicted of forging documents and indicted for bribing a judge. Surely, the king could find someone more trustworthy to send on a mission of this sensitivity, and with so much hanging in the balance.

It is puzzling that Vergennes would have recommended Beaumarchais under any circumstances. Vergennes must have thought that Beaumarchais had some unique quality that could persuade d'Eon, yet d'Eon had never met Beaumarchais. It may be that Vergennes hoped Beaumarchais could charm—or even seduce—d'Eon to surrender the papers. Perhaps Vergennes believed the stories that d'Eon was a woman, or, alternatively, perhaps he thought that d'Eon was a man who preferred men. Certainly, Vergennes and the king would have known about Beaumarchais's relationship to Pâris-Duverney, which may have at least appeared to suggest that Beaumarchais had seduced the older man. (Indeed, the Comte de La Blache had charged that Beaumarchais had used "undue influence" to steal from his wife's uncle.) Vergennes may have deduced that a man like Beaumarchais, who was known to dazzle men and women alike with his handsome face and his brilliant wit, might be able to win the chevalier's heart, whether d'Eon was male *or* female. That might explain why Vergennes persuaded the king that Beaumarchais was uniquely suited for this delicate mission.

Whether Beaumarchais understood or agreed with Vergennes's calculations would make no difference. He did not have much choice in deciding if he wanted to go. If he remained in France, he faced the likelihood of further criminal prosecution for his role in the La Blache affair, as well as his mounting debts. If he succeeded in obtaining the correspondence, the French king would restore his title and office. Thus, Beaumarchais gratefully accepted the secret mission to persuade the tempestuous and puzzling Chevalier d'Eon to surrender Louis XV's secret correspondence. It was his last chance to prove his worth to Louis XVI and to rescue himself and his family from ruin.

SIX

TICONDEROGA

Hartford, August 1774–May 1775

E ven the August heat could not dampen their excitement. The Massachusetts delegation to the First Continental Congress paraded into the Hartford town common with carriages, horses, and colonial militia cheered by a throng of well-wishers. The delegates included John Adams, his cousin Sam, Elbridge Gerry, Robert Treat Paine, and Thomas Cushing. Sam Adams led the procession, looking uncomfortably overdressed for the weather in a bright red coat, fancy silver-buckled shoes, and a new powdered wig topped by a stylish hat. The delegates were dusty and perspiring after their long ride under a broiling sun. They stopped off on their way to Philadelphia to meet with the Connecticut colony's leaders. Silas Deane, who was a member of the Connecticut delegation to Congress, rode four miles to Hartford to greet them, along with his twenty-one-year-old stepson, Samuel Webb. While Adams and the others had heard of Deane from his work as the secretary to the Connecticut Committee of Correspondence, they had never met.

Five years had passed since Deane was first elected to the Wethersfield Committee of Correspondence. Since then, the rising wave of resistance to British rule drew him deeper into politics. He was now a member of the Connecticut General Assembly and secretary to the Connecticut Committee of Correspondence. His practical experience as a merchant, his legal acumen, and his spirited work coordinating the boycott of British imports impressed many, not just in Connecticut, but throughout New England. Though Deane initially resisted British rule as an interference with his own business, over time he recognized that more was at stake than mere commercial interests. The brutality of the British military occupation of Boston and the general corruption of the British administration convinced Deane that liberty itself was jeopardized. Perhaps Deane was too quick to rush to judgment, but he concluded earlier than most Americans that only independence from Britain could preserve those rights cherished by Englishmen. He may also have been motivated in part by the commercial opportunities of opening trade with other European countries—trade that was restricted by Britain.

After the British Parliament adopted a set of laws known as the "Coercive Acts" to punish Massachusetts for the Boston Tea Party, the colonies agreed to send representatives to Philadelphia to discuss the growing crisis with England. The Connecticut Assembly appointed Deane and two Superior Court judges, Eliphalet Dyer and Roger Sherman, to represent them in Philadelphia.

From their first meeting in Hartford, John Adams was impressed by Deane's keen intellect and his strong commitment to supporting Massachusetts in its struggle. Superficially, the two men had much in common: Adams was just three years older than Deane and had grown up in a small New England farming village, much like Deane. Adams's ancestors, like Deane's, were part of the Puritan wave that arrived from England in the 1600s. Adams attended Harvard College, and, like Deane, he had thought seriously of becoming a minister and supported himself as a schoolteacher before he became an attorney. But while Adams had made a career as a practicing attorney outside Boston, Deane had abandoned law practice for a much more lucrative career as a merchant.

Yet, it was surprising how easily they got along, considering their different temperaments. Deane was convivial and easygoing. He possessed a warm, open personality; he did not expect or demand much of others and was forgiving to a fault. People liked him. Although he was generally modest and plainspoken, his one vanity was his taste for elegance and fashion. By contrast, Adams was more reflective, sober, and pedantic. He paid little attention to his appearance, though his ego was legendary. He would not suffer fools, or anyone else who disagreed with him. He was obstinate and rigid to the point that it was difficult for other delegates to work with him. In his own words, Adams was "obnoxious, suspected and unpopular."

After their first meeting Adams described Deane to Abigail as his "brother." Deane's sunny personality and natural enthusiasm were infectious, even to a man as somber and serious-minded as Adams. Deane exuded optimism. He was effusive to the point that he could not resist the temptation for overstatement. He extolled the Continental Congress as "the grandest and most important assembly ever held in America." Congress's decisions, Deane predicted, would be compared to "the laws of the Medes and Persians."

The next day the Massachusetts delegates rode out to Wethersfield to visit Deane again before heading on their way. He welcomed them warmly, and Deane's wife, Elizabeth, served punch, wine, and coffee in their spacious sitting room. To Adams, Deane's elegant home must have seemed ostentatious. As the summer evening cooled, Deane walked the men across the yellowed town commons to the newly constructed whitewashed Congregational meetinghouse. They climbed the narrow, twisting staircase to the top of the steeple and looked out over verdant rolling hills and ripening orchards on both sides of the Connecticut River. Even John Adams was moved by the majesty of the Connecticut River valley. He marveled that it was "the most grand and beautifull Prospect in the World, at least that I ever saw." Deane had business to finish up and could not leave with the Massachusetts delegates that evening, but he was brimming with anticipation as he watched the proud procession march off toward Middletown.

A week later, on Monday morning, August 22, Deane began the long journey by carriage to Philadelphia with his stepson Samuel. Deane had never been outside Connecticut, and he was thrilled by the chance to meet political leaders from the other colonies and visit far-off cities he had only read and heard about. They were accompanied by a parade of well-wishers who marched twelve miles south with them, as far as Middletown. Deane rode in relative comfort in his plush coach known as a "leathern conveniency," but the days were hot and the roads were rutted and dusty.

In New Haven, Deane met up with his fellow delegate Eliphalet Dyer from Windham County. Dyer had graduated Yale College twenty years before Deane and practiced law before becoming a judge on the Superior Court. Dyer was a well-respected judge, but he was notoriously loquacious; certainly, spending days traveling with such a man would test Deane's patience. In Fairfield they picked up Judge Roger Sherman. Sherman was one of the leading political figures in New Haven, which competed with Hartford as the cultural and economic center of the colony. He was known for being prickly. In the Connecticut General Assembly, Deane had supported someone else as a delegate to Congress, and Sherman was still smarting from Deane's opposition. By Thursday evening, the three Connecticut representatives reached New York City, dirty and exhausted.

They found a room for the three of them at Robert Hull's Tavern on lower Broadway at the sign of the bunch of grapes. Though Hull welcomed the delegates from Connecticut and Massachusetts, he remained a Loyalist throughout the Revolution.

Deane was stunned by the size and wealth of New York City, with its more than twenty thousand inhabitants, thousands of wood-frame and redbrick buildings, and three hundred stores. Hartford was a small provincial town by comparison. That evening the three delegates were escorted to the stock exchange in lower Manhattan, where the leading merchants of New York hosted all the delegates on their way to Philadelphia. After dinner each man introduced himself and congratulated the others on their appointment. Then they passed around a glass of wine for each to sip. "The glass had circulated just long enough to raise the spirits of every one to that nice point which is above disguise or suspicion," Deane later noted. He "saw that it was an excellent opportunity to know their real situation." He later assured his wife, Elizabeth, that he had remained sober while "sharing in the jovial entertainment." Ever the convivial storyteller, Deane mixed easily with his colleagues. He began quietly sounding out the others on the question of independence. Deane "found many favorable to the cause and willing to go any length."

The cramped conditions in the tavern required that Deane share a bed with his fellow delegate Judge Sherman. The judge's loud snoring kept Deane up all night, although he was too polite to mention it to Sherman. Deane thought Sherman was an odd man—stern-faced, socially inept, and inflexible. Sixteen years older than Deane, Sherman was born in Newton, Massachusetts, ten miles west of Boston. His father was a farmer , and as a child, Sherman had been apprenticed to a cobbler. Sherman's family moved to New Milford, in western Connecticut, on the New York border. Despite a lack of formal education, he possessed a commanding knowledge of Scripture, and he was as prolific as he was devout—after his first wife died, leaving him with seven children, he had eight more children with his second wife. At forty, Sherman moved to New Haven, where, like Deane, he would own a shop. The religious differences in New Haven between traditional Congregationalists ("Old Lights") and the new evangelicals ("New Lights") divided neighbors. Sherman was originally an establishment Old Light, but his business and political interests drew him toward the more overtly religious New Lights. In time, he became treasurer of Yale College and was elected to numerous positions in New Haven County, including justice of the peace, county judge, member of the upper and lower houses of the General Assembly, and judge of the Superior Court.

On Sunday evening, as the weather cooled, Deane prepared to cross the Hudson by ferry, but Sherman insisted that the three delegates should not travel on the Sabbath. Obliging Sherman, Deane waited until Monday morning to make the forty-mile trip, with the result that he was forced to drive under a "scorching sun." This incident irritated Deane, whose religious convictions were tempered by practicality. He had no patience for what he termed "religious canting." Deane began to regret that Sherman had joined him. Though "Mr. Sherman is clever in private," Deane observed, "he is as badly calculated to appear in such company as a chestnut burr is for an eyestone." Other delegates, including Adams, shared his view that Sherman was difficult.

Sherman probably felt just as uncomfortable with Deane, who did not hide his wealth or intellect. Sherman thought Deane was ambitious, prideful, and showy. Deane was disrespectful toward Sherman's religiosity and failed to show appropriate deference for the judge's seniority. Deane's gregarious personality struck Sherman as superficial and pushy. The emerging tension between these two men would have profound and far-reaching consequences.

DEANE WAS EXHILARATED and awestruck arriving in Philadelphia as a member of the Congress. "We are in high spirits," he reported to Elizabeth, "when the eyes of millions are upon us, and consider posterity is interested in our conduct." At the opening session, Deane wore a fashionable new suit he purchased in New York City. He considered his fellow delegates men of "firmness, sensibility, spirit, and thorough knowledge of the interests of America." Deane gushed that the minister's invocation offered at the opening session of Congress "was worth riding one hundred miles to hear; even Quakers shed tears."

By 1774, Philadelphia was the world's second-largest English-speaking city after London, and had grown rapidly over the previous decade. Despite the insufferable summer heat, the clamor of carriages on cobblestones, and the filth that lined the streets, the city shimmered with prosperity. The outdoor stalls ran about twelve-hundred feet down Market Street and were crowded with commodities. Packed side by side were horses and cattle, earthenware and stockings. Though there was a large assortment of dry goods, everything in Philadelphia was expensive, and there was less fresh produce, fowl, and fish than what he could find in Hartford. On the whole, Deane thought that the inhabitants were haughty. They "think nothing is right but what is in this city and province," and "they look on me mad when I tell them that I have seen more good pasture, clover, meadow, oxen, and cows, in a circle of three miles in Connecticut, than is here to be met within thirty." Yet, he found the people of Philadelphia "really extremely civil, and vastly industrious; in both of these I think they must take rank."

For nearly two months, September through October of 1774, the Continental Congress debated how to respond to the Coercive Acts that Britain had adopted in 1774 to punish Massachusetts after the Boston Tea Party. These acts had closed the port of Boston, restricted trade, and abolished representative government in the Massachusetts colony. Most delegates were not yet willing to support independence. Deane understood at the outset that it would take time to win over a consensus for independence, but his excitement soon soured into impatience. He could not deny his disappointment when, at the end of October, all that Congress could agree to were a "Declaration and Resolves" appealing to the king and Parliament to repeal the Coercive Acts and calling on the colonies to raise militias and enforce the colonial boycott against British imports. Though most delegates agreed that Britain had abused its colonies, the majority hoped that it was not too late for the damage to be undone; war was not inevitable. The delegates remained loyal subjects of King George III. Congress was merely asking George III to protect his faithful subjects against a corrupt and brutish Parliament. Deane returned to Hartford dejected and somewhat embittered by the outcome of the Congress. The only reason for optimism was that the delegates had agreed to reconvene to discuss further measures if Britain did not redress their grievances by May 1775.

George III was incensed by Congress's Declaration and Resolves. In the king's eyes, the British had expended a huge sum for the defense of these ungrateful colonies, and, after repeated efforts to raise revenues from the Americans, Parliament had lifted most of the offending tariffs and taxes. Now the Continental Congress had the audacity to ask for more concessions. George III was convinced that the only thing the colonies would understand was the firm hand of the mother country. Instead of addressing Congress's grievances, the king declared that the colony of Massachusetts, which had been at the center of the storm, was in open rebellion, and he authorized military measures to suppress the uprising.

In response, the colonial assemblies agreed to call a Second Continental Congress beginning May 10, 1775, to discuss the future of relations with Great Britain. The Connecticut Assembly again chose Deane, Sherman, and Dyer as their representatives. Even before Deane left Connecticut for the long journey back to Philadelphia, events took a dramatic turn.

ON THURSDAY, April 20, 1775, Thomas Shelton, a merchant from Hartford, arrived breathless at Deane's door with a letter from Joseph Palmor, a member of the Massachusetts Committee of Safety. The address was scrawled in a hurried hand, "To S. Deane, Wetherfield." Deane turned it over and cracked open the seal. Palmor wished to inform Deane, as a member of the Committee on Correspondence, that early the previous morning, regular British troops had fired on a number of colonists at Lexington and killed six of them. The British forces were continuing their march toward Concord.

Deane was stunned. How had the Bostonians responded? Where would the troops go next? Had anyone alerted the Assembly? Deane called a town meeting for that night to prepare Wethersfield against a British attack on the Connecticut colony, and then he rushed to Hartford to notify the leaders of the General Assembly.

Deane later learned that the British general Gage, who was occupying Boston, had ordered 700 soldiers to capture a cache of arms in Concord. As the redcoats approached Lexington, scouts alerted the militia. While rebel leaders like Samuel Adams and John Hancock fled for their lives, a small contingent of the militia confronted the redcoats on Lexington Green. The British marched on to Concord to seize the arms depot. As news of the fighting spread around Boston, hundreds more patriots grabbed their guns and rushed to attack. By day's end, nearly 300 British regulars and 100 militiamen had been killed or wounded. Though the British military commanders viewed the confrontation as a riot, rather than an uprising, to most New Englanders, the British troop movements were a provocation. Within days nearly 10,000 colonists volunteered for their state militias in what some called a "*rage militaire.*" The bloody confrontations at Lexington and Concord demonstrated that the British were determined to keep arms from the rebels. Unable to manufacture or import guns or gunpowder in any significant quantities, the rebels were compelled to seize their armaments from British armories.

One of the most potent stores of British arms was at Fort Ticonderoga. Ticonderoga was once known as the "gateway to the Continent." The fort sat at a strategic point at the base of Lake Champlain just north of Lake George and the Hudson River. An army invading from Canada would pass this point to reach the Hudson and New York City. The fort was a massive stone-and-wood fortress situated high above the lake. It was originally built by the French in a star formation with thick walls surrounded by heavy earthworks. The earthworks were covered by tall timbers with sharpened branches protruding out against any invader. Within its two-story stone walls, impenetrable to cannon fire, was an armory packed with gunpowder. When the British general Jeffrey Amherst captured the fort from the French in 1759, Fort Ticonderoga assumed almost mythic proportions in the public mind, embodying the invincibility of the British military.

By 1775, the reality of the fortress was quite different. After the French had withdrawn from Quebec in 1763, the crown saw little use for the fortress. The British stationed only a token number of men there to guard supplies. For more than a decade the British neglected the fort. Ticonderoga crumbled from disrepair. "I beg leave to inform you," the fort's commandant had reported to London months earlier, "that the commissary's room is fallen in." Yet Parliament refused to appropriate any money for repair. The ditches surrounding the once-mighty fort were filled with foul-smelling garbage. The filthy, ruinous fort offered scarcely any protection from the elements, let alone from an invading army. It squatted over a barren plain commanding a view of mountains stripped bare of forest with no sign of human or animal life as far as the horizon.

On the Thursday following the battles at Lexington and Concord, Benedict Arnold, a captain in the Connecticut Militia's Footguards, was on his way to defend Boston with a small contingent of men from New Haven. Captain Arnold was a striking-looking soldier with gun-metal gray eyes, a Roman nose, and a strong chin. Thirty-four years of age, he owned an apothecary in New Haven and sold medical books to Yale students on the side. He was a casual friend of Deane's, and he possessed a dazzling mind, a genius for military tactics, and insatiable ambition. On the road, he encountered Samuel Parsons, a colonel in the Connecticut Militia and a member of the Connecticut Assembly. Parsons, just returning from business in Massachusetts, was headed to an urgent meeting in Hartford in response to Concord and Lexington. They discussed recent events in Boston, and Parsons expressed his anxiety over the need for more arms. Arnold mentioned that he had heard that the great cannons of Ticonderoga were guarded only by a token force and might be vulnerable to capture by the patriots. Colonel Parsons was intrigued and hurried to Hartford to discuss this possibility with Connecticut's leaders.

That afternoon Parsons met with Silas Deane and Colonel Samuel Wyllys, all members of the Connecticut Committee on Correspondence, to plan an attack on Fort Ticonderoga. They knew that the British intended to send reinforcements, and so speed and the element of surprise were vital. To finance the attack, Deane withdrew three hundred pounds from the Connecticut colonial treasury on behalf of the Committee of Correspondence. Deane considered it a "loan," though he had no authority to borrow money from the colony, and there's no evidence he repaid it. Obviously, if Deane had asked the Assembly for authorization, the plan would be uncovered. An attack by Connecticut militiamen on a British fort was treasonous, but Deane believed his actions in defense of the colony were justified by the exigency of the moment. With this financial backing, a dozen Connecticut militiamen left the next day from Hartford for Bennington, Vermont. There they met at Stephen Fay's tavern with Ethan Allen, the legendary leader of the Green Mountain Boys, to plan an attack. Captain Arnold also met with the Massachusetts Committee of Safety, which the British had outlawed. The Committee of Safety elevated Captain Arnold to the rank of colonel and commissioned him to raise a militia to take the fort.

Ethan Allen and Benedict Arnold agreed to lead the charge jointly—Arnold, in a scarlet dress uniform with gold braids, led about one hundred Massachusetts volunteers, and Allen led about eighty Green Mountain Boys, in their deerskin and homespun. On the night of May 10, 1775, they crossed Lake Champlain in darkness and silently crept up the side of the embankment around the fort's battery, then made their way under the ramparts and through a large unguarded gap in the south wall. When the single sentry at the gate tried to fire at Allen, his gun jammed, and he ran away. The entire contingent of colonists entered the fort unhindered, aimed their guns at the barracks where the British troops were sleeping and shouted to wake them. Only one guard tried to attack, and Allen knocked him to the ground with the flat of his sword. Not a single shot was fired, and there were no casualties. Within ten minutes two hundred untrained and lightly armed citizen-soldiers had seized the symbol of the British Empire's conquest of North America.

As soon as the fort was captured, chaos broke out. Ethan Allen and his men began looting the premises. They threatened to kill the terrified British men, women, and children they held captive. Arnold tried to impose order on the marauding Green Mountain Boys, but Allen refused to control his men, whom he felt were entitled to take whatever booty they wanted, which was mostly alcohol. Arnold was outraged at this undisciplined behavior. He fiercely defended the safety and property of their British captives. When one of the Green Mountain Boys tried to steal a woman's sewing table, Arnold fought back, literally grabbing the table away. Allen's men continued their looting for several days—just long enough to finish off all the British liquor—and then stumbled home to Vermont, leaving the fort in a shambles under the command of Colonel Arnold.

Despite the absence of resistance and the humble condition of the fort, the capture of Ticonderoga was an extraordinary symbolic, psychological, and strategic boost to the Americans—the first victory in what became a long struggle for independence. It sent a shock wave through the colonies, cheering patriots, assuaging the doubters, and worrying the Loyalists. Most significantly, the capture of Ticonderoga provided some arms that were desperately needed to defend Boston. Captain Arnold quickly dispatched the fort's ample supply of cannons and ammunition.

News of the capture of Ticonderoga sailed down the Hudson at about the same time that the delegates were beginning to gather for the Second Continental Congress in Philadelphia. Even before the news reached the delegates, there was a palpable sense that something extraordinary was about to happen. Deane and the other New England delegates were mobbed by well-wishers the whole way to Philadelphia. As they approached the city, a large parade of about two hundred men on horseback and many more uniformed militia- and riflemen on foot, with swords drawn and bayonets fixed, greeted them. Deane could not believe the sight: "rolling and gathering like a snow-ball, we approached the City," where they were met by enormous crowds, larger than any he had ever seen. "[T]he bells all ringing and the air rent with shouts and huzzas. My little bay horses were put in such a fright that I was in fear of killing several of the spectators."

When a letter reporting Captain Arnold's triumph at Ticonderoga reached the Congress on May 17, the delegates erupted with cheers. They credited their colleague Deane as one of the strategic architects of this victory. Though Deane had clearly violated the law by misappropriating money from the Connecticut Treasury to underwrite Arnold's mission, he was now hailed by the delegates. He had risked being charged by the crown with treason to defend the colonists against British tyranny. His grateful colleagues even called him "Ticonderoga" as an expression of their admiration for his cunning and bravery.

For one sunny moment, Silas Deane basked in the light as one of the heroes of the struggle against British tyranny. Deane was elated to share the reflected glory of this iconic victory with his neighbor Benedict Arnold. But the warm sun of approbation soon slipped behind a dark cloud of jealousy.

SEVEN

THE CHEVALIER

London and Paris, April–September 1775

After his meeting with Foreign Minister Vergennes in April 1775, Beaumarchais departed at once for London to negotiate with the Chevalier d'Eon. To avoid detection, he had chartered a small boat from Boulogne on his own and rowed all night. A strong east wind held him off the English coast. After seventeen hours on rough waters he landed far south at Hastings on the coast of East Sussex, and from there he journeyed north to London, still feeling a bit queasy.

In London he pretended to be engaged in his own private business. Rather than pursue the chevalier overtly, Beaumarchais waited patiently for the opportune moment to meet him. He expected that d'Eon could be an intransigent negotiator, and he did not want to appear too eager or to make his intentions obvious. He did not have to wait long.

D'Eon knew Morande, the blackmailer with whom Beaumarchais had maintained a friendship since his previous mission to London. On April 20, 1775, the very day that British troops fired on militiamen at Lexington, Massachusetts, d'Eon asked Morande to introduce him to the famous playwright. D'Eon had read Beaumarchais's "Memorials" attacking the French judiciary, which gave d'Eon "reason to suppose, judging by the boldness of his style and opinions, that there was still a man left in Paris." D'Eon, himself a cult figure who boldly challenged convention, was curious to meet the man who had revolutionized timekeeping, satirized the aristocracy, and exposed a corrupt judiciary. "Both of us probably felt drawn to each another by the kind of natural curiosity found in all extraordinary animals," d'Eon later explained. More to the point, d'Eon also had a hunch that since Beaumarchais had been sent once before to London to pay off Morande for his false libels, he might have authority to buy back the king's papers from d'Eon. Morande directed d'Eon to Beaumarchais's flat.

D'Eon arrived at Beaumarchais's door at Ploone Street without an appointment. Even at forty-seven, d'Eon cut an athletic figure. He was short and trim, with thick light-brown hair, smooth skin, sparkling blue eyes, and fine features. He wore the green-and-crimson uniform of a captain in the king's regiment of dragoons. On his chest he displayed the *Croix de Saint-Louis*, France's highest honor for military service, which Louis XV had awarded him for his service as an officer and a spy. He introduced himself in French. Despite years in the diplomatic service, d'Eon still spoke with the soft provincial accent of Burgundy.

The chevalier's poise did not disguise his anxiety. After they exchanged pleasantries, and d'Eon acknowledged his admiration for Beaumarchais's writing, he bluntly announced that he had come to open negotiations with the king. Beaumarchais feigned ignorance. He claimed that he was visiting London on personal business; he was no longer in the king's employ, and he had no commission to negotiate on the king's behalf. The chevalier did not believe him and insisted that Beaumarchais, who, after all, had paid off the vulgar libeler Morande, surely must have something to offer an officer and minister plenipotentiary who had loyally served his king. The chevalier assured Beaumarchais that he had come to him in good faith, but Beaumarchais replied that he "was not seeking either his friendship or his trust." D'Eon could beg him to accept the former, but he could not force him "to be the repository of the other."

The playwright clearly was toying with him, and they both knew it. D'Eon was profoundly shaken by Beaumarchais's sangfroid. D'Eon had come believing that Beaumarchais was in London to end his estrangement from his king and country. His voice began to quaver as he told Beaumarchais that if Versailles had been willing to talk, "I would have been back in my country a long time ago . . . and the King would have received all the important papers relative to the secret of Louis XV, which must not remain in England." For a man as proud as the chevalier to be reduced to begging a convicted criminal for help was a sign of his growing desperation. Deserted by the king he had served faithfully, d'Eon felt "like a drowning man abandoned . . . to the current of an infected river." Morande had warned him that Beaumarchais was a tricky negotiator, and d'Eon knew better than to trust the playwright. But he also knew that his only chance for rescue depended on Beaumarchais, and so d'Eon begged Beaumarchais to help him. As d'Eon remarked years later, he grabbed hold of "the boat of Caron [Beaumarchais] as I would to a red-hot rod of iron." In the end, he came to regret his dependence on Beaumarchais. "Although I took the precaution to protect my hands with gauntlets, I had my fingers burnt after all."

As d'Eon became more agitated, Beaumarchais remained implacable. Beaumarchais was not going to make it easy on the chevalier. He persisted in pretending that he had no idea what d'Eon was asking, and he denied that he had any authority to act as an agent for Louis XVI. The more Beaumarchais demurred the more intensely d'Eon entreated him to save him. Beaumarchais coolly moved to end the interview, but the chevalier refused to leave his flat.

After years spent dodging his creditors and hiding from the king's agents sent to capture or kill him, d'Eon could take no more abuse. He was at the end of his rope. Everything he had done was in the service of his king, and all he asked for was a chance to retire in dignity. It was too much for the chevalier to bear. He became hysterical resisting Beaumarchais's efforts to show him the door. He began to sob uncontrollably. Suddenly, he exclaimed, "*Je suis une femme malheureuse!*" ("I am an unhappy woman!")

FOR A MOMENT, Beaumarchais was stunned by d'Eon's sudden admission. Of course, Beaumarchais had heard the rumors that d'Eon was a woman, but he did not necessarily believe them, and, in any event, he surely would not have expected her to confess her gender to a complete stranger. Yet, as the *chevalière* collapsed in his arms, weeping, there could be no doubt of her gender. She had a woman's voice. Her face was smooth, her hands and feet were small for a man, and though she showed her age, she retained something of her beauty. Beneath her military uniform, she felt small and light, nothing like a man. Despite the strong odor of tobacco and the medals on her chest pressing against Beaumarchais, she had a sweet vulnerability. How was it possible that this decorated officer, diplomat, and spy could be a woman?

As d'Eon later explained in her *Memoirs,* her older brother had died before she was born, and her father desperately wanted a son to replace him. D'Eon was the youngest of two daughters, and her

disappointed father insisted on baptizing her as a boy. She was christened with the names of five male and one female saint. According
to d'Eon, her mother acquiesced in her father's decision only because her grandmother, a wealthy noblewoman, promised her
mother the sum of 12,000 livres if she had a son.

From d'Eon's early years she was as good at athletic pursuits as
any boy. She quickly realized at a young age that, dressed as a man,
she had greater opportunities than she would as a woman. She
"would prefer to keep my male clothes because they open all the
doors to fortune, glory, and courage." As she watched her older sister's life constricted by her gender, d'Eon was keenly aware of the
ways that she was spared an unhappy fate. She excelled at fencing and
riding, while her older sister could only watch. "Dresses close all
those doors for me. Dresses only give me room to cry about the
misery and servitude of women," d'Eon later mused. It was not a life
for someone who was "crazy about liberty." D'Eon had dressed and
behaved as a man for four decades. The only hint that she was different from other men was her apparent indifference to women.

As Beaumarchais held her in his arms, he smiled to himself, certain that he knew how he would persuade her to surrender the king's
correspondence. He would now regain the king's confidence and a
position at court. At last, Beaumarchais had found his salvation, and
it was a woman.

EIGHT

THE CHEVALIER'S GHOST

London, June–October 1775

At least since she had left her home in Burgundy, d'Eon had never told anyone that she was female. Beaumarchais was deeply moved by her naked vulnerability. He wrote to Louis XVI that "When one thinks that this creature, so much persecuted, belongs to a sex to which one forgives everything, the heart is touched with a sweet compassion." Beaumarchais was already ensnared in d'Eon's emotional web. He could not disguise his feelings towards the *chevalière*, but he felt sure that he could capture both her heart and the king's papers. "I do assure you, Sire," Beaumarchais wrote to Louis, "that in taking this astonishing creature with dexterity and gentleness, although she is embittered by twelve years of misfortune, she can yet be brought to enter under the yoke, and to give up all the papers of the late King on reasonable conditions." Though he sounded confident Beaumarchais underestimated the will of this determined woman.

In June, Beaumarchais returned to Versailles to discuss with Foreign Minister Vergennes the terms for resolving d'Eon's blackmail
threat. Beaumarchais informed Vergennes that d'Eon wished to return to France with a guarantee of her safety and freedom, but first
she insisted on having a formal audience with George III to bid
farewell in her capacity as minister plenipotentiary. Beaumarchais
realized that she was quite capable of saying anything and that it
would be impossible to control her behavior in such a situation.
Allowing d'Eon to appear before the British monarch as the emissary of Louis XVI would risk embarrassing both France and England. Beaumarchais suggested to Vergennes that if d'Eon were
required to declare openly that she was a woman, it would make it
impossible for her to continue to claim she were the minister plenipotentiary. She would have to admit that she was a fraud, and she
would be compelled to return to France quietly without a formal
meeting with George III. In this way, a potentially embarrassing
diplomatic scene could be avoided.

Vergennes agreed that if d'Eon admitted publicly that she was a
woman, it would no longer be an option for her to have an audience
with the king of England. "If M. d'Eon is willing to adopt the cos-
tume of his sex," Vergennes advised Louis XVI (unsure of his pro-
nouns), "there will be no objection to his return to France. But
under any other circumstances, he should not even express that
wish." Over the last decade of her public battle with the French government, the *chevalière* had offended a number of prominent
Frenchmen, particularly her rival, Ambassador Guerchy. Vergennes
worried that if d'Eon returned to France as a man, d'Eon's enemies would seek revenge, but if d'Eon returned as a woman, there
would be no need to settle old scores. "If Mr. D'Eon wanted to
wear women's clothes, the matter would be over."

There was another, more important reason for demanding that

d'Eon acknowledge her feminine identity: Vergennes and Louis XVI had every reason to fear that even if d'Eon returned the correspondence to Beaumarchais, d'Eon would still be in a position to continue blackmailing Louis XVI with the knowledge that his grandfather had planned to invade London. The only way to silence d'Eon permanently—short of murder—would be to compel her to declare publicly that she was female. Once d'Eon was forced to admit she was a woman disguised as a man, who would believe anything she said? She would have no credibility with which to threaten Louis XVI in the future.

D'Eon must have realized that if she publicly acknowledged she was female, she would lose her power to threaten the king in the future as well as any hope of returning to government service. On the other hand, there is evidence that long before Beaumarchais had arrived in London, d'Eon had been preparing the way for coming out as a woman. Years earlier, she had begun purchasing corsets, jewelry, and other female garments, presumably for her own wardrobe. And she may have started the rumors herself about being female. Her actions suggest that perhaps she was tired of dressing as a man, and Beaumarchais presented her with the opportunity to free herself from the bonds of her male disguise. If that were the case, then perhaps she only resisted Beaumarchais's proposal that she declare herself female in the hope that she could squeeze more money out of Louis XVI.

By July, Beaumarchais reported to Vergennes that he had almost concluded his negotiations with the woman he affectionately called his "*Amazone*." That was an exaggeration. In fact, negotiations had barely begun, and d'Eon was enjoying Beaumarchais's attention too much to allow him to bring the negotiations to a rapid conclusion. As a gesture of her good faith, d'Eon presented Beaumarchais with the key to an iron chest in which she promised she had deposited her secret correspondence with Louis XV. D'Eon gave the chest to her friend Lord Ferrers for safekeeping while she did her utmost to prolong their negotiations.

By personality and expediency the *chevalière* and the playwright were two contradictory individuals uniquely suited to each other. Both were brilliant social outlaws and, at the same time, social climbers; both duplicitous secret agents of the monarch and yet they saw themselves as champions of the common man; both charming raconteurs who were loathed and discredited by many powerful people. Beaumarchais and d'Eon each needed the other in their quest to win the king's approval. Without d'Eon, Beaumarchais would return to France without title, property, or the rights accorded citizens. Without Beaumarchais, d'Eon would remain in political exile, impoverished, unwelcome in her own country. Thus began a strange courtship.

WHILE NEGOTIATIONS BETWEEN Beaumarchais and d'Eon dragged on, half a world away events were coursing swiftly toward revolution. In June, two thousand British regulars attacked Massachusetts militiamen holding Breed's Hill over Boston Harbor. The British succeeded in capturing the heights, but lost half their men. This battle, known popularly as "Bunker Hill," was the first significant military confrontation between British and American forces. In response, the Second Continental Congress meeting in Philadelphia established the army of the United Colonies, which later became known as the Continental Army and selected the Virginian delegate George Washington as commander-in-chief in June, 1775.

At forty-three, Washington was painfully aware of his own limitations as a military commander. He had no formal military education and only limited military experience two decades earlier. Despite Washington's shortcomings, John Adams nominated him as commander-in-chief in order to win support from other southern delegates for independence. After assuming command of the ragged Continental Army camped in Cambridge across the Charles River from Boston in July, Washington wrote, "Could I have foreseen what I have experienced and am likely to experience, no consideration on earth would have induced me to accept the command."

Though Washington had been promised an army of 18,000 men, he had barely 13,000 men, including nearly 600 drummers and fifers. It was an army in name only. The colonists were undisciplined and inexperienced. Beyond the deficiency in training and numbers of men, Washington's army lacked the most basic implements of war. Supply shortages, combined with Congress's routine failure to pay the soldiers what was due them, would lead to mass desertions, further undermining the army's strength. Colonists without guns, bullets, uniforms, or boots practiced playing soldier with broomsticks. At the time Washington took command, the Massachusetts regiments had only 36 barrels of gunpowder, less than half a pound per man, and there were less than 100 barrels of gunpowder in all of the colonial militias combined. If the British attacked with their vastly superior forces, each man could fire at most nine times before the entire stock of powder in rebel hands would be exhausted. Moreover, the colonies had no capacity to manufacture significant quantities of gunpowder or muskets. All of the army's ammunition and guns would have to be imported—around the British blockade.

Back in Philadelphia, in July 1775, the delegates adopted the Olive Branch Petition, appealing for reconciliation with Britain; but when the petition was presented to George III, he refused to even accept it. Instead, the king declared the American colonies were in open rebellion. Recognizing the military weakness of the colonies, the British were determined to settle the dispute once and for all by force of arms.

THROUGH THE AUTUMN of 1775 Beaumarchais and d'Eon danced a curious *pas de deux*. Beaumarchais sought to win her trust using every masculine charm and artifice. He boasted to a friend that he could offer "a head, a heart, two arms and no tongue" with which to persuade d'Eon. For a master of the game of seduction like Beaumarchais, the *chevalière* posed an interesting challenge. Beaumarchais was d'Eon's frequent companion and confidant. Both were seen out in London as regular guests at the homes of prominent Whigs, many of whom, like d'Eon, were Freemasons at the Lodge of Immortality at the Crown and Anchor in the Strand. For her part, d'Eon continued in her masculine disguise, alternately intransigent or vulnerable, threatening or plaintive. How far could she push the playwright? And how far would she permit him to go without offending either her feminine modesty or her masculine honor?

That autumn, rumors again began circulating in Lloyd's and other London coffeehouses that d'Eon was a woman. There were even whispers of an affair between d'Eon and a certain unnamed French playwright. Indeed, it may be that Beaumarchais started these rumors for reasons that became clear only later.

D'Eon was flattered by Beaumarchais's apparent interest in her, but she was also amused that a forty-seven-year-old soldier could touch the heart of the handsome younger man. What she saw in her looking glass was not a blushing ingénue but a tough battle-scarred veteran, a daring spy, and an aging diplomat. As one of her contemporaries noted, her sinewy arms looked better suited for carrying a sedan chair than a fan. But d'Eon appreciated and encouraged Beaumarchais's attention. She called him her "guardian angel." She gave him her portrait as a token of her affection and asked for his in return.

Was Beaumarchais genuinely attracted to her? We cannot know for sure. Most of Beaumarchais's biographers dismissed the idea that he was romantically interested in d'Eon, but it was not impossible. D'Eon was no longer an androgynous beauty, but her wit and charm were undiminished. Beaumarchais was just three years younger, and he had already shown a preference for middle-aged women. If his wife were still alive, she, too, would be in her forties. Beaumarchais's correspondence with d'Eon was often affectionate and playful: "I am giving over the evening to Venus," the goddess of love, Beaumarchais wrote to d'Eon, "when do you want me to embrace Minerva?" Minerva, the goddess of war, would seem to refer to his *chevalière*. On another occasion, after one of their arguments, Beaumarchais wrote to d'Eon that he looked forward to seeing her "with all my heart and I will consider myself so happy if I can still contribute to your future happiness."

Regardless of how Beaumarchais really felt about d'Eon, she was obsessed with him, and her writing suggests that she had formed a deep emotional attachment. For d'Eon, who all her life had denied herself any opportunity for love, Beaumarchais had changed everything. "My heart which has been closed to other men," she wrote to him, "naturally opens in your presence, like a flower spreading itself out in a ray of sunshine." She teased Beaumarchais affectionately. In one letter he was "the shrewdest and nicest monkey" she had ever met. She even quoted back to him his own writing: "I repeat what Rosina says in Le Barbier de Seville, you are made to be loved!"

Beaumarchais acknowledged to Vergennes that "Everybody tells me this madwoman is crazy about me." He could not deny the humor in it: "[H]ow on earth could I imagine that, to serve the King zealously, I would have to become a gallant knight to a captain of dragoons?"

Some biographers have suggested that d'Eon was merely manipulating Beaumarchais's ego with flattery, but d'Eon was not a cold calculating woman. She was highly emotional and romantic, even when her sentiments worked to her disadvantage, as they often did. If d'Eon had been better able to control her emotions in the first place, she would have avoided alienating the French king and his advisers, and she could have kept her diplomatic job. It was precisely because d'Eon was so readily swayed by her heart's desire, rather than by rational self-interest, that she found herself in this predicament.

By the end of October 1775, after months of negotiating, cajoling, threatening, and wooing, Beaumarchais had finally persuaded d'Eon to return Louis XV's correspondence. Their agreement, which they referred to as "the Transaction," was part legal contract, part narrative, and part apologia. It stipulated that d'Eon would receive from Louis XVI an annual pension of 12,000 livres (about $92,000 today) for her past military and diplomatic service. In addition, Louis XVI would assume most of her debts from the time she was minister plenipotentiary. She agreed to surrender her military uniforms and arms to Beaumarchais, and she was promised an allowance of 6,000 livres (about $46,000 today) to pay for a new feminine wardrobe. She was allowed to keep only one complete uniform of her regiment—with her helmet, saber, pistol, rifle, and bayonet—as a souvenir of her military service, and she was permitted to wear the distinguished *Croix de Saint-Louis* on her dress as a tribute to her gallantry.

In exchange, the agreement provided that d'Eon, a "spinster of full age," would surrender all of the king's papers and abandon "that disguise which has hitherto hidden the person of a woman under the appearance of the Chevalier d'Eon." Beaumarchais was at pains to absolve d'Eon of any moral culpability for her deception by specifying in the agreement that her "parents alone are guilty." The document somewhat incongruously praised "the rare example of this extraordinary girl," who, like Joan of Arc, "bravely fulfilled all the dangerous duties" of a professional soldier "in man's attire," and recognized her "modest and virtuous, though vigorous and manly, manner in which she has always conducted herself in her adopted garb." The time had come, therefore, to resolve "the uncertainty about her sex, which up to now has been an inexhaustible subject of indecent bets and salacious jokes." To appeal to her vanity, Beaumarchais added that by assuming women's clothing "it can only make her appear more interesting in the eyes of both sexes which her life, her courage and her talents have equally honored." In addition to paying her pension and debts, the king guaranteed her safe return to France. At d'Eon's suggestion they agreed that the contract would be back-dated to October 5, her forty-seventh birthday, signifying her rebirth as a woman. In a dramatic flourish, the playwright exhorted "the ghost of the Chevalier d'Eon" to "vanish forever."

Beaumarchais soon learned that ghosts are not so easily exorcised.

NINE

THE JUDGE

Philadelphia, June–December 1775

I n June, the weather in Philadelphia turned tropical. It was an effort just to breathe the thick, moist air, and enormous black mosquitoes tormented the delegates, who were soon covered with itchy red welts. In their black wool stockings, powdered wigs, and waistcoats, the delegates were ill prepared to face summer in Philadelphia. They met on the first floor of the handsome redbrick Pennsylvania State House, which would later become known as Independence Hall. The delegates sat at small tables in pairs on assorted dark Windsor chairs. Each table was covered with a green cloth, and running from left to right the tables were grouped into New England, mid-Atlantic, and southern colonies. They faced a large fireplace and a raised platform where the president of the Continental Congress sat at a long table. The three tall double-hung windows on the front and back of the building were kept closed and shuttered much of the time to preserve the secrecy of the proceedings. As a result, the room temperature hovered between eighty and one hundred degrees much of the summer.

Among the men sweltering in the Assembly room were the most distinguished leaders of the colonies. There were prominent financiers and statesmen, large landowners with long pedigrees and famous attorneys noted for their brilliant oratory. Silas Deane, by contrast, was a shopkeeper and the son of a blacksmith from a small New England town. He was less well known and less politically experienced than any of the other New England delegates. Among such glittering company, Deane might have been expected to sit quietly in the background, as the young Virginian Thomas Jefferson was inclined to do. Yet, after the victory at Ticonderoga, Deane quickly emerged as one of the leaders in Congress. His stout support for independence and his intellect impressed many, and Congress acknowledged Deane's abilities by selecting him for numerous important committees. Among other assignments, he was appointed to the Committee on Trade, the Committee of Ways and Means, which he chaired, and, most important, the Committee of Secrecy, which had the critical responsibility of obtaining gunpowder, cannons, muskets, and uniforms from Europe. This committee, better known as the "Secret Committee," became the primary source of funding for arming the military.

It soon became clear that Deane was gifted at building coalitions across regional lines. John Adams wrote to his wife, Abigail, that Deane was "a very ingenious Man and an able Politician." Adams remarked that "There is scarcely a more active, industrious, enterprising and capable Man, than Mr. Deane." On a typical day, Deane would rise at six, write letters to his wife and business associates for an hour, and then dress and eat. He would start his committee work at eight, for a couple of hours before Congress convened at ten.

Congress continued right through lunch until four, when he would dine with several of his colleagues and discuss the day's work. After dinner he would spend several hours at more committee meetings. He would have a light supper before going to bed at eleven. Congress exhausted him. "My time is all taken up," he wrote his wife. "Well as I love the busy scenes of politics, . . . I have had more than my share of such business."

Deane's hard work and popularity bred jealousy among some of the delegates. His ceaseless energy and his close relationships with the leading figures in Congress—Adams, Franklin, and Washington— probably made some of the other delegates self-conscious about their own modest contributions and influence. They saw his fierce commitment to independence as an excess of ambition. Some of the delegates—especially among the New England Puritans and the southern planters—were inherently suspicious of members of the new mercantile class. To these delegates, Deane epitomized the new wealth that arose not from land or craft, but from foreign trade. For them, thrift was a religious virtue, and Deane's taste for luxury evidenced a character flaw.

Ever since his time at Yale, Deane had worked hard to be well liked, and he was overly sensitive to the opinions of some delegates. "People here, members of Congress and others, have unhappily and erroneously thought me a schemer," Deane lamented to Elizabeth.

My principles are (the eyes of my God knows them, and the most envious eye of man or the bitter tongue of slander cannot find anything in my political conduct to contradict them) to sacrifice all lesser considerations to the service of the whole, and in this tempestuous season to throw cheerfully overboard private fortune, private emolument, even my life,—if the ship, with the jewel Liberty, may be safe. This being my line of conduct, I have calmness of mind which more than balances my external troubles, of which I have not a few.

One of Deane's chief troubles was Judge Sherman, who became increasingly jealous of Deane's growing influence in Congress. Partly it was a matter of personality. Deane radiated good cheer and a ready wit. He spoke sparingly, but when he did, his speeches were punchy, practical, and persuasive. The judge, by contrast, glowered. He had no patience for friendly banter among delegates. Sherman, in John Adams's words, spoke "often and long, but very heavily." Sanctimonious and often rude, he was "the Reverse of Grace," Adams joked. Adams thought that Sherman seemed ill at ease, as if his body were a compressed spring ready to pop. He would stand up to speak with his right hand holding his left clenched tightly into an angry fist. At random intervals, he would jerk his arms upward with his fist still clenched. Adams described Sherman's manner as "Stiffness and Awkwardness itself. Rigid as Starched Linen or Buckram. Awkward as a junior Bachelor or a Sophomore." While most delegates may have respected Judge Sherman, nearly all would have preferred to dine with Deane.

Underlying the differences between Deane and Sherman were class and regional conflicts. In the 1600s, New Haven had been the headquarters of the New Haven colony—separate from the Connecticut colony. The two colonies later joined, and for a time New Haven and Hartford were co-capital cities. By the 1770s, Hartford had eclipsed New Haven as the provincial capital. The two cities bitterly vied for influence in the colonial Assembly. Sherman was one of the leading politicians in New Haven, and he saw Deane as embodying the Hartford elite. Deane was far better educated, more politically prominent, and financially more successful than the judge. Deane felt sorry for Sherman, whom he regarded as irritating

but harmless. Sherman, by contrast, could not distinguish their regional rivalry from their personal differences. For Sherman to succeed, he believed, Deane had to be crushed.

A bitter division between Deane and Sherman arose over the
appointment of officers to the Continental Army from Connecticut. Following Washington's commission as commander-in-chief,
Congress appointed four major generals under him. For political
reasons, Congress set aside one of these top posts for an officer from
the Connecticut militia. The Connecticut General Assembly had
voted to recommend Connecticut's Major General David Wooster
for the post, and Sherman, who was Wooster's friend and neighbor,
strongly favored him. Deane, however, thought Wooster, at sixty-six,
too elderly to serve as second in command of the Continental Army.
In Deane's eyes, Wooster's religiosity, his oversized wigs, and his
ill-fitting hats marked him as old-fashioned and eccentric. Deane
found Wooster "totally unequal to the service" and said so openly
before Congress. Deane preferred Captain Israel Putnam, a tough-
talking tavern owner and a hardened soldier-farmer from northeast-
ern Connecticut. Putnam was beloved by his men, who affectionately
called him "Old Put." Though he ranked below Major General
Wooster in the Connecticut Militia, Putnam was a more experienced and more successful officer than Wooster—or even Washington. In Congress, Deane led the fight to appoint Putnam over the
objections of Sherman and the Connecticut Assembly. While he recognized the political risk, Deane did what he thought was right for
the army. He wrote to Elizabeth that "[I] am determined to do my
duty, and will on no occasion sacrifice the good of my country to
the whim of any old man, or old woman rather, or their sticklers."
Persuaded by Deane, Congress unanimously endorsed Putnam. It
was a stunning victory and evidence of Deane's growing influence
in Congress. But Sherman and Wooster were furious, and Deane was

savagely attacked by the friends of Wooster and Sherman in the
Connecticut Assembly.

DEANE PAID a high price for his support of Putnam. Despite
Deane's effectiveness in Congress, the Connecticut Assembly did not
reappoint Deane as a delegate in 1776. Deane was "confoundedly
Chagrined at his recall," according to his Connecticut colleague
Eliphalet Dyer, who was also denied reappointment. Dyer expressed
his surprise at Deane's recall, noting that Deane "is really Very Use-
full here and much esteemed in Congress." Ezra Stiles, a Congregationalist minister and future president of Yale College, remarked
that the Assembly recalled Deane and Dyer "for this principal Reason that they think Liberty most secure under frequent changes of
Delegates & they determine to set an early Example & Precedent."
But Stiles, too, felt compelled to acknowledge that Deane was "a
most useful Member in Congress." In fact, Stiles's explanation is not
convincing, since the Connecticut Assembly continued to reappoint
other delegates, including Sherman. Sherman most likely played
some role in defeating his two colleagues, as Deane's friend John
Trumbull reported from Connecticut. While there is no record of
the reasons the Assembly recalled Deane, the most obvious explanation is that many members of the Assembly wanted to punish
Deane for opposing Wooster.

Deane tried to accept his recall gracefully. He wrote Elizabeth
that he was "quite as willing to quit my station to abler men; and
who they are, the Colony knows, or ought to know, best." He was
"unfit for trimming, courting, and intrigues with the populace," and
he wondered "how I ever became popular at all. What therefore I
did not expect, I have too much philosophy to be in distress at losing." To his opponents he wished "no other punishment than a con-

sciousness of the low, envious, jealous and sordid motives by which they are actuated."

Deane did not seek revenge against Sherman for engineering his recall. He tried to maintain a cordial relationship with the judge, but Sherman remained frosty. In private, Deane confided to his wife his annoyance with "that malevolent prig in buckram, who is secure from my serious resentment in consequence of the supreme contempt I have ever, and still hold him in." In Deane's eyes, Sherman had betrayed his country by sacrificing a dedicated public servant for political gain. In public, Deane would not criticize Sherman, and unlike the judge, he was not the sort of man to carry a grudge. More than anything, he pitied Sherman's lack of social grace. Once, Deane loaned Sherman his coach, and the judge returned it badly damaged without even offering to pay a portion of the repairs. Deane shrugged off the incident and took the opportunity to refit the carriage as a more capacious phaeton. With characteristic magnanimity, Deane wrote to his wife that Sherman was not really at fault; rather, Sherman was "peculiarly unfortunate."

Deane knew others were plotting against him in Connecticut and in Congress, but he treated everyone respectfully. When warned that a friend and neighbor in Wethersfield had spoken out against him, Deane replied coolly "that I should sooner suspect my own conduct than his honor and friendship." Deane concentrated on the cause of independence. His civility and hard work were rewarded with the support and appreciation of nearly all the delegates. Franklin, in particular, continued to be impressed by Deane's energy and commitment.

With the encouragement of his colleagues, Deane continued serving in Philadelphia for several months after he was recalled. Congress unanimously appointed Deane to a committee to establish a navy. In late 1775 and early 1776, Deane, with help from Robert

Morris, Franklin, and John Jay, planned, acquired, and equipped the first ships to sail under the American flag. During months of frenetic activity, Deane built the navy from scratch. He rode back and forth between Philadelphia and New York City to talk to shipbuilders and review sketches. He searched for outfitters and chased down suppliers. All this time Deane kept promising Elizabeth he would return to Connecticut as soon as he had completed his work, but Congress's need for a navy was more urgent than his own family's need for him.

Had events turned out otherwise, Silas Deane would have returned to Wethersfield, but Deane's retirement from politics was postponed indefinitely when a mysterious visitor appeared in Philadelphia.

TEN

THE LORD MAYOR

London, September 1775

The first week in September, Beaumarchais and d'Eon were invited to dine with the Lord Mayor of London, John Wilkes, at his official residence, Mansion House. Beaumarchais was curious to meet Wilkes, who was an outspoken critic of the prime minister, Lord North. The Lord Mayor probably invited Beaumarchais as a favor to d'Eon, who was his good friend. Beaumarchais was joined by his personal secretary, Paul-Philippe Gudin de La Brenellerie. Beaumarchais had kept his dealings with d'Eon secret even from Gudin. Once seated at the Lord Mayor's sumptuous banquet table, Gudin leaned over and asked the Lord Mayor's daughter, Polly, who was "that man with a woman's voice?" Gudin was intrigued by the mysterious d'Eon. D'Eon seemed at once aggressive and vulnerable, powerful and feminine. Some time later that evening, d'Eon privately confessed to Gudin in tears that she was, in fact, a woman.

Gudin had not yet heard all the rumors about d'Eon. Some London newspapers had linked d'Eon romantically to Lord Mayor

Wilkes and even reported that d'Eon had given birth to Wilkes's child in the lobby of the House of Commons. In fact, Wilkes was as unsure of d'Eon's gender as the rest of the world was. Wilkes's daughter Polly once wrote to d'Eon, boldly posing the question that all London was asking: "Miss Wilkes presents her compliments to Monsieur the Chevalier d'Eon, and is very anxious to know if he is really a woman, as everybody asserts, or a man." Years later, after the *chevalière* had declared that she was a woman, the Lord Mayor continued to welcome her to his home. Unperturbed by this news, Wilkes's notations in his diary switched from "dined with the Chevalier d'Eon," to "dined with the Chevalière," as if it were merely a change in spelling.

Theirs was a peculiar friendship. The effete, prudish d'Eon had little in common with the populist politician Wilkes. Wilkes was a radical libertine: he was promiscuous, indecent, and heretical. He belonged to the notorious Hell Fire Club, a secret society that ridiculed the Church while conducting sexual orgies in the ruins of an old abbey. The king called him "that devil Wilkes," and most gentlemen, including Benjamin Franklin, when he lived in London, spurned him. His astonishing popularity with the "middling sort" was a testament to his wit and eloquence. Wilkes was purportedly "the homeliest man in London," but he joked that he needed only twenty minutes with a woman to "talk away my face." When John Montagu, the Earl of Sandwich, remarked that Wilkes would die either of venereal disease or on the gallows, Wilkes fired back, "that depends, my lord, whether I embrace your mistress or your principles." The son of a malt distributor, Wilkes made a career of insulting aristocrats and rousing the rabble. Once when Wilkes was invited to join a card game, he replied, "Do not ask me, for I am so ignorant that I cannot tell the difference between a king and a knave."

Wilkes and d'Eon were both unlikely folk heroes, whose eccentric behavior pushed the limits of personal liberty against the constraints of society. Political expediency drew them together. Wilkes hoped that d'Eon would provide him with secret information about the diplomatic negotiations between France and Britain that would embarrass Lord North's cabinet, while d'Eon hoped to gather intelligence from Wilkes for the French king. Both could profit from exploiting their relationship. When d'Eon feared that the French government would try to assassinate her, Wilkes offered her protection by posting supporters to keep a constant vigil outside d'Eon's house on Golden Square in Soho.

Wilkes had launched his political career in 1762 by founding a radical newspaper, *The North Briton,* which was highly critical of the then–prime minister, Lord Bute. Wilkes's platform called for extending voting rights to the common man, making Parliament more representative, punishing corrupt politicians, and protecting free speech from government censorship. In April 1763, Wilkes published the famous issue number 45 of *The North Briton* in which he excoriated the king's ministers as "tools of despotism and corruption." Soon after, Wilkes was arrested for publishing seditious and treasonable statements against the crown and briefly held in the Tower of London. After his release from the Tower, he was expelled from Parliament and charged with obscenity for a poem he had written years earlier for the Hell Fire Club. Wilkes fled to France, and an English trial court convicted him in absentia of obscenity. He remained in France several years, until he could no longer afford to live abroad and feared his creditors would catch up with him. Wilkes returned to London in 1768 as a hugely popular fugitive. Across London, residents stenciled the number "45" on their front doors as an expression of solidarity with Wilkes and his publication. When he was arrested again, mobs demanding his immediate release took to the streets, chanting, "Wilkes and liberty!" The government was unable to restore order even by force of arms.

Wilkes remained in King's Bench Prison for two years. There he inhabited a comfortable ground-floor suite of rooms with a view of St. George's Field and London Bridge where he received a constant flow of distinguished visitors. During that time he won election to Parliament as a radical reformer four times, and four times the government voided the election on the grounds that a convict could not serve in Parliament. The ongoing battle kept Wilkes in the public eye and ensured that the Wilkites continued to control London's streets. All over London Wilkes was lauded as a champion of liberty. Pubs were renamed for him. Women sent him love letters. Friends lavished gifts on him: a barrel of Yorkshire ale, 240 bottles of wine, silver, pet turtles, pork, turkey, salmon, forty-five hogsheads of Virginia tobacco, and, on his birthday, a dozen smoked tongues from a certain admiring chevalier. D'Eon enclosed a note with the gift, wishing that "the tongues might have the eloquence of Cicero and the nicety of speech of Voltaire." After his release from prison, Wilkes won election as Lord Mayor of London and as member of Parliament in 1774.

Wilkes had begun his political career as a staunch defender of the empire; he even supported taxing the American colonies to pay for British troops. However, as the political winds shifted, so did his view of the American conflict. In 1775, Wilkes repeatedly stood up in Parliament to defend the colonies' right to representation, and he received a warm response from many Americans who identified his cause with theirs. Americans embraced the mottoes "Wilkes and Liberty" and "Number 45" in opposition to a tyrannical Parliament. When George III proclaimed, in August 1775, that Massachusetts was in rebellion, Wilkes warned that the king "draws the sword unjustly against America." Wilkes and his friends believed that Britain would be better served by concentrating its resources at home rather than spreading its forces in a remote wilderness. Wilkes declared that the American colonies viewed Britain "as a tyrannical, unprincipled, rapacious, and ruined nation," while America was a "sure asylum" for liberty. By the autumn of 1775, the Lord Mayor's Mansion House had become the de facto headquarters of the opposition to British colonial policy. Wilkes gathered around him an unorthodox circle of social and political outlaws operating on the fringe of London society.

Beaumarchais and d'Eon were frequent guests of the Lord Mayor that season. Since Beaumarchais could not speak English, he often depended upon d'Eon to translate for him. Beaumarchais admired Wilkes's criticism of British colonial policy. More than a decade earlier, Beaumarchais's patron, Pâris-Duverney, had implanted in him the idea of avenging France's defeat by severing the North American colonies from the British Empire. As Beaumarchais moved among Wilkes's exotic circle of luminaries and iconoclasts, that seed began to germinate in his fertile imagination.

ELEVEN

THE FOREIGN MINISTER

Paris, September 1775

Charles Gravier, the Comte de Vergennes, had spent a lifetime preparing himself to become foreign minister. His father was the president of the Parliament of Dijon, his uncle was a respected diplomat, and his brother was the president of the French Senate. Before Louis XVI ascended the throne, Vergennes had served Louis XV for more than three decades in various diplomatic posts, including thirteen years in the sensitive position of ambassador to the Ottoman Empire.

At fifty-five, he looked like a harmless bureaucrat. His plump face revealed nothing more than a vague sort of pleasantness. But this surface blandness masked a passionate intellect, a wry wit, a penchant for intrigue, and a natural talent for duplicity. Once, while serving as ambassador to Sweden, he engineered a coup that installed a more Francophile government in Stockholm. As foreign minister he would tell the most shameless lies to the British ambassador and later laugh about them. Yet in his private life, he was devoutly religious, scrupulously honest, and, perhaps unique among his peers at the French court, faithful to his wife. Vergennes, though jaded by the cynicism of eighteenth-century diplomacy, still cherished the quiet time he shared with his family and friends.

Six years before becoming foreign minister, Vergennes had been fired from his post as ambassador to Constantinople by Louis XV's foreign minister, the Duc de Choiseul. The immediate cause of his dismissal was that Vergennes had married without first obtaining Choiseul's permission. Vergennes's decision to marry for love was not merely considered peculiar in the court of Louis XV; it was insubordination. Choiseul felt entitled to control the public and private conduct of his ambassadors. The rupture between Choiseul and Vergennes was rooted in class and policy differences. Choiseul, stout, homely, and red-faced, traced his aristocratic lineage back through one of the most elite families in France. He lived in a vast palace near Versailles and amused himself with his own orchestra and troupe of entertainers. He spent obscene sums on trinkets for himself and his statuesque mistress, who towered over him. Choiseul sneered at Vergennes, whose family were relatively obscure petty nobles.

It wasn't just Choiseul's snobbery that offended Vergennes. He objected to Choiseul's style and policies as foreign minister. Where Choiseul was bellicose and boorish, Vergennes was cautious and discreet. Vergennes questioned Choiseul's controversial decision in 1754 to reverse French foreign policy and align France with her former enemy Austria. For more than a century, France had defended Poland against Austria's territorial ambitions. The bitter competition for hegemony between France and Austria had long divided the Continent. Choiseul, however, thought that Britain posed a much greater danger to France. Choiseul believed that an alliance with Austria would counterbalance Britain's military superiority. To solidify this "*renversement des alliances*," Choiseul arranged the marriage of Louis XV's grandson to Marie Antoinette, daughter of the empress of Austria. Vergennes strongly disapproved of the *renversement* and believed it threatened both the French monarchy and the peace of Europe.

Privately, Louis XV shared Vergennes's doubts about Austria's intentions, and about Choiseul as well. When the king established the network of spies known as "*le secret du roi*" (the Secret), Foreign Minister Choiseul knew nothing about it. Vergennes, like d'Eon, was one of the king's secret agents, quietly working against the policies of Choiseul.

Choiseul's tenure as foreign minister was a failure marked by military defeat and a loss of diplomatic influence across Europe. The Seven Years' War, which ended in 1763, shattered the French Empire. Britain forced France to concede all its territory in North America east of the Mississippi. She retained only the port of New Orleans, a portion of the West Indies, and two tiny fishing islands off the coast of Newfoundland. In addition, France lost her military bases in India, effectively conceding the subcontinent to Britain. France was left without a strong navy capable of defending against any future British invasion. Louis XV and Choiseul lusted for revenge against Britain, but France had neither the military strength nor the finances to fight. Meanwhile, the *renversement* had undermined French influence on the Continent. France watched helplessly as Russia, Austria, and Prussia attacked and carved 80,000 square miles out of Poland. By 1770, Louis XV had had enough of Choiseul, and he dismissed him from office.

Four years later, in 1774, Louis XVI succeeded to the throne on the death of his grandfather. (His father had died when he was eleven, and his mother died two years later.) The twenty-two-year-old monarch felt unprepared for the job. "I feel the universe is going to fall on me," he predicted with startling accuracy. At the urging of his aunt, Princess Adélaide, one of his first decisions was to appoint the Comte de Vergennes as foreign minister. Vergennes tutored the young monarch in the dangers and opportunities posed by France's adversaries.

Vergennes's worldview was shaped by France's humiliating defeat in the Seven Years' War and the partition of Poland. His foreign policy was founded on the fear that France was losing influence on the Continent and was vulnerable to attack by Britain. Certainly, France could not face Britain alone. The alliance with Austria had alienated France's traditional allies, and France could no longer depend on Spain. The Spanish were too preoccupied by their rivalry with Portugal to care much about the threat Britain posed to the Bourbon monarchs. The French navy was still decimated and could not even defend French shipping or the French West Indies. Louis XVI listened carefully to Vergennes's advice to strengthen French defenses and restore traditional alliances against Britain, but he did not act. The king seemed timid and equivocal. Vergennes understood that he would have to tailor his policies to fit an indecisive monarch.

Vergennes's first priority was to rebuild the navy. He knew that France needed a navy to counter British aggression and restore the balance of power in Europe. Louis XV's predatory ambitions had destabilized Europe and undermined French security by alienating potential allies against England; Louis XVI would have to expand French influence by renouncing territorial ambitions. Vergennes doubted the intentions of Austria, but he knew that Marie Antoinette would oppose any shift away from the alliance with her native country.

Vergennes argued that while France maintained the alliance with Austria and honored the peace treaty with Britain, France should also reaffirm the Bourbon Family Compact with the Spanish king,

Charles III. That would not be easy. The Family Compact was a series of treaties by which the two Bourbon powers, France and Spain,
had pledged to resist Austria and Britain. Each country promised to
regard any attack on the other sovereign or its colonies as an attack
on itself. Moreover, relations with Spain were complicated by Spain's
territorial ambitions in Gibraltar and South America and its obsession with Portugal. Spain also felt that it had already paid too high
a price for its alliance with France during the Seven Years' War: Britain had forced Spain to surrender Florida.

Spain's most pressing concern was preserving her colonies in
South America against encroachments by Portugal, a British ally.
Spain's King Charles III thought this was the right moment to strike
Portugal, while the British were tied down fighting the Americans.
Charles III expected France to join him against Portugal. The Spanish foreign minister, the Marqués de Grimaldi, wrote Vergennes in
1775 proposing a preemptive war against Portugal. He argued that
a quick, small, local war now against Portugal could prevent a much
larger war later, saving lives and money while restoring honor to the
Bourbons. Though it might seem odious to us that a great power
would propose an alliance for the purpose of launching an unpro-
voked attack on a smaller country in the name of preemption, diplomacy in the eighteenth century was far less civilized than in our
own time. Weaker states were, in the words of a Spanish minister,
"sliced like Dutch cheeses."

Vergennes knew that "*une petite guerre*" might quickly draw in
other European powers and become a much wider war. He responded to Grimaldi sympathetically, but he was not ready to risk
French soldiers in a war in which France had little to gain. Vergennes
wrote to the Spanish ambassador Aranda that the mere possibility
that Portugal might attack Spanish possessions at some point in the
future could not justify a preemptive strike. A preemptive war would

"soil oneself with a notorious injustice, which would be invincibly repugnant to the feelings and principles of the two monarchs." An unprincipled attack on a sovereign state would antagonize other European powers and undermine France's long-term interests in maintaining the balance of power. The argument for preemptive war was as tempting as it was dangerous. A wise leader would never commit his country to a foreign war in the name of preemption when no imminent threat existed.

Vergennes warned that "The spirit of revolt, wherever it breaks out, always gives a dangerous example." Revolution in North America threatened monarchy everywhere. Vergennes reassured England that France would not "take advantage of the difficulties which England faces with respect to her American colonies. . . ." Privately, Vergennes may have hoped for a long, drawn-out, indecisive war that would preoccupy Britain, expend her blood and treasure, and ensure that the colonies remained defiant and hostile to British interests—when and if they ever gained independence. He certainly was not prepared to help the Americans in any way to win independence. That would be a violation of France's treaty with Britain. It would be tantamount to a declaration of war, and France had neither the will nor the capacity to fight Britain.

BEAUMARCHAIS RETURNED to Versailles on September 20, 1775, to meet with Vergennes about d'Eon. But d'Eon was not the only subject Beaumarchais was interested in discussing. The talk around Lord Mayor Wilkes's table in London was all about the coming war in North America. Restless with ambition, Beaumarchais hoped to expand his portfolio to advise Vergennes about policy toward the American colonies. Since August, when George III issued a royal proclamation declaring that the colonies were in open rebellion, war between Britain and her colonies appeared unavoidable. Beaumarchais reported all this to Vergennes and impressed upon the foreign minister the necessity for France to take action to sustain the American rebels. Since the French king was about to leave for his hunting retreat at Fontainebleau, Beaumarchais drafted a report overnight that summarized his observations.

Beaumarchais reported that he had heard from an American who recently arrived from Philadelphia that the rebels had a well-armed and disciplined army of 38,000 men surrounding Boston and another 40,000 men scattered around the colonies. (In reality, Washington had at that time no more than 13,000 poorly trained and mostly unarmed soldiers who were compelled to return periodically to their farms to tend their fields.) Beaumarchais wrote that "All sensible people are therefore convinced in England that the English colonies are lost for the mother country." The opposition Whigs were calling the government's colonial policy a "masterpiece of folly." The opposition believed that the king's ministers could hold on to power only if they threw seven or eight members of Parliament into the Tower. Beaumarchais's good friend Lord Rochford, the Secretary of State for North America, told him that "winter will not pass without a few heads rolling, either in the King's party or in the Opposition."

Beaumarchais argued that France faced the possibility of war no matter what the outcome in America. He claimed that both the present British government—even the opposition Whigs, if they gained power—intended to steal the very profitable French sugar islands in the Caribbean. The French sugar islands, particularly Saint-Domingue, Martinique, Guadeloupe, and Saint Kitts, produced a vast share of the sugarcane consumed in Europe and yielded enormous profits for France.

Beaumarchais stopped short of recommending any particular

course of action to Louis XVI, but it was clear that he was arguing that France should intervene on behalf of the Americans. It was also clear that Beaumarchais was strategically leveraging his influence with the king, who needed Beaumarchais's help now to clear up the problem with d'Eon. What is less clear is whether there was any genuine threat that Britain would seize the French Caribbean islands. Most probably Beaumarchais concocted, or at the very least exaggerated, any threat in the hope of inducing Louis XVI to aid the Americans. Beaumarchais cautioned that "Our ministers, poorly informed, look stagnant and passive on all those events that couth our skin." Beaumarchais obliquely criticized the French ambassador to Britain and urged the king to appoint someone better suited to the position: "A superior and vigilant man would be indispensable in London today." There was no question what man Beaumarchais had in mind for this job, yet it was folly for him to think that Louis XVI would appoint him as ambassador.

At this point, Vergennes would not consider recommending any action on the war in North America. Vergennes knew that Louis XVI was cautious and idealistic and believed that France should focus its energies on improving the lives of its citizens and respecting its treaties with Britain. Moreover, Vergennes feared that any involvement in the British colonies risked sparking a war that could only end in defeat and humiliation for France. He had already received a report on the matter from Ambassador Guines, who had replaced Ambassador Guerchy at the French embassy in London after Guerchy was accused of trying to poison d'Eon. Ambassador Guines had reported that the Americans were well armed, which was entirely untrue. Guines's opinion mattered little to Vergennes, who thought the ambassador was a fool. But if Guines was correct, then the Americans did not need France to beat the British.

Beaumarchais waited in Paris for a reply from Versailles to his report. Days passed without a response. He did not know what to do. "All the sagacity in the world cannot help someone who remains without an answer about what he must do," he wrote to Vergennes. "Must I wait for your reply here, or must I leave without any? . . . [A]m I a useful agent for my country or only a deaf and dumb traveler?" But Vergennes remained mute. Even the king's ministers did not know what Vergennes was really thinking.

Three weeks before Beaumarchais arrived at Versailles, Vergennes had dispatched a secret agent to meet with the Continental Congress. While Beaumarchais returned to his *Amazone* in London, thinking that he had failed, Vergennes was waiting for a report from Philadelphia, hoping it would confirm Beaumarchais's optimistic appraisal of the Americans' prospects.

TWELVE

A SECRET LIAISON

Philadelphia, December 1775

I t was the time of the winter solstice, and the sun could not set soon enough for Benjamin Franklin. He watched the sunlight withdrawing behind the shuttered windows of the Pennsylvania State House as the other delegates droned on ceaselessly. Since the battles of Lexington and Concord the previous April, Congress, sitting in Philadelphia, was still dithering on the question of independence. In October, George III, addressing Parliament, had in effect declared war on the colonies, but still the delegates hesitated to sever their ties to Britain. Instead, the delegates bickered over the minute details of governing the colonies, endlessly postponing the overarching question of independence. The issue before them now was how much Congress should spend on clothing for prisoners of war. Franklin listened with growing impatience. Another hour passed as the candle at his desk melted into a waxy puddle. The last seven months in Philadelphia had been a mere prelude. Franklin knew what must be done, and he wondered whether this night could change history's course. When, at last, Congress adjourned for the day, Franklin's restlessness turned to anticipation.

As they filed out of the State House into the cold night, Franklin exchanged glances with another delegate, who nodded and walked away quickly. He then dined with a few friends, but he could not keep his mind on the subject of the conversation. After dinner, telling no one where he was headed, Franklin quietly slipped down Chestnut Street, his walking stick lightly tapping the cobblestones. He had been in London for most of two decades, and despite his worldwide fame, he would not be recognized by most Philadelphians. At Third and Chestnut, Franklin entered the first floor of Carpenters' Hall, the meeting place for the local trade guild.

There he was met by four other delegates who were members of the Committee of Secret Correspondence, which Congress had appointed to negotiate secretly for recognition and support from Europe. These delegates included John Dickinson, John Jay, Thomas Johnson, and Benjamin Harrison. Three of them, Dickinson, Jay, and Johnson, were well-educated distinguished attorneys. Dickinson, forty-three, also from Pennsylvania, had, like Franklin, spent time in London, where he studied law at the Inns of Court. He was one of the richest men in Congress and the eloquent author of *Letters from a Farmer in Pennsylvania*, which set out the colonists' grievances with Britain. Dickinson doubted the colonies would be able to achieve independence without foreign allies to support their struggle. Jay, representing New York, was, at twenty-nine, one of the youngest and most able delegates. Though New York was a stronghold of Tory sentiment, Jay was firmly committed to independence. Johnson served in the Maryland Assembly, where he distinguished himself as a leader opposing British taxation. In his mid-forties, Johnson was relatively quiet, but was an unshakable supporter of independence. Harrison, fifty, of Virginia, was a patrician farmer who had defied the royal governor by opposing the Stamp Act. Harrison must have regarded Franklin, the man who tamed lightning, with a special awe: he had the misfortune of losing both his sisters and his father to a freak lightning bolt. Of these five men, only Franklin and Dickinson had any experience abroad or knowledge of foreign politics. Franklin and Dickinson were also members of the Secret Committee, which was responsible for purchasing arms, and even members of the Secret Committee sometimes confused it with the Committee of Secret Correspondence, resulting in overlapping responsibilities.

Just days before their meeting, Franklin had received an intriguing message from Francis Daymon. Daymon was a Frenchman living in Philadelphia, and he had tutored Franklin in French and worked as the librarian for Franklin's Library Company, which occupied the second floor of Carpenters' Hall, where the first Continental Congress had met. Without knowing of the existence of the Secret Committee, Daymon informed Franklin that a French visitor had arrived in Philadelphia with a message for him from the French king. Some months earlier, Daymon had been approached by that Frenchman, the Chevalier Julien-Alexandre Archard de Bonvouloir. Bonvouloir was an ambitious French military officer from a noble family. He had heard that Daymon ran a French school in Philadelphia where the sons of wealthy Americans studied. Bonvouloir had a vague sense that Daymon could introduce him to the right people and that somehow Bonvouloir might serve as a liaison between the French government and the American colonies. Bonvouloir stayed with Daymon for a brief time before hurrying back to France.

Bonvouloir had now returned to Philadelphia for a second visit. He claimed that he was representing the French foreign minister, the Comte de Vergennes, on a secret mission and asked Daymon to arrange a meeting with Franklin. In fact, Bonvouloir had never met Vergennes. Bonvouloir was a former officer in the French army's elite Regiment du Cap. After leaving the army, he had visited America and Britain. In London, he had impressed the new French ambassador to Britain, the Comte de Guines, as someone with important connections in America. (In truth, his only connection was to Franklin's employee, Daymon.) Ambassador Guines wrote to Vergennes, recommending that he send Bonvouloir as an observer to report back on the circumstances of the Continental Congress and the American rebels.

Vergennes thought Ambassador Guines a flamboyant and supercilious buffoon. Stories circulated that Guines wore trousers so tight that he needed the assistance of a ladder and two valets to hoist him in, and then he was unable to sit down. Nevertheless, Ambassador Guines had been clever enough to curry favor with the French queen, Marie Antoinette, who found Guines *amusant*. Over Vergennes's strenuous objection, Louis XVI had appointed Guines as ambassador to London in order to placate his headstrong wife.

Despite his misgivings, Vergennes assented to Bonvouloir's mission to America, but he insisted on keeping him on a tight leash. He instructed Bonvouloir to make clear that he was *not* an official representative of the French government. Bonvouloir should try to gather as much information as possible to assess the Americans' intentions and military strength. He should express France's sympathy for the cause of independence; however, he should not offer any substantive military support. The French could not be seen as interfering with British colonial policy. After France's humiliating defeat in the Seven Years' War, France had pledged to stay out of North America and to maintain peaceful relations with Great Britain. If Britain knew that France was even discussing relations with the rebels, it could provoke a war for which France was unprepared.

For the delegates even to meet with a representative of a foreign government to discuss independence and military alliances against the British could be punishable as treason. Franklin knew there was a risk that Bonvouloir could be a spy for the French, or, worse, for the British. His sudden appearance in Philadelphia raised suspicion. Bonvouloir arrived with no credentials—not even a letter of introduction. Was it a mere coincidence that the name of this messenger translated as "goodwill," or was it an alias? Jay and Franklin agreed that they needed to know where France stood and that under the circumstances they had no choice but to meet with the mysterious visitor. However, they needed to take every precaution to keep the nature of their meeting secret and unofficial. They would not tell Congress. They would make no commitments, and they would be careful to avoid disclosing too much.

The second floor of Carpenters' Hall was divided between Franklin's laboratory, filled with his equipment and notebooks, and the Library Company, which Franklin had incorporated in 1731 as the first subscription library in America. Glass cabinets filled with books lined the walls of the reading room. The library's motto was displayed prominently: *Communiter Bona Profundere Deum Est* ("To pour forth benefits for the common good is divine").

Franklin's French teacher, Francis Daymon, who served as translator, welcomed the committee members and introduced Bonvouloir. Bonvouloir described himself as a military officer, which was true, and a businessman from the West Indies, which was not. Though he could not speak for the French government, he indicated he had "valuable acquaintances" in Versailles who might listen to him as a supporter of the American cause.

The four men were perplexed by their mysterious visitor. He claimed to be the twentysomething son of a French aristocrat, yet he did not appear to be wealthy, well-bred, or even young. Jay later described him as "an elderly, lame gentleman, having the appearance of an old, wounded French officer." In reality, Bonvouloir was a twenty-six-year-old unemployed veteran living in London and hoping for a pension that would never come. He walked with a limp, not from combat, but from a childhood injury. Perhaps Bonvouloir was wearing a disguise, or perhaps Jay, who was excessively worried that British spies might intercept his private papers, was trying to mask Bonvouloir's identity.

The men warmed themselves around a table set near a fireplace. Their faces were half cast in shadow, and candlelight reflected off the glass cabinets, adding to the sense of intrigue. No one at the meeting was permitted to take notes. The only record of their conversation is a report written days later by Bonvouloir. The meeting lasted several hours, and two more meetings were held the following week. The five delegates asked if France would support independence for the colonies. Bonvouloir replied obliquely, "Possibly she might," but he "could not tell at all." He assured the delegates that France would act "on just and equitable conditions." He could only commit to carry their requests to certain unnamed friends. He could "promise, offer and answer for nothing." Bonvouloir ventured that "France was well-disposed towards them," but he cautioned that asking for assistance was "a ticklish step." Bonvouloir thought that France might be willing to trade arms for crops, like tobacco. So long as they did not attract too much attention to their trading, "France would shut her eyes."

But then Bonvouloir, recalling his instructions from the king, seemed to reverse himself: Congress should not depend on his word, he told the delegates. He warned them that he "was nobody." With growing frustration after three nights of questions and evasive answers, Franklin asked if the time were ripe to send a representative to France. Bonvouloir discouraged that. It would be "premature, even dangerous, because everything of what was going on in France was known by London." Of course, Bonvouloir also hoped to maintain his role as the exclusive liaison between Congress and Versailles.

Bonvouloir had told the delegates nothing they did not know already, and he had learned very little of value from them. Yet both parties came away from these sessions hearing what they wanted to hear. The Americans concluded that France would support the colonies in a war for independence, and Bonvouloir concluded that the Americans were ready to fight and would be victorious. Bonvouloir hurried back to his lodging to write a report to the foreign minister. He drew a wildly exaggerated picture of the Americans and their prospects for defeating the British. He wrote to Vergennes, via Ambassador Guines:

> Everyone here is a soldier, the troops are well clothed, well paid, and well armed. They have more than 50,000 regular soldiers and an even larger number of volunteers, who do not wish to be paid. Judge how men of this caliber will fight. They are more powerful than we could have thought, beyond imagination powerful; you will be astonished by it. Nothing shocks or frightens them, you can count on that. Independency is a certainty for 1776; there will be no drawing back. . . .

In fact, at the time Bonvouloir was writing, the number of active enlisted men in the Continental Army was perhaps one-tenth the figure he cited, barely 5,000 men. The soldiers had only the arms, ammunition, and training they brought with them. Perhaps Franklin and his committee had overstated the strength of their army, or, more likely, Bonvouloir simply wanted to believe that the Americans could whip the British. By embellishing the state of America's military preparedness, Bonvouloir was trying to persuade the French government that he could be a valuable source for information.

In case the report was intercepted by the British, Ambassador Guines had instructed Bonvouloir to write any sensitive material in milk so that when it dried it became invisible. Using milk to disguise secret correspondence was not unusual for diplomats at the time. The recipient would apply a warm object to the page so that the milk would scald and reveal the secret writing. In this instance, however, Bonvouloir forgot the milk and hurriedly wrote his complete report in ink. When the bumbling Guines received the letter he stuck a shovel in the fireplace and then applied it to the envelope so ineptly he scorched the pages. The singed papers were forwarded to Vergennes, who for good reason doubted Bonvouloir's judgment and hesitated to act.

Bonvouloir left Philadelphia for London, expecting to see Ambassador Guines. But by the time he arrived, Guines had finally drained the king's patience, and Louis XVI had recalled him. Bonvouloir waited in London for a few months for further instructions from Vergennes. He received none. Without Guines, Bonvouloir had no access to the foreign minister. In time, Bonvouloir grew tired of waiting for a reply from Vergennes. Unable to support himself, he accepted a commission to serve with the English army in India, where he died after a brief fever.

Though the would-be diplomat did not persuade France to help the Americans, he nonetheless served an essential function: he had unwittingly convinced the Secret Committee that the time had come to send an American representative to Versailles.

THIRTEEN

AN IMPROBABLE
EMISSARY

Philadelphia, January—March 1776

Franklin and Jay knew the perfect man for the job: Silas Deane. Steadfast in his commitment to independence, energetic, intelligent, and resourceful, Deane commanded respect in Congress. He had practical experience from owning a successful business and could pose convincingly as an anonymous Connecticut merchant purchasing French goods for import. Deane understood maritime shipping, mercantile financing, and the supply needs of the army and navy. Having been recalled by the Connecticut Assembly and no longer a delegate to Congress, Deane could credibly claim to be acting as a private merchant on his own account.

That was not to say that Deane was an obvious choice to represent the colonies to Louis XVI. Until his appointment as a delegate to Congress, he had never ventured beyond the borders of Connecticut. Despite his Yale education, Deane was a plainspoken man without affectation. He knew nothing about royalty, diplomacy, or European politics. And though he was trained in classical Greek,

Latin, and Hebrew, he did not speak a word of French. There were other more prominent men in Congress, like John Jay, Ben Franklin, and John Adams, who had more political experience and influence and came from more important colonies. They were known in Europe, and at least Franklin could read and converse in French. Nevertheless, Franklin thought that Deane was the ideal candidate, in part, because he was such an improbable emissary. The British would never suspect him of being a secret agent for the American rebels.

SOMETIME IN LATE FEBRUARY, Franklin asked Deane if he would consider serving as Congress's secret emissary to France. Franklin told Deane about the clandestine meetings with Bonvouloir, who had convinced the Secret Committee that Louis XVI would be receptive to the American cause. Deane deeply admired Franklin, just as Franklin had enormous faith in Deane.

Having worked for months to purchase ships and military supplies, Deane understood as well as anyone the urgency of French aid. Washington's army was in desperate need of gunpowder, guns, and artillery, none of which could be manufactured in large quantities in the colonies. There were shortages of food, tools, tents, blankets, uniforms, and boots as well. "Congress have left it in the power of the States to starve the Army at pleasure," one officer wrote. John Adams described the army as "disgraced, defeated, discontented, diseased, naked, undisciplined, eaten up with vermin; no clothes, beds, blankets, no medicines; no victuals, but salt pork and flour." One soldier complained that "We were absolutely, literally starved." The soldier recorded seeing other men "roast their old shoes and eat them." The men who had rushed off to join the Continental Army came without a change of clothing, outer coat, or blanket. There was no uniformity in their dress, and after several months of hardship, their clothing was tattered and smelly. Soldiers shivered through the cruel New England winter without coats, boots, socks, or hats. Many soldiers lived essentially outdoors without tents, sleeping on snow and mud. As a result of these deprivations, the army was plagued by mass desertions. (Over the eight years of war, nearly a quarter of all enlisted men deserted annually.)

Shortages were exacerbated by corruption and theft. Soldiers stole goods to sell for cash or drink. To make matters worse, soldiers regularly took their guns and powder when they returned home, as compensation for their service, leaving new recruits without weapons. Washington's men were forced to cannibalize supplies for different purposes than were intended: blankets were sewn into coats; tents were cut into blankets. Scarcity bred waste: guns that would not fire were abandoned; broken wagons were left behind; shoes that needed mending were discarded.

Franklin did not need to persuade Deane to accept his commission. Though it meant a long absence from his family and time spent overseas in an unfamiliar place, totally isolated, and at great personal risk, Deane accepted this dangerous mission enthusiastically. More than anything, he wanted to be useful to his country.

On March 2, 1776, the Secret Committee issued Deane's commission "to transact such business, commercial and political, as we have committed to his care in behalf and by the authority of the Congress of the thirteen united colonies." Specifically, the committee authorized Deane to acquire in France all the arms, uniforms, and equipment for an army of 25,000 men on credit. The committee instructed Deane to travel to France "in the character of a merchant." Congress wanted to win support from the Indian tribes, which had been valuable allies to the French against the British in the French and Indian War. For this purpose, the committee gave Deane $200,000 in Continental paper currency to buy gifts in France for the Indian tribes. (It was roughly equivalent to $4.9 million today, but the Continental dollar quickly lost most of its value.)

It was essential to the success of Deane's whole mission that he continue to conduct his own private trading business as a cover. For this purpose, Pennsylvania delegate Robert Morris, a wealthy Philadelphia merchant, offered Deane a position as export agent for his firm, Willing and Morris. Morris and Deane had developed a close friendship in Congress. Morris became a critical figure in financing the American Revolution, and Deane was pleased to form a business relationship with him.

In addition to agreeing to pay Deane's expenses, the Secret Committee promised to pay Deane a five-percent commission on all purchases he made on behalf of Congress. That would be the only compensation paid by the government for Deane's services as diplomat and arms broker. Beyond that, Deane would depend on his work for Morris to support himself for however long he would be abroad. In this way the committee unwittingly created the possibility of a conflict of interest between Deane's public responsibilities and his private dealings. Though later many critics and historians would accuse Deane of commingling his private business with the government's procurement, Deane used the same books for both accounts in order to conceal his arms purchases.

Franklin gave Deane letters of introduction to two French friends who were sympathetic to the American cause, Comte de Chaumont, a wealthy aristocrat, and Jacques Barbeu-Dubourg, a respected physician who could arrange a meeting with Vergennes. Franklin instructed Deane that in exchange for French aid he should offer the foreign minister a preferential trade relationship. Franklin suggested that if Vergennes seemed reluctant, Deane should give him time. Once Deane established a relationship with Vergennes, he should inquire whether France would be willing to recognize the Americans and sign treaties of commerce and alliance if the colonies declared independence. Franklin stressed that Deane was not simply a messenger. He urged Deane to be an advocate for independence and to respond "to the several calumnies thrown out against us" by the British. If the colonies declared independence, Congress would rely upon Deane alone to secure French recognition and support.

The importance of France's recognition cannot be overstated. Without some acknowledgment of their legitimacy, the colonies were merely rebels, traitors, and pirates; recognition would transform them from criminals to statesmen, diplomats, and privateers. Other European powers would quickly follow French recognition. It would afford the Americans opportunities for trade relations, loans, and alliances throughout Europe that were essential to securing and maintaining independence.

Franklin also suggested that Deane contact one of his American friends in London, Dr. Edward Bancroft. Coincidentally, Bancroft had been one of Deane's pupils when Deane was a schoolteacher in Hartford. Deane also knew Bancroft's stepfather, David Bull, who owned the Bunch of Grapes tavern in Hartford, where the Committee of Correspondence often met. Bancroft supported the American cause and could provide Deane with intelligence about the British government from his contacts in London. Deane was no doubt delighted and relieved to have someone familiar to him only a few days' travel from Paris.

SILAS DEANE WROTE to Elizabeth informing her of his decision to leave for France at once. There was no time to return to his family. Washington's army needed arms and ammunition as quickly as possible. As Deane sat down to write Elizabeth, he knew that the trip to France posed many dangers and deprivations. He did not know when, if ever, he could return. If his ship were captured by the British, or if he were discovered by British spies in Paris, he could be imprisoned and hung as a traitor. He would be traveling alone, knowing no one and unable to converse in French. He had no way of knowing how the French government would receive him, if at all. Without any way of proving his bona fides, he was expected to purchase arms, gunpowder, and uniforms for an army of 25,000 men, all on credit, and he would need to arrange for this massive shipment without arousing suspicion by the British. Finally, without any diplomatic training and scant instructions, he was expected to negotiate treaties on behalf of a country that did not yet exist.

Meanwhile, how would his business in Wethersfield fare during his long absence? And how would he support himself in France with pocketfuls of rapidly depreciating Continental currency, especially if the European banks would not give him credit? Congress promised to reimburse his expenses, but when and with what, as Congress was already in debt? Even if he did manage to return to Hartford, what would he return to? The war might soon spread throughout New England. The British had threatened to burn the rebels' homes. Elizabeth and his son, Jesse, were both frail and might not survive the deprivations of the war. All these anxieties crowded his mind.

Elizabeth had not seen him all winter, and now she learned he was leaving on a risky voyage to France without returning home first to see her. Recognizing the need for secrecy, he cautioned Elizabeth, "It will be no purpose to write to me, until you hear from me, and then not a word of politics." Deane felt compelled to contain his genuine sentiments. "You will not imagine I am unfeeling on this occasion,—but to what purpose would it be to let my tender passions govern, except to distress you?" Hardly what Elizabeth hoped to hear from her departing husband. He recognized the risks he faced. He assured her that he would be careful, but if he fell into the enemy's hands, "I am prepared even for the worst, not wishing to survive my Country's fate, and confident, while that is safe, I shall be happy in almost any situation." He regretted "the pain I must give you by this adventure," and thanked her for being "one of the best of partners and wives, while on my part, by a peculiar fatality attending me from my first entrance into public life, I have ever been involved in one scheme and adventure after another." He gently explained that he could not bear to say goodbye in person. "The present object is great. I am about to enter on the great stage of Europe and the consideration of the importance of quitting myself well, weighs me down, without the addition of more tender scenes."

Only a few months earlier he had written to her that "[h]e that has the least to do in public affairs stands the fairest chance of happiness." Now, he was prepared to sacrifice even his family's happiness to the nation's interests: "I wish as much as any man for the enjoyments of domestic ease, peace, and society, but am forbid expecting them soon." It would be "criminal in my own eyes, did I balance them one moment in opposition to the Public Good and the Calls of my Country."

In closing, Deane questioned the ironies of political life.

. . . [A]re not the ways of Providence dark and inscrutable to us, short-sighted mortals? Surely they are. My enemies tho't to triumph over me and bring me down, yet all they did has been turned to the opening a door for the greatest and most extensive usefulness, if I succeed; but if I fail,—why then the Cause I am engaged in, and the important part I have undertaken, will justify my adventuring.

Providence would prove more inscrutable than Deane could have imagined.

FOURTEEN

THE DINNER PARTY

London, October–November 1775

Beaumarchais and d'Eon were in a celebratory mood when their coach drew up to Mansion House on the evening of October 25. As usual, she was dressed smartly as a man in her captain's uniform. It was the night before the traditional opening of Parliament, and Lord Mayor Wilkes had invited a glittering circle of friends to toast a momentous confrontation that was about to take place.

For months Wilkes had been fiercely defending the Americans. He had bitterly denounced the king's proclamation that Massachusetts was in open rebellion, and now his rhetoric had reached a fever pitch. Just days before this gathering, Wilkes, who still retained his seat in Parliament, had delivered his most virulent speech on the floor of the Commons, describing the British military occupation of Massachusetts as "unjust, felonious and murderous." King George III and his government were incensed. All London was holding its breath, waiting to see if Wilkes had finally gone too far. A crowd of Wilkites was planning to disrupt the king's address to Parliament the following morning. Wilkes hoped to provoke a parliamentary crisis that would topple Lord North's corrupt government and sweep Wilkes to power, but the plan was risky. Lord North had already arrested Wilkes's associate Stephen Sayre and other members of Parliament on questionable charges of treason. Wilkes's guests at Mansion House all wondered if Wilkes would be arrested next.

But for a man who might reasonably anticipate spending the following night in the Tower, Wilkes seemed remarkably upbeat. There was a sense that history was about to be made. As things turned out, Wilkes and his dinner guests were on the cusp of a historic moment, but not for the reasons they imagined.

Mansion House, the Lord Mayor's official residence, was built in the grand Palladian style. Lord Mayor Wilkes presided over a lavish dinner evoking a Roman banquet in the gilded Egyptian Hall. In addition to d'Eon and Beaumarchais, Wilkes's guests that evening included, among others, London alderman William Lee and his younger brother, Arthur Lee. The Lee brothers were frequent guests of Wilkes and outspoken supporters of his political machine, the Bill of Rights Society, which, despite its name, was organized for the express purpose of paying Wilkes's debts from his legal troubles rather than advocating for any specific freedoms.

The Lees came from one of the leading families in the Northern Neck of the Tidewater region of Virginia. The family plantation, known as Stratford Hall, was an imposing two-story redbrick manor with a commanding view overlooking the Potomac. It had been built by their grandfather Thomas Lee, a tobacco farmer and land speculator who had served both as a member of the ruling Council of Virginia and as acting governor. In its prime, Stratford Hall had nearly 150 slaves plus indentured servants and transported convicts to work the fields, a grist mill, and a substantial wharf from which it exported tobacco to Europe. Altogether, the family owned about

16,000 acres in Virginia and Maryland. Like other southern barons, the Lees self-consciously imitated the lifestyle of English aristocrats. The furniture, china, crystal, and silver were all imported from the best craftsmen in England. There were liveried servants, elegant coaches drawn by four white horses, fancy dress parties, equestrian events, fox hunts, and exquisitely manicured English gardens. Sons were sent to England for their education and service to the Crown was regarded as a high calling.

Arthur Lee, the youngest of eight children, was raised by a slave woman and had had little contact with his parents, who died when Arthur was nine. Arthur was left to the supervision of two older brothers—the mean-spirited Philip and the indifferent Thomas— who thought it convenient to ship Arthur to boarding school in England when he was scarcely eleven. Though his father's will had bequeathed Arthur 1,000 pounds and other property, Philip and Thomas refused to honor the will. Arthur grew up feeling deeply aggrieved throughout his life and wallowed in self-pity. He matured into a brittle and paranoid young man, unable to form genuine friendships or romantic relationships. Instead, he fixated on the rich and famous. And when he drew close to someone, he almost inevitably became resentful and envious. His own dark soul cast suspicion on everyone he knew.

After English public school, Arthur earned a medical degree from the University of Edinburgh. He returned to Virginia briefly to practice medicine, but grew quickly bored and decided to return to London to become a barrister like his two oldest brothers. While he was studying law in London, Lee began writing articles critical of the British government's colonial policy. These were published in the *London Evening Post* and other papers, usually under the pseudonym "Junius Americanus." Over the course of five years he produced nearly eighty articles and a number of pamphlets, most famously, "An Appeal to the Justice and Interests of the People of Great Britain." Lee's talents as a propagandist commanded attention on both sides of the Atlantic and raised concern among the British government.

Yet Arthur remained in the shadow of his five older brothers. The oldest, Philip Ludwell Lee, who inherited Stratford Hall, was one of the twelve members of the Virginia Council. The next brother, Thomas Ludwell Lee, belonged to the Virginia House of Burgesses. Richard Henry Lee and Francis Lightfoot Lee also served in the House of Burgesses and were selected as delegates to the Continental Congress. Arthur's other brother, William, lived in London, where he had a lucrative trading business before being elected a London alderman. Throughout his life Arthur remained largely dependent upon whatever modest support the family provided, and he struggled to compete with his older siblings for prestige.

While Arthur was still a law student, his brother Richard Henry lobbied unsuccessfully for Arthur to be appointed colonial agent to the crown for the Virginia House of Burgesses and the Massachusetts Assembly. Both groups found him unsuitable; Arthur Lee already had a well-deserved reputation for being outspoken and hotheaded. Instead of Lee, the Massachusetts Assembly chose the world-famous Dr. Franklin, who was then in London serving as the agent for Pennsylvania. As a concession to Lee's supporters, Arthur Lee was named Franklin's substitute in case the sixty-five-year-old were unable to continue.

During his years in London, Franklin tried to befriend the young Lee. After Lee wrote a paper on the medicinal properties of a certain bark, Franklin sponsored Lee for admission to the Royal Society of London. Yet instead of being grateful for the older man's support, Arthur rewarded Franklin's generosity with mistrust and malevolence. During his five years in London, Lee persistently tried to undermine the old man and publicly sniped at him at every opportunity. Lee's antagonism toward his more experienced colleague evoked, once again, the sense of betrayal he had experienced at the hands of his older brothers at losing his inheritance.

Lee, like his brothers, was also an outspoken critic of the slave trade. In 1764, he wrote "An Essay in Vindication of the Continental Colonies of America." The essay was written in response to the Scottish intellectual Adam Smith, whom Lee had met and disliked as much as he disliked all Scots. Lee argued that the institution of slavery was unjust, but it would be a mistake to conclude from this that Lee had an enlightened view of Africans. To the contrary, like many slaveholding Virginians, he thought that Africans were an inferior and depraved race. Moreover, his objections to slavery were partly rooted in his fear that Virginian whites were outnumbered by Africans, which was not literally true. Moreover, Virginia planters, including the Lees, had supported curbs on the import of slaves. They worried that the slave trade was contributing to an overproduction of tobacco and driving down prices. Though his eloquent opposition to slavery was notable, Lee was motivated by his family's economic interests at least as much as he was by higher principles.

Shortly after arriving in London in 1768, Arthur Lee met Wilkes while Wilkes was in the King's Bench Prison, and he soon joined the Bill of Rights Society to express his support. Lee became a bridge between Wilkes and the "Real Whigs," a circle of influential American and British writers critical of British colonial policy. The Real Whigs included among others Benjamin Franklin, the scientist Joseph Priestley, and the leading Whig intellectual the Earl of Shelburne, not all of whom supported Wilkes. Lee acted as a sort of publicist for Wilkes and wrote numerous articles for American newspapers portraying Wilkes as a friend to the colonies and linking the cause of Wilkes's freedom to America's.

In fact, Wilkes's position with regard to American policy had been more ambiguous than Lee acknowledged, but Lee spun Wilkes's public image as one of the leading advocates for the colonies. Once Wilkes was deluged with favorable correspondence from colonial leaders like John Hancock, he began to identify with the Americans' cause. Wilkes considered Arthur Lee "his *first* and *best* friend," and, indeed, no man ever had a more steadfast supporter.

It is puzzling that Lee, who was constantly disappointed by holding good men to impossible standards, nonetheless forgave Wilkes all his obvious flaws. While Franklin excoriated Wilkes as "an outlaw, an exile, of bad personal character, not worth a farthing," Lee praised Wilkes for his "courage, calm and . . . flowing wit, accommodating in his temper, of manner convivial and conversable, an elegant scholar." He overlooked the fact that Wilkes ruthlessly pursued his personal political ambitions by any means. Lee saw a great deal of himself in Wilkes. Deprived of loving parents, siblings, or partners, Lee identified with Wilkes's hunger for affection and recognition. He recognized in Wilkes a reflection of his own sense of being misunderstood, unappreciated, and persecuted. His obsession with Wilkes reflected his own narcissism.

Before their meeting at the Lord Mayor's dinner party, Lee probably was not known to Beaumarchais. Naturally, the two writers had something in common, and as the evening progressed, Beaumarchais found himself in conversation with Lee. Beaumarchais had an easy, convivial manner, whereas Lee appeared dour and uncomfortable. When Lee opened his small, tight mouth to speak, Beaumarchais could see his yellowed teeth. Lee's squinty green eyes, ash-gray complexion, and long bony fingers gave him a ghoul-like appearance.

When the two could speak privately, Lee boasted that he represented Congress's interests in Europe and that he was interested in obtaining arms for the Continental Army. (This was an idle claim.

In fact, the Secret Committee did not contact Lee until a few months later, but it was typical of Lee to fabricate stories to exaggerate his own importance.) Lee probably knew from either Wilkes or d'Eon that Beaumarchais had friends at Versailles. It is likely that Lee even asked Wilkes to set up the chance meeting with Beaumarchais so that he could raise the question of buying arms for the Americans. It would seem improper for Wilkes to participate in a conspiracy to aid the Americans and the French at the expense of Britain on the eve of his effort to become prime minister; but Wilkes was comfortable living with contradictions, so long as they did not get in the way of his ambitions. Lee wanted to know if Beaumarchais could assist him in arranging for French military support for the rebels. Such talk excited Beaumarchais, who had already written to Vergennes the previous month about the American cause. Beaumarchais and Lee planned a secret meeting for a few days hence.

The conversation that took place around Wilkes's table that evening would have far more historic consequences than Wilkes's planned demonstration for the opening of Parliament. In fact, his dinner guests would soon realize that Wilkes's political career had already peaked. The dinner stretched long into the evening, and the guests paid no attention to the worsening weather until it was time to make the ride home in a heavy downpour. Throughout the night, the rain and wind were fierce and continued gathering force. By morning, Wilkes's plot had been rained out. The king proceeded to Parliament down deserted streets in a drenching rain. The anticipated mobs of Wilkite agitators stayed home rather than disrupt the king's speech to Parliament. When the sun reappeared, it was clear that the government had survived the storm, and the looming constitutional crisis had evaporated in the mist.

Beaumarchais, of course, had no authority to negotiate with Lee on behalf of France. He wrote to Foreign Minister Vergennes for instructions, but Vergennes would not authorize Beaumarchais to negotiate on his own. Vergennes and the king were far more concerned with concluding the settlement with d'Eon. Vergennes insisted that Beaumarchais include another prominent Frenchman, the Comte de Lauraguais, in any discussions with Lee. Vergennes hoped that Lauraguais would act as a brake on Beaumarchais's enthusiasm for the Americans. Lee, Beaumarchais, and Lauraguais agreed to meet at Lee's flat later in the week to discuss the prospect of French aid. Instead, what emerged from those discussions was a secret plan to smuggle French aid to the Americans without implicating the French government.

FIFTEEN

THE MIDDLE
TEMPLE CONSPIRACY

London, November 1775

Arthur Lee rented a modest flat at the Middle Temple, one of the four Inns of Court where English barristers practiced and often resided. The Middle Temple was originally founded around the fourteenth century as the headquarters of the Knights Templar, established to protect Christians on pilgrimage to Jerusalem. By the end of the fifteenth century the Middle Temple was overrun by lawyers, who drove out the Templars. (It had taken the Turks centuries longer to achieve the same result in Jerusalem.) Lee, who had little interest in practicing law, enjoyed living in this ancient gentlemen's fortress where two of his older brothers had also belonged. He would enter the Middle Temple's extensive grounds through the massive doors of the gatehouse off Fleet Street and proceed down Middle Temple Lane past the windows of Abram and Sons stationery shop. The lane was bordered on one side by a long, crooked row of wood-frame buildings that appeared to sag under the weight of so many plump barristers. Every morning Lee could check the time on a sundial with the sobering motto *Pereunt et Imputantur*—"Things are passing and reckoned." Middle Temple Hall stirred thoughts of chivalry with its dark Elizabethan paneling garnished with ancient coats of arms of the Knights Templar, and the great oak-beamed ceiling that towered overhead. Lee's chambers were adjacent to the Hall. His flat was bright and airy, overlooking a private garden lined with elms and offering a magnificent view of the Thames. It was an idyllic scene for a conspiracy.

Beaumarchais and Comte de Lauraguais met with Lee in his rooms several times over the following weeks. In their conversations Beaumarchais saw an opportunity to do well by doing good: he wanted to help the Americans, and he also recognized the possibility of a substantial sales commission from the export of arms. He proposed to establish a phony trading company that would appear to be a legitimate business while secretly arming the Americans. From his long association with Pâris-Duverney, who had made his fortune selling weapons during the Seven Years' War, Beaumarchais knew something about the arms trade.

More important, Beaumarchais now had access to Vergennes and Louis XVI, who needed his help to settle the d'Eon affair. Once he returned d'Eon's incriminating correspondence to Versailles, he would have the king's confidence and gratitude. He had proved that he could operate in secret as the king's agent in a sensitive diplomatic matter, and he had shrewdly declawed d'Eon from ever again blackmailing the king by making her promise to dress as a woman when she returned to France. He would ask the king for a substantial amount so that he could purchase arms directly from the French military and resell them to the colonies. Beaumarchais would disguise the origin of the arms so that it would never appear that the French government was involved.

For his part, Lee negotiated with Beaumarchais as if he had the full authority of the Continental Congress behind him—which he did not. Lee, however, saw an opportunity to profit financially as well as to enhance his prestige and influence. Beaumarchais would ship gold and gunpowder to the French West Indies, where Lee would arrange for it to be loaded onto an American ship. Only Lee and Samuel Adams would know about the shipments. In exchange for this support, Lee agreed that the Americans would export to France top-quality Virginia tobacco. Whether it was Lee who first suggested that the Americans would pay for the arms with the Virginia tobacco is unclear. But he certainly saw that selling tobacco to France could help economically distressed Virginia plantations like his brothers'. Since the British did not allow the American colonies to export directly to France, good-quality Virginia tobacco was not widely available on the Continent and commanded a high price. Lee's brother in London, William, imported tobacco to England, and he could act as agent. Thus, the Lees would profit directly from the sale of tobacco in exchange for arms. The tobacco would be resold by Beaumarchais on behalf of the French government. Beaumarchais would use the profits to enable him to purchase more supplies for the Americans. In this way an initial loan of one million livres (nearly $8 million today) from the French government could be multiplied to provide a continuing stream of arms and ammunition to the Americans.

After a few meetings, Beaumarchais and Lee began to suspect that the Comte de Lauraguais, who enjoyed wine to excess, might be keeping his friend the Earl of Shelburne, a leading Whig intellectual, informed of their discussions. Lee decided to exclude the tipsy comte from further discussions. The result was that the comte did everything in his power to try to undermine Beaumarchais with the French government. Unfortunately, Lee overlooked a more obvious threat to their plot—his close friend, and sometimes roommate, Paul Wentworth.

FOR THE PAST FIVE YEARS, Lee and Wentworth had been nearly inseparable. Wentworth, a wealthy American with a plantation in British Guiana, took an interest in the young law student practically from the moment that Lee first began publishing his critique of British policies as Junius Americanus. Lee was no doubt flattered by the older man's attention, especially given the fact that Wentworth was one of the best-connected Americans living in London. Wentworth had done very well investing in British stocks at a time when many in the aristocracy disdained the vulgar "stock jobbers," but the leading statesmen, aristocrats, and scientists flocked to the lavish parties at his home on Poland Street and spent weekends at his country manor, Brandenburgh House in Hammersmith. Wentworth was not merely rich; Lee knew that Wentworth was a cousin of the royal governor of New Hampshire, John Wentworth, and also of the Marquess of Rockingham, Charles Watson-Wentworth, one of the richest and most influential men in Britain.

In fact, Wentworth's famous lineage was a carefully spun lie. His genteel manners and polished appearance masked an imposter. Paul Wentworth was born to a planter on Barbados, and as a young man he made his way to New Hampshire with letters of introduction to the family of the then–royal governor Benning Wentworth, who is today known as the father of Bennington, the first town in the territory of Vermont. He somehow persuaded the Wentworth clan that he was a long-lost relative, and he formed a lasting friendship with the governor's young nephew John Wentworth, who later became governor himself.

Paul Wentworth returned to the West Indies, where he married a rich widow who died soon after, leaving him heir to a large sugar plantation in Guiana. Wentworth was quickly bored by plantation life and moved to London, where now-governor John Wentworth appointed his "cousin" agent for the Colony of New Hampshire and a member of the New Hampshire Council. Paul Wentworth leveraged his relationship with the governor to gain access to the Marquess of Rockingham, and no one, including Rockingham, questioned how Wentworth was related to the governor. Much later, after the American Revolution, the governor entrusted Wentworth with managing his own estate, and Wentworth absconded with the governor's assets back to the West Indies, where he was never heard from again.

When Arthur Lee was a hungry law student, Paul Wentworth had invited him to move into Wentworth's fashionable Poland Street mansion. And after Lee could afford his own room at the Middle Temple, Wentworth sometimes spent the night there. In May 1775, shortly after Lee had published his "Second Appeal" to the British people, Wentworth offered Lee 300 pounds (about $55,000 today) to stop publishing. The impoverished Lee accepted the payment, which he considered a "loan," though it is doubtful that Lee ever repaid Wentworth. Lee was also promised that he would be appointed to an official post in London, and that his brother Richard Henry would be named to the Virginia Council—if he cooperated. Though Lee later claimed he had rejected Wentworth's offer, Wentworth insisted that Lee took the money. Lee was apparently so dazzled by Wentworth's social standing, and so grateful for his financial support, that he had never questioned Wentworth's political loyalties when he accepted the payment. Lee published only one more critical essay, in 1776, before silencing Junius Americanus forever.

Lee, who tormented himself with suspicion of nearly everyone he encountered, and who never hesitated to accuse innocent men of being spies, did not immediately reveal Wentworth's bribe to Congress or abandon his friendship. Instead, while Lee secretly conspired with Beaumarchais to smuggle arms, he continued to confide in his friend Wentworth, oblivious to the fact that Wentworth had already betrayed him to the British government. Wentworth gave Lee access to the highest reaches of the British government. For all his ability and enthusiasm for independence, Lee was always guided by naked self-interest. But he never questioned his own motives. As one historian noted, Lee "might have played a fine part in the American Revolution if his self-esteem had not been in vast excess of his public spirit."

From the outset, Lee's relationship to Wentworth compromised the secrecy of the conspiracy to smuggle arms. The British government knew that Lee and Beaumarchais were plotting to smuggle French aid to the Americans even before Versailles or Philadelphia knew.

SIXTEEN

THE BET

London and Paris,
November 1775–January 1776

November brought miserable weather to London. The city suf-
focated in a thick fog of coal dust that hung in the damp air
for days. A bronchial epidemic swept through the city, and Beaumarchais was sick for weeks. On November 4, Beaumarchais and
d'Eon finally signed their contract, which they referred to as "the
Transaction," and d'Eon gave Beaumarchais the iron coffer filled
with documents. D'Eon celebrated the completion of the Transaction by purchasing a black silk gown, which years later remained one
of her favorite outfits. Nursing a cough and high fever, Beaumarchais headed back to Paris with the coffer containing the king's precious papers still sealed. D'Eon gave Beaumarchais a worn copy of
Montesquieu's *Spirit of the Laws.* The book was hollowed out and
contained a secret compartment into which d'Eon had stuffed Louis
XV's instructions to her as an agent of the king's Secret network.
(Twenty years before d'Eon had used the same book to carry into

Russia the king's correspondence to Empress Elizabeth.) Beaumarchais wasted no time before claiming his prize: he wanted Vergennes to provide him with the money he needed to smuggle arms to the Americans.

At Versailles, Beaumarchais was greeted warmly by Vergennes and his friend, Antoine de Sartine, who had been elevated from Paris police chief to minister of the navy. They congratulated Beaumarchais on the return of the damaging correspondence and assured Beaumarchais of the king's gratitude. Beaumarchais could now expect that the king would restore his status at Versailles, but he wanted more. As he and Lee had agreed, Beaumarchais proposed that the king loan him one million livres to set up a phony trading firm with Lee to provide financing, arms, and ammunition to the Americans. The firm would appear to be acting on its own, without involving the French government, so that the English could not hold France responsible. First, he would exchange half a million livres for Portuguese gold pieces. The gold would be sent to Congress to finance the issuance of its own paper currency. The other half-million livres would be used to purchase gunpowder secretly from the French armory at a discount. The Americans would cover the one million livres by sending tobacco, which Beaumarchais hoped to resell for three million livres. He would use the profit from tobacco sales to purchase more supplies for the Americans. By this geometric progression, Beaumarchais hoped to triple the amount of aid available to the Americans with each transaction. Beaumarchais suggested to Vergennes that it would be a nice twist to pay for the initial one million livres by taxing British imports.

Vergennes reacted coolly. While there is some evidence that he considered aiding the Americans, he knew that the king would be unwilling to take any action, even covertly, that would jeopardize the peace with Britain. The king felt morally and legally obligated to respect the spirit and the letter of the 1763 peace treaty. He was resolutely opposed to aiding the Americans.

Beaumarchais would not take no for an answer. He could not. He begged Vergennes for an audience with the king, confident that in "15 minutes" he could persuade Louis XVI of "the certainty of succeeding, and the immense harvest of glory and peace that must result for his reign from the smallest seed so timely sown." When Vergennes refused, Beaumarchais returned to the Jouy Hotel. With characteristic temerity he wrote a strongly worded memorandum directly to the king. The fact that Vergennes passed Beaumarchais's memorandum to the king indicates that Beaumarchais had acquired access to the king through his role in settling the d'Eon affair. Perhaps it also suggests that Vergennes, himself, was quietly becoming convinced of the value of aiding the Americans.

In Beaumarchais's memorandum he argued that the king's highest duty was not to follow his personal morals; the highest duty of the sovereign was to "look at himself as a stranger to any other people and a father to his own [nation]." Politics was inherently amoral, he counseled, and so the king must accept the responsibility to use whatever means in his power to punish Britain for humiliating France.

> If men were angels, no doubt, one would have to despise, even hate politics. But if men were angels, they would have no need for religion to enlighten them, kings to rule them, for magistrates to restrain them, for soldiers to subdue them, and earth, instead of being a living picture of hell, would itself be a heavenly place.

Despite Beaumarchais's impassioned appeal, Louis XVI was unmoved. In frustration, Beaumarchais wrote to the king several more times, expressing his disappointment and impatience. He warned the king that "you will one day recognize my views were right, when all that is left to us is to regret bitterly not to have followed them." A few days later he complained to the king that "from now on ask someone else to do this job which brought me neither thanks, nor honors, nor profit." He chastised Louis XVI for ignoring "my reports, after I have met with all kinds of unpleasantness to spare them to everyone else." What kind of man would write a letter like that to his monarch and expect to be rewarded? Beaumarchais's reputation for speaking his mind was legendary. An Englishman once addressed an envelope simply, "To Beaumarchais, the only free man in France," and the post knew exactly to whom to deliver it.

The French monarch was unaccustomed to being addressed with such audacity, yet the king remained silent. Beaumarchais had already proved his value, and Louis XVI could not afford to slam the door on him. Close inspection of the contents of d'Eon's iron coffer had revealed that certain incriminating letters were missing, and Beaumarchais was needed to continue negotiations with d'Eon to obtain the balance of the papers. The king's continued reliance on Beaumarchais gave him some future leverage, but he also felt that the king was not listening to him. After lingering in Paris and Versailles for several weeks, he returned to London in a huff, dejected and annoyed, but determined to retrieve d'Eon's documents and to persuade Louis XVI of the urgency of aiding the Americans.

BACK IN LONDON the d'Eon affair was quickly unraveling. Beaumarchais's friend Charles Morande leaked to the newspapers word that d'Eon was about to reveal her gender. Morande himself had bet that d'Eon was female and hoped to improve his winnings. One London paper reported the exact terms of the Transaction and promised its readers that "it is absolutely decided that she is a woman, and intends very soon to take the habit of her gender." As a result, betting on d'Eon's gender reached a frenzy in London. In a fit of indiscretion d'Eon posted a notice that the public was being scammed by people who knew d'Eon's real gender and that "he would never manifest his sex until such time as all policies shall be at an end." D'Eon also hinted that she had reached a settlement of sorts with Louis XVI. These public statements were inconsistent with the terms of the Transaction, and they only sparked greater interest in the betting.

D'Eon began to suspect Beaumarchais's role in the renewed betting. It's unclear whether Beaumarchais did in fact wager on d'Eon's gender. There is at least one letter that reported to Vergennes that Beaumarchais had bet as much as 100,000 pounds (approximately $18.5 million today), but that seems exaggerated. Beaumarchais needed to make some easy money, and he may have been tempted to bet something, but if he did he risked exposing his secret negotiations, raising d'Eon's ire, and damaging his credibility with Vergennes.

Sometime in late December, d'Eon was invited to a dinner party at the home of Charles Morande. D'Eon had mixed feelings about associating with this infamous blackmailer, but Morande was a good source of gossip, which was his stock in trade. Morande told d'Eon that while Beaumarchais was visiting Paris earlier in the month the playwright had informed people that he intended to marry d'Eon. At various soirées Beaumarchais even entertained guests with love songs he wrote for the captain of the dragoons. Morande's gossip was soon confirmed when d'Eon began receiving letters from friends in Paris asking her if it was true that she was really female and intended to marry Beaumarchais.

In a fit of pique, d'Eon stormed off to Lord Ferrers's estate, Staunton-Herald in Leicestershire, about one hundred miles northwest of London near the center of England. From there she mailed

Beaumarchais a series of angry letters. "[A]s to our approaching marriage," she wrote, "according to what I hear from Paris, it can only be regarded by me as mere persiflage on your part." It was unclear whether d'Eon objected to Beaumarchais announcing their "approaching marriage" before she had agreed to reveal she was female, or whether she had never agreed to marry him at all. "If you have made a serious matter of a simple pledge of friendship and gratitude," she wrote, "your conduct is pitiable." In any case, she expected more discretion from him: "A woman of Paris, however much she might submit to the morals in fashion," would not have pardoned this offense; "even less a woman whose virtue is as uncivilized as mine, and whose spirit is so haughty when the good faith and sensibility of her heart are wounded." Though it is uncertain if Beaumarchais actually announced their engagement in Paris, he did not deny to her either that they were engaged or that he had made such an announcement.

Beaumarchais wrote to d'Eon, alternately pleading and threatening. He was desperate for her to return to London and declare herself a woman, as required by the Transaction. Until she complied, there was still the risk of her blackmailing Louis XVI with the missing letters. Beaumarchais gave her a week to calm down and apologize, or he would be "compelled to leave and break off all relations with you." Beaumarchais seemed wounded by her behavior: "My only sorrow will be to go back to France carrying the cruel conviction that your enemies knew you better than your friends." He warned her that if she did not honor all the terms of the Transaction by turning over all sensitive documents and publicly disclosing her gender, "it is with the most painful sorrow that I would force myself to change titles from your defender to your most implacable prosecutor."

D'Eon sent a fiery reply. Beaumarchais could not complain about her failure to produce all the documents; how would he know what secret documents existed? No one but d'Eon could know if any documents were missing; not even the foreign minister had records of her secret communications with the king. The Transaction depended upon her "good will," and she would comply with it only if she were treated fairly. He had abused her trust and taken advantage of her sex. He had made her "look ridiculous" by telling everyone in Paris they were engaged and performing love ballads to her in salons. She had placed in him "blind trust," and had found in him "the master of my sex." She had regarded him as "the most virtuous of men" who had persuaded her that he "has some respect for my position," but he had mocked their relationship.

> Why did I not remember at that moment that men are only good in this life to deceive girls and women? Alas, there are injustices that are so wounding and outrageous when they come to us from those to whom we are the most sincerely attached that it forces even the most prudent person to lose control. . . . I thought only of acknowledging your merit and of admiring your talents and your generosity. There's no doubt that I loved you! But I was so naive about this situation.

She accused him of covering her with "shame." Among other outrages, she alleged that Beaumarchais had contracted a venereal disease in London that he had spread all over Paris. Yet she was ready to forgive. She now demanded that the king pay for her new feminine wardrobe. If the king would agree to buy her a new *trousseau* as her "dowry," then "harmony will be restored between us." She was prepared to forgive Beaumarchais and promised to "return to London to embrace you."

There were no more tender embraces. Beaumarchais had had enough. He decided he could no longer deal with d'Eon, and he asked Morande to continue the negotiations on his behalf. It must have seemed more than a bit bizarre for Morande, who had himself blackmailed Louis XV, to approach d'Eon on behalf of Louis XVI. Yet, d'Eon set aside her own disdain for the slimy Morande and invited him to dinner at her flat in early April with a few friends. D'Eon was famous for serving her guests large quantities of Burgundy and at some point in the evening, perhaps under the influence, Morande blurted out that he and Beaumarchais had indeed gambled a large sum on the question whether d'Eon was a woman.

D'Eon's worst suspicions were now confirmed, and she refused to negotiate further with either of them. Instead, she wrote to Vergennes, expressing her outrage that a "virtuous maiden" like herself should be expected to negotiate with scoundrels like Morande and Beaumarchais. When Morande threatened to publish an article about her secret, d'Eon challenged Morande to a duel, and when he refused to fight a woman, she brought a libel suit against him before Lord Mansfield, the same distinguished jurist who had heard her claim against Ambassador Guerchy for poisoning her. Though the suit was later dismissed on the grounds that she was equally guilty of libel, the rupture among d'Eon, Morande, and Beaumarchais was now irreparable. It would take another year of cajoling and threats by Beaumarchais and Vergennes before d'Eon would agree to honor the Transaction.

SEVENTEEN

THE KING MUST DECIDE

London, Paris, and Philadelphia,
January–March 1776

That winter was one of the coldest anyone could remember. Temperatures plunged below zero degrees Fahrenheit, freezing the lake in St. James's Park and transforming the Thames into a glacial plain with shrieking winds. Starving animals struggled to claw through layers of granitic snow and ice, vainly searching for grass, and birds dropped, lifeless, from icy limbs. In Sussex a flock of sheep disappeared for a fortnight under a deep blanket of snow, until the astonished animals were miraculously rescued by a vigilant sheepdog. Humans, too, suffered terribly, shivering in their drafty quarters and listening to the wind's mournful howls. With Thames traffic halted, food was scarce. Prices soared, and there was a shortage of coal for heating and cooking. Those who plied their trade on the water—ferrymen, sailors, fishermen—had no work for a month and were reduced to begging. Ashes were scattered over the icy streets of London to make walking less treacherous, and coal dust settling on snowdrifts imbued the city with a funereal hue.

Since Beaumarchais's return to London in January, he and Arthur Lee continued to meet regularly, often over dinner with Wilkes, who became so embroiled in the conspiracy that he, too, ran the risk of committing treason. The Secret Committee in Philadelphia wrote Lee, asking for his advice on how it could communicate secretly with America's friends in England. Lee interpreted this to mean he had been appointed the secret agent for Congress, which was not the case. Lee and Beaumarchais discussed what could be done to persuade the French government of the urgency of providing arms to the Continental Army. Lee warned that if France denied the Americans any help, France would "become the victim of England and the laughing-stock of Europe." Beaumarchais wrote a long memorandum to Vergennes, reporting on his discussions with Lee. Beaumarchais recounted that the Americans were willing to "offer France, as a price for secret aid, a treaty of commerce which would let her enjoy, for a certain number of years, all the profits" that had once enriched England and a guarantee to defend the French sugar islands from British attack.

Lee's offer to help France defend its Caribbean colonies was, of course, preposterous: the Americans did not have the firepower, ships, or men to defend the French sugar islands, and Congress would hardly be prepared to fight for French colonialism in its own hemisphere. Most probably, Beaumarchais cooked up this argument. He felt that if they could somehow convince Louis XVI that the real prize Britain coveted was the French sugar islands, Louis XVI would help the American rebels.

Beaumarchais laid out four possibilities for Vergennes to consider. First, if England defeated the colonies, it would be saddled with a huge war debt, and the easiest way to repay the debt would be to steal the French possessions and "become in this manner the exclusive merchants of the precious commodity of sugar." In the second scenario, if the Americans won, their standard of living would be so diminished without British trade that they would be motivated to seize the French West Indies to support themselves. Alternatively, if the English granted independence to the colonies, they would "be more able to grab our islands which they will no longer be able to do without, if they want to keep a foothold in America." Or, fourth, if Wilkes and his friends took power in England and made peace with the colonies, then the Americans would likely join England against France to appropriate their islands and punish France for denying them aid for independence. Thus, there was no point in trying to avoid war with Britain. Beaumarchais concluded that "the fine precautions that you were taking to keep your possessions were the very same ones that were to deprive you of them forever." Instead, the only way to keep the peace, Beaumarchais argued, would be to aid the Americans just enough "to balance their forces with those of England, and nothing more." In other words, Beaumarchais was arguing that the longer France could prolong a bloody struggle between England and her colonies, the more France could drain England's strength and better protect her own possessions in America.

It was an ingenious argument, worthy of the playwright who made aristocrats laugh at themselves: France should support America, not because Americans loved France, but because either an independent America or an America restored to the mother country posed a greater threat to France. In reality there was little evidence that the British or the Americans lusted after the sugar islands. It is unclear whether Vergennes really believed that Britain threatened France's Caribbean possessions. Other sources of intelligence would have cast doubt on Beaumarchais's assertions of British intentions. Vergennes was astute enough to appreciate when Beaumarchais was playing him, and the sugar islands were already well prepared to defend themselves from attack. If Vergennes were truly worried that the British might attack, he could have merely sent additional reinforcements.

On the other hand, Vergennes probably recognized that Beaumarchais offered him an argument that might persuade the reluctant Louis XVI to take action now.

On March 2, 1776, the Secret Committee gave Silas Deane his secret commission to go to France and acquire all the supplies for an army of 25,000 men. Only six days later, Deane began his circuitous journey from Philadelphia by pilot boat to Chester, Pennsylvania, on the Delaware Bay. There he boarded a large merchant brig that set sail, but adverse winds repeatedly forced it back to shore and damaged the vessel beyond repair. For several frustrating weeks, he waited near Cape May, New Jersey, while another "Leaky & sickly" sloop was being outfitted in Maryland. In the meantime, Congress sent a guard of twenty soldiers to protect Deane from capture by Loyalists.

While Deane waited, events were moving rapidly toward a full-scale war. The Continental Army had sat helplessly in Cambridge all winter, camping in muddy squalor, while across the Charles River, Boston remained under the firm hand of British general Sir William Howe and his men. Since the capture of Fort Ticonderoga by Benedict Arnold and Ethan Allen the previous spring, the Continental Army had little to cheer about. Colonel Arnold had sent all the guns and ammunition stored by the British at Ticonderoga to assist the army. But moving the heavy artillery from Ticonderoga across hundreds of miles of forest and mountains was slow and difficult.

Washington's artillery commander, Colonel Henry Knox, a rotund twenty-five-year-old bookseller from Boston, showed remarkable fortitude and ingenuity, transporting the cannons from Ticonderoga by boat across Lake George and then by ox-drawn sled over the snowy Berkshire Mountains. It took until February to drag all the artillery 200 miles south and east to Cambridge. Under cover of night on March 4, the guns were deployed on Dorchester Heights, from which vantage point Washington aimed them menacingly at the British fleet anchored below in Boston Harbor. Washington could now command an attack at any time on the British forces in Boston, while the British guns could not strike Washington's position. When the sun rose the next morning, General Howe saw no option but to retreat. On March 17, the British troops withdrew to Nova Scotia, along with one thousand Loyalists, who, fearing reprisals, immigrated to Britain. The guns of Ticonderoga had proved decisive.

From Canada, Deane's friend General Benedict Arnold wrote to Deane from his camp on the Plains of Abraham, just below Quebec. Arnold reported that the American forces which Congress had sent to "liberate" Canada were hopelessly outnumbered and lacked basic supplies. Arnold complained that "we have never had more than seven hundred effective men on the ground, and frequently not more than five hundred." Moreover, the New England troops had contracted smallpox and "not one-quarter" were fit to serve. "Our Surgeons are without medicine; our Hospitals are crowded, and in want of almost every necessary." The Canadian invasion proved to be a colossal failure, despite Arnold's heroism and bold maneuvers.

To make matters worse, Lord Dunmore, the last royal governor of Virginia, who was despised among the colonists as a "bloody butcher" for offering freedom to slaves who joined the Loyalists and for encouraging Indian tribes to attack Virginians, was now menacing the waters of the Chesapeake Bay. At the same time, British general Henry Clinton was sweeping down the coast, and 2,500 British troops were reportedly en route from Ireland. It looked likely that the British would be able to take New York City. By the time Deane's ship was outfitted, the British navy might be too close to outrun.

More than a month passed in Cape May before Deane could climb aboard the *Betsy*. The sloop was loaded with a cargo of salt pork, which Deane intended to trade for hard currency in France. Ten days later, the *Betsy* landed in Bermuda, where Deane was delayed again by an argument with the customs house. The customs officer compelled Deane to sell the pork in Bermuda at a lower price than he had anticipated receiving in France. From Bermuda, Deane had to sail to Grand Turk Island in the Caribbean, and then on to Jamaica to obtain more cargo to sell in France. Another month passed before the *Betsy* finally set out across the open water for France.

IT WAS NOW MARCH, and sitting on Vergennes's desk alongside Beaumarchais's memorandum was the recent memorandum from Bonvouloir, the secret envoy to Philadelphia who had met with Franklin and the Secret Committee in December. Bonvouloir's wildly inflated numbers of American troops bolstered Beaumarchais's claim that the Americans were well prepared to take on the British forces. But Bonvouloir did not necessarily have much credibility in Vergennes's eyes. After all, Vergennes did not know or trust Bonvouloir and had only reluctantly agreed to dispatch him to America at the urging of Ambassador Guines, whom Vergennes had since fired.

While neither Bonvouloir nor Beaumarchais had conclusive evidence to support their claims, the two reports together seemed to buttress the proposition that the Americans might actually succeed in their struggle with Britain. Vergennes was less interested in whether the Americans would succeed than he was in the ability of the Americans to prolong the war. He was probably persuaded by Beaumarchais that France's objective should be to entangle Britain in a long and costly war that would weaken them militarily and economically. In addition, Vergennes might have hoped that if the Americans ever won their independence, they would be more inclined to open their markets to France.

Vergennes would have to convince the other cabinet ministers—and the excessively cautious Louis XVI—that Beaumarchais's plan to arm the colonists could succeed without entangling France in another disastrous war with Britain. The foreign minister prepared a memorandum to the cabinet, outlining the costs and benefits of aiding the Americans. He used Beaumarchais's argument that the French sugar islands were threatened by Britain. He pointed to the advantage to France from prolonging Britain's troubles in North America. Vergennes argued that this was France's opportunity to revenge all the humiliation that Britain had inflicted on France. By encouraging American resistance, France would drain Britain's economic and military power, while at the same time France would continue to rearm against Britain. He was not arguing in support of independence or representative government. Supporting the Americans were merely a useful gambit by which France could restore the balance of power on the Continent. Vergennes proposed that France provide secret arms and funds to the rebels while maintaining the appearance of neutrality.

Obviously, Vergennes was not bothered by the moral niceties involved in violating France's treaty commitments. On the one hand, he denounced the British for their "habitual breach of good faith, violation of treaties, and disregard of that observance of the sacred laws of morality which distinguish the French." On the other hand, without a trace of irony, he recommended that France should continue to mislead the English with respect to their true intentions. Although Vergennes's memorandum did not mention Beaumarchais by name, it is clear that he had adopted Beaumarchais's plan as his own.

The French minister of war, Claude Robert, the Comte de Saint-Germain, a tough old soldier, responded enthusiastically, *"Si vis pacem, para bellum"* ("If you wish for peace, prepare for war"). The more cautious comptroller-general, Anne-Jacques-Robert Turgot, the baron de l'Aulne, waited several weeks before venturing the opinion that France could not afford war with Britain. Turgot, a brilliant economic reformer, was convinced that the Americans would succeed without France and that the cost of supporting the Americans and possibly being dragged into a full-scale war with Britain would ruin the economic reforms he had envisioned. In fact, Turgot's judgment proved accurate. The staggering cost of the American Revolution would eventually push France into bankruptcy and thereby necessitate the excessive taxation that sparked the French Revolution. Turgot's opposition to aiding the Americans was particularly ironic because, unlike Vergennes, the liberal-minded Turgot was actually sympathetic to the principles of the American revolutionaries. The other ministers were generally supportive of Vergennes's plan.

Vergennes responded to Turgot's arguments for fiscal prudence by blaming England for "the impoverishment, humiliation, and ruin of France." By favoring the colonies, France would take commerce away from Britain for itself and thus increase its own wealth. Vergennes warned that whether Britain retained or lost her colonies, unless weakened, Britain would attack the French West Indies. War was inevitable, and therefore, it would be preferable to make common cause with the Americans.

Louis XVI had no sympathy for American colonists opposing monarchy, and he felt deeply conflicted over France betraying its treaty obligations. Even more, he feared leading his country into a war it was not prepared to win. But the king relied on Vergennes as his mentor and trusted his judgment above that of others. He found Vergennes's arguments persuasive, and he also now regarded Beaumarchais as a faithful agent who could conduct the smuggling operation in secret.

After a few weeks of hesitating, Louis XVI agreed to set aside his objections to supporting the American colonists. France was finally prepared to exact revenge on Britain for the punitive terms of the peace treaty that d'Eon had negotiated ending the Seven Years' War. The king ordered Turgot to supply Beaumarchais with one million livres to finance his smuggling operation. Turgot's reluctance to support Vergennes's proposals helped to convince the foreign minister that the comptroller-general Turgot must go, and by late spring the king dismissed Turgot.

France had found a way to stab Britain in the back. Not to make America independent, but to bleed Britain dry. And Vergennes would ensure that the hand that held the knife would be Beaumarchais's.

EIGHTEEN

THE BRITISH
ARE WATCHING

Philadelphia and Paris, March–July 1776

Deane left Philadelphia on March 8, and after about two months of delays, he set out on the *Betsy* for France in late April. Though Deane owned a schooner and had prospered from trade with the West Indies, he had never sailed on the ocean before. He missed the luxuries of home and the comfort of the familiar. For six weeks he suffered the deprivations of life at sea—the blustery damp wind, the nauseating odors belowdecks, the dark cramped cabin, the coarseness of the seamen, the salty overcooked food, and the daily monotony broken only by violent storms.

Deane had no way of knowing whether his family was safe, or whether he would reach Paris before the British crushed the Continental Army. He worried that at any point they would be stopped and boarded by the British navy. In the event he was seized by the British, he kept among his papers a letter from Captain William Hunter, a British officer captured by Benedict Arnold at St. John in New Brunswick, Canada. Hunter was being held prisoner at Wethersfield under the supervision of Deane's brother, Barnabas. Hunter wrote to any British officer who might capture Deane to treat him with "as much Politeness" as the British officers had received from Deane's friends.

On June 6, 1776, after three months at sea Deane sailed into the Bay of Biscay and arrived in Bordeaux, having evaded the British navy's watchful eye. Now his mission began in earnest.

Deane had never seen a place as old or as lively as Bordeaux. Along the banks of the Garonne he was jostled by wealthy wine merchants and sweaty dockworkers rushing from ship to ship. The old city, surrounded by a medieval wall and dotted with spires, was one of Europe's leading ports. Shops and stalls crowded the Basilica of St. Michel with merchants offering their wares in a strange tongue. The noise of the stone cutters and the smell of the tanneries overwhelmed Deane's senses. He spent a few weeks in Bordeaux, hoping to purchase cloth, blankets, and other essentials for the army. He found some English-speakers among the prosperous merchants, especially in the Chartrons quarter, but generally, he avoided Englishmen. Goods were far more expensive than he expected, and he decided to wait until he reached Paris before procuring supplies. He wrote to Franklin's contacts in France and England to inform them of his impending arrival in Paris.

The three-hundred-mile journey by coach from Bordeaux to Paris took two weeks. The road was slow and bumpy and often crowded with peasants and soldiers. He passed majestic stone châteaux that glowed pink with the setting sun, and fields of gnarly vines submerged in a green sea of ripening grapes. The summer air seemed almost intoxicating. Each day, Deane's excitement grew with the anticipation of meeting the French monarch and his court. As the coach lumbered north he watched peasants in the field bent over their crops, tending animals, and carrying firewood to their modest cottages. Deane's carriage crossed a bridge over the clear rushing water of the Loire and entered the ancient Gallo-Roman city of Tours, where he stayed overnight. He saw the splendid gothic Cathedral Saint-Gatien in the center of town. The enormous stone façade seemed too massive to hold itself up. Inside, the damp cool air offered a welcome relief from a hot June afternoon. The scent of incense, the chanting of monks, and the gaudy display of gold and silver were unlike anything he had ever experienced. No Yankee Congregationalist could imagine praying in a church like that. Just outside the cathedral stood the skeletal ruins of a Roman fortress—a reminder of the impermanence of empires. For a man who had lived his whole life within the narrow circumference of colonial Connecticut surrounded by fellow Congregationalists, it must have felt both exhilarating and lonely to be in a place so remote and exotic.

Finally, the moment came when Deane could make out a dark line at the horizon. "*C'est-ça. Paris,*" the coachman shouted. To the son of a Connecticut blacksmith who was once thrilled by the romantic notion of New Haven, Paris was mythic. As the coach approached the city, the road improved considerably. The clatter of wheels rumbled louder on stone pavement. The thin dark line at the edge of the horizon grew taller and wider. Spires soared overhead. The road widened and then narrowed as the carriage rumbled across a bridge.

After nearly four months of travel, Deane at last arrived at the Porte d'Orlean gate to Paris on July 6. He had no idea that Congress had declared independence just days before, and that he was now the sole foreign representative of a new government. Not comprehending any French, he watched in puzzlement as the rude customs officials poked his few small bags with poles, searching for contraband. They did not discover his secret instructions hidden in a hollowed-out volume. He had left Philadelphia in a hurry with only the clothes he had brought with him to Congress the previous September. There had been no time to be fitted for a new suit in which to present himself to Louis XVI. Once inside the city gates, Deane continued to the Hôtel du Grand Villars at 31 rue Saint-Guillaume.

Neither New York nor Philadelphia could rival the density or beauty of Paris. The street sounds of horses, carriages, church bells, and street hawkers enveloped him. The foul smell of humans living in close quarters mingled with the sweet aromas of bakeries and vegetable stalls. The city was glorious, filthy, refined, and disordered. The magnificent palaces and the elegance of the gardens contrasted markedly with the people he saw on the streets. Hungry men, women, and children stretched out their hands to passing carriages. Occasionally, Deane might glimpse through the window of a passing coach the profile of a woman powdered white as a ghost with a tower of hair adorned by gold brooches, diamond pins, feathers, or even small birds. Splendor took no notice of despair. Aristocrats seemed to inhabit another city entirely.

Deane passed his first few days there in wonder, glorying in the magnificence and the strangeness of Paris. He took long walks, marveling at the strange foods and customs. He stammered a few phrases in French; merchants stared back, uncomprehending. He found a wine merchant and ordered one bottle of every varietal, curious to sample everything. (After a few weeks, he ordered only Burgundy.) He crossed to the Ile Saint-Louis and gazed at the boats as they passed under the arch of the Pont Neuf. The Seine was not nearly as broad or as fast-moving as the Connecticut River. He stood for a time admiring the rose window of Notre Dame and wished he could share this experience with someone.

Deane found himself in peculiar circumstances, which, he thought "no man now living in Europe or America, and but few in any nation or age of the world, ever found themselves in." It was not just that he lacked any rudimentary knowledge of French or diplomatic etiquette; he was an unofficial representative of a nonentity asking the French monarch for support against the British crown. Unaware that Congress had already declared independence, he felt obliged to state that he was a loyal subject of George III. "I could not therefore solicit for the aid which I was commissioned to procure from the court of Versailles on the ground of our having declared ourselves independent," he later wrote, nor could he even suggest "our intentions to do so." Instead, he was compelled to argue that no sovereign had the right to tax his subject without their consent and that the colonies had resorted to arms solely "to enable us to bring the King and Parliament of Great Britain to recede from these their unwarrantable claims, and to accede to reasonable terms of accommodation." The awkwardness of this argument was apparent: the French king was unlikely to agree that discontented subjects had a natural right to rebel against their sovereign.

Though Franklin thought that Deane could escape suspicion, practically from the moment Deane landed, the British ambassador to France, Lord Stormont, knew of his presence. Stormont had informants posted at various French ports reporting on the arrival and departure of vessels. Any American arriving in France was immediately suspect. Deane noticed two Englishmen, whom he had seen when he arrived in Bordeaux, trailing him in Paris. Stormont had sent them to watch Deane and prevent him from meeting with French officials. He plotted to have Deane seized if he tried to return to America. Deane wrote that Paris "swarmed with Englishmen" who followed him everywhere, causing him "heartrending anxiety." Deane could trust no one.

It was not idle paranoia. Paris was lousy with British spies. Less obtrusively, the French police chief Jean-Charles-Pierre Lenoir was also watching Deane and reporting all this British espionage regularly to Foreign Minister Vergennes. Marveling at Britain's economic competitiveness, Vergennes remarked that the British government was hardly "economical" when it came to espionage. Spying on foreigners was not uncommon, but Vergennes mused that only a government as free as England's would be so suspicious of its own subjects.

NINETEEN

THE FOREIGN
MINISTER WINKS

Paris, July 1776

The Secret Committee had advanced 200,000 Continental dollars to Deane and Robert Morris as a down payment on the purchase of arms, ammunition, and clothing for 25,000 troops, 100 brass field pieces, and presents for the Indian tribes. Deane soon realized that the 200,000 Continental dollars would not go far in France. Though a Continental dollar was supposed to have the same value as a Spanish silver dollar, which was often used in the colonies, the Continental dollar lost value as soon as it was printed. There was no gold or foreign currency backing up the value of the Continental dollar, and Congress had not even declared independence by the time it was printing Continental dollars, which was prohibited by British law. While originally the face value of 200,000 Continental dollars would have equaled the purchasing power of nearly $5 million today, by the time Deane reached Paris, it was worth about one-tenth that amount, assuming he could find someone willing to accept his dollars. It was hardly enough money to finance an army, and Deane had already spent a substantial portion of his cash on his four-month-long journey. Most of the advance was in the form of large bills drawn by Congress on a bank in London, but banks had no reason to trust the credit of a Congress that was operating without legal authority from the British sovereign. When Deane presented the bills for deposit to a bank in Paris, nearly all of the notes were returned unpaid. Within days of his arrival in Paris, Deane had no means to purchase more supplies for the army, and for his travel and living expenses he was forced to rely on bills drawn against his own private business.

On July 8, a few days after Deane's arrival in Paris, a visitor called on him at his hotel. It was Dr. Edward Bancroft, whom Franklin had recommended as a contact for Deane in London. Bancroft arrived still feeling the ill effects of a virus. Deane had not seen Bancroft since he had been Deane's pupil back in Hartford, sixteen years earlier, and he was eager to hear all about Bancroft's adventures since. After leaving Deane's tutelage, Bancroft had apprenticed to a doctor in Connecticut, but he yearned for more excitement and soon ran off to sea. Coincidentally, he worked on a plantation in Guiana owned by Paul Wentworth, Arthur Lee's friend in London. Wentworth had become a kind of patron to Bancroft. In Guiana, Bancroft learned about obscure native plants and developed an expertise in native dyes, medicines, and poisons. After a few years he moved to Britain, where he received a medical degree from the University of Aberdeen. He also wrote *An Essay on the Natural History of Guiana, in South America.* He found work writing reviews of recent American publications for the *Monthly Review*, and in that capacity he had befriended Franklin, America's most famous publisher, while Franklin was living in London in the 1770s. He also knew Lee in London, and Bancroft may have introduced Lee to his friend Wentworth when Lee was a law student. With Franklin's support, Bancroft had been elected to the Royal College of Physicians and the Royal British Society. Bancroft had also written a strong critique of British colonial policy, which had impressed Franklin.

Now thirty-two, Bancroft was well known in London as a scientist and a popular author. He had written an epistolary novel on the evils of religion and civilization called *The History of Charles Wentworth, Esq.* It tells the sordid tale of a young man who impregnates a woman, abandons her to a life of prostitution, and runs off to find adventure in Guiana. Some people probably wondered if Bancroft used the name of the former British prime minister Charles Watson-Wentworth, the Marquess of Rockingham, as a political satire. But Bancroft may have been writing about someone else entirely. Rockingham, a leading critic of the present government's colonial policy, was also the cousin of Bancroft's friend and patron, Paul Wentworth, who had much more in common with Bancroft's amoral hero. As charming as he was sophisticated, Bancroft captivated nearly everyone who met him, and Deane was no exception. Bancroft, who spoke French fluently, offered to help Deane get settled in Paris and make contact with Foreign Minister Vergennes.

The following day Deane and Bancroft called on Dr. Jacques Barbeu-Dubourg with a letter of introduction from Franklin. Dr. Dubourg was one of Franklin's closest friends in France. He was a distinguished physician and botanist who spoke English fluently and had translated the first French edition of Franklin's works—*Les Oeuvres de M. Franklin.* Dubourg was a wealthy gentleman with access to the highest reaches of the French government, and he was sympathetic to the American cause. Dubourg had already tried to help Congress by sending an agent, Monsieur Pinette, to Philadelphia with an offer to sell the Americans 15,000 muskets from the French government. Deane had met Pinette in Philadelphia before he left for France, and they had agreed on terms for the purchase. But

Dubourg did not have Louis XVI's blessing, and the deal collapsed. Despite this setback, Dubourg still hoped to become the chief arms dealer for the Americans.

Dubourg's sympathy for the American cause was eclipsed by his own avarice. He insisted that Deane must procure arms exclusively through him. He told Deane that Vergennes would not see Deane, because Vergennes feared offending the British ambassador, Stormont. Indeed, Stormont had already warned Vergennes that France should not interfere with the American colonies, but Deane saw through Dubourg's self-serving scheme and firmly insisted that Dubourg must arrange for him to meet with the French foreign minister immediately. Dubourg reluctantly agreed to write a letter to Vergennes asking to arrange a meeting with Deane at Versailles the following week.

WHEN DEANE, BANCROFT, and Dubourg arrived at Versailles on July 11, Vergennes was not expecting them. Though Vergennes's spies had informed him of Deane's arrival in Paris, he had not received Dubourg's letter of introduction. Nevertheless, the French foreign minister met with them for two hours in his well-appointed villa known as "La Solitude," a short distance from the palace. There British agents would be less likely to observe their meeting. News that Congress had already declared independence had not yet reached Europe. Vergennes's English was no better than Deane's French, but the minister's chief secretary, Conrad-Alexandre Gérard, spoke English well and acted as translator.

Deane began by informing Vergennes of his secret mission: to solicit France's friendship, commerce, and support in the guise of a private merchant. Aware that he did not know what behavior would be expected of him in these circumstances, Deane modestly asked the foreign minister to forgive him for his ignorance of diplomatic etiquette. Vergennes assured Deane that he found Deane's simplicity and sincerity agreeable. Vergennes responded that an open acknowledgment of the independence of the colonies or an assertion of a right to trade with North America would antagonize Britain and could lead to war. This issue could not be addressed without discussions with the king and his other ministers after the colonies declared their independence and proposed terms for commerce and alliance. Independence, in the minister's words, "was an event in the womb of time," and it would be improper for him to "say anything on that subject until it had actually taken place."

What was France likely to do if the colonies declared independence? Vergennes expressed his personal view that it was not in France's interest for the British sovereign to defeat the Americans and establish absolute control over North American trade. Vergennes assured Deane that the American cause had "the unanimous good Wishes of the Government and People of France." The minister extended to Deane "the King's Protection" from any threat or action by the British. Vergennes worried that the British ambassador might learn of Deane's mission, and he cautioned Deane to maintain his disguise as a private merchant and to act discreetly to avoid compromising French neutrality. Vergennes told Deane that he should maintain contact with Vergennes's secretary, Gérard. If Deane needed to see the foreign minister, Vergennes would be happy to meet him someplace away from the palace.

Deane's visit to Vergennes bore fruit immediately. Deane had impressed Vergennes both with the urgency of his appeal and his discretion. First, Vergennes informed Deane that 13,000 small arms were being shipped at once to Congress from Nantes. This was the shipment Dubourg had arranged with Pinette but which the French government had earlier stopped. Second, Vergennes wrote to Deane

a few days after their initial meeting to suggest that Deane contact a
Monsieur Beaumarchais, who ran an import-export firm in Paris.
Vergennes claimed that Beaumarchais could offer Congress military
merchandise at good prices on credit, up to three million livres
(roughly $25 million today). Since he spoke no French, Deane prob-
ably would not have heard of the famous playwright. Dubourg was
puzzled by the suggestion that a comedic playwright was now heading a trading firm large enough to finance such a transaction, and
he warned Deane that Beaumarchais, "though confessedly a man of
abilities, had always been a man of pleasure and never of business."
Relying on Dubourg's judgment, Deane decided not to contact the
playwright.

Deane followed his meeting with Vergennes by submitting a
lengthy memorandum to the minister on the commercial advantages of trade with North America, part of which he had composed
during his long ocean voyage. On the morning of July 20, Deane,
Dubourg, and Bancroft returned to Versailles to meet with Vergennes and Gérard to urge the French to provide military aid. Deane
showed the foreign minister extracts from Franklin's instructions.
He needed arms and uniforms for 25,000 soldiers and 200 light cannons. He offered to pay for them on credit or to replace them at
some future time. Vergennes said he did not have sufficient uniforms to offer, but he would see what could be done. The French
government could not provide guns or cannons directly, but perhaps Deane could buy these from a private firm.

Deane asked if France would consider forming an alliance with
the Americans against Britain. Vergennes cautiously replied that
Deane "could not expect anything of the kind." Any assistance would
be inconsistent with the explicit terms of the 1763 treaty ending the
Seven Years' War with Britain. Vergennes appeared to close the door
on providing any overt material support. Vergennes added with a

knowing smile that "the ports of France were open" for all trade, other than military goods. And even arms shipments "might be winked at if conducted with prudence."

Toward the end of their conversation, Vergennes repeated his suggestion that Deane should meet Beaumarchais. Deane was still uneasy about meeting with the playwright, given what Dubourg had told him. Dubourg's criticism of Beaumarchais may have been based on the contemporary rumors about Beaumarchais's unconventional romantic life or his theatrical productions, like *The Barber of Seville*, which skirted the line of good taste. Or Dubourg's judgment may have been clouded once more by his own self-interest. He wanted to control commerce with the Americans, and it must have seemed preposterous to Dubourg to be displaced by a comedy writer. Vergennes and his secretary, Monsieur Gérard, assured Deane that Beaumarchais really was financially secure and could readily sell merchandise on credit to the Americans.

Deane agreed to contact Beaumarchais, unaware that Beaumarchais was already his secret ally in Louis XVI's court.

TWENTY

THE COUNTERSPY

Paris and London, July 1776

An envelope addressed in an elegant hand to "Mr. Deine" arrived at the Hôtel du Grand Villars. Beaumarchais had written to Silas Deane in French, hoping that Deane could find someone to translate for him. Edward Bancroft, who spoke fluent French, was happy to oblige. Beaumarchais began that he "cherished the desire to aid the brave Americans to shake off the British yoke," and for this purpose he had established a firm that could provide military supplies through private channels to the Americans. He alluded to his prior conversation with Arthur Lee, whom he had not heard from in some time, and he now questioned Lee's bona fides. Moreover, since Vergennes had welcomed Deane as Congress's emissary, Beaumarchais preferred to negotiate with Deane. There may be other Frenchmen, like Dubourg, who could offer Deane supplies, Beaumarchais conceded, but when Deane compared these offers with Beaumarchais's "own disinterested ardor for the cause of

America," he would see the difference between dealing with "the common run of agents" and "the pleasure of finding a generous friend."

Beaumarchais and Deane met for the first time on a warm Friday afternoon, July 19, 1776. Since Beaumarchais could not speak English, it was necessary for Bancroft to be present to translate. Beaumarchais introduced Deane to his trading firm, Rodriguez Hortalez and Co., which, Deane was unaware, Beaumarchais had recently established for this purpose only. They agreed that in exchange for uniforms, guns, and ammunition sufficient to arm 25,000 men, Congress would ship to Rodriguez Hortalez and Co. ten to twelve thousand hogshead or more of the finest Virginia tobacco. (A hogshead was a large wooden barrel, which, when full of tobacco, weighed roughly one ton.) Beaumarchais did not disclose to Deane that his operation was secretly underwritten by a loan of one million livres from Louis XVI and another million that Vergennes had squeezed out of the king of Spain with vague assurances about the Bourbon alliance against Portugal. (The total of two million livres would be worth about $15 million today.) Although Deane may have suspected later that the king was financing Beaumarchais, it is unclear whether Deane ever realized the full extent to which the French government was Beaumarchais's silent partner.

Beaumarchais boasted to Deane that Rodriguez and Hortalez was "well established and I have allocated many millions to your trade alone." He would take care of every detail of their commercial arrangements, and he claimed that he had agents in every French port to assist them. He explained that despite Louis XVI's "overt opposition" to helping the Americans, Beaumarchais would do his "utmost to clear up difficulties, soften prohibitions, and in short pave the way" for providing military aid on favorable terms.

It is doubtful that Beaumarchais had any of the capabilities he claimed, but he never doubted that his capacity could rise to meet his confidence. Whether out of excessive zeal or blind ambition, Beaumarchais now acted as if he were operating as a kind of shadow government. He advised both the American Congress and Versailles on foreign relations and finances. Though he was virtually unknown in America, Beaumarchais boldly wrote to the Continental Congress, advising the delegates of the merits of appointing a dictator during wartime. In a similar vein, he wrote to Louis XVI, proposing a new tax system to finance a war with Britain. Beaumarchais did not have a modest opinion of his own genius.

In fact, Beaumarchais remained frustrated with his own government's tentative measures. "I am even more unfortunate than Cassandra, whose prophecies no one believed because she always announced calamities," he complained. Even though he predicted only success for the Americans, his predictions were dismissed as confusing reality with his "overheated imagination." At least, he had the good sense to acknowledge his clumsiness. He knew that he could offend ministers. "I did not promise you to do my best in politics," he wrote Vergennes, "but to do the best that can be done. You can judge if I intend to keep my word." He asked the foreign minister not to "take my impatient remarks as insubordination." Rather, he explained, "It's only zeal."

A WEEK AFTER Deane's first meeting with Beaumarchais, Bancroft left Deane to return to London. He promised to visit again with fresh information when his affairs permitted. Deane was sorry to see his friend leave. He paid Bancroft's travel expenses out of his dwindling advance and agreed to employ him as a secret agent for information about British politics and military movements. Deane gave Bancroft an advance of thirty pounds on an annual salary of 300 pounds (about $56,000 today).

Dr. Bancroft arrived by coach at his townhouse at number 4 Downing Street on July 26. Deane would have been surprised by the elegant lifestyle that Bancroft enjoyed in London. Bancroft's expenses far outstripped his income as an author or physician, so he supplemented his income by "stock-jobbing," or speculating short-term in stocks. Through his friend Samuel Wharton, a very successful American financier, Bancroft had been involved in a number of speculative adventures with varying success. A few days after he returned to London, Bancroft saw Wharton and mentioned to him that perhaps some of the information provided by Deane about the progress of the Americans' cause could be useful to Wharton's investors. Wharton, indeed, thought that Bancroft's intelligence on the negotiations between France and America could be a source of profit, and he agreed to pay Bancroft for this inside information.

Bancroft also contacted his former patron from Guiana, Paul Wentworth. Bancroft thought that perhaps his information could be useful to Wentworth as well. Wentworth was very interested to hear Bancroft's news of the arrival of Silas Deane and the willingness of the French to aid the Americans, and he had news of his own: Wentworth had taken a plum job in the foreign ministry, with a promise of a baronetcy, a seat in Parliament, and a position on a government board—if he performed well. Wentworth, who spoke flawless French, would be working for the British ambassador in Paris and hoped to see Bancroft there.

A few weeks after Bancroft's visit, Wentworth invited him to a private meeting with the British secretaries of state, Lords Weymouth and Suffolk. At the meeting Bancroft told them everything he knew about Deane's commission and Deane's meetings with Vergennes. He had written down a precise narrative of all his dealings with Deane, which he handed to the secretaries, who were delighted to receive a detailed account of the discussions between the American emissary and the French foreign minister. The precise dates and times of Deane's meetings with Dubourg and Vergennes, as well as the substance of the conversations, were all recorded in Bancroft's fluid hand. Bancroft said he was acting out of loyalty to the crown with no expectation of any financial reward. Lord Weymouth encouraged Bancroft to maintain his contacts with Deane, and he was prepared to pay him a generous salary for providing regular information on Deane's activities. Bancroft cheerfully accepted. His British code name would be "Edward Edwards."

Thus, Edward Bancroft became a double agent. While Deane had agreed to pay him 300 pounds annually for information about British politics, the director of the Secret Service, William Eden, eventually offered Bancroft 500 pounds—later increased to 1,000 pounds annually (about $185,000 today) to report on Deane. Living well in London did not come cheap.

Though Deane and Franklin always believed that their friend Bancroft was a true American patriot, they should have read to the end of his novel. At its conclusion, the hero, Charles Wentworth, vows never to revisit his native country. He declares, "I boast of no patriotism, which at best is but an extended selfishness."

With no genuine loyalty to any country, Bancroft was happy to spy for both the Americans and the British. His relationship to Franklin and Deane had created an opportunity for Bancroft both to profit personally and to determine the course of Anglo-American history. He was now the one person ideally situated to destroy Deane and prevent France from arming the Americans.

TWENTY-ONE

A TANGLED WEB

Paris, July–August 1776

Over the next six months, Deane and Beaumarchais would move heaven and earth to load eight ships with cannons, guns, ammunition, saltpeter, powder, cloth, blankets, shovels, tents, belt buckles, and boots. Wary that some of this cargo might be captured by the British, Deane exceeded his original instructions to supply 25,000 men and increased the amount by twenty percent. To hoard this quantity of supplies without directly raiding the French military or arousing too much suspicion required Rodriguez Hortalez to engage in a staggering number of small transactions. In Bordeaux, Beaumarchais purchased ships and some armaments from the nearby arsenal at Château-Trompette, but the French War Ministry objected, and it took many visits to Bordeaux to persuade them to release the guns. The 200 cannons Beaumarchais procured could not be shipped until the king's coat of arms was carefully removed from each so that they could not be traced back to the French armory. The frustration of trying to obtain large quantities of military supplies without attracting attention tore at Beaumarchais. He complained that he was "sick at heart when I see how everything is going, or rather not going at all." He was repeatedly forced to cancel contracts; find new suppliers; unravel one day's work and start fresh. Exasperated by French bureaucracy, he fumed, "How quickly harm is done, how slow good is!"

By August, Rodriguez Hortalez had purchased 200 tons of cannon powder, 20,000 guns, and an indeterminate number of brass mortars, bombs, cannonballs, bayonets, plates, cloth, linen, and lead. To add to the difficulty of moving this quantity of supplies from various locations to the ports at Le Havre and Nantes, they were hounded by British spies and French police every step of the way. Beaumarchais cautioned Deane that they must "slip between everyone's fingers and not cause anyone to squeal."

Vergennes had warned Deane that he was being watched. Deane noticed when a gentleman followed him too closely along the quay or if a customer at his favorite wine merchant's shop strained to overhear his conversation. Dr. Dubourg suggested that Deane disguise himself and change his name, but Deane thought that would only make him more suspicious. As a merchant he appreciated the importance of trading on one's reputation. He could not expect other merchants to trust him if he appeared to be hiding something. It was not in his nature to suspect others or to behave suspiciously.

Meanwhile, Vergennes vacillated under the stern warnings of the omnipresent British ambassador in Paris, Viscount David Murray Stormont. A commanding Scotsman with a mercurial temperament, Lord Stormont complained repeatedly to Vergennes that the peace between France and Britain was threatened by Frenchmen seeking to aid the American rebels. Vergennes vigorously denied any French involvement. The British ambassador knew that Vergennes was lying, but he presented no evidence to support his accusations, because he did not want to disclose his sources of information. Bancroft kept Stormont well informed about Deane's relationship to Beaumarchais, and Beaumarchais's well-financed new trading company. Stormont also suspected that Wilkes was somehow involved in the initial effort to establish the smuggling operation, and he probably knew of Arthur Lee's involvement as well from Lee's close friend Paul Wentworth. For the time being, Stormont thought it was useful to allow France to believe it had deceived Britain about its involvement with the Americans. "I must not appear to have the least suspicion since it is evidently wise to dissemble our knowledge of the duplicity of France," Stormont wrote to the British secretary of state, Lord Weymouth. If he revealed all he knew, France "might at once throw off the mask which in the present Circumstance might have dangerous Consequences." Stormont had resolved to meet France's "deceit and artifice" with "seeming Credulity."

Beaumarchais went to great lengths to create the appearance that Rodriguez Hortalez was a serious trading company, while at the same time maintaining his own career as a playwright. He leased one of the grandest mansions in the Marais, at 47 rue Vieille-du-Temple, the Hôtel des Ambassadeurs de Hollande. The magnificent baroque structure, built in 1660, had once been home to the Dutch ambassador. When Huguenots, like Beaumarchais's family, were forbidden to worship in France in the early 1700s, the Dutch ambassador welcomed hordes of Protestants into his home to attend church services there. The sculptor Thomas Regnaudin carved the imposing outer doors with a terrifying head of Medusa, representing a shield against evil. Jean-Baptiste Corneille painted the rich murals in the main gallery that recounted the story of Psyche's marriage to Cupid. The windows were modeled after the royal palace at

Fontainebleau, and the inner doors were adorned by the sculptor Jacques Sarazin. No one would question the financial resources of the firm of Rodriguez and Hortalez.

Beaumarchais's life was divided between his often frantic efforts to help the Americans and his life as a dramatist. He ran the arms business downstairs, in his ornate public rooms, while upstairs he found time to write a sequel to *The Barber of Seville*. In his new comedy, *The Marriage of Figaro*, a comte covets the fiancée of his servant Figaro. The wily Figaro outwits the comte by disguising another man as his fiancée. At one point the hapless comte, recently appointed ambassador to London, admits to his wife that "We men think we know something of dissimulation, but we are only children." Women would make better diplomats, the comte concedes, because they are so much better at "the art of controlling their demeanor." (Beaumarchais may have been poking fun at the Chevalière d'Eon; Beaumarchais knew from personal experience just how effective a woman could be as a cross-dressing emissary.)

Deane and Beaumarchais felt increasingly isolated and dependent on each other. Deane knew that spies might at any moment seize or murder him. Indeed, Ambassador Stormont had already proposed to Lord Weymouth that the British should kidnap Deane. He avoided all English-speakers—they might be British agents—yet he could barely speak any French. "[H]e is the most silent man in France, for I defy him to say six consecutive words before Frenchmen," Beaumarchais joked to Vergennes. With Beaumarchais's secretary acting as their translator, the two partners conferred regularly in Beaumarchais's elaborate dining room over a simple lunch of fish soup. While Deane worried for his physical safety and liberty, Beaumarchais worried about his rapidly depleting finances. What could Beaumarchais tell the French government when it demanded repayment of its loan, which had grown to three million livres? Beaumarchais unburdened himself to Deane: "[P]ray the wind to blow toward us over a few tobacco loads, for I shall be broke."

The two men became good friends over the succeeding months. Both were hard-working and ambitious entrepreneurs endowed with sufficient charm to rise past their social betters. Though Deane could not understand French dialogue, he would have appreciated Beaumarchais's literary talent. Beaumarchais, in turn, respected Deane's character and appreciated his business and political acumen. Beaumarchais and Deane both understood that each needed the other to vindicate themselves in the judgment of their respective governments. Most important, they shared a passionate commitment to a single purpose: American independence.

AMONG OTHER OBSTACLES in both men's way stood Dr. Dubourg. He continued to object to Beaumarchais's involvement with the Americans and spread rumors that Beaumarchais was amoral and unqualified to handle business matters. Beaumarchais accused Dubourg of trying to profit from the Americans and warned Vergennes that Dubourg was a "deadly scatterbrain," whose bumbling indiscretions jeopardized the secrecy of the whole operation. He even threatened to punch the venerable doctor. When Dubourg wrote to Vergennes, accusing Beaumarchais of living beyond his means with several much younger women, Beaumarchais retorted sarcastically:

> The women I've been keeping for twenty years ... I have only three to keep now, two sisters and my niece, which is still quite an extravagance for a fellow like myself. But what would you have said, if, knowing me better than you do, you had been aware that I was scandalous to the point of keeping men as well—two pretty young

nephews and even the poor father of so scandalous a pimp? And my ostentation is even worse. For the past three years, believing lace and embroidery to be too paltry for my vanity, I have been arrogant enough to adorn my wrists with the finest plain muslin!

Vergennes's secretary, Gérard, decided to intervene and invited Dubourg, Deane, and Beaumarchais to a meeting in Versailles. There Gérard made it plain, on behalf of Vergennes, that Deane could rely on whatever Beaumarchais said. Dubourg was chastened, and Beaumarchais was satisfied. At the same meeting, Gérard warned both Deane and Beaumarchais that Arthur Lee had disclosed too much about Beaumarchais's operations to Comte de Lauraguais, who was notoriously indiscreet. It was reported that the unreliable Lauraguais had been back in Paris asking people about Deane and had returned to London to share this information with his friends. After this meeting, Deane wrote to Lee to warn him against any further dealings with the loose-lipped comte. Deane explained that he was now working with Beaumarchais and that the French foreign minister was concerned by Lee's involvement with Lauraguais.

Arthur Lee was furious. Beaumarchais and Lee had an arrangement; how was it possible that Beaumarchais was now working exclusively with Deane? Beaumarchais had written using Lee's pseudonym, "Mary Johnson," several times in June and July to confirm the details of the smuggling operation, and yet behind Lee's back he was dealing with this Connecticut shopkeeper. Deane's letter triggered Lee's fury. Lee wanted to rush to Paris and confront Beaumarchais, but he was afraid that if he left London suddenly, he would arouse further suspicion. Lee wrote to Deane, whom he did not know, and *directed* him to arrange at once for a private flat—not one of those public hotels, where he might be noticed. He would be traveling under the pseudonym "Mr. Johnson." (Apparently, like her friend d'Eon, "Mary Johnson" switched her gender when necessary.) Deane knew that all Englishmen and Americans were carefully watched from the moment they arrived in France. Using an assumed name would only serve to confirm in the mind of the British ambassador that Lee was acting strangely.

Lee was a slave to his own neuroses. He spotted enemies in every corner. He kept a list of prominent Americans, including members of the Continental Congress, whom he suspected of disloyalty to the American cause. He had only recently added to this list Paul Wentworth, in whose home Lee had lived for some time in London and in whom Lee had almost certainly confided all the details of his relationship to Beaumarchais. He was so confident of his own righteousness that anyone who disappointed or slighted him must assuredly be a traitor to his country.

Lee's overreaction to Beaumarchais's reneging on their deal was a sign of what was to come. Something in Lee's mind had snapped. "The scale is coming so near to a ballance that a little treachery may turn it to our destruction, and the ruin of public Liberty," Lee warned darkly in a letter to Deane.

Deane was a tolerant man. (After all, he even forgave his colleague Roger Sherman for all the trouble he had caused Deane in Congress.) But nothing offended Deane more than Lee's accusations against the men Deane had served with in Congress. Without evidence—or even a particular allegation—Lee asked Deane to write to Congress to inform them that certain delegates were traitors to the American cause. Lee's allegations were reckless and untrue, but if they were believed, these delegates might be hung for treason. Struggling to control his outrage, Deane informed Lee plainly that he would not become "a second hand accuser of men of Character."

When he received this response, Lee inferred that Deane, too, must somehow be part of a wider conspiracy. Lee came to view Deane either as a mere creature of Dr. Franklin's nefarious designs or as the cat's paw of the French government.

Deane had little patience or time to worry about Lee's feelings. Though he had not received any formal instructions from the Continental Congress for months, he was still the sole emissary representing Congress, and he was compelled to mediate his way through the exotic politics of Versailles while seeking financial assistance from other European governments. At the same time, he had a long list of items to purchase, not merely arms, but all the pots and pans, flints, matches, tents, shovels, linen, blankets, shoes, socks, caps, buttons, and handkerchiefs that an army requires. To complicate matters further, he was still charged by the Secret Committee with buying goods for trade with the Indian tribes, and he had his own trading business with Robert Morris to juggle. On the same day that Deane was buying and shipping saltpeter and sulfur to Washington's army, he was also importing flour to Portugal, exporting cloth for the Indians, and sending large orders of oil, capers, olives, and claret to Morris's customers in Philadelphia. All these exchanges were recorded in the same account books, so that Deane could disguise his secret mission, as he had been instructed by the Secret Committee.

Deane made sure that if his account books ever fell into the hands of the British, they would not be able to untangle the web of transactions that he was weaving. That was the beginning of his undoing.

TWENTY–TWO

THE DECLARATION GOES MISSING

Paris, August–October 1776

July 1776 passed with no word from Congress since the May 15 resolution. Deane was worried by the progress of the war, and he was unsure how to conduct himself. No one in Europe yet knew that the Americans had declared independence. The Secret Committee had not yet received word that Deane had reached Paris, so the delegates had no idea that already there were plans to send six ships loaded with supplies in the coming months. Deane tried to focus his mind to the task of persuading France to form an alliance with the Americans. To that end, he drafted a long and thoughtful memorandum on the commercial opportunities for France that would follow from diplomatic recognition and a military alliance. In truth, Deane was improvising while he waited for a ship to arrive with some message from Congress.

On Saturday, August 17, Beaumarchais had a dinner at his home for Deane, Deane's newly hired personal secretary, the American William Carmichael, and two French military experts, Colonel Tronson du Coudray and General Jean-Baptiste de Gribeauval. The Paris newspapers were finally reporting that the Continental Congress had declared independence from Great Britain. Unable to read French himself, Deane would have been among the last in Paris to hear that he was now the de facto emissary of a new country. Though he had long anticipated this moment, Deane was dumbstruck. He had not received any instructions or news from the Secret Committee since his arrival six weeks earlier. Now his situation had become even more awkward. Shouldn't he have informed Louis XVI personally? He did not even have the text of the Declaration to deliver to Versailles. Was it possible that Congress had forgotten him? Or was another emissary en route to replace him?

Congress, it turned out, had not forgotten him. Deane was very much on Congress's mind. "When, in the course of human events, it becomes necessary for one people to dissolve the political bonds which have connected them with another," Congress had declared, "a decent respect to the opinions of mankind requires that they should declare the causes which impel them to the separation." The Declaration was written in large part to persuade Europeans, particularly the French, of the justice of the American cause. Almost immediately after signing the Declaration, Congress commissioned a copy to be printed and sent to Deane to present to the French king. Somehow, the Declaration was either lost in the mail or intercepted by British naval vessels. Perhaps in hindsight Congress should have found a more reliable courier to carry the Declaration to Deane, or else held off issuing a public declaration until instructions could be received in France.

That same week, Deane received word that Lee had landed in France and would be in Paris the next day. He quickly scribbled a note to Vergennes, warning him not to receive this interloper. Deane feigned surprise to Vergennes that Lee would venture to Paris. He could think of "no particular affair that might call him here," and he worried that Lee's presence as Congress's agent in Britain would attract unwarranted attention from the British ambassador. Deane was already predisposed by Beaumarchais to dislike Lee, and he was hoping to send off the first arms shipments to the colonies within days. He felt he could handle the arms trade without Lee. Neither Vergennes nor Beaumarchais wanted to meet with Lee, who upon his arrival was vexed to learn that Deane had already secured contracts on supplies worth three million livres.

Lee's visit was an inauspicious beginning to the destructive rivalry between the two American agents. Lee returned to London jealous of Deane's position at the French court and suspicious of Deane's financial activities and relationship with Franklin. Soon after his return to London, he began writing to his brothers in Congress, Richard Henry and Francis Lightfoot, and to his friend Samuel Adams, cautioning them against Deane and Beaumarchais. Lee falsely claimed that he "had several conferences with the French ambassador," and that as a result the foreign minister had sent Beaumarchais to London to offer him 200,000 pounds sterling worth of arms and ammunition as a gift to the Americans. He accused Deane and Beaumarchais of fraudulently billing Congress for free arms and warned members of Congress not to pay for the arms.

As he wrote this, Lee knew it was a lie. He knew that Beaumarchais expected to be paid with tobacco in exchange for the arms. Months earlier, Beaumarchais had written to Lee, reporting that he was about to send a ship loaded with cannons and ammunition worth 25,000 pounds sterling in exchange for good Virginia tobacco. In his reply Lee did not contradict Beaumarchais's understanding that the Americans would pay for arms with tobacco. After all, that was precisely what Lee had agreed to do when he negotiated with Beaumarchais the previous November at the Middle Temple.

Lee simply wanted to get even with Beaumarchais and Deane, whom he felt had betrayed him. In Lee's distorted mind, their betrayal justified his lies. Lee wrote Congress repeatedly, denying that the arms were in exchange for tobacco. While months would pass without a single delivery of tobacco, Deane and Beaumarchais had no idea that Congress was receiving misinformation from Lee. Lee knew that the financial survival of Beaumarchais's company depended on the tobacco shipment to pay for more arms. Without the tobacco, it was unlikely the French government would continue to send arms. Lee was guilty not merely of bad faith, but of betraying the Revolution itself. From Lee's deceptions grew an enormous controversy that would divide Congress, jeopardize the French alliance, and place the entire outcome of the Revolution in doubt.

In MID-SEPTEMBER troubling news arrived from London. Bancroft often wrote Deane juicy letters filled with small tidbits of political gossip—just enough to convince Deane that he was getting something for his money. Now Bancroft warned that Deane's name had surfaced in Parliament. Late Wednesday afternoon, September 11, the former prime minister, the Duke of Grafton, stood up in the House of Lords and demanded to know if the secretary of state for the American colonies, Lord Weymouth, knew that Silas Deane was a regular visitor to Versailles. Grafton pointedly asked the secretary of state if he knew that Deane was smuggling arms to the Americans out of Nantes. While Grafton's purpose was to embarrass the king's ministers, the implications for Deane were more serious. The British government was now on public notice that Deane was involved in treason, and the British government would be under pressure to seize and prosecute Deane in order to silence its critics at home.

How could the Duke of Grafton be so certain of these details?

Most likely the information had been confirmed by Bancroft himself. Having betrayed Deane to the British government, Bancroft was now sending Deane news of his betrayal as a way to bolster Deane's trust in him.

CONGRESS'S LONG SILENCE TOWARD France raised concern among the French court that the Americans—and Deane in particular—were secretly negotiating with the British. Stormont and others probably helped to spread these rumors as a way of discouraging the French from supporting American Independence. Deane wrote Congress, warning that Vergennes was "extremely uneasy at your absolute silence." Deane tried to reassure his hosts that no such negotiations "would or could take place." While Vergennes trusted Deane, he remained suspicious of Congress.

Vergennes was also worried by the increasingly belligerent meetings with Stormont, who was openly accusing France of shipping arms to the Americans. Vergennes warned Deane and Beaumarchais to be more cautious about their smuggling activities. Beaumarchais demurred. It was not their fault, he told Vergennes. He suspected that his rival, Dr. Dubourg, had behaved indiscreetly. "[T]he Doctor is continually writing public works on this subject," he wrote the foreign minister. "If while we shut the door on one side the window is open on the other, it is quite impossible for the secrets not to get out."

In the face of Stormont's thinly veiled threats of war, and Congress's silence, Louis XVI became cautious and issued an order forbidding all military shipments to the Americans. France would not risk war with Britain on behalf of a nation that could not even pay its debts. Deane's entire mission looked doomed. None of the arms they had acquired would reach the colonies.

In response to this crisis, Deane sat down and carefully composed a long memorandum to Vergennes, setting out in the clearest terms the reasons for declaring independence, though he still had not heard from Congress in almost three months and had not received the text of the Declaration. Deane wrote a powerful brief for the American side: the revolution, he argued, was a broad popular uprising, not a narrow effort instigated by a few ambitious landowners to seize power, as the British Foreign Ministry argued. The Americans "are not an ignorant unprincipled rabble, heated and led on to the present Measures by the artful and Ambitious few," Deane wrote. Rather, they were "bred from their Infancy in what they conceive to be the fundamental principles of their liberty."

Deane's argument reviewed the events that had led up to independence, justifying the colonists' action as a last resort. The colonists had not betrayed their sovereign, Deane pointed out. It was George III who had betrayed his subjects. Americans had not declared their independence "[u]ntil they saw their Commerce ruined, . . . their defenceless Towns in flames, their Brothers bleeding, Savages courted & Slaves instigated to Butcher and Assassinate without Distinction of Age or sex."

Deane knew better than to suppose it made any real difference to Louis XVI whether the Americans had "rebelled," or whether George III was politically shortsighted. But Deane offered Louis XVI a point-by-point counterargument to Stormont's allegations that the Americans were in open rebellion and needed to be suppressed. He appealed to the king's own sense of dignity: "Divine Will" had placed in the hands of the French monarch the power to determine the outcome of this revolution by deciding whether to grant "Aid or Countenance" to the Americans. It was "impossible that any Events in the Course of human affairs can be more interesting to France," because of the opportunity to open up the American market to

French trade and to deny Britain the power "ever hereafter to disturb her repose on the Continent or insult her on the Ocean." America was France's "most natural ally." Deane's memorandum may have been one of the most cogent arguments for independence written then or since—and one that history has inexplicably ignored.

In a postscript probably added by Beaumarchais, Deane directly addressed the French government's fear that if France entered the war and the Americans sued for peace with Britain, France would be left vulnerable to British retaliation. Deane argued there would be no need for the Americans to reach an accommodation with Britain if they were supplied by France. To the contrary, Deane warned, only if France failed to aid the Americans might they be forced to settle with the British, and if that happened, a more powerful Britain would be tempted to seize the French islands in the West Indies. (This was the same argument Beaumarchais had used before.) The British had already demonstrated their disdain for French sovereignty by imposing the humiliating treaty that ended the Seven Years' War and stripping France of its North American colonies. Would Britain's "regard to Justice, and the Laws of Nations," Deane asked sarcastically, prevent her from taking the French sugar islands merely because Britain cannot prove France aided the Americans?

Deane's arguments apparently won the day. Less than a week later, after a further intercession by Beaumarchais, Vergennes reversed the order and allowed shipments to the Americans to proceed, albeit quietly. How much longer could Deane rely on Vergennes's patience? Deane's ability to persuade France to form an alliance with the new republic would depend on swift action from Congress. But Congress remained inscrutably mute on how he should proceed. What were his colleagues thinking, and how could they have abandoned him on a foreign shore? Deane tried to imagine what had happened. Were his letters lying at the bottom of the ocean? Or had his letters been received and ignored for more sinister reasons? Was Philadelphia occupied by British troops? Had Congress disbanded? Were his colleagues in jail—or worse? Had Washington's army collapsed?

Sometimes it seemed as if America were merely an invention of his own fevered imagination.

TWENTY-THREE

THE FRENCH OFFICERS

Paris, October–December 1776

F or Heaven's sake," Deane chastised the Secret Committee in a
letter, "if you mean to have any connection with this Kingdom,
be more assiduous in getting your letters here." All through October,
as Deane purchased hundreds of tons of powder on credit, there was
still no word from Congress. He wrote the Secret Committee nearly
every day, hoping for a response. Each letter grew more despairing
and bitter. News of the Declaration, he wrote, "has given this Court,
as well as several others in Europe, reason to expect you would in
form announce your Independancy to them, and ask their friendship." After three months, Congress's silence had "given me the most
inexpressible anxiety, and has more than once come near frustrating
my whole endeavors." Deane could not have known that none of his
letters to Congress had been received. The British blockade of Philadelphia had kept both Congress and Deane in the dark as to the
other's activities.

October's arrival cast a cloud over Deane's mood. October felt both comforting and sad, like a visit from an old friend one does not expect to see again. The blazing colors of the Tuileries, the damp scent of leaves, and the long afternoon shadows made him wistful for Connecticut. He missed his young son and his frail wife, Elizabeth. He thought of the view from his front door, across the town commons lined with elms and the profile of the church steeple against a cloudless sky. In the market, the smell of pears and apples reminded him of the puddings and ciders that Elizabeth served their guests. He wondered if and when he would return to Wethersfield, and what he would return to.

In letter after letter he pleaded with Congress for some sign that they were aware of the difficulties he faced, but he was greeted only with silence. He knew that success "depended on the friendship and aid of powers on this side of the globe," and the probability of winning the friendship of the Europeans was now seriously diminished. He had tried to make excuses for Congress "until my invention is exhausted," and when other vessels from America arrived in French ports without a line from Congress, his credibility was undermined. America's friends were asking if Congress "were in earnest, and unanimous in their Independence." Even if Congress needed no support from Europe, "common civility" required Congress to announce their independence formally. He concluded glumly that Congress's lost opportunity risked "the ruin of the greatest cause in which mankind were ever engaged."

The one American whose letters reached Deane's desk was the last person Deane cared to hear from: Arthur Lee. When Lee sent him a code book so that he could encode his letters to Lee, Deane tossed it aside. As Deane had no intention of writing to the meddlesome Lee, he hardly needed a code book.

Deane was preoccupied by another Lee—Captain John Lee—no relation to the irksome Arthur. News had arrived that Spain had seized Captain Lee, an American privateer, at the port of Bilbao in northwest Spain. Captain Lee was commanding a schooner with a letter of marque from Congress. Letters of marque were written authorizations to privateers to seize enemy ships and their contents. Privateering was, in effect, licensed piracy on the high seas, and it was considered a legitimate way for countries to wage war. Privateers operated like mercenaries for a percentage of the sale price of the enemy's vessels and cargo.

Captain Lee had seized five British ships and their crews. When he arrived at Bilbao, the British captives charged that Captain Lee was a pirate—rather than a duly licensed privateer—and the Spanish government decided to arrest him. The incident raised fundamental questions about the sovereignty of the United States under international law. Since Spain had not recognized the United States, it did not regard Captain Lee's letter of marque as official. His mission to seize British ships looked like the crime of piracy, and under Spanish law it would be punishable by death.

The situation threatened American relations with Spain, which government Deane hoped would support the Americans. If Deane had had some instructions from Congress, formally appointing him ambassador for the new republic, perhaps he could negotiate for Captain Lee's release. Deane fretted: "I confess I tremble to think how important a question is by this step agitated, without any one empowered to appear in a proper character, and defend." Compelled to improvise, Deane approached Vergennes. Deane promised that American privateers would avoid French and Spanish ports in the future. In exchange, Vergennes agreed to intercede with France's Bourbon ally, and eventually, Spain agreed to release the American.

Hoping to evade the British spies who continually monitored his front door, Deane changed residences. He moved to a spacious apartment occupying the first floor of the Hôtel d'Entragues at numbers

2–4 rue de l'Université, near the Pont Royal. Despite this move, British agents continued to trail him. Meanwhile, French police kept an eye on both the British agents and on Deane. Deane's new flat was large enough for a live-in valet. Beaumarchais helped him find a servant who spoke fluent English and could assist as a translator and bodyguard. Deane thought the valet fiercely loyal, if perhaps excessively suspicious of anyone who came near him. He never suspected that the fellow's education and language ability probably indicated that he, too, was an agent for the French government.

As news of the Declaration of Independence spread, many French military officers wanted to enlist in the Continental Army to fight the British. Both Vergennes and Beaumarchais persuaded Deane of the need to send French-trained military engineers and artillery men as well as arms to the Americans. Vergennes saw this as an opportunity for France to consolidate its influence over the Americans without having to commit French troops. He proposed to Deane that Congress appoint the Comte de Broglie, who had led the French army—to defeat—in the Seven Years' War, to replace Washington as commander-in-chief of the Continental Army.

Deane agreed to meet General Broglie only as a courtesy to Vergennes. Broglie brought Baron de Kalb with him as his translator. De Kalb had visited America and spoke fluent English. He was a large Prussian who hid his peasant origins by calling himself "Baron." During the meeting in Deane's flat, Broglie imperiously presented Deane with a list of sixteen French officers whom he wanted Deane to commission, and he insisted that they should receive ranks and salaries above their equivalent ranks and salaries in the French army. Broglie explained that this was how Europeans purchased the services of a foreign military officer. Deane had no authority from Congress to

commission any officers, but he felt obliged to accommodate Vergennes, who insisted that he issue these commissions. Deane commissioned Baron de Kalb as Major General, the rank just below
Washington, which would ordinarily have required a vote of Congress, and Kalb was given the handsome sum of 6,000 livres for expenses and another 6,000 livres as an advance (totaling about $92,000
today). As far as Vergennes and General Broglie were concerned,
Kalb's principal mission would be to explain to Congress the absolute
necessity of replacing Washington with General de Broglie.

Whatever Deane thought about the value of commissioning
these officers, he must have recoiled at the suggestion of replacing
General Washington. Deane idolized Washington, whom he regarded as the living embodiment of republican virtue. Washington
had been a guest in Deane's home in Connecticut. It is unlikely that
Deane actually agreed with Vergennes's proposal to replace Washington, but Deane was desperate to maintain good relations with
France, and he believed that he was obliged to communicate the
French government's views to Congress. Therefore, Deane wrote to
Congress passing along Vergennes's suggestion of appointing General de Broglie commander-in-chief. Deane explained that the appointment of a French nobleman with the experience and acumen
of Broglie would solidify the French alliance and alarm the British.
He was quick to add, "I only suggest the thought and leave you to
confer with Baron de Kalb on the subject at large." This was one of
Deane's letters that managed to slip through the British blockade. When it was received in Philadelphia, many of Washington's
admirers were outraged. Deane's letter only served to undermine his
support in Congress.

Word soon spread through Paris that Deane was commissioning
officers on behalf of the Continental Army. The sons of French aristocrats, or purported aristocrats, quickly lined up outside Deane's

door to offer their services. Many of these men were mere adventur-
ers, and Deane had no criteria for judging who was truly qualified to
help the American cause. He had to rely on his own instincts and
the recommendations of others. As visitors in uniform streamed
into his sitting room, Deane abandoned any hope of living anonymously. The flock of young men visiting Deane's apartment could
not have escaped the notice of even the most inattentive spy, and
Stormont grew increasingly frustrated observing Deane's activities.
But Deane's recruitment activities became the source of a diplomatic tempest for other reasons.

Among the men who found their way to Deane's doorstep were
the nineteen-year-old Marquis de Lafayette and two of his friends,
the Vicomte de Noailles and the Comte de Ségur. All three came
from exceptionally wealthy and influential aristocratic families.
Lafayette was a powerful-looking young man with beautiful features and an intense gaze. His parents had died when he was a boy,
leaving him with a huge fortune. He had been trained in military
science and riding at the elite Académie de Versailles, where he befriended Noailles and Ségur. Noailles's father, one of the richest and
most powerful men in France, had selected Lafayette to marry his
adolescent daughter, which only further assured Lafayette's social
position. The three glittering young men, however, had other plans.
They had joined the Masons and become followers of the social
reformer Abbé Guillaume Raynal, who disdained the aristocracy,
colonialism, and the Church. Lafayette and his friends rejected the
decadent lifestyle of their parents and embraced the American
Revolution as the struggle for human dignity. When the three young
men showed up at Deane's apartment to volunteer, Deane hesitated
to add their names to his growing list of commissioned officers.
They appealed to him as a fellow Mason, and he allowed himself
to be persuaded by Lafayette's idealism and boyish charm. Deane

allowed himself to imagine that these three might inspire a generation and ensure France's continued support for the American struggle. Unfortunately, Deane did not fully appreciate the high position
these men occupied in French society and the risk their enlistment
posed to Franco-American relations.

The families of Lafayette, Noailles, and Ségur reacted immediately
and angrily to the news that their sons had joined the Continental
Army. Lafayette's pregnant young wife and his father-in-law, who was
also the father of Noailles, accused the French government of col-
laborating with the American rebels. To make matters worse,
Noailles's uncle was in the awkward position of having recently been
appointed ambassador to London. Vergennes feared that Britain
would view the enlistment of these three famous aristocrats as a declaration of war. He prohibited any ships carrying French officers or
arms to America from leaving port and ordered the arrest of the three
young officers before they could escape to America. Unsatisfied by
French actions, the British blockaded the French coast and threatened
to cut off all trade. Deane and Beaumarchais faced financial ruin, and
it appeared that Deane's mission had once more collapsed.

To complicate matters further, the impetuous young Lafayette
could not be stopped, even by the French government. He evaded
arrest, secretly purchasing and outfitting his own warship, *La Victoire*, to carry him and the other French officers to America. Despite
Vergennes's best efforts to prevent him from reaching the ship. Lafayette sailed from Bordeaux, leaving behind a diplomatic brouhaha,
a pregnant sixteen-year-old wife and a two-year-old daughter, an
enraged father-in-law, an anxious General Broglie, and a bellicose
British ambassador.

Members of Congress would later harshly criticize Deane for
many of the nearly sixty commissions he issued. Congress did not
understand how circumstances had compelled Deane to make snap

judgments about whom to appoint. He knew that he was acting without authority, but he felt he had to act in the absence of any further instructions from Congress, and he wanted to ensure France's support. It was true that some of these officers were underqualified, and that some American officers resented the inflated ranks and salaries awarded to some of the French. Yet Deane's critics never credited him with the enormous contributions made by many of the French officers. Deane was responsible for sending to Washington two of his most valued generals: Baron de Kalb, who proved to be perhaps the greatest tactician in the Continental Army, and Lafayette, whom Washington came to love as a son. While it is true that Deane acted without authority, these soldiers would ultimately help secure victory for Washington's army. By then, however, it was too late to redeem Deane's reputation.

TWENTY-FOUR

THE SABOTEUR

Paris and London,
November 1776–March 1777

One day in early November, Deane was working in his study on the rue de l'Université when he overheard a commotion in the front hall. His valet was shouting in English at someone who was trying to push past him into the vestibule. Deane peeked out of the study to see who was making such a disturbance. Was Deane being arrested? Was this a British agent planning to assassinate Deane? Or was it another soldier wanting to go fight for the Americans? His valet informed him that a strange-looking man was demanding to see him. The same man had twice before come to Deane's door demanding to see the American emissary, but the valet had refused him entrance. "You never saw a worse looking fellow in your Life," the valet explained to Deane. The man looked like a beggar or a criminal, and the French valet added that "he speaks English so strangely that I can hardly understand him, and I think if he was honest he would speak plain." Curious, Deane told his valet to admit the stranger. Reluctantly, the valet acquiesced, but insisted that he would remain within earshot in case the stranger threatened Deane.

In the light of his study, Deane could see the man more clearly in all his peculiarity. He was a scrawny-looking twenty-five-year-old with long, unkempt, reddish hair down to his shoulders and a reddish face marked with freckles. He wore a filthy, ill-fitting jacket the color of dried blood, a fantail hat, and a long watch chain (most likely stolen). "His dress," Deane later quipped, "no way recommended him at Paris." For several moments the man stammered incoherently. Deane labored to understand his broad Scottish accent. His name was James Aitken, but he was commonly known as "John the Painter." He would not disclose his purpose because he was afraid that the valet was listening. Deane tried to press him to explain himself. "[I]f a Man is ill used," Aitken responded cryptically, "has he not a right to resent it and to seek revenge or retaliation on those who have injured him?"

"This is a droll question," Deane replied. "[G]o into the Fields and tread on the meanest insect and see if it do not at least try to turn upon you."

"Right, right," Aitken responded excitedly, his eyes darting wildly. "Your honor has cleared up every doubt in my Mind; I have been most grossly injured, and I will be most signally revenged." Then, somewhat presumptuously, he asked what rewards might be available for someone who served Congress with distinction.

What was this man raving about? Deane grew impatient with Aitken's way of talking in riddles. Congress would reward all those who served it, Deane assured him, but "I have not any time to lose, and therefore come at once to the point," Deane insisted.

Aitken said he had lived in America and had "foolishly" sided with the British Crown, serving in the forces of Virginia's royal governor Lord Dunmore against the rebels. After being treated poorly by Dunmore, he decided to join the Americans and fight for liberty. So Aitken claimed that he had returned to Britain to help the Americans in any way he could.

As Deane would later learn, most of Aitken's story was a lie. Aitken was actually an itinerant house painter, a pyromaniac, a common thief, and a highwayman who had robbed homes and coaches throughout England. His secret ambition was to be a military officer, for which he had no obvious qualifications. In 1773, he had journeyed to America, looking for honest work, and when the Revolution exploded, he sided with George III and took refuge in North Carolina, where many other Scottish loyalists lived. Several months later, he returned to Britain, hoping for an officer's commission in the British army. When the British army refused him, he decided to offer his services to the Americans in hopes that they would commission him.

Aitken perhaps appreciated the incredulity with which Deane received him. "[T]hough I may appear to your honor a very weak, and insignificant creature, yet if you will give me another audience, I will shew you from the intelligence which I can give you that I can strike a blow . . . as will need no repetition." His eyes rolled wildly. Aitken meant to punish Britain in a way unimaginable, but he was not prepared to reveal his plan with the French valet hovering so close. He merely hinted that he had some information about Britain's ports that would interest Deane. Though Deane did not know what to make of this strange man, he was curious as to what Aitken was really talking about and told him to return the next day at the same hour.

The following day Aitken returned and waited patiently outside of Deane's hotel until Deane left for his morning stroll. Aitken followed Deane silently down the rue des Saints-Pères three blocks to the Quai Malaquais, turning right, as did Deane, along the river.

He did not speak to Deane until they were crossing the Pont Neuf, headed to the Ile de la Cité. Beneath them boats sailed by, laden with wine and flour. The cold wind blew Aitken's unruly hair over his face. He spoke so softly in his brogue that Deane had to stand close to hear him.

Aitken's plan was to destroy the British navy by destroying the Royal Navy dockyards throughout England. He planned to burn down all the dockyards at Portsmouth and Plymouth, on the west coast, and at Chatham, Deptford, and Woolwich, near London. It sounded like madness for one man to attempt to destroy even a single dockyard, but Aitken understood that the dockyards were entirely vulnerable to fire. The trick was to be able to set a large blaze in multiple locations throughout the dockyard and still manage to escape undetected before the fires were noticed. He had designed a small incendiary device that could be concealed in a pocket and would ignite hours after he left the scene. Aitken's device was a primitive time bomb. By placing a few incendiary devices at strategic locations, he could create a massive fire without being present at the scene.

Deane was too shocked to respond. He did not quite see how Aitken's plan could work, but he saw no reason to discourage him on the off chance that it might succeed. Deane could see that for Aitken such an act was clearly criminal arson, but for Deane, as a citizen of a foreign country presently at war with Great Britain, he was bound only by the laws of war, not by the criminal law of Britain. An enemy's naval dockyard was an appropriate military target, even if the means of attack were unconventional and the attacker was an unstable pyromaniac. Deane regarded himself as a patriot, defending his country in time of war. Deane later argued that anyone of common sense must approve of his motives, "motives no less than a desire to weaken a declared enemy, and to preserve my country, by every means in my power, from the horrors, and distress of fire and desolation."

Deane made no effort to stop Aitken, but he provided Aitken only nominal assistance. Perhaps facetiously, he assigned Aitken the code name "Zero," which may have represented Deane's assessment of Aitken's likelihood of success. Though Aitken asked Deane to finance his operation, Deane would only agree to pay 72 livres (a little more than $500 today), to cover Aitken's travel expenses. He foolishly suggested that if Aitken were in trouble he might contact Deane's friend Bancroft while in London. Aitken would later claim that Bancroft was supposed to pay him another 300 pounds (about $55,000 today) for his attacks on the dockyards, but there is no evidence to support that, and both Deane and Bancroft denied it. In addition, the British later alleged that Deane supplied Aitken with a "passport" purportedly signed by Vergennes on behalf of Louis XVI. If that were true, it is puzzling why Vergennes would have signed such a document. The passport would not have offered Aitken any protection, and it had the consequence of linking Aitken's terrorism to the French government. It is possible that Deane hoped that if Aitken were captured by the British, the passport would be enough to spark a confrontation between Britain and France, but that would not explain why Vergennes would have endorsed it. It is perhaps more likely that the passport was a fraudulent document concocted by the British Foreign Ministry to link Aitken to Deane and Vergennes.

Aitken returned to England in mid-November and immediately set out to effectuate his plan. He hired a tradesman in Canterbury to construct the incendiary devices out of tin, according to his simple drawings. He created a combustible mixture of turpentine and other paint products that could smolder for hours before bursting into full flame. Each device was less than ten inches long and three-by-four inches around and looked like a small rectangular lantern. He began in Portsmouth on December 6, setting one fire in the dockyard and two in a neighboring residential area as a diversion. Contrary to what he had told Deane, he planned to destroy not only the military target, but the entire city. Aitken's cheap matches failed to catch flame, however, and he was able to set only one of the fires in the dockyard before he escaped. The fire burned down a factory that produced rope for naval rigging, but did not succeed in destroying the dockyard or the city.

The next day Bancroft was surprised to find a crazed-looking stranger in his front parlor at Number 4 Downing Street. Bancroft had no idea that Deane had recommended him to Aitken. Aitken began by boasting that he had just come from burning down the royal dockyard at Portsmouth. He claimed that Deane had sent him to destroy all the Royal Navy dockyards around the country and had told him that Bancroft would give him whatever money he needed and provide him with a safe place to hide.

Bancroft was terrified. He had no intention of risking his neck to protect a wild man who cheerfully boasted of committing arson. He had no way of knowing whether Aitken had burned Portsmouth or had ever met Deane. Yet, he was caught in a classic dilemma of a double agent: he needed to respond in a way that would neither raise the suspicion of Aitken and Deane as to his loyalty to the Americans, nor the suspicion of his British patrons as to his loyalty to the crown. Bancroft told Aitken that he could not allow him to stay nor would he give him any money. Bancroft might have warned Aitken that Bancroft's home was monitored by British spies to ensure his loyalty to the British. Bancroft's one concession was to agree to meet Aitken again.

They met at the smoky Salopian Coffee House on Charing Cross Road the evening of the following day. This seemed like a particularly indiscreet meeting place. The crowded coffeehouse was frequently patronized by naval officers leaving work across the street at the Admiralty Office. Aitken appeared more nervous than he had the previous day. Anyone there might have been a government agent watching them from a nearby table. Had Bancroft led him into a trap? Bancroft himself felt trapped by Deane's indiscretion. Perhaps Deane and Aitken were testing his loyalty?

Speaking in a quiet voice and leaning forward so that he could be heard above the din, Bancroft told Aitken that as much as he admired and liked Deane, he could not involve himself in Deane's schemes so long as he lived under the British Crown. He would not help Aitken and asked him never to return to his home. He discouraged Aitken from any further attacks on the dockyards, but assured him that in any case he would not divulge his identity. Aitken became red-faced and indignant. He accused Bancroft of deceiving Deane as to his true intentions and swore that he would continue the fight against the British government. Rising from the table, he looked Bancroft squarely in the eye and warned him that he would soon be hearing of his deeds at Plymouth. As Aitken stalked out of the coffeehouse, Bancroft worried more about Aitken's capacity to destroy him than any threat he might pose to the Royal Navy.

One month later, Aitken was captured after two failed attempts to burn down the naval yard at Bristol. The trial of "John the Painter" in early March drew large crowds and wide publicity. The chief prosecution witness was an informer to whom Aitken had confessed all his crimes and implicated both Deane and Bancroft. On the stand the prosecutor's witness falsely testified that Deane had given Aitken 300 pounds to carry out his plot. The prisoner tried to interject something to protect Deane. He shouted out, "Consider in the sight of God what you say concerning Silas Deane!" The prosecutor turned to the witness and reassured him, "You need not be afraid, Silas Deane is not here"; but, he added, "he will be hanged in due time."

When news of the trial spread, many in Bancroft's social circle denounced him as a traitor to the nation. All this gossip against Bancroft incensed Paul Wentworth, Bancroft's patron and spymaster, who had reason to know on which side Bancroft's loyalties truly lay. Over dinner at his club in Pall Mall with Thomas Hutchinson, the former governor of Massachusetts, Wentworth heatedly defended Bancroft. It was impossible, Wentworth insisted, that "anyone should suppose Doctor Bancroft anyway capable" of spying with John the Painter. Wentworth's assurance may have persuaded Hutchinson, but Wentworth knew better than to suppose that men were exactly as they seemed. Wentworth added that "Bancroft had told 20 of his friends what John the Painter said to him." Wentworth coyly speculated that perhaps Bancroft was actually a spy for the British government.

As Wentworth's ironic remark suggests, Bancroft had already informed the British about Aitken. Bancroft had visited the clueless Aitken in prison and encouraged him to confide more details of the plot, which Bancroft then disclosed to the prosecution. That explains why the British government made no effort to arrest Bancroft. To the contrary, the British Foreign Ministry had offered Bancroft a life pension of 200 pounds if he would move to Paris and offer his services as a personal secretary to Deane. Aitken's arrest offered Bancroft the perfect opportunity to carry out this plan. He would write Deane that Aitken told the British that Deane had instigated the arson and that he had implicated Bancroft. Under the circumstances Bancroft had no choice but to flee to Paris. As Bancroft predicted, Deane offered him a job as his secretary. Now Bancroft would be uniquely placed inside the American operations, able to report every move Deane made. Deane looked to Bancroft as his confidant and friend. "Doctor Bancroft has been of very great service to me," he reported. "No man had better intelligence in England, in my opinion, but it costs something." The price was higher than Deane could have imagined.

On the afternoon of March 10, 1777, a day after Aitken was convicted and sentenced to die, he was escorted to the gate in front of the Royal Navy dockyard at Portsmouth. Though it was nearly spring, it was still exceptionally cold, but that did not deter a crowd from gathering. From the gallows Aitken had a clear view of the dock and the ships—unmistakable evidence that his wild conspiracy had failed utterly to undermine British naval power.

The only thing Aitken had unwittingly accomplished was that he had placed Bancroft in the perfect situation to destroy Silas Deane and prevent the Americans from ever obtaining French aid.

TWENTY–FIVE

INVISIBLE INK

Paris, November–December 1776

Paris in November grew gloomier every day. From his sooty window he could see a patch of purplish-gray spreading like a bruise across the sky. The Seine looked opaque, and the rains turned the narrow streets into a swamp of brown mud that caked his boots and splattered his stockings. The stale air smelled of fungus and coal dust. Melancholy enveloped him as he sat in his study, scratching out yet another desperate letter to Congress. Five months had passed without a word from Congress. He dipped his pen and wrote in the invisible ink that John Jay's brother had provided to him:

Paris, 9th November, 1776.

   Gentleman,—I have written to you often and particularly of affairs here. The want of intelligence retards every thing. As I have not a word from you since the 5th of June last, I am well-nigh distracted.

He chastised his colleagues as he had done for months:

> All Europe have their eyes on the States of America, and are
> astonished to find month after month rolling away without your
> applying to them in form. I hope such application is on its way;
> nothing else is wanting to effect your utmost wishes.

He signed the letter with his neat signature and watched as the ink
dried, and the text disappeared until not the faintest trace of his
name remained. The mountain of pages he had penned to Congress
since July were blank to the naked eye. Yet, the invisible ink gave him
little assurance that his letters were not somehow being intercepted
and read by British agents.

Only days later, on the evening of November 16, Deane finally
received a letter from Congress. A copy of the Declaration of Independence, mailed August 7, came with the first news from Congress
since Deane had arrived in France in early June. The Congress had
begun consideration of a proposed treaty of alliance with France.
Elated, Deane wrote to Vergennes requesting a meeting to deliver the
official Declaration. Deane also conveyed a copy to Spain through
the Spanish ambassador. Painfully aware of Congress's languid pace,
Deane did not wait for more instructions. He wrote to Vergennes as
"a private individual" proposing a treaty of alliance between the
United States and the Bourbon powers of France and Spain.

To Congress Deane expressed his concern that they had shown
little respect for "the dignity of old and powerfull States" by waiting
two months to send the second copy of the Declaration, relying on
a sea captain to deliver it when he "thinks of it or has nothing else
to do," and failing to enclose some more formal communication to
the French monarch.

By presenting Vergennes with the official Declaration, Deane gained new stature and importance in the French court as the de facto representative of his government. His natural optimism returned. Despite news that the British were threatening Philadelphia, he assured one friend that "America must come off, in the end, triumphant." Deane waxed philosophical: "Whatsoever disappointments I may meet with, I will never despair of my country, for which I shall count it my glory to suffer all things, if it receive any advantage therefore." Even if the revolution failed, "I shall, at least enjoy the pleasure, the unalienable pleasure, resulting from a consciousness of having done all in my power for its happiness, and, connectedly, for the happiness of mankind in general." He exulted, "The temper of the times is in favour of America, and it is now as fresh and as striking an object to Europe, as when first discovered and called the New World."

AS DEANE STEPPED into his public role on the diplomatic stage, Rodriguez Hortalez quietly moved thousands of tons of supplies and equipment from every corner of France to Le Havre, where three ships—the *Amphitrite*, the *Seine,* and the *Romain*—were being readied to sail to America. Sixty tons of cannon balls were barged down the Seine from Abbeville and Gravelines, near the Channel. Thousands of tents, grenades, and muskets were carted from Douai, Sedan, and Mézières, near Lille in the far north. Dozens of cannons were brought from military stores in Metz and Strasbourg, near the eastern border. Twenty-four tons of gunpowder were delicately loaded on wagons and carefully shipped long distances over bad roads. All this Herculean activity took place in secret, often under the cover of night, to avoid detection by British agents, who were hungry for evidence that the French were smuggling weapons to the Americans.

In November the *Amphitrite* was ready to load its precious cargo. It was a large 400-ton frigate. Under the command of French captain Fautrel, the *Amphitrite* was bound for New England. The *Amphitrite* would also carry a team of newly commissioned French officers led by Colonel Tronson du Coudray, whom Deane, at the insistence of Vergennes, had elevated to the rank of major general in the Continental Army. Du Coudray was a prima donna who had already strained Beaumarchais's patience. Du Coudray had recently learned that the British had defeated Washington's forces in New York City, and he feared that he might find himself on the losing side. He was now procrastinating at Versailles, threatening to hold up the voyage as he got cold feet. As du Coudray hesitated, Beaumarchais steamed. "I have not heard from him for three days," he complained to Vergennes. "Everything is ready to go, everything is waiting. I am on needles."

By December, du Coudray finally returned to his ship, and Beaumarchais arrived in Le Havre to supervise the final details. More than a hundred men worked for two solid nights loading the *Amphitrite* and the *Seine*, in a scene of wild confusion. At the risk of causing a massive explosion, the men nervously loaded twelve tons of gunpowder on the *Amphitrite*. Goods ended up on the wrong ships, and bills of lading listed supplies on one ship that were in fact loaded on the other. (This would later complicate any effort by Beaumarchais to obtain compensation from Congress.) When they were done, the *Amphitrite* sat low in the water, with nearly 500 tons of equipment and supplies and 130 men on board. In addition to arms and ammunition, there were 3,388 spades, 300 axes, 4,954 pickaxes, 7,200 knee buckles, 8,545 pairs of black stockings, 320 blankets, 52 carriages, and 15,264 pocket handkerchiefs. At that point the military officers unexpectedly demanded their full year's salary paid in advance. Beaumarchais hastily arranged it, careful

enough to ensure that no crew member or officer had any incriminating papers on him in case they were stopped by British ships. To
the British, it must appear that this ship was merely bringing supplies to the French sugar islands and any interference with the shipment would look like an act of war.

While he was in Le Havre, Beaumarchais traveled incognito
under the name "Durand." If the British knew that he was in the
port city they would try to stop the ships from leaving. One evening
Beaumarchais attended a dreary local production of *The Barber of
Seville*. Beaumarchais was so disappointed that he could not resist
the temptation to critique the direction of his play. The fate of the
American Revolution seemed somehow less urgent than the fate of
Figaro at the hands of these amateurs. Beaumarchais told the director he would take a few days to rehearse the cast himself. Soon word
leaked out that the famous playwright was directing the local production, and tickets began selling briskly. Even General Baron de
Kalb and his military entourage, who were in Le Havre, preparing
to leave on the *Romain*, took time to attend the production.

The revised production was well received. Figaro and his companions brought howls of laughter and roars of approval from the
audience, and Beaumarchais was delighted by his directorial success.
But news of his presence at the port city quickly reached the British
ambassador. Beaumarchais had blown his cover. Stormont raced
back to Versailles in a fit and demanded that Vergennes stop these
ships from leaving the port. Vergennes could no longer deny Beaumarchais's involvement or the staggering amounts of military supplies that had been gathered in Le Havre. There was no doubt that
Britain now had good cause to accuse France of intermeddling in
their North American colonies in blatant violation of the express
terms of the Treaty of 1763. Figaro's triumph literally had brought
Britain and France to the brink of war.

Faced with the prospect of war with Britain, Vergennes issued an order to stop any of Beaumarchais's ships from leaving Le Havre. His messenger, however, was delayed and did not arrive at Le Havre until Sunday evening, December 15—too late. The *Amphitrite* had already left the previous afternoon on a crisp light breeze coming off the Channel. The port commissioner wrote to the minister of the navy that it would be impossible for any ship to overtake the *Amphitrite*, but he ordered the *Seine* and the *Romain* seized. Beaumarchais held out hope that Vergennes would release the vessels eventually. It was left up to the British navy now to try to capture the *Amphitrite* before it could reach New England.

On December 4, 1776, just as the *Amphitrite* was reaching the open sea, Deane received more unexpected news: Benjamin Franklin had landed at the small fishing village of Auray, in Brittany. Franklin wrote to inform him that Congress, recognizing the importance of their relationship to France, had appointed Franklin, Thomas Jefferson, and Deane as co-commissioners to negotiate a treaty of commerce and an alliance with France. Finally, Deane had an official title and status as a United States emissary.

Congress had sent with Franklin indigo worth 3,000 pounds sterling for trade and 7,000 pounds sterling in currency to support their mission (totaling about $1.85 million today). Though Franklin had intended to travel to Paris secretly, that proved impossible. Franklin's fame was so great that practically the moment he stepped onto the French shore, he was swamped by a wave of adulation—and Franklin enjoyed it too much to forgo. Crowds cheered his passing carriage. He was mobbed everywhere he went. The throng of admirers was greater than even the king could expect, and it slowed Franklin's progress toward Paris to a crawl. As Deane read Franklin's letter he was overcome with relief and joy. He would not be alone anymore. In the same letter announcing his arrival, Franklin added a postscript: Jefferson had declined Congress's nomination. His wife was sickly and he preferred to remain behind with her in Virginia. In his place Congress had appointed Arthur Lee as co-commissioner to France.

Deane stared at the letter hard. His long isolation was finally over, yet he would now have to contend with the obnoxious Lee as a colleague. Deane consoled himself that at least he could always rely on his one true friend, Bancroft.

As events transpired Arthur Lee and Edward Bancroft became bitter enemies. But the two men shared a common purpose—to destroy everything Deane had labored to accomplish: the one by spreading lies; the other, by revealing secrets.

TWENTY–SIX

ODD MAN OUT

Paris, December 1776–March 1777

Benjamin Franklin gingerly lowered himself into a steaming bath of mineral water. He held on to the sides of the tub as the wind gently rocked the room, splashing the sudsy water from one side to the other. The Poitevin was the first floating bathhouse in Paris. It was easy to find. The smell of sulphur wafted from the whitewashed wooden boathouse at the Pont Royal, across the Tuileries. Franklin arrived at the dock at six in the evening by hackney coach and climbed aboard. He thought that the Poitevin was a salubrious spot both for relaxation and discreet negotiations. Naïvely, perhaps, the world's most famous American imagined that no one would recognize him indulging in a steamy bath, even though his image was ubiquitous, and strangers applauded his passing carriage on the street. At the Poitevin, the other patrons may have been less inclined to notice the elderly foreign gentleman; they were preoccupied with pairing off in the shadows of Paris's most notorious rendezvous for men who prefer men. Franklin seemed insensible to the muffled laughter, ghostly moans, and sudden gasps from adjoining rooms. British spies and the undercover Paris police were much more likely to observe the frequent visits of the American commissioner and puzzle over Franklin's preferences.

Franklin leaned his long stringy hair back into the warm water and stared up at the swaying ceiling. He felt exhausted by the challenges he confronted since his tumultuous welcome in December. He had arrived in Paris with his seven- and seventeen-year-old grandsons, Benjamin Bache and Temple Franklin, on December 22. He stayed with Deane on the rue de l'Université, and Arthur Lee joined them there the next day. Franklin knew Lee from his time in London and did not especially care for him, but he was happy to see his old friend Deane. Deane was so delighted to have Franklin by his side that he would not allow the sour Mr. Lee to spoil his joy. Franklin was deluged with well-wishers, fellow scientists, celebrity hounds, vendors hoping to export to America, young soldiers offering their services, aristocrats, and the most powerful grandes dames in Paris. It was evident that Deane's hotel would not be adequate to the task of receiving Franklin's public, and a few weeks later the three commissioners moved to more comfortable quarters at the Hôtel de Hambourg in the St. Germain district on the rue Jacob, where they enjoyed a garden view and the proprietor prided himself on his English.

On December 28, the three commissioners met with Vergennes to present their credentials in a secret location in Paris. The first meeting went badly. From America there was news that Washington had lost another important battle at White Plains, New York, and that the army was once again in retreat. It was an inauspicious moment to ask the French for an alliance. Moreover, Vergennes had already received complaints about Franklin's presence in Paris from the British ambassador, and he took pains to avoid the appearance

of any official contact with the Americans. The commissioners requested a commercial treaty, which Deane had proposed months
earlier, and Vergennes responded coolly that France would continue
to trade with the Americans *only* to the extent consistent with her
treaty commitments to Britain. To underline his point, Vergennes
read to them the treaty article that prohibited privateers from using
French ports. The commissioners were off to a bad start with their
French host.

To make matters worse, the *Amphitrite*, which had left France on
December 15, returned to Port Louis in southern Brittany on January 5. The ship's captain had failed to provide enough supplies for
the crew, and a storm had ruined some of the food that had been
improperly stored. The ship's 49 passengers and 160 crew members
faced the prospect of weeks of hunger and thirst. General du Coudray, who was also unhappy with his quarters, ordered the captain to
return to France. By then, the ship's mission had been publicized in
British newspapers and denounced in Parliament. Facing threats
from Stormont, the French government immediately imposed an
embargo, detaining all of Beaumarchais's ships indefinitely. Deane
and Beaumarchais could not believe that their hopes once again had
been dashed by circumstances and the failure of the French Foreign
Ministry to stand up to Stormont's bullying.

On the morning of Sunday, January 5, the commissioners took
a carriage to Versailles, hoping to see Vergennes again and clarify
their needs. They asked for a meeting on Monday morning. Vergennes hesitated. He worried that the mere presence of the commissioners in close proximity to the palace would be reported to the
British ambassador, and he did not want to do anything to further
to anger Stormont. Vergennes refused their request for a meeting.
But Deane would not be put off so easily. He wrote to Vergennes's
secretary, Gérard, that he was too ill to go out and needed to meet

at his hotel at once. Gérard immediately replied that he would be happy to see his friend at Deane's hotel in Versailles. Thus the commissioners met with Gérard at the Hôtel de Joue in Versailles the following morning. They wanted the foreign ministry to release the *Amphitrite* and Beaumarchais's other ships and to provide eight armed and manned vessels, more cannons, muskets, and bayonets, all delivered under the protection of a French convoy. Contrary to what Lee later wrote to members of Congress—namely, that the arms were all gifts from France—the commissioners agreed that Congress would pay for all the ships, men, and supplies. Gérard assured them that France would soon release all the ships, including the *Amphitrite*, and France would loan the Americans directly two million livres (roughly $15 million today). However, Gérard regretted that France could provide neither ships nor men under the terms of its treaty with Britain. Negotiations reached an impasse.

One of Franklin's friends in France was Jacques-Donatien Le Ray, the Comte de Chaumont, a squat giant of a man who had made a fortune trading in leather, textiles, glassware, stone, minerals, grain, and that most lucrative commodity, government contracts. Chaumont invited Franklin to live in his hilltop villa, the Hôtel de Valentinois, on the rue Raynouard in the tiny village of Passy, only half an hour's carriage ride from the heart of Paris. Today, the free offer of a home to an American diplomat might seem to raise the potential for a conflict of interest, especially when the host sought and received contracts for supplies from the American and French governments. However, the commissioners' finances were strained, and the Hôtel de Valentinois would afford them the opportunity to conduct business behind its walls without being observed by British spies. The sprawling eighteen-acre estate featured a neoclassical design around a courtyard and a terraced garden with a view of Notre-Dame. There was a team of liveried servants who attended to the commissioners' comfort, and an impressive wine cellar of more than a thousand bottles for entertaining. The lively Madame de Chaumont presided over elaborate dinners every afternoon at which the commissioners and their guests gorged themselves. Franklin lived like a prince, with a monthly food budget of about 1,500 livres (roughly $11,000 today). The famous exponent of thrift and savings admitted that "Frugality is a virtue I never could acquire in myself." In gratitude for Chaumont's hospitality, Franklin erected one of his lightning rods over the villa. Franklin preferred not to venture beyond his neighbors' châteaux, except for an occasional ride to Paris to the tony salon of the Marquise du Deffand in Saint-Germain, a meeting of the Academy of Sciences, or one of his warm baths at the Poitevin. Franklin embraced the inscription over the entry gate to Valentinois as his own: *Se sta bene non se muove*—"If it's going well, don't change it." It was an ironic signpost for the diplomatic mission of a revolutionary republic.

Franklin understood public relations as well as any man of his century. He had built a fortune as a printer and publicist. From the moment he arrived in France, he consciously tried to personify the American Enlightenment. To the aristocracy—powdered, wigged, and frilly—Franklin appeared simple, natural, and wise. He was the Sage of Pennsylvania, and the French imagined Pennsylvania as a sort of natural utopia populated by good Quaker farmers prospering from their honest labor on the rugged frontier. Franklin was no farmer. He was a cosmopolitan, urbane man of science and industry, who had lived in large cities his whole life. And he certainly was no Quaker, but he was willing to play one if that was what it took to win over France. He made a point of wearing the same plain brown coat every day with a white linen blouse. He carried a walking stick and covered most of his long gray hair under a round fur cap that looked as if he might have shot and skinned it himself. "Think how

this must appear among the Powder'd Heads of Paris," he chuckled
to an English lady friend. Franklin could certainly afford to dress à
la mode, but he was playing to his audience, who wanted him to
look exotic. His host Chaumont had hundreds of medallions
stamped with Franklin's portrait for his adoring fans. Franklin understood the power of his celebrity and believed he could be more
effective as a figurehead, winning the hearts of the most powerful
women and men in the capital. While Franklin posed for painters
and sculptors, he left to Deane the details of negotiating, financing,
equipping, raising, and arming a fighting force. Even the British
spies reported that between Franklin and Deane, Deane was "the
more active and efficient man."

Franklin spent his days preoccupied by the political, the scien-
tific, the social, and even the frivolous. The flood of candidates for
military commissions now went to Franklin rather than Deane, who
had been criticized for issuing commissions without authority. In
the basement of his villa he installed a printing press so that he
could publish pamphlets that would build public support for the
Americans. He wrote a regular column for a monthly French magazine, *Affaires de l'Angleterre et de l'Amérique*, which was secretly controlled by the French Foreign Ministry. All this while Franklin
continued a lively correspondence with a staggering number of serious thinkers and flirtatious women.

For the same reasons that the French found Franklin charming,
Lee regarded his famous countryman as self-indulgent. Franklin,
now seventy, was not quite the man he had known in London. Lee
thought that Franklin was losing his edge, growing soft, and cor-
rupted by French influence. Franklin spent too much time chasing
younger—and often married—women, including his neighbor's
wife, the charismatic Madame Brillon. Though Franklin's relations
with Madame Brillon may have remained chaste, there was little

doubt of the passion he felt for her. Their correspondence was more than suggestive. Franklin confessed to her that he was "constantly" violating the commandment "which forbids Coveting my Neighbour's Wife." Nor was Franklin at all discreet in his pursuit of this young beauty. "Do you know, my dear Papa," as she often called him, "that people have criticized my sweet habit of sitting on your lap, and your habit of soliciting from me what I always refuse?" Franklin thought nothing of playing chess in her bathroom as Madame Brillon admired him from her tub. At thirty-six, Lee, who apparently had little interest in women and remained chaste throughout his life, probably regarded Franklin's extracurricular activities as a distraction that potentially could endanger their mission. Franklin, in turn, thought Lee too dour for a man his age.

While Franklin took charge of the public diplomacy, and Deane was up to his elbows in the smuggling operation, Lee felt bored and underemployed. He was the odd man out. He wanted to travel to Madrid and Berlin to seek additional assistance. Franklin and Deane were delighted to oblige their irritating colleague by sending him far afield. They probably did not expect much from Lee's diplomacy, although the Spanish ambassador to France, the Conde de Aranda, had encouraged them to believe that the Spanish foreign minister, the Marqués de Grimaldi, might be prepared to help. Lee was enthusiastic about taking on these diplomatic missions, convinced that he alone had the character and intellect to forge alliances.

Lee left for Spain in February of 1777. On the way he stopped over at the French port city of Nantes, where he met Thomas Morris, whom Deane had appointed as the American commercial agent at Nantes, charged with arranging shipments to Congress. Morris was the half brother of Robert Morris, Deane's most powerful ally in Congress and his commercial partner. Lee found that commercial affairs under Thomas Morris were "greatly deranged." During their meeting Morris was noticeably inebriated; Lee thought he was "a sot . . . a man who could not get a month's employment in any counting house in Europe." Privately, Lee was probably gleeful to find evidence confirming his suspicions of Deane's incompetence and possible corruption, especially concerning the brother of Robert Morris. Robert Morris was one of the leading opponents of the "Lee-Adams Junto" in Congress led by Richard Henry Lee and Samuel Adams. Anything that would weaken Morris—and the clique of mercantile men he associated with in Congress—would strengthen Lee's brothers, Richard Henry and Francis Lightfoot. On his own Lee wrote to Congress that Thomas Morris was unfit, and he recommended that Congress appoint his brother William Lee to oversee all of America's commercial interests in Europe.

To his credit, when Deane learned that Thomas Morris was a drunk, he dismissed him despite Deane's close relationship with Robert Morris. Deane and Franklin reported to Congress the reason for dismissing Thomas Morris, and their report embarrassed and angered Robert, who wished they could have handled the matter more discreetly. Franklin replaced Thomas Morris with his grand-nephew Jonathan Williams. Franklin's nepotism infuriated Lee; after all, to Lee it was obvious that his brother William was the most qualified man for the job.

Deane's public disclosure of Thomas Morris's drunkenness opened a significant rift between Deane and Robert Morris, his chief ally in Congress and business partner. Morris wrote to Deane accusing him of betraying their friendship and "Blasting [Thomas's] character in the most Public manner, and exposing me to feelings the most Poignant I ever knew." By embarrassing the Morris brothers, Lee had sown the seeds for dividing Deane's supporters in Congress.

By the time Lee reached Spain in late February, Conde de Floridablanca had replaced the Marqués de Grimaldi as Spanish foreign minister. Nonetheless, Lee met with Grimaldi in early March at Vitoria, Spain, in the Basque country near the French border. At the request of the foreign ministry the meeting was held out of the capital city to avoid alarming the British ambassador. Lee, never a man to take a hint, insisted that he should be allowed to go to Madrid. He warned Grimaldi that if he were not received in Madrid it would damage the credibility of the American commissioners in Europe. The English ambassador had no right to object to his visiting a "neutral court." Lee told the foreign minister that this "is the moment in which Spain and France may clip [Great Britain's] wings and pinion her forever." Grimaldi growled back at Lee, "You have considered your own situation and not ours. The moment is not yet come for us."

Grimaldi warned Lee that there would be no point in proceeding to Madrid. The new foreign minister, Floridablanca, who was cautious and conciliatory by nature, wanted to negotiate a peace that would avoid war with Portugal or Britain. Though Grimaldi personally opposed American independence as a threat to the Bourbon monarchy, he saw the Americans as a convenient means to an end. His goal was to defeat Portugal, Britain's ally, and expand Spanish influence in South America. In other words, by overthrowing British colonialism, Grimaldi hoped to strengthen Spanish colonialism. Grimaldi promised Lee that Spain would provide some aid, but it was never clear how much or in what form. Spain eventually delivered 30,000 blankets to New Orleans for the Continental Army, but whether they actually provided arms or ammunition is doubtful. Spain also offered to loan the Americans an unspecified amount of money, but the Spanish king had already decided to make that offer before Lee's arrival. Though Lee considered his mission a brilliant success, the Spanish crown thought otherwise.

Lee returned to France, where he learned that the Lee-Adams
Junto in Congress had appointed him emissary to Spain and Prussia
and appointed his brother William emissary to Austria. This was no
more than naked nepotism. The Lee-Adams Junto believed in "militia diplomacy"—that is, sending representatives out to every capital regardless of whether there was any reason to believe their
credentials would be recognized. Rather than wait for the right time
and situation when a foreign power expressed a willingness to open
talks with the Americans, these diplomatic militiamen would simply
arrive at a foreign capital and insist on recognition and treaties of
friendship and commerce. Militia diplomacy was more of a buck-
shot approach to diplomacy than a narrowly defined deliberate
strategy. Franklin, who had more diplomatic experience than any
other American, thought that "A Virgin state should preserve its
virgin character, and not go about suitoring for alliances, but wait
with decent dignity for the application of others." Franklin was correct. Militia diplomacy was presumptuous, promiscuous, and as
things turned out, fruitless.

Lee had no talent for diplomacy. His ability as a propagandist
flowed from his absolute certainty of the righteousness of his convictions; diplomacy demanded nuance and empathy, not bombast
and zealotry. He was handicapped not only by a prickly personality,
but by poor judgment. Though he chastised Franklin for his lax attitude toward secrecy, Lee showed no discretion in his first diplomatic
foray as emissary to Spain and Prussia. He traveled to Berlin accompanied by Wilkes's friend Stephen Sayre, who had been arrested and
tossed into the Tower of London for his alleged conspiracy against
George III. Sayre's company guaranteed that Lee would attract the
suspicion of British spies. After their arrival in the Prussian capital,
Lee and Sayre went to dinner, leaving Lee's personal papers behind
in a room with an open window. While the two men ate, Lee's diary

was snatched and secretly copied by a British agent who delivered it to London. By the time Lee approached the Prussian government, the Prussian emperor had already heard from the British, and he had no interest in what Lee had to offer.

Deane and Franklin thought that Lee did more to tax their efforts than to assist. Neither the Spanish nor the French liked dealing with Lee, whom they regarded as too English. Lee, for his part, distrusted all things French, including the language, which he refused to learn. His years spent growing up in Britain had infected him with Anglophilia. Lee returned to Passy, where he was furious to learn that, in his absence, Franklin had invited his friend Deane to join him in his elegant quarters, leaving Lee to live miles away in much humbler accommodations in Chaillot. Lee envied Deane's closeness to Franklin; even as he distrusted them, he wanted their trust. Lee was restless to be at the center of the action, and he continually proposed new plans that were impractical and impolitic: having failed to win support for the American cause in Prussia, the militia diplomat now proposed a diplomatic mission to China. Leaving aside the logistics of transporting diplomats to, or arms from, China, he had apparently failed to calculate just how sympathetic the Chinese emperor was likely to be to the revolutionary sentiments of the Declaration of Independence.

In Lee's absence Deane negotiated a secret deal with Vergennes to obtain another million-livre subsidy for the Americans (nearly $8 million today). To keep the subsidy secret, it was in the form of a contract to import tobacco. Deane and Franklin promised to sell five million pounds of Virginia tobacco for one million livres, a price that was substantially discounted from the price on the French market. When Lee learned of this contract he accused Deane and Franklin of making a bad business deal and suggested to Congress that they must have had a personal stake in it. More than likely, Lee understood that the contract was merely a ruse to hide the French subsidy, but he chose to mischaracterize the transaction to embarrass Deane and Franklin.

What Franklin and Deane did not know is that Lee was secretly undermining their efforts, even at the risk of betraying the Revolution. At the end of December 1776, Lee privately wrote to the Secret Committee about France's military aid. "The politics of Europe are in a state of trembling hesitation," he cautioned Congress. As a consequence, "I find the promises that were made to me by the French agent in London [Beaumarchais] . . . have not been entirely fulfilled." Lee charged that Deane had intervened and undone all of Lee's good work. Though Lee still hoped that Congress might receive some of what was promised to him, the goods were "infinitely short" of what was promised. Implicit in Lee's message was that Congress had no obligation to pay for the goods by shipping tobacco to Beaumarchais.

Though they did not yet know the full extent of Lee's treachery, Deane and Franklin realized that Lee was rowing the boat in the opposite direction. They would have to row harder.

TWENTY-SEVEN

THE OHIO COMPANY

The bleak prospects for their diplomatic mission strained relations between Lee and the other commissioners, but there were other personal and familial explanations for Lee's behavior. As a Virginia gentleman from a leading Tidewater family, educated at Eton, Edinburgh, and the Inns of Court, Lee felt destined to lead. Instead, he had been elbowed aside by the pushy New England sons of a candle maker and a blacksmith who, to his mind, were too eager to enrich themselves any way they could. Lee wrote to a friend that the appointment of commissioners "who were neither bred [n]or born gentlemen . . . was either a great folly or a great contempt of those to whom they were sent."

And there was another motive behind Lee's animosity, especially toward Franklin. It was rooted in the bitter competition between the Lee family and Franklin over the development of the Ohio River valley.

By the early 1700s the Lee family, like many Virginia planters, had a difficult time maintaining their extravagant lifestyle from tobacco alone. Tobacco exhausted the soil, and farmers had not learned to rotate crops efficiently. Tobacco prices were unstable, and there was competition not only from other English colonies, but from Spanish Florida as well. The Navigation Acts prohibited the export of tobacco except to Britain. To gain access to European markets Virginian tobacco growers were compelled to consign their crops to English merchants, who skimmed off most of the profit. These merchants advanced credit to planters against their future tobacco sales and also filled orders for manufactured goods from Europe. The availability of credit encouraged planters to live far beyond their means, but when tobacco prices fell, the laws gave English creditors swift and brutal remedies against debtors.

Like many Tidewater growers, the Lees could not maintain their lifestyle from their tobacco sales, and they were constantly threatened with insolvency. And so the Lees turned to real estate development as a new source of wealth. In 1747, Thomas Lee, Arthur's father, organized the Ohio Company, a land syndicate, to settle 500,000 acres of the fertile region along the Allegheny River and north and south of the confluence of the Ohio and Mississippi rivers in what is now parts of Illinois, Missouri, Indiana, Kentucky, Ohio, and Pennsylvania. Lee's plan was to sell off plots to new immigrants to develop a new territory. The syndicate included leading Virginians like George Washington and George Mason, another Virginian planter who was a member of the Continental Congress. In 1748, Lee became the president of the Virginia Council. Shortly after that the British Board of Trade, the powerful committee of the Privy Council that oversaw land grants, awarded Lee's company 200,000 acres and promised Lee another 300,000 acres after he built a fort and began settlements.

John Robinson, the powerful Speaker of the Virginia House of Burgesses, ran a competing land syndicate known as the Loyal Land Company and viewed Thomas Lee as an impediment to both his political and financial ambitions. After the Loyal Land Company received a grant of 800,000 acres in what is now Kentucky, Thomas Lee decided to seek a larger land grant for the Ohio Company. In 1749, he became acting governor for the colony. Not without reason the Board of Trade feared that greedy land developers were encroaching on Indian lands and risked sparking a war with the tribes. Lee pressed the Board of Trade for more land—without success. The Board of Trade viewed the competition between the Robinson faction and the Lee faction as destructive to the peace of the colony and decided not to grant Lee any additional land. When Lee died in 1750, the Ohio Company's claim to more land remained unsettled.

That is not to say that the Ohio Company had no historical significance other than building a few forts and settlements. In 1753, Virginia governor Dinwiddie, who had also invested in Lee's Ohio Company, was concerned by reports of French forces occupying land that Parliament had granted to the company. He dispatched a twenty-one-year-old surveyor named George Washington with six men to find the French military camp and ask them to leave. When the French refused, the Virginia House of Burgesses sent Washington, who had no military experience, and a force of 300 men to confront the French. Washington established a makeshift stockade, which he named "Fort Necessity." The French dispatched a small patrol of 32 men to negotiate with Washington, but the young commander could not speak French, and his Indian allies, who understood French but did not care about diplomatic niceties, proceeded to massacre and scalp the French commander and his men. French forces from Fort Duquesne retaliated against Washington and killed more than one-third of his force before compelling him to surrender. Ironically, Washington's first retreat occurred on July 4, 1754. Washington's defeat at Fort Necessity became the opening battle of the Seven Years' War, which was waged in Europe and the Americas and which Americans call the "French and Indian War."

At the conclusion of the French and Indian War in 1763, the British wanted to avoid future tensions with the Indian tribes. King George III issued the Royal Proclamation of 1763 that annulled all of the colonies' western land claims, reserved all the land west of the Allegheny Mountains for the Indian tribes, and prohibited colonial settlements or land purchases. The king's proclamation called a halt to westward expansion. It appeared to put an end to the Lee family's dream of settling the Ohio Valley. But almost immediately, the Board of Trade agreed to grant some limited licenses for western settlements.

By then, Virginian planter John Mercer and his family had wrested control of the Ohio Company from the Lees. The Mercers submitted a new petition for a land grant. The Lees and the Mercers agreed to send the eldest Mercer son, George, to London to petition the crown for an exception from the king's ban on settling western lands. For two years George Mercer sought audiences with the British government to obtain a new land grant, but he was unsuccessful. Without the land grant, the Ohio Company and the Lee family faced a dim financial future, and the Lee brothers bitterly blamed the Mercers for this failure. They were determined to regain control of the company and obtain the land grant at all costs.

In 1765, the British Parliament issued the Stamp Act requiring colonists to purchase stamps from British agents to authenticate certain kinds of documents. The stamps were essentially a tax on transactions. As a concession to the colonists, the prime minister appointed a number of Americans as stamp distributors, effectively granting them the power to earn sizable commissions on the sale of stamps. Both Franklin and Richard Henry Lee sought to be appointed stamp distributors, but both were denied. George Mercer, still in London representing the Ohio Company, was appointed as the stamp distributor for Virginia, and in this new official capacity he returned to Virginia in October 1765.

This was an opportunity for the Lees to humiliate the Mercers and eliminate them as competitors for the land. Richard Henry Lee, who was still smarting over being rejected for the position himself, now denounced Mercer as "an execrable monster, who with parricidal heart and hands, hath concern in the ruin of his native country." No doubt his commission as stamp distributor for Virginia would have significantly contributed to his family's income, and he was especially disappointed to lose the position to a member of the Mercer family. Richard Henry, untroubled by his own hypocrisy, led a demonstration against Mercer as an agent of British taxation in which the crowd, composed largely of Lee's own slaves, pulled a hangman's cart carrying an effigy of Mercer with signs reading, "Money is our God" and "Slavery I love!" The slaves were dressed up like the radical supporters of Lord Mayor John Wilkes and carried menacing clubs. At the end of the parade the effigy of Mercer was hung and burned. When that did not suffice to intimidate Mercer into resigning, Lee instigated a mob that confronted Mercer on his arrival in Williamsburg. Shaken by the angry demonstration and the threat of further violence, Mercer decided to quit and returned to England at once. Richard Henry had made it appear that his attack on Mercer was based on the principle of no taxation without representation. But later, when the *Virginia Gazette* disclosed that Lee had acted from self-interest, he was forced to admit that he had wanted the job as stamp distributor himself. The incident left a toxic rivalry between the Lees and the Mercers, and at one point, the young Arthur Lee even challenged John Mercer's brother

James to a duel. (Happily for Arthur, who was nearsighted and a poor athlete, James arrived late for the duel, and Arthur declared himself the victor.)

By now the Lee family had abandoned any hope of regaining control of the Ohio Company and instead organized a new competing land company called the Mississippi Company. The Lees hoped to use their political influence to carve out an exception from the Royal Proclamation for the Mississippi Company. They petitioned the British Board of Trade for an even more ambitious plan: 2.5 million acres between the Wabash, Ohio, and Tennessee rivers, including parts of what now includes Indiana, Illinois, and Kentucky. When it became obvious that the British stood firm on their policy against westward expansion, the Lee family's ceaseless appetite for western land brought them into irreconcilable conflict with Britain.

The Lee brothers appointed Arthur Lee as agent and lobbyist for the Mississippi Company with discretion to distribute shares of the company to buy support for the land grant from members of Parliament. This placed Arthur in the unique position of trying to curry favor with Lord Hillsborough, the president of the Board of Trade and later the Secretary of State for Colonial Affairs, while at the same time he was anonymously scribbling articles as Junius Americanus attacking Hillsborough's colonial policy. The Lees were happy to offer Hillsborough a financial stake in the Mississippi Company, if that is what it took to build their family's western empire.

By then there were several other rival land syndicates competing with the Mississippi Company for land grants from the Board of Trade. There was still the Loyal Land Company, which was now led by Thomas Walker, a physician, explorer, and, coincidentally, legal guardian of Thomas Jefferson and close relative of Meriwether

Lewis. And in Connecticut there was the Susquehanna Company, which included among its influential boosters Silas Deane, who had negotiated on behalf of the company to avoid a war between Pennsylvania and Connecticut over competing land claims.

The most significant rival was the Indiana Company, based in Philadelphia. The Indiana Company's shareholders included Benjamin Franklin and his illegitimate son, William, who was royal governor of New Jersey; the wealthy Philadelphia merchant Samuel Wharton; and Edward Bancroft, Deane's assistant. The Indiana Company eventually merged into the Illinois-Wabash Company, which in turn merged with the remnants of the Ohio Company to form the Grand Ohio Company. The Grand Ohio Company laid claim to an area that stretched from what is now Pittsburgh south to what is now Boonesborough, Kentucky. It was bounded by the Potomac on the east and the Ohio River on the west and it occupied much of what is now West Virginia and healthy slices of Virginia, Pennsylvania, Kentucky, and Ohio. In a naked effort to curry favor with George III, the Grand Ohio Company named this wilderness empire "Vandalia" after Queen Charlotte, who claimed that her ancestors were Vandals.

Throughout the 1770s, while Franklin and Arthur Lee were representing the Massachusetts colonial Assembly to the British Parliament, they were also representing rival land syndicates competing for a grant to the same western land. Though Franklin's reputation and access gave him great influence, and though his son was royal governor of New Jersey, Lee had cultivated relationships with well-connected men like Lord Mayor John Wilkes and Paul Wentworth. The Lee family would not yield, and each time the Privy Council rejected their petition, the Lee family increased the size of their request. But the Earl of Hillsborough, Secretary of State for Colonial

Affairs, opposed land speculation in principle and shrewdly played the demands of the Mississippi Company off against Franklin's Grand Ohio Company.

The two competing bids between Franklin and the Lees ultimately canceled each other out, and neither grant was ever made. The embittered Lees blamed Franklin and Wharton for their financial difficulties. The Mississippi Company's loss could not have come at a worse time for the Lees. By 1772, the price of tobacco had collapsed, losing half of its value and plunging the Virginia Tidewater into a deep recession. The financial panic over tobacco prices was the worst experienced since the South Sea Bubble of 1720. Planters like the Lees could no longer service their debts, and many debtors faced foreclosures and imprisonment.

The Lee family regarded the Ohio Valley as their birthright. It was not merely a land deal. In the face of a declining tobacco fortune, their wealth and status as one of Virginia's leading families depended on their ability to realize the dream of Thomas Lee. For the Lees, this competition was nothing less than a tribal struggle to survive. Their animosity was not just reserved for Franklin and his land syndicate. Silas Deane's professional relationship with Franklin, his personal interest in the Susquehanna Company, and his financial relationship with Wharton made him suspect as well. Indeed, while Deane was serving as commissioner he allegedly was negotiating with Wharton to invest in the Grand Ohio project. The Lees would continue their bitter rivalry with Franklin and Deane until it erupted into a full-scale war in Congress.

TWENTY–EIGHT

TURTLE'S PROGRESS

Paris, January–July 1777

Arthur Lee's feud with his diplomatic colleagues was further fueled by his brother William and their associate Ralph Izard, who had been appointed by Congress to the courts at Berlin and Tuscany, respectively. William Lee found nothing inconsistent in serving both as a London alderman and as the American commissioner to Berlin. Izard was the spoiled son of a rich southern plantation owner. He constantly found fault with Deane and Franklin. Though he nominally served as commissioner to Tuscany for nearly two years, he never actually visited Tuscany and instead supped daily at Franklin's table. Bored and cynical, William Lee and Ralph Izard had nothing better to do than to languish in Paris, stirring the pot of Arthur Lee's paranoia.

Lee went behind his colleagues to complain to members of Congress about Franklin and Deane. He accused them of conspiring to destroy him. He believed that Deane, Bancroft, and Deane's personal secretary, William Carmichael, were spies. He complained that

Franklin and Deane spent public funds, made contracts for the delivery of arms, and reached decisions without involving him. Lee suspected both Deane and Franklin of profiting at the expense of the public. He urged Congress to move Franklin to Vienna and Deane to Holland, leaving Lee alone in Paris. Although he had accused both Deane and Franklin of cronyism and nepotism, he proposed that Congress put his brother William in charge of all commercial affairs in Europe and name his cousin Edmund Jennings as emissary to Madrid.

For his part, Deane struggled to understand Lee and hold his temper. After a particularly nasty series of exchanges, Deane wrote to Lee that he was not "insensible to the manner in which he has been treated in Mr. Lee's two last Billets, or to the insinuations which have been for many months since made by Mr. Lee, respecting his conduct." But Deane had no wish to "resent" Lee and expressed instead his wish that Lee "have the Candor to Communicate to him in Person the grounds of his Jealousies & uneasiness; in which Case Mr. Deane pledges his Honor that Nothing on his Part shall be wanting to remove them." Despite Deane's efforts, Lee's hostility and suspicions continued to fester.

While Lee complained that he had too little to do, Deane and Beaumarchais were racing around, trying to persuade France to allow Beaumarchais's ships—the *Amphitrite*, the *Amélie* (formerly the *Romain*), the *Seine*, and now the *Mercure*—to leave for North America. Moreover, Deane now feared that the supplies aboard the ships were either in poor condition or badly stored and insisted on reinspecting all the cargo. Beaumarchais resented Deane's insistence on checking the cargo of each of the ships. He felt that Deane's suspicion was unwarranted and served only to delay the mission. "Sir, by what right have you become so difficult regarding my engagements when you have so far failed to fulfill any of yours toward me?" Beaumarchais quickly apologized for his foul mood, but explained that "I have exhausted myself in money and in work, without being able to know by now if anyone but you appreciates it at all." Beaumarchais's efforts certainly were not appreciated by Lee or Franklin "who deny the most simple civilities to their country's most useful friend." Beaumarchais was especially cross that Franklin had never invited him to dine at the American headquarters at Valentinois.

While all this was going on, General du Coudray decided to take an excursion to Paris, abandoning the *Amphitrite* and his officers, to denounce Beaumarchais to the commissioners. Du Coudray accused Beaumarchais of being responsible for delaying the *Amphitrite* and not supplying the ships properly. He hinted that Beaumarchais had skimmed profits from the shipment. Du Coudray's slanders aroused Lee's suspicion that Beaumarchais and Deane were somehow profiting, though Lee knew perfectly well that the Americans had not paid for any of the supplies. Lee's suspicion was of course absurd. Beaumarchais had not received any payment for his expenses, travel, or time since the operation had begun eighteen months earlier, and his trading company, Rodriguez and Hortalez, was teetering on insolvency. Deane was so angered by du Coudray that he tried, but failed, to stop him from departing for America.

Beaumarchais wrote to Vergennes, asking why the shipments were so delayed and confused. Vergennes claimed that he had no idea and that the ministry had done nothing to delay the delivery of arms. This was patently false. Vergennes did not want to admit that he was afraid of Stormont's reaction. Neither did he want to discourage Beaumarchais. He hoped that Beaumarchais and Deane would find a way to outwit the French government so that he could plausibly deny to Stormont any responsibility for the delivery of arms. But Vergennes's denial was too much for Beaumarchais, who exploded with anger: "[A]fter swallowing one disgusting thing after the other without complaining, this one sticks in my throat and strangles me." He complained to Vergennes that "while evil advances with giant steps, good drags on like a turtle."

Soon after, the embargo was suddenly and inexplicably lifted, and by the end of February all four vessels had departed. By April 1777, three more ships, the *Thérèse,* the *Concorde,* and the *Marquis de la Chalotais,* had set out from Paimboeuf, a small harbor just south of Nantes. Beaumarchais hoped that the British would be less likely to keep an eye on such a small harbor. Together these seven ships carried enough muskets, lead, powder, flints, cannons, bombs, uniforms, caps, boots, stockings, buttons, buckles, tents, blankets, spades, carriages, and matches to equip an army of 30,000. These were the first of approximately forty ships that Beaumarchais sent to the Americans during the Revolution.

Even before the ships weighed anchor the British ambassador appeared at Versailles with a precise list of the cargo and crew of the *Amphitrite.* He told Vergennes that he knew of five ships that Beaumarchais and Deane were readying to carry supplies to the American rebels. Vergennes feigned surprise, but Stormont knew he was lying. Humiliated at being caught, Vergennes blamed the commissioners and Beaumarchais for being indiscreet. Clearly, the British ambassador must have had sources inside Valentinois who could provide such reliable information.

Deane and Beaumarchais had labored for nine months to launch these ships for America, but now Deane had a new worry: The British knew the ships were carrying guns and ammunition and would be looking to intercept them. The safest way to avoid capture at sea was to sail far south, which would take longer. But then the ships would reach the American shore just as the days were lengthening and the number of British ships cruising in the Atlantic coast would be increasing. If the ships were lost or captured, the commissioners would not know for months. The commissioners did not know whether Congress had received their communications about when and where the ships would arrive. If they were intercepted or sunk, the commissioners would not find out until it was too late to send more ships to supply Washington's desperate troops.

IN THE THREE MONTHS since Franklin's arrival in France, in December 1776, the commissioners had heard nothing from Congress. Deane was all too familiar with this situation, but Franklin found it unacceptable. The commissioners had to rely mostly on newspapers to follow the progress of the war. The Secret Committee, now with the more dignified name the "Committee for Foreign Affairs," wrote only sparingly. "Though it must be agreeable to you to hear frequently from us," the committee warned the commissioners, "when you hear not so often as you wish, remember our silence means our safety."

From newspapers and occasional letters from friends in America, the commissioners knew that the Revolution was going poorly. Most of the American navy had been damaged or destroyed by the British on Lake Champlain in October. During the month that followed, General Howe's massive army drove Washington from New York after a string of defeats and thousands of casualties at White Plains, at Fort Washington on Manhattan, and at Fort Lee in New Jersey. More than 2,600 American soldiers were taken prisoner at Fort Washington, where General Cornwallis chased Washington's terrified troops from the battleground, leaving hundreds of scarce muskets, cannons, and barrels of gunpowder behind. In December, the British captured the naval base at Newport, Rhode Island. Washington continued his retreat across Delaware and Pennsylvania. By mid-December, British forces controlled most of New Jersey and were poised to march on Philadelphia. Anticipating the fall of the city, Congress evacuated in panic to Baltimore.

At the same time that the military effort was failing, so was the ability of Congress to finance the war and manage the economy. The Continental Congress had no treasury to finance a war and possessed neither the legal authority nor the practical means to collect taxes or mint coins. It could only recommend, request, and entreat the states to provide material support for the war effort. "Congress have left it in the power of the States to starve the Army at pleasure," one officer wrote.

All Congress could do by way of finance was to print paper currency, and this it did with a vengeance, pouring nearly $200 million on what had been an agrarian barter economy. The value of the currency, which was questionable from the outset, fell precipitously, so that within a few years a soldier's monthly pay was scarcely enough for a bottle of cheap rum. When merchants refused to accept Continental currency for supplies, soldiers sometimes resorted to "impressment," a euphemism for extorting supplies from civilians. Washington rightly feared that popular support for the Revolution would be lost if the army failed to respect private property. Rapid inflation eventually forced Congress to repudiate the Continental currency in 1780.

War imposed severe economic hardships on most Americans, testing support for Washington's army. The price of beef shot up four hundred percent in a single year. "People are now so afraid of the money that it is almost impossible to Purchase Grain at any rate," lamented one officer. While the elite in New York and Philadelphia dressed in the latest French and British fashions and savored lavish banquets, tradesmen and farmers struggled to survive. Civilians, no less than soldiers, faced shortages of food and manufactured goods. "Great frugality and great industry are now become

fashionable here," Franklin had observed ironically. "Gentlemen
who used to entertain with two or three courses, pride themselves
now in treating with simple beef and pudding. By these means, and
the stoppage of our consumptive trade with Britain, we shall be better able to pay our voluntary taxes for the support of our troops."

Washington knew that his men needed encouragement after a
long string of defeats. On Christmas Day 1776, he crossed the ice-
choked Delaware and staged a raid at daybreak on a group of Hes-
sian mercenaries at Trenton, New Jersey, a small village of no
strategic value. Twenty-one Hessians and no rebels were killed in a
brief exchange during which 2,400 rebels captured nearly 900 Hessians. Trenton was the first of a painfully few victories that Washington won—albeit against sleepy mercenaries with Christmas
hangovers. The victory at Trenton, followed by another at Princeton
in early January, helped rally Americans during the hard winter
months. By the spring thaw, however, Washington's army had melted
away to barely 1,000 men.

The commissioners later learned that while the British massed
to drive the rebels out of New York and New England, Congress
slipped back into Philadelphia in March. Still, the reports from
home grew ever more dire. In June, British general Burgoyne and
nearly 8,000 men sailed down from Canada across Lake Champlain,
headed for Fort Ticonderoga and Albany. At the same time, General
Howe had 15,000 men under orders to march north toward Albany,
link up with Burgoyne's forces, and mop up what remained of the
rebel army.

In July, Burgoyne chased the Americans from Fort Ticonderoga
without firing a shot. Two thousand badly clothed and unfit soldiers, many of them mere boys, tried to outrun the relentless redcoats in a series of teeming thunderstorms that lasted days. They left
behind them 128 cannons, cartloads of scarce ammunition, and

rusting muskets. Now the only military obstacle between the British and Albany was a thousand ill-equipped soldiers under the command of General Philip Schuyler, who was blamed for the loss of Ticonderoga and eventually dismissed. His men were deserting or falling ill in astonishing numbers. They had two cannons to defend Albany against Burgoyne's 9,000 battle-ready troops. They had no shelter from constant rainstorms punctuated only by merciless heat, and their food and ammunition were nearly gone. The fall of Ticonderoga was a crushing blow to American morale. It was not just the strategic value of the fort and the loss of tons of gunpowder and dozens of cannons, but the symbolic significance of Ticonderoga in the public's imagination. No one would have felt this loss more keenly than Deane, who had helped engineer and finance the capture of the fort at the start of the Revolution. That victory had been the signal event in Deane's career at the Continental Congress, where some still called him by his nickname, "Ticonderoga." For the three commissioners in Paris, the loss of Ticonderoga also meant it would be nearly impossible to persuade the French to side with the Americans.

In July, General Howe decided for reasons of his own to disobey his orders to link up with Burgoyne and instead sailed from New York to Chesapeake Bay with the goal of recapturing Philadelphia. In September, Washington suffered still another demoralizing defeat at Brandywine, Pennsylvania, clearing the way for General Howe to roll into Philadelphia. Congress fled again—this time west, to York, Pennsylvania—where it watched in frustration and horror as the massive invasion of British troops in Pennsylvania and New York threatened to snuff out the last remnants of Washington's army.

The staggering cost of the war tested the courage of every American. "Our people knew not the hardships and calamities of war when they so boldly dared Britain to arms," Robert Morris wrote to the commissioners. "[E]very man was then a bold patriot ... equal to the contest ..." But now, "when death and ruin stare us in the face, and when nothing but the most intrepid courage can rescue us from contempt and disgrace," Morris continued, "many of those who were foremost in noise shrink coward-like from the danger, and are beggin pardon without striking a blow."

TWENTY-NINE

MESSAGE IN A BOTTLE

Paris, January–October 1777

A world away from the Revolution, Franklin and Deane tried to keep up appearances around the immaculately pruned gardens of the American headquarters at Valentinois. Franklin regularly attended the salon of the Marquise du Deffand, where he flirted with the ladies and boasted about the prospects for the Revolution, knowing the truth was quite the opposite. Deane never acknowledged his own doubts in public. If the French government thought that the American cause was futile, it would never agree to an alliance. But behind the elegant façade of Valentinois, the Americans were deeply worried about the future of the Revolution and began to wonder whether they should make a separate peace with the British. Franklin and Deane secretly wrote to Stormont, proposing a prisoner exchange. The ambassador returned their unopened envelope with the reply that "The King's Ambassador receives no applications from rebels unless they come to implore his Majesty's mercy." Yet the British Foreign Ministry sent a secret envoy to meet Franklin to discuss terms for a settlement, and Franklin was happy to oblige: he suggested they meet in his favorite spot for privacy and intrigue—the Poitevin bathhouse.

Franklin and Deane saw the possibility of negotiations with the British as a way of pressuring the French into action. Beaumarchais told Vergennes that unless France stepped forward quickly, the Americans would be forced to come to terms with Britain, and France would miss the chance to strike a blow against the British Empire. Beaumarchais suspected that British agents were speaking to Franklin already, over Deane's objections to negotiating. Beaumarchais warned Vergennes that the British were planning to kidnap Deane and prosecute him for John the Painter's arson attack. Stormont viewed Deane as an obstacle to a negotiated settlement.

One bright piece of news arrived in late May: the first of Beaumarchais's ships, the *Mercure*, had arrived safely at Portsmouth, New Hampshire, on March 17 with 12,000 muskets, 1,000 barrels of powder, 34 bales of woolen stockings, 2 cases of shoes, and bales more of woolen caps, linen, cloth, blankets, and other items. Two more ships arrived at Falmouth, Massachusetts, and two others reached the West Indies. The *Amphitrite* reached Portsmouth a month later and hastily unloaded a wealth of supplies including 32,840 cannon balls, 129 barrels of powder, 52 cannons, nearly 9,000 grenades, and 219 chests of small arms. The question remained whether the arms would reach the Continental Army in time to stop Burgoyne from plowing through New York.

Almost as soon as word reached the commissioners in Paris that the shipments had arrived safely, the British ambassador had a precise copy of the cargo lists. Nothing at Valentinois escaped Stormont's notice. The accuracy of his information was uncanny. Each time Stormont confronted Vergennes with more evidence of the activities of the commissioners, he fueled Lee's suspicions that someone in Valentinois was working as a spy for Britain. When Lee accused Bancroft of spying, Bancroft was incensed and challenged Lee to a duel, which only Franklin prevented. Franklin and Deane were outraged that Lee would question the honor of a man who had already proved his patriotism by sacrificing his comfortable life in London to serve as the secretary to the American commissioners. Franklin and Deane were convinced that Lee was mentally ill. Lee "must be shaved or bled, or he will actually be mad for life," Deane exclaimed. "It is very charitable to impute to insanity what proceeds from the malignity of his heart; but the Doctor [Franklin] insists upon it. . . ." While it was true that Lee was tormented by many demons he had imagined, Bancroft was not imaginary.

ON TUESDAYS, Bancroft worked late at his desk in Valentinois. He left after dark, carrying a plain satchel, which contained letters he had written to an anonymous woman with whom Bancroft appeared to be carrying on an illicit affair. The lines were carefully spaced in his broad fluid script. He rode by carriage from Passy along the right bank of the Seine into the city, stopping at the Tuileries a little before half past nine. It was not far from the bathhouse where Franklin bathed on Tuesday evenings, but Bancroft was careful to walk in the shadows and avoid the festive lights of the Poitevin. The garden was mostly empty at this hour. Bancroft walked purposefully to a certain tree on the south terrace. Other people did not notice that there was a narrow hole partially obscured under the tree's roots. The hole was made visible in the darkness by a small white card held by a peg, and the peg was tied to a string about one yard in length. Bancroft knelt down and carefully pulled the string, which was tied to a bottle at the other end. He placed his amorous letters into the bottle, corked it, and then quickly lowered it back into the hole under the tree. Before returning to his carriage, he stopped at a nearby boxwood under which another bottle was placed containing instructions for him from Stormont. A short time later, someone from the British embassy arrived to retrieve the letters from the first bottle.

Bancroft was not having an affair with anyone; between the lines of his love letters he had inscribed secret messages in invisible ink. When Stormont brushed a chemical solution onto the pages, the secret messages appeared. All these letters were signed "Dr. Edward Edwards," Bancroft's British code name.

Neither the British Foreign Ministry nor the master spy Paul Wentworth trusted Bancroft entirely. Bancroft had no idea that the ministry had posted other spies who observed the commissioners as well. In this way the British double-checked the accuracy of the information that each spy provided.

One of the other British spies was Joseph Hynson, a sea captain from Maryland. Captain Hynson was a close friend of Deane's personal secretary, William Carmichael. Carmichael was another Marylander visiting Paris when he met Deane in the fall of 1776 and came to work for him. Carmichael lived at the same address as Wentworth at the Hôtel Vauban on the rue de Richelieu. He was a young man from a well-off family who hungered for excitement. He spent an inordinate amount of his free time trolling the seedy side of Paris for adventure, and in such environs he met a lot of seamen. Deane found that Carmichael's taste for disreputable sorts could be useful in recruiting men for the smuggling operations and privateering. Hynson was one of the men Carmichael recruited.

Hynson and Carmichael were soon inseparable friends and roommates. Deane chose Hynson to operate a packet ship that would convey mail expeditiously between Paris and Philadelphia. Deane did not know that Hynson was delivering his mail to the

British for a salary of 200 pounds per year (about $37,000 today). Curiously, Carmichael apparently knew that Hynson was a British agent, yet he remained intimate with Hynson and never exposed his treachery to Deane. Whatever magnetic power Hynson possessed over Carmichael, Carmichael kept his secret. It was not until late 1777 that Deane suspected Hynson was a spy and promptly dismissed him. When he was finally discovered, Hynson confessed and offered his services as a counterspy—for a price—against the British. But Deane refused to speak to him and ordered Carmichael never to see Hynson again. Despite the fact that Hynson was working to undermine their mission, Carmichael continued to meet Hynson in secret.

Lee blamed Deane for the lapse of secrecy caused by Hynson's betrayal, and he continued to suspect Carmichael and Bancroft. The only man Lee trusted completely was his own devoted secretary, John Thornton; yet Thornton was also a British agent. He had been recruited by the British when he went to England to inspect the conditions of the American prisoners of war. Lee himself regularly wrote to his friend Lord Shelburne, in the prime minister's cabinet, describing the latest progress in their talks with France and Spain. Of the three commissioners, only Franklin employed a secretary who was not employed by the British Foreign Ministry—his grandson, Temple Franklin. Franklin and Deane knew the British and the French were spying on their activities, and even if they did not know who was a spy, they did not allow their fear to paralyze them. Franklin acknowledged it was impossible to prevent spying, but he felt he had nothing to fear; there were "no Affairs that I should blush to have made publick." So long as the commissioners behaved honorably, the more that was known of them, the more their reputations would grow. Franklin once commented that even if he knew that his valet were a spy, he would not fire him if he were otherwise a good valet.

———

IN JULY, Ambassador Stormont confronted Foreign Minister Ver-gennes with irrefutable evidence from his spies that two privateers outfitted in France and commissioned by the Americans had seized or destroyed at least eighteen British ships. He accused France of violating its treaty commitments and gave Vergennes one final warn-ing to stop aiding the Americans or Britain would declare war on France. Vergennes was furious with the commissioners for flaunting their activities and jeopardizing France's neutrality. He had warned the commissioners that France could not permit privateers to enter their ports, and they had promised him none would. By violating their pledge, the commissioners had embarrassed Louis XVI. Ver-gennes ordered that the privateers and their ships be detained in France and that the captured vessels be returned to Britain.

Franklin and Deane wrote to Vergennes to apologize for bringing France to the brink of war with Britain—which was, of course, the whole point of their diplomatic mission—and assured Vergennes that American privateers would not attempt to enter French ports in the future. "We are very sensible of the protection afforded to us and to our commerce since our residence in this kingdom," the letter began. "[A]nd it gives us real and great concern when any ves-sels of war appertaining to America, either through ignorance or inattention, do anything that may offend his majesty in the smallest degree." The commissioners would make it known to "our friends residing in your ports" that "our armed vessels" were not welcome in France and should return directly to America "without making any other cruises on the coasts of England."

With the growing threat of war between France and Britain and the fall of Fort Ticonderoga, the British sent a peace envoy to Louis XVI, and the French promised not to provide any assistance to the

Americans. As the London stock exchange roared its approval of the peace accord, the commissioners fell into a deep despondency. Events were moving swiftly against them, and the commissioners were not sure they would be able to persuade France to join an alliance.

Privately, Vergennes wrote to Louis XVI that the time had come either to form an alliance with the Americans or to cut them off completely. France could no longer pretend to be neutral while continuing to wink at the arms smuggling, which had proved wholly inadequate in effecting the outcome of the war. Contrary to the rosy predictions of Beaumarchais and Bonvouloir, it was now clear that the Americans could not win without a commitment of French forces. Nor could France wait to act in tandem with Spain. The new Spanish foreign minister, Conde de Floridablanca, was firmly opposed to war with Britain. If France were prepared to act, she must act on her own. Vergennes was not necessarily arguing in favor of war; but he recognized that the moment of decision had arrived, and that the king could no longer vacillate.

But Louis XVI was not a decisive leader. While he wavered, his ministers quietly began making preparations for war.

MEANWHILE, THE COMMISSIONERS, unaware that Vergennes was moving toward war, were losing hope that France and Spain would ever agree to ratify treaties of commerce and alliance. "There is nothing better to do here than drink," Franklin remarked. "How can we fool ourselves that France might understand America better than Britain? How can we fool ourselves that a monarchy will help republicans, [who have] revolted against their monarch?"

While Deane wrestled with his dark mood, he received a letter the first of October that his wife, Elizabeth, had died the previous

June after a long illness. He had not seen her in almost two years. Though few of their letters survive, there is no doubt that he loved and respected his wife deeply. His only son, Jesse, now age twelve, was left in the care of Deane's brother Barnabas. The distance from his home in Wethersfield only magnified the loss. His brother Simeon, who happened to be visiting Paris on business, tried to comfort him, but grief was a luxury Deane could not afford. The pressure of work and cascading events allowed him no time to dwell on the loss of his wife. "[T]he situation of my Country is sufficient to engross my whole attention, yet the loss I have met with is not the less heavy on my spirits, nor does it fall the lighter on me for coming attended with publick misfortunes & distress." At a time when the Revolution seemed to be failing, he could not permit himself the indulgence of showing "too much Distress & Grief on any thing which effects me individually." Perhaps Deane's stoical attitude to the loss of a loved one was a symptom of his own despondency or of his profound faith that he might hope to see her again in heaven.

Elizabeth's death was a vivid reminder of what Deane had sacrificed to serve his country, and of his distance from home and family. He wrote to his brother Barnabas in Wethersfield asking him to send his sickly son, Jesse, to Europe to be near him. Deane proposed that his son go to London on an English ship, which would presumably be safe from English privateers, and from there be brought to Paris. Jesse was all that Deane had left, and he prayed that the English would not take his son for his father's crimes.

THIRTY

MADAME D'EON'S
TROUSSEAU

Paris, August–October 1777

On a warm evening in mid-August 1777, the Chevalière d'Eon left her home at 38 Brewer Street in Soho and climbed into a carriage in the green-and-crimson uniform of a captain of the French dragoons. She had waited until nightfall to escape London undetected. D'Eon rode down Golden Square and headed toward the docks. For the first time in fourteen years she was heading home to France. The *chevalière* had had enough of England. She still refused to comply with the requirement in the Transaction that she declare her true gender and dress as a woman. One of the people who had wagered she was female was now battling in the English courts to collect, and while she refused to appear in court, the plaintiff, Mr. Hayes, had produced a motley assortment of witnesses who testified in the most humiliating manner as to their personal knowledge of her female anatomy. The whole spectacle had become a farce. She was embarrassed and offended by the proceedings and feared that one of the parties might try to prove their case by having her kidnapped or killed.

In court, Lord Mansfield, the most illustrious judge of the eighteenth century, struggled to remain stone-faced before the parade of witnesses. The blackmailer Morande testified that d'Eon on one occasion had opened her blouse to reveal her breasts, and on another occasion he had found d'Eon in bed one morning and teasingly asked her whether she was male or female. According to Morande, she replied, "Come here and give me your hand," and then surprised him by placing his hand under the covers, which one of the lawyers called "a very singular instance of French levity." One doctor told the court in French that he had examined d'Eon for a "woman's disorder." A surgeon and male midwife claimed that he had examined her "in the very place from which the knowledge of her sex was to derive." The genteel d'Eon refused to corroborate or deny any of it. Lord Mansfield was disgusted with the entire proceeding and expressed the wish that both sides might lose. However, he could find no basis for holding that the wager was illegal or fraudulent. The jury found that d'Eon was indeed female, and awarded the plaintiff 700 pounds (about $129,000 today) for his wager. The day after the jury's decision, d'Eon left London.

According to her account, she went straight to Versailles to clear her name from various slanders against her and to defend her right to wear her military uniform. She also hoped to expose Beaumarchais's duplicity to the king. At Versailles she was ushered into the office of Vergennes, whom she had never met. She wore on her uniform the *Croix de Saint-Louis* to remind the foreign minister of her service to Louis XV. Vergennes was polite but cold. He was unhappy to see that she was still wearing her uniform, which contravened the terms of the Transaction. She requested an audience with the king, but Vergennes insisted that first she must permanently abandon her male identity. D'Eon objected that she had nothing but rags to wear, and no money to buy a new *trousseau*. Vergennes demanded that she change her appearance immediately. To underline this point, the king issued an order two days later prohibiting her from appearing "in any clothes other than those proper to women." D'Eon later wrote that Vergennes also insisted that she undergo an examination by the physicians to the king and queen. D'Eon explained modestly that "in the presence of these two respectable chief doctors, the ghost of Captain d'Eon disappeared like the shadow of the moon. ..." The doctors reported to Vergennes that her "nether regions" were in "good order as if they had always been protected by the House of Austria." D'Eon wrote these words as if to assure her reader that she remained a virgin.

It was vital to French policy that d'Eon complete the transformation into a woman. Only then could Louis XVI be confident that the planned invasion of England would remain secret, and war with Britain could be avoided. For this reason, Vergennes wanted to keep an eye on d'Eon to ensure her compliance with the king's order, and so he arranged for d'Eon to remain at Le Petit-Montreuil, the home of the chief administrator of the foreign ministry, Edmé-Jacques Genet. Marie Antoinette took pity on d'Eon and arranged for her own dressmaker, the incomparable Mademoiselle Rose Bertin, to design d'Eon's new *trousseau*. D'Eon readily accepted the queen's generous offer, and soon d'Eon was being fitted by one of the most famous dressmakers in Europe. D'Eon had corsets designed for her by Madame Barmant, and hats by Mademoiselle Maillot. She went to the wigmaker Sieur Brunet for a three-tiered headdress. Louis XVI spared no expense. D'Eon was no doubt dazzled by the finery and probably delighted once again to be the center of attention. In her memoir she described the experience of putting on a dress for the first time: "All that I know is that my transformation has made me into a new creature!"

As d'Eon later recounted, on October 21, the feast day of Saint Ursula, the patron saint of virgins, Mademoiselle Bertin arrived at seven in the morning accompanied by her two assistants wearing identical straw hats with pink ribbons and carrying d'Eon's new *trousseau.* D'Eon at first was reluctant to undergo the transformation. She feared that women would laugh at her for being "dressed in style and done up like a doll or at the very least like a Vestal Virgin." Mademoiselle Bertin reassured her: "Put aside your concerns about what others will say. Must what the mad say prevent us from being wise?" If d'Eon refused to dress as the king commanded, she would be forced into a convent. "Isn't it better for you to be dressed by me, who has the honor of dressing the Queen," Mademoiselle Bertin remarked, "than by some witch in a convent?" It took more than four hours for d'Eon to be sufficiently scrubbed, brushed, combed, powdered, laced, and dressed to appear for the first time as a woman. Mademoiselle Bertin was delighted with her own creation. "I am glad about having stripped you of your armor and your dragoon skin in order to arm you from head to toe with your dress and finery," she said. D'Eon looked startling in a rich blue satin skirt the color of her eyes. Her blouse revealed large breasts and thick muscular arms bulging through her sleeves. Though d'Eon may have embroidered some of these details, it is known that Bertin dressed d'Eon for the first time as a woman in October 1777.

In order to prepare her to be presented to the king and queen at Versailles, d'Eon was tutored intensively by Madame Genet in the manners, dress, and toilette of a lady. "What does it matter that I was tormented in every conceivable way," d'Eon later recounted, "since it all turned out well for me, and I was not embarrassed in any matter as I tried day and night to resemble my virtuous Duchesse in every way." Her valet was replaced by one of Mademoiselle Bertin's plump maids, who bandaged d'Eon's rough hands at night so that she could have "paws of velvet" with which to greet the queen.

After a month of lessons, d'Eon was ready to be received by Louis XVI and Marie Antoinette. She wore her blue gown with diamond necklace and earrings. Proudly pinned to her chest was the *Croix de Saint-Louis*. Either out of nervousness or lack of practice, she seemed to be teetering in heels, her three-tiered headdress balanced precariously on her head. The king and queen seemed curious, if not entirely charmed to meet the person whom Voltaire called the "Amphibian." To the disappointment of some, d'Eon appeared more masculine than they expected. Her muscularity, assertiveness, and voice seemed incongruous in her frilly dress.

D'Eon's miraculous conversion was the talk of Paris. D'Eon's image was reproduced and widely distributed. She was variously portrayed as a beautiful young woman, the goddess Athena, a bizarrely costumed hermaphrodite, or a grotesque mannish woman. The public embraced her as a contemporary Jeanne d'Arc, a maiden soldier who fought bravely for her country.

When she returned to see her mother in her hometown of Tonnerre, the townspeople celebrated with a huge party and fireworks. Convents around the country invited her to join them, and she stayed for some time with the sisters at Saint-Cyr, a school west of Versailles, for poor noble girls. She liked the lovely setting and was well-received by the sisters, but d'Eon was not yet prepared to take her vows.

D'Eon had become a popular icon. In the finest salons in Paris, men and women came costumed as d'Eon. They performed comic skits mocking Beaumarchais with tasteless scenes of their lovemaking and celebrating d'Eon's feats of strength and heroism. She lunched with Voltaire, supped with aristocrats, and shared box seats with the king's courtiers. Now she boasted that she had triumphed as a woman who proved that "the qualities and virtues by which men are so proud have not been denied our sex."

Madame d'Eon used her new prominence to attack Beaumarchais. She proclaimed that "I owe nothing but contempt to the man who wanted to empty the pockets of English gamblers and make an infamous fortune out of my sex." In a published manifesto she denounced him "to all the women of my day for having tried to enhance his reputation by ruining a woman's," and she mocked anyone "stupid enough to imagine that I would let Pierre-Augustin Caron de Beaumarchais marry me." More ominously, d'Eon publicly referred to Beaumarchais's "embassy to America in order to export enough tobacco from it to make the entire audience [at *The Barber of Seville*] sneeze." D'Eon's public tirade unwittingly threatened to expose the American smuggling operation, which might have forced Vergennes to shut it down. It was one thing for Stormont to suspect France's deception; it would have been something entirely different for all the world to know that France had violated its treaty obligations and lied about it.

D'Eon's slurs infuriated Beaumarchais. He complained bitterly to Vergennes that she was trying to ruin him, but Beaumarchais already knew that she was not a creature who could be silenced. If he reflected on it for a moment, he would have to concede that he would not have been in a position to help the Americans at all had it not been for her intransigence. Vergennes and Louis XVI would not have needed Beaumarchais's intervention but for d'Eon's stubborn refusal to surrender the secret correspondence or her reluctance to appear in a dress.

In any event, Vergennes would not lift a finger against the *chevalière*. There was much more than Beaumarchais's reputation at stake. The king had paid dearly for her transformation. Now that she had publicly appeared as a woman for the first time, she had surrendered her power to blackmail the king in the future. Her allegations that Louis XV had plotted to invade England would no longer seem credible. The king's correspondence would remain secret.

THIRTY-ONE

A LITTLE REVENGE

Paris, December 1777–March 1778

While Paris glowed with the spectacle that d'Eon created, the mood at Valentinois darkened. Rumors circulated that the British had captured Philadelphia, and the despondent commissioners wondered if Congress had escaped. Washington had not won a single battle in almost a year. The last remaining troops in New York were stuck at Saratoga, without arms or ammunition, and faced the onslaught of 9,000 well-armed British regulars under the command of General Burgoyne. The French and Spanish were still unwilling to sign a treaty with the Americans. With few good options, the commissioners now discussed seriously whether to open negotiations toward reconciling with Britain.

On the morning of Thursday, December 4, 1777, Beaumarchais headed to see the commissioners at Valentinois in an angry mood. After unloading arms in New England, Beaumarchais's ship the *Amphitrite* had returned to France with a cargo of rice and indigo. Beaumarchais believed that this cargo, sent by Congress, rightfully belonged to his firm, Rodriguez Hortalez, as partial compensation for the arms shipment. Lee, who was writing to Congress that the arms shipments were all gifts from France, insisted that the rice and indigo were the property of Congress for sale by the commissioners.

Beaumarchais arrived at a particularly inopportune time: the commissioners were having a sobering meeting with their banker, who informed them that their credit was nearly exhausted. In addition, they had recently learned that Captain Lambert Wickes, who had brought Franklin to France, had been lost with his ship and crew off Newfoundland. The Americans' mission was collapsing.

Shortly before noon, the commissioners and their guests heard a disturbance outside. A messenger had arrived in a chaise pulled by three horses with news from America. The messenger, Jonathan Loring Austin, had left Boston Harbor on October 31 on the *Perch* and arrived at Nantes with a message from Congress. The commissioners ran outside. Without waiting for Austin to dismount, Franklin shouted, "Is Philadelphia taken?" Austin replied that it was, and the crestfallen Franklin folded his hands in resignation and turned to walk away. Austin quickly added, "But, sir, I have greater news than that." Franklin could not have imagined what came next. "General Burgoyne and his whole army are prisoners of war!"

The commissioners were too stunned to react. It was impossible that the British commander had surrendered at Saratoga. Hadn't the British general Burgoyne and a massive army surrounded the Continental Army at Saratoga, New York, above Albany? The commissioners had not expected the Continental Army commanded by General Horatio Gates (who had replaced General Schuyler after his humiliating loss of Ticonderoga) to survive this assault. How could Gates have captured Burgoyne's army?

BEAUMARCHAIS'S SUPPLIES had arrived in Portsmouth in May and June of 1777, and the supplies slowly made their way inland through dense forests over the Green Mountains of western Vermont to the Continental soldiers stranded in Saratoga. As news spread that the Continental Army had enough guns, cannons, powder, and uniforms for 30,000 men, a huge number of volunteers flocked to Saratoga. During the month of September the numbers of American troops at Saratoga swelled to more than 12,000.

"Gentleman Johnny" Burgoyne's army lumbered down from Canada, crossing rivers, mountains, and dense forests until its supply line was stretched beyond its limits. Vain, pompous, and foppish, Burgoyne, at fifty-two, was more of a politician, a bon vivant, and a frustrated playwright than a gifted military leader. He did not allow his military duties to distract from his enjoyment of food, drink, and debauchery. And he brought with him to war his mistress, who was married to one of the commissaries. The general did not travel lightly. He marched with more than forty tons of personal baggage carried in thirty wagons pulled by horses and men who often did not have enough to eat.

The American rebels ahead of Burgoyne drove off cattle and burned crops to prevent the British from getting fresh supplies. Burgoyne decided to concentrate his forces by abandoning Fort George, Fort Edward, Lake George, Fort Anne, and Skenesborough. It was a clear signal to General Gates that "the General's Design is to Risque all upon one Rash Stroke." The British had no idea that as their supplies were dwindling, the Continental Army had been reinforced with more than ten thousand fresh soldiers, well armed for the first time since the war began.

It did not help that General Burgoyne made a number of poor

tactical decisions as well. In August, he realized that he could not continue without more horses to carry baggage for himself and his troops. Rather than abandon excess baggage, he sent more than a thousand men on a raid to Bennington, Vermont, to capture horses and other supplies. On August 16, the British forces were trapped in the thick forests around Bennington, where they were attacked by 600 well-armed rebels in a blaze of gunfire. As many as 900 of Burgoyne's troops were killed or captured by rebels, and tons of British supplies were lost.

By October, Burgoyne's army had dwindled to roughly 6,000 men, and a substantial portion of those remaining were German mercenaries who spoke no English. With General Howe's troops occupying Philadelphia, Burgoyne had to rely upon General Henry Clinton, who was guarding the British bases on Rhode Island, to provide reinforcements. Clinton, however, could not believe that Burgoyne really needed the reinforcements and sent only a token force up the Hudson River. In the event, Clinton's troops became stuck in the shallows of the Hudson and never reached Burgoyne.

As the two armies began to form lines outside of Saratoga, the American general Gates quarreled with General Benedict Arnold over tactics. While Gates was competent, he lacked imagination and fought defensively rather than offensively. Arnold, by contrast, an aggressive risk-taker, was one of the most brilliant and experienced tacticians in the Continental Army. Weeks earlier, Gates had refused to credit Arnold in a report to Congress for his prior success, and Gates wrote to the president of Congress that he had given Arnold permission to leave his command. Arnold became enraged and the two men had a furious row on the eve of battle. Out of vanity and jealousy "Granny" Gates dismissed Arnold.

This blunder could have cost Gates victory were it not for the fact that Arnold was too audacious to be bullied by his commanding officer. Nearly all the general officers signed a petition asking General Arnold to stay, and so he did even though Gates had dismissed him. On the morning of October 7, as the British began their attack, General Gates was at breakfast. Arnold asked for permission to advance, and Gates refused him. As the battle unfolded Arnold raced to the front line, shouting at the men to follow him. Gates sent a messenger ordering him to return to camp, but Arnold ignored the order and drove his men right through Burgoyne's line. The British beat a hasty retreat. Arnold would not quit. He charged forward in a storm of grapeshot with his men close behind. He was only stopped when his horse was shot and collapsed on him, breaking his leg. He had been shot and was bleeding heavily. By then the British forces were entirely surrounded, and the battle was over. Ten days later Burgoyne and nearly 6,000 British and Prussian troops surrendered with 42 cannons and nearly 7,000 muskets. Burgoyne was taken prisoner and later exchanged for 1,000 American prisoners of war.

When he returned to London Burgoyne was harshly criticized for his military leadership, but, he found a more receptive audience in the theater. Like Beaumarchais, Burgoyne eventually triumphed as a comic playwright. The critic Horace Walpole wrote that "Burgoyne's battles and speeches will be forgotten; but his delicious comedy of 'The Heiress' still continues to the delight of the stage."

SARATOGA WAS the Americans' single greatest victory and the turning point of the Revolutionary War. After Saratoga, the Revolutionary War effectively ended in the northern states, and the British were confined to the South. Without the armaments sent from France, it would never have happened.

The stunned commissioners wasted no time sending a message to Vergennes announcing the capture of Burgoyne and his army.

They hoped that this was the moment that might finally persuade France to form an alliance. While the commissioners composed a letter asking Vergennes to meet with them as soon as possible, Beaumarchais took care of some personal business. He rushed back to Paris in his two-horse carriage apparently with the intention of profiting by dumping British bonds on the Paris stock exchange before the British defeat became widely known. Traveling at a reckless speed, the carriage hit a rock and overturned, nearly killing Beaumarchais. He suffered a serious concussion and lost so much blood that he was confined to bed for several days. Recuperating at home, Beaumarchais would not let the chance to influence the foreign minister pass. He wrote Vergennes that "The charming news from America spread a balm on my wound." And he was now more hopeful that France would do the right thing: "[S]ome God whispers in my ear that the King will not let such auspicious events to be marred by a total desertion from the true friends of America."

Vergennes was listening to the same God. He sent his secretary Gérard to meet with the commissioners at Valentinois to discuss the possibility of an alliance, just forty-eight hours after Austin's surprise announcement. The commissioners responded with two draft treaties based partly on the drafts submitted by Deane the previous year. First, there was a treaty of commerce to establish trade relations between the two countries. Second, there was a treaty of alliance pledging to provide military aid to the Americans. To avoid detection by the British, the commissioners met Vergennes a few days later at a private house outside Paris. The foreign minister warned them that France still would not act without Spain, and that they would require at least three weeks to send an envoy back and forth between Versailles and Madrid.

The commissioners did not want to wait. They despaired that Spain could be persuaded to act and feared that the moment would pass if France did not commit itself at once. But at this moment luck favored the Americans.

The British agent Paul Wentworth reentered the scene with a secret message for Silas Deane from the British foreign minister. Wentworth wrote to Deane that his hackney coach would be waiting for him the next morning at the gate to Passy. If Deane did not arrive there, Wentworth would look for him at the exhibition in the Luxembourg Gallery, and if they did not meet there, he would be waiting at the Poitevin Baths that evening at six. He would leave a note with the number of his room at the bathhouse. Deane hesitated. Although Franklin thought the bathhouse an ideal location for secret diplomatic negotiations, the venue was a bit too furtive for Deane's tastes. Besides, Lee had forewarned him that Wentworth could not be trusted, and the British ambassador had already discussed the possibility of kidnapping Deane. With Franklin's blessing, Deane responded that he would be at the flat he used in Paris at the Hôtel de Coislin, on the corner of the rue Royale and the Place Louis XV at ten the following morning and would be "glad to see anyone that has Business with Him" then.

Wentworth and Deane met at least twice in Paris, but he made sure that Franklin and Lee were aware of these meetings. On one occasion Wentworth met Deane at the Café St. Honoré, where Deane was having breakfast with Lee and Franklin. Deane excused himself and left with the British agent. There was no question that Deane was behaving openly in front of his colleagues. Wentworth told him that the British government was ready to negotiate to restore the *status quo ante* 1763, allowing the Americans a full measure of home rule under the king. Wentworth offered Deane personal inducement—money, a title, and a government position—if he would help to effect an armistice to end the Revolution.

Though Deane was undoubtedly offended by Wentworth's

clumsy attempt to buy his honor, he shrewdly played along—again, with Franklin's blessing. Franklin also agreed to talk to Wentworth so long as he understood that Franklin would not entertain any offer of personal gain. (Wentworth didn't even consider talking to his former roommate Lee.) Wentworth's subsequent discussion with Franklin was not productive, and Wentworth was surprised by the intensity of Franklin's bitterness toward Britain. He wished that he had a better read on what the commissioners were really thinking and how close they were to an agreement with France, but his sources were engaged elsewhere. Wentworth's chief spy, Bancroft, was himself in London at this moment, trying to unload his government bonds before news of a Franco-American alliance was made public.

It was fortunate that Bancroft was away. He might have warned Wentworth that Deane and Franklin were engaged in a clever deceit. They knew that wherever they went, Louis XVI had spies watching them. Louis would surely know that they were negotiating with the British. France did not want to act without Spain's participation, but the commissioners expected that Spain would not act without France. The only way to induce the French to act was to convince them that the opportunity for defeating Great Britain was passing. Deane and Franklin were feigning interest in a negotiated settlement in order to spur France to action. Deane made sure that Beaumarchais dutifully informed Vergennes of the commissioners' meetings with Wentworth. Beaumarchais urged Vergennes to act quickly before the Americans succumbed to negotiations with Britain.

The ploy worked. Worried that the Americans were on the verge of a settlement, Vergennes persuaded his government to sign the treaties immediately in exchange for a promise that the Americans would never make a separate peace with Britain.

Then, on the eve of the meeting of the French Cabinet to approve the two treaties, a new wrinkle appeared: Versailles learned that the Elector of Bavaria, Maximilian Joseph, the duke who ruled Bavaria under the Holy Roman Empire, had died. There was no chosen successor, and the Austrian Hapsburgs now claimed Bavaria. Frederick the Great, the emperor of Prussia, was prepared to go to war to stop Austria. The Austrian emperor, Joseph II, brother of Marie Antoinette, expected his ally France to join with him in a war against Prussia at exactly the moment that France was committing to fight Britain.

As usual, Louis XVI wavered. The king felt pulled by his obligation to his Austrian-born queen, Marie Antoinette, and his ally Austria. Moreover, Austria could offer France a healthy slice of Flanders as a tempting inducement to fight Prussia. Britain hoped that France would indulge its natural appetite for Flanders and be drawn into a costly war with Prussia, rather than form an alliance with the Americans.

Vergennes, however, resisted temptation. Instead, he proposed that France mediate the dispute between Austria and Prussia. The Austrian emperor might have objected to mediation, except for the fact that he was now facing the risk of war with Russia as well. The Russian empress, Catherine the Great, sided with Prussia and sent 30,000 troops into Galicia to compel Austria to negotiate. As a consequence, Austria and Prussia agreed to mediation; the resulting peace agreement at Teschen averted war on the Continent and ensured that France could devote its full attention to defeating Britain in America.

Once Louis XVI approved the alliance, Vergennes proceeded swiftly to conclude treaties of alliance and commerce with the commissioners. The terms of these treaties were very close to Deane's original proposal in 1776. The treaty of commerce gave both countries the right to export goods to the other on the most favorable terms. The secret treaty establishing a military alliance provided that

if France went to war with Britain, the two parties would not negotiate separately with Britain. France specifically agreed to renounce
any future claim to Canada, while the Americans agreed to respect
French sovereignty over the sugar islands in the West Indies. In addition, the French agreed to loan the Americans another three million livres (approximately $23 million today).

The treaties were signed by all three commissioners on February
6, 1778, at a quiet ceremony in the foreign ministry at the Hôtel de
Lautrec. Franklin put aside his customary brown jacket to wear a
slightly threadbare blue velvet coat to the ceremony. Deane thought
it odd that Franklin did not dress formally for the occasion and
asked him about the worn jacket. Franklin explained that when
he was the agent for Pennsylvania in London, he had worn the same
coat on the day he was subjected to a humiliating inquiry by the
British Parliament. Franklin explained that he wore the coat now
"[t]o give it a little revenge."

The French intended to keep both treaties secret until they were
ratified by both parties. It would take at least until late spring for the
ratified treaties to be returned from America. (The ratified treaties
were eventually exchanged at Versailles on July 17.) No matter what
rumors circulated about these two treaties, the French government
would deny everything. Still, the French had an obligation to inform
their closest ally, Spain. The Spanish foreign minister, Floridablanca,
was visibly angered when he learned that France had acted unilater-
ally. The British government learned about the treaties almost immediately, courtesy of Bancroft.

Though the three commissioners signed the treaties, Lee was
deeply conflicted about the treaties and showed it. First, he complained bitterly that Deane and Franklin had left him out of the
negotiations, which was probably true. Later, he claimed that he had
negotiated them essentially on his own. At the signing ceremony he

squabbled with Deane. Lee insisted that he should sign the treaties twice—as the commissioner to Spain as well as France. Vergennes's secretary Gérard settled the matter: one signature would be sufficient. Even after the signing, Lee was troubled. He secretly wrote to his close friend Lord Shelburne, a member of the prime minister's cabinet, informing him about the treaties, in violation of the pledge to keep both treaties secret for the time being. Lee wrote to Shelburne that "If the old one [Britain] wishes to preserve some interest it should act without delay." Apparently, Lee hoped that Shelburne would offer the commissioners a negotiated settlement with Britain to spare America from entering into an entangling alliance with France. By disclosing the treaty in this manner, Lee risked sabotaging the alliance at the outset.

Deane realized that Lee and his allies in Congress might try to undermine the alliance with France. Seizing the opportunity, Deane pressed the foreign ministry to make the treaty public as a way of putting Britain on notice and making it harder for the Lee-Adams Junto to reverse course. On March 10, 1778, the French ambassador to London, Noailles, officially informed Lord Weymouth, the British secretary of state, of the treaty of commerce with the Americans. Even though Weymouth already had the complete texts of both treaties, he vented his outrage. France, he fumed, had insulted Britain by interfering in the American colonies in violation of treaty commitments. George III declared that the treaty was an act of aggression and recalled Ambassador Stormont from Paris. That was precisely the response that Vergennes had hoped to elicit from the British king, and he breathed a sigh of relief to be rid of Stormont and his incessant demands. Stormont left so quickly he had no time to pack all of his household goods. Instead, he placed an advertisement in the Paris papers, listing all the items for sale, including "A large quantity of table linen, which were never used." The French joked that the thrifty ambassador had never used his tablecloths because he never fed anyone.

Now that the treaty of commerce was no longer secret, Louis XVI felt that he could formally acknowledge the American emissaries. On the first day of spring, 1778, the commissioners arrived at the king's apartments at Versailles. Deane and Lee wore the prescribed formal dress for the occasion; Franklin, however, insisted on wearing his trademark brown coat and white blouse to make a statement to the French monarch about American democratic values. Louis XVI, however, was even more casually attired than Franklin: the king received the commissioners in his dressing room at Versailles with a small circle of his ministers. The king did not look like he was ready to receive foreign dignitaries. His hair hung down undressed to his shoulders. In this intimate setting, the king told the commissioners, in French, that "I shall be very happy that Congress be assured of my friendship," and then he left. The commissioners were somewhat bewildered by this display of informality. Lee was especially offended by the lack of dignity accorded to the Americans, but Franklin and Deane shrugged it off. Afterward, Foreign Minister Vergennes led the Americans past a cheering crowd to a formal luncheon in his apartments at the palace.

For Silas Deane, this day was the crowning achievement of years of solitary and anxious effort. It was, he wrote to an associate, "a glorious day for America." The alliance was secure. The French would soon be fighting side by side with the Americans. The Revolution would survive.

THIRTY–TWO

BETRAYED

Paris, March–April 1778

Unfortunately, Deane could not linger long on his moment of triumph. A fortnight before the commissioners' reception at Versailles, Deane had received a letter dated December 8 from the Committee of Foreign Affairs informing him that he was being recalled to Philadelphia. Congress had appointed John Adams to take his place. Deane showed the letter to Franklin. There was no explanation. None was needed. It was clear to Deane and Franklin that his recall was the consequence of Lee's unrelenting attacks on Deane contained in Lee's letters to his brothers and the growing influence of the Lee-Adams Junto in Congress. Neither Franklin nor Deane bothered to inform Lee that Deane had been recalled; they would not give Lee the satisfaction of knowing he had vanquished his rival.

Ten days before his dressing-room audience with the king, Deane personally informed Vergennes's secretary, Gérard, of his recall. Gérard was sorry to see Deane recalled, and he worried that the Lee-Adams Junto would try to undermine the alliance. Deane seized the opportunity to ask the foreign ministry to give the American navy ships to replace dozens of vessels lost to the British navy. After some discussion, the French Cabinet agreed to make the Americans a gift of an entire fleet of ships under the command of Vice-Admiral Comte d'Estaing. The fleet would bring Deane home triumphantly with an additional gesture of France's recognition—the first French minister plenipotentiary to the Americans, Vergennes's own secretary, Conrad-Alexandre Gérard. By sending Deane home with the French ambassador and a fleet of powerful warships, France was making a bold gesture of support for Deane in recognition of his singular role in forging the alliance.

When Deane informed Beaumarchais of his recall, the Frenchman bitterly blamed Lee. Beaumarchais wrote to Vergennes that Lee had been jealous of Deane from the outset. From the first time Beaumarchais had met Lee over dinner at the Lord Mayor's mansion, Lee had made it clear that "His design has ever been to choose between France and England the power that would more surely promote his fortunes." To that end, Lee needed to "dispose of a colleague so formidable, because of his intelligence and his patriotism, as Mr. Deane."

Beaumarchais also wrote to Congress in support of Deane. "I certify that if my zeal, my money advances and shipments of munitions and merchandise have been agreeable to the noble Congress, their gratitude is due to the indefatigable exertions of Mr. Deane throughout this commercial affair." In the same letter, Beaumarchais exposed the inconsistencies in Lee's allegations against Deane. First, Lee alleged that all the arms were a gift from France to America. Beaumarchais wrote Congress that he had coded letters in which Lee had first negotiated with Beaumarchais to send supplies to the Americans in exchange for top-quality Virginia tobacco. Second, Lee charged that Deane had abused his power by commissioning military officers over

Lee's objections. But Beaumarchais responded that Lee had written to Beaumarchais from London asking him to send engineers and military officers to aid the Americans. Beaumarchais's conclusion was that Lee was simply lying to discredit Deane.

Once Deane received Congress's order to return to Philadelphia, both Deane and Franklin greeted Lee with silence. Franklin knew that Lee had conspired against both of them and wanted nothing to do with Lee. In response, Lee accused Franklin of trying to hide Deane's recall from Louis XVI by not disclosing it prior to the king's reception at Versailles. (Lee did not know that Deane had already been to see Gérard.) Franklin tried ignoring Lee, which agitated Lee even more. Lee blamed Franklin for keeping him in the dark about Deane's recall, and even accused Franklin of intentionally misleading him. "Had you studied to deceive the most distrusted and dangerous enemy of the Public," Lee wrote to Franklin, "you cou'd not have done it more effectually." Lee insisted he had a right to know and that Franklin's continued silence was an "indignity" and one of the "many affronts of this kind which you have thought proper to offer me."

Franklin replied, "I am old, cannot have long to live, have much to do and no time for Altercation." After suffering months of Lee's outbursts, however, Franklin's patience was finally exhausted, and he decided it was time to tell Lee honestly what he thought of him:

> If I have often receiv'd and borne your Magisterial Snubbings and Rebukes without Reply, ascribe it to the right Causes, my Concern for the Honour and Success of our Mission, which would be hurt by our Quarrelling, my Love of Peace, my Respect for your good Qualities, and my Pity of your Sick Mind, which is forever Tormenting itself, with its Jealousies, Suspicions and Fancies that others mean you ill, wrong you, or fail in Respect for you. If you do

not cure your self of this Temper it will end in Insanity, of which it
is the Symptomatick Foreruner, as I have seen in several Instances.

Franklin was disgusted by Lee's attacks on Deane and wanted to set
the record straight, even though he realized Lee was targeting him
as well. He wrote to the president of Congress, Henry Laurens, a
member of the Lee-Adams Junto, in defense of Deane. Franklin attributed Deane's recall to "some misrepresentations from an enemy
or two at Paris and at Nantes." Franklin could not have been clearer
that he was referring to the Lee brothers. Though Franklin was
confident that Deane would vindicate himself, as a "witness of his
public conduct," Franklin judged him "a faithful, active, and able
Minister, who, to my knowledge, has done, in various ways, great
and important services to his country."

As the day of Deane's departure approached, Vergennes sent
Deane a note for the president of Congress "to give my testimony to
the zeal, activity, and intelligence with which [Deane] has merited
the esteem of the King." Vergennes wished Deane well and prayed
"that you may find in your own country the same sentiments which
you inspired in France." As an expression of the king's regard for
Deane, Vergennes enclosed a gold snuffbox set with diamonds and
painted with Louis XVI's portrait. The foreign minister added, "You
will not, I presume, Sir, refuse to carry to your country the image of
its most zealous friend."

Without saying goodbye to Lee, Deane left Paris secretly on
April 1. The French feared that the fleet would be attacked by British
ships if they knew when it was leaving and where it was headed.
As Deane was leaving Paris he did not know that John Adams had
just arrived on the frigate *Boston* at Bordeaux. Adams was accompanied by Deane's thirteen-year-old son, Jesse, whom he was

bringing to see his father for the first time in two years. Deane missed them entirely.

Deane traveled by coach, under an assumed name, first to Aix and then through Marseilles to the tiny port of La Seine on the Bay of Toulon, where he met Gérard. On the evening of April 13, when the wind blew favorable, a small boat picked him up to take him a mile out to the *Languedoc*. This ninety-gun vessel was possibly the greatest warship of its time. Under the command of Vice-Admiral d'Estaing, the *Languedoc* would be the flagship of a fleet that included 4,000 troops on twelve ships of the line with at least seventy-four guns each and four swift frigates. The British had no ships as big or as powerful as these.

The evening breeze felt warm, and in the moonlight Deane could make out a forest of masts with their sails billowing open. Soon they were under way, and Deane felt a strange sense of calm. He knew they might be stopped by the British blockade; he knew that he faced a hostile inquisition in Philadelphia. Still, he found comfort knowing he was coming home at last with an armada "which will convince America and the World of the Sincere Friendship of France." He was "happy at the great prospect" before him. Under a sky flecked with stars he headed swiftly into darkness.

THIRTY—THREE

TO OPPOSE A TORRENT
IS MADNESS

Philadelphia, July—December 1778

I n later years Deane could look back in amazement on the cascade of events that tumbled after the first shipment of French arms arrived in New Hampshire: the capture of Burgoyne at Saratoga, the treaties of commerce and alliance with France, and the arrival of the French fleet. These events were followed in July with France's declaration of war against Britain. Within the year, Spain had entered the war as well. Later Britain declared war on the Netherlands for supporting the French and the Americans. Soon Britain would be fighting in the West Indies, India, Africa, and the Mediterranean. In the space of two years, the American War of Independence became a world war with Britain fighting on many fronts, and Britain's victory was no longer assured.

On July 2, after a year in exile, Congress rode back into Philadelphia with great fanfare. The British forces occupying the city had heard that Admiral d'Estaing was approaching with a French fleet, and they marched from Philadelphia to New York City to avoid being trapped by the French. The redcoats left the city in ruins. Hundreds of shops and homes, including Franklin's, had been looted or destroyed by the British. Remnants of buildings were strewn in the streets. Market stalls were emptied, and what few goods were available were too expensive for the few inhabitants who had remained behind—the poor, sick, wounded, and elderly. Congress had to postpone returning to Independence Hall for several weeks until the building was thoroughly scrubbed. The British had used the building as a military hospital and left behind an insalubrious pile of rotting corpses to greet the returning delegates. The war had proved far costlier than Congress had ever imagined in the first intoxicating breath of independence.

A week later a fleet of magnificent ships flying the flag of France sailed into Delaware Bay below Philadelphia. From his cabin Deane wrote to the president of Congress, Henry Laurens, that the *Languedoc* had landed under the command of Admiral Comte d'Estaing and carried His Excellency, the French minister plenipotentiary, Conrad-Alexandre Gérard. Deane tactfully advised Congress on the appropriate protocol for receiving a foreign diplomat, including the proper form of salute, and asked Congress to advance the French minister the equivalent of 20,000 livres (about $154,000 today) for his expenses. That Sunday, members of Congress, attired in their best suits and sweating profusely under a blazing sun, rode down the river on a barge rowed by a dozen soldiers in scarlet uniforms trimmed with silver. When the assembled delegates caught sight of the ships' towering masts shimmering in the heat like a mirage, they gasped. Americans had never seen ships this large with so many powerful guns. Four thousand French troops crowded the decks of the sixteen vessels—a number equal to roughly half of the entire Continental Army at that time.

To Gérard, who was accustomed to the grandeur of Versailles, the homely scene of the seat of government floating on a barge might have seemed somewhat comical. These Americans were as unpretentious as Franklin's fur cap. They looked like children pretending to be grown up. But he found their sincerity and humility deeply affecting. Gérard was received with a fifteen-gun salute at a ceremony chaired by Laurens, whose South Carolina accent must have sounded incomprehensible to French ears. Despite the heat, the crowd roared enthusiastically, and after the ceremony they proceeded into Philadelphia, where the delegates toasted the French monarch over drinks at the City Tavern, on Second Street.

Gérard's arrival could not have been better timed to renew a sense of dignity and hope to the people of Philadelphia after suffering so much hardship. "Who would have thought," gushed a correspondent from one local paper, that the American colonies "claimed by every pettyfoging lawyer in the house of Commons, and every cobbler in the beer houses of London, as part of their property," would after three years of war "receive an Ambassador from the most powerful monarchy in Europe."

Over dinner that night Deane sat next to his old friend General Benedict Arnold, the hero of Saratoga, who was now posted to Philadelphia as military governor. Arnold had not seen Deane since they had conspired to capture Fort Ticonderoga three years earlier. Their public service had complemented each other: Deane had provided financing for the assault on Ticonderoga and arms for the battle at Saratoga, the two victories that had secured Arnold's military reputation. Arnold invited Deane and Minister Gérard to stay with him until they found suitable accommodations, and they accepted gratefully. Some people already suspected that Arnold was secretly sympathetic to the British Crown, but that seemed patently absurd to Deane. Only later would Deane's friendship with Arnold prove inconvenient.

Once settled into Arnold's comfortable home, Deane was eager to address Congress and clear his name. Congress, however, was not interested in hearing from him. They did not expect an explanation or a defense of his conduct. It was far from clear, even to Congress, why they had recalled Deane. There were so many insinuations against Deane, but no specific allegations or solid evidence of any kind. A vague cloud of doubt had enshrouded Deane, and neither he nor Congress could see a way out of it.

Meanwhile, delegates in Congress were openly questioning Arnold's loyalty. The attack was led by Joseph Reed, an influential delegate who became President of Pennsylvania. Reed was single-minded in his pursuit of suspected Loyalists, and not coincidentally, he was also an outspoken opponent of Deane and Robert Morris. Reed was especially outraged that Arnold was courting the daughter of a prominent Loyalist. (She later became his wife.) Moreover, Arnold as the military governor of Pennsylvania represented a potential challenge to the authority of the state government and to Reed himself. Reed arranged to publish scurrilous assaults on Arnold's character in the *Pennsylvania Packet*. Eventually, Reed pressured Congress to order that Arnold be subject to court-martial on a range of dubious criminal charges. Feeling falsely accused and unjustifiably maligned, Arnold in May 1779 sold himself to the British as a secret agent. Deane's association with Arnold further tainted his own reputation.

ONE OF THE REASONS often mentioned for Deane's recall was that he had issued military commissions without authority. American military officers resented the generous terms Deane had offered to some French officers. Of course, Deane commissioned these officers at the request of Vergennes, on whom Deane depended for the continuation of arms. Congress did not appreciate that these commissions helped to cement the relationship with France.

Samuel Adams objected that Deane had no authority to issue any commissions "and yet he sent us over Majors, Colonels, Brigadiers & Majors General in Abundance & more than we knew what to do with, of his own creating, till at length mr. Du Coudray arrivd." Major General du Coudray was the last straw. Deane was hardly surprised to hear that du Coudray was as inept as he was demanding; after all, Deane had tried to prevent du Coudray from ever leaving France.

Rather than acknowledge the many *talented* officers Deane had recruited—including some of Washington's most valued generals, Lafayette, de Kalb, and Steuben—the Lee-Adams Junto exploited the appointment of du Coudray as a pretext for recalling Deane. And if Congress were genuinely opposed to these commissions, why didn't Congress object to the dozens of commissions that were subsequently issued by Franklin after he arrived in France?

In truth, Deane's recall was a naked power grab by the Lee-Adams Junto, which for the moment held the balance of power in a deeply polarized Congress. The junto included most of the southern and New England delegates, who viewed men like Deane, Franklin, and Morris as constituting a dangerous alliance of commercial and financial interests based in New York and Philadelphia. Planters, like the Lees and their southern brethren, had long felt that they were exploited by the mercantile class that controlled foreign trade out of cities like Philadelphia. The economic difficulties brought on by the Revolution and the collapse of the Continental currency had sparked a backlash against financiers. The Lees still wanted revenge against Franklin and his cronies for upending their development plans in the Ohio River valley. The Lees and the Adamses shared a deep suspicion of France, and they wanted control of foreign policy.

The Lee-Adams Junto saw no need for a congressional inquiry into Deane's conduct. No matter what Deane said in his own defense, his critics had already judged him. And they condemned Deane for a bad character rather than for any specific crimes. Richard Henry Lee dispensed with even the pretense of civility: "The wickedness of Deane and his party exceeds all belief, and must in the end fail them notwithstanding the Art with which they clothe themselves."

The real goal of the Lee-Adams Junto was to recall both Deane and Franklin and to strip Morris of his power in Congress; Deane was merely the first step. Richard Henry Lee thought Franklin was "immoral" and assured his brother that "The Doctor is old and must soon be called to account for his misdeeds." Similarly, Ralph Izard wrote Congress that Franklin's

> abilities are great and his reputation high; removed as he is to so considerable a distance from the observation of his constituents, if he is not guided by principles of virtue and honor, those abilities and that reputation may produce the most mischievous effects. In my conscience I declare to you, that I believe him under no such internal restraints, and God knows that I speak the real unprejudiced sentiments of my heart.

But the attacks on Franklin's integrity were a tactical mistake. The Lees and their party were overreaching; the delegates were not about to condemn their most distinguished colleague. Eventually, the assault on Franklin's character gave Deane and his allies the opportunity to argue that the junto was now threatening a genuine American icon.

AFTER BEING ORDERED to return to Philadelphia at the earliest possible opportunity, Deane waited more than a month before Congress agreed to allow him to appear. His testimony was then postponed three times before he was invited to address Congress in late August. Over two humid mornings, Congress listened as Deane reported on his two years of service. He spoke from a few notes and memory, but he was not allowed to take questions from delegates. In his thick drawl President Laurens warned Deane darkly that he would reserve judgment until Congress heard from the "other side," although it was far from clear what the "other side" would have to say. No one had alleged that Deane had done anything wrong, apart from appointing too many French officers at high salaries. Deane then withdrew to await Congress's orders. But none came.

In September 1778, Arthur Lee and Ralph Izard wrote to Congress accusing Deane for the first time of financial improprieties. Their letters contained only general statements about Deane's character and their suspicions, without pointing to any specific transaction or offering any proof. More significantly, Richard Henry Lee came forward to announce that William Carmichael, Deane's secretary, was in Philadelphia and possessed information about Deane's financial abuses. Specifically, Carmichael claimed that Deane had used public funds to purchase the privateer *Tartar* and that Deane would receive a share in the profits from the vessel's privateering. (In fact, Deane and Morris together had invested their own money in the *Tartar* for a share of its profits, which was a perfectly legitimate form of investment that posed no conflict with Deane's public role.) Richard Henry had learned of Carmichael's allegations through two

American merchants who had dealings with Carmichael in France. Deane had retained Carmichael in his employ despite Carmichael's questionable relationship to the British spy Captain Hynson, and Deane had defended Carmichael against Arthur Lee's charge that Carmichael himself was a British spy. Now the troubled young man had turned against Deane, and Richard Henry was confident that he could provide the evidence needed to establish Deane's guilt.

Congress called Carmichael to testify about Deane's finances, but under questioning from Deane's critics, Carmichael's confused allegations collapsed. In fact, Carmichael confessed that he knew of no particular instance in which Deane abused the public's trust for his own advantage. Deane's critics quickly realized that Carmichael was not helping to build a case against Deane. James Lovell, a delegate from Massachusetts and one of Deane's harshest critics, admitted that "Mr. Carmichael seems rather to perplex than clear our Views." Richard Henry Lee suspected that Carmichael had changed his story and now accused his own witness of conspiring with Deane to hide his crimes.

For Deane, defending himself against unspecified allegations of improper financial dealings seemed nearly impossible. He had left France in March not knowing of these allegations, which were not made until the following September. If he had known, it might have been possible to assemble all the financial records and receipts for hundreds of purchases, but the documents he needed were scattered among vendors and agents all over France. Even if Deane had gathered the documents, it would have been foolish for him to travel past British naval lines carrying documentary evidence of his smuggling operations, and it would have been nearly impossible to explain hundreds of transactions to Congress's satisfaction in any case. He had been instructed by the Secret Committee to maintain the appearance of a private merchant and to continue his private business.

For example, he had contracts to purchase goods for the Indians on behalf of the Congress. Were these public or private transactions? Deane had purposefully commingled funds so as to make it impossible for spies to track his arms dealing.

What made the allegations against him especially outrageous was the fact that Congress had never transferred any funds to Deane or paid for any of the arms Deane procured. The Secret Committee had promised Deane a sales commission of five percent on such transactions to support himself while he was in Europe, but nothing was ever paid. The Secret Committee had advanced Deane $200,000 in Continental currency to buy gifts for the Indians, but Congress knew that their paper money had proved nearly worthless. Congress also knew that most of the notes it had given Deane had been rejected by the banks, so that Deane was forced to rely on his own funds and credit to get by until Franklin arrived. Franklin brought with him goods and currency worth nearly 10,000 pounds sterling (about $1.85 million today), and those funds were overseen by all three commissioners. Deane provided Congress with a detailed statement by the commissioners' banker, Ferdinand Grand, who handled all their funds. Grand's statement showed that the commissioners had received a total of 3.75 million livres during Deane's time in Paris and had expended 4.05 million livres (roughly $31 million today). Contrary to Arthur Lee's charges, Lee had access to these figures and had approved nearly all of the expenditures during his time as commissioner. In fact, Lee himself had complained he could not survive on his stingy allowance as commissioner of 3,000 livres (roughly $23,000 today).

If Deane had taken public funds, what did he do with them? He clearly had not spent significant funds on his living expenses. He lived modestly throughout his tenure in Paris, and since Franklin's arrival he had lived free at Valentinois. He had spent far more of his own funds to support himself and to acquire supplies than he had received from Congress. Although two years earlier Deane was a wealthy merchant, his own finances now showed that he was seriously in need of money and depended on the support of his friends, including Franklin.

Some of Deane's contemporaries also charged that Deane invested some of his own money with Bancroft and Beaumarchais in the London stock exchange hoping to profit by short selling British stocks when the British suffered defeats in North America. There is no evidence that Deane received significant profits from stocks. Moreover, even if this charge were true, there would have been no conflict between his duties as an American agent and his willingness to short British stocks.

After more than five months and a dozen unanswered appeals to Congress for an opportunity to respond to the charges against him, Deane decided that he would appeal to the public directly. Deane thought that the public should know about the factionalism that divided Congress. "I feel it a Duty which I owe my honest and abused Countrymen," Deane explained to his brother Barnabas. In December, Deane published a blistering broadside in *The Pennsylvania Packet* attacking the Lee-Adams Junto and exposing to public view for the first time the machinations of Congress's foreign policymaking. In a 3,000-word essay Deane exposed the nasty underside of American foreign policy and the fractious politics of the Lee-Adams Junto in Congress. Deane wrote that he had decided to make public his grievances not for his own purposes, but to protect the "general weal" from being subordinated to the ambitions of certain individuals. "While it was safe to be silent, my lips were closed. Necessity hath opened them, and necessity must excuse this effort to serve, by informing you." In an age when it was still routine for even major figures like Hamilton and Franklin to publish under pseudonyms, Deane's address was a daring move.

Deane described his relationship to his two colleagues in Paris: "honored with one" and "saddled with another." He bluntly traced the long history of his difficulties with the Lee brothers: "I shall make no other observation on the fruitful topic of their manners and deportment than this, that unfortunately for you [the public], those gentlemen so highly elevated, and so widely entrusted, gave universal disgust to the nation whose assistance we solicited." Deane disclosed that Arthur Lee had shared secrets with Lord Shelburne and expressed his "contempt" for France, causing the Americans great embarrassment. Lee "was dragged into the treaty [with France] with the utmost reluctance," and even though the commissioners had agreed to keep it secret, Lee disclosed it to the British government through Lord Shelburne.

Deane explained how Lee's misrepresentations had led to his recall, and how Lee's friends in Congress had denied Deane any opportunity to respond to the unsubstantiated charges made against him. Yet Congress never inquired into the allegation, made by Deane, that Arthur Lee was involved with Dr. William Berkenhout, an alleged British spy jailed in Philadelphia who was mysteriously released with the intervention of Richard Henry Lee. In closing, Deane warned his countrymen that the Lees and their friends were threatening to undermine America's reputation in Europe.

The effect of Deane's broadside was unimaginable.

THIRTY–FOUR

SAFETY LIES
IN SILENCE

Philadelphia and Paris,
December 1778–May 1781

Still in Paris, John Adams read Deane's broadside and thought that it was "one of the most wicked and abominable productions that ever sprang from a human heart." Deane had blown the whistle on Congress's dirty secrets. There was now "no alternative but the ruin of Mr. Deane or the ruin of his country." Adams wrote that Deane should be "hunted down for the benefit of mankind." President Laurens accused Deane of insulting the dignity of Congress, and he demanded that Congress appoint a committee to censure him. When Congress hesitated, Laurens resigned as president in an angry huff. The next day the delegates chose New York delegate John Jay, who happened to be a good friend of Deane's, as the new president.

Thomas Paine, who was a friend of Richard Henry Lee, retaliated against Deane's broadside in a series of vicious articles attacking Deane. Paine repeated the charges that Deane was unfit for public service and had confused his personal affairs and official business at the public's expense. Further, Paine, the fiery author of *Common Sense* who had helped to mobilize the people for revolution, now accused Deane of disturbing the peace by publishing his views. A diplomat, wrote Paine, "ought to be as silent as the grave." "[W]ho would trust a person with a secret," Paine asked, "who shewed such a talent for revealing?"

Paine accused Deane of amassing a fortune from underhanded deals with Willing, Morris, and Co. Paine's charges were too much for Robert Morris. He responded that in fact Deane had only three commercial transactions with Morris's company, and all of these involved the purchase of armaments for the war. Morris attacked Paine, and then Laurens attacked Morris. The insults and counter insults eventually led to a duel between Laurens and another delegate.

Months of bitter back-and-forth charges between the allies of Deane and Lee fractured any semblance of consensus in Congress over the conduct of diplomacy and exposed the conflict to the public. For the first time, two parties had emerged in Congress with opposing views regarding foreign affairs: the radical Lee-Adams faction favored "militia diplomacy" and keeping a cautious distance from all European powers; the friends of Deane, Morris, and Franklin supported a pragmatic engagement with France and other governments wherever useful.

There in a nutshell was the real issue: America's relationship with France. Deane, Franklin, and Morris welcomed the support of the only ally that could check Britain's military superiority. The Lee-Adams Junto viewed France through the lens of English history as morally tainted. They feared the corrupting influence of the French monarchy, the Catholic Church, and Continental politics. They might reluctantly accept French aid, but they suspected French motives. It was an emotionally uncomfortable situation to be compelled to depend upon a foreign nation you regarded as anathema to English government, culture, and religion. This was especially true for Anglophiles like the Lees. Since Deane and Franklin were primarily responsible for the Franco-American alliance, the bitterness of their attacks on Deane may have been in part a consequence of their displaced anxiety toward France.

Without a trace of irony the Anglophile Lees and their friends characterized Deane's supporters—who leaned toward France—as "Tories" while describing themselves as "Whigs." And they blamed the Tories for polarizing Congress by forming their own political party. Samuel Adams charged that "artful Tories, who would cordially receive such a character [as Deane] into the Bosom of their councils," were conspiring to undermine independence against the "honest and zealous Whigs." (Years after the Revolution, some of the members of these factions of Whigs and Tories formed the twin nuclei of the Federalist and Republican parties, respectively, and they remained bitterly divided over the question of Franco-American relations.)

Deane's broadside had another more immediate consequence: his complaint that he had been denied the opportunity to defend himself against unsubstantiated charges shamed the delegates into agreeing to hear his side of the story. On Wednesday, December 23, 1778, Deane arrived at Congress at nine in the morning. It must have given him some comfort that the president's chair was now occupied by Jay. He was also surprised and pleased to see his friend, General Washington, who happened to be visiting. Snow was expected. The weather outside was biting cold, and inside extra logs were tossed on the fireplace.

For three days, as the logs crackled and embers flew, Deane read into the record a narrative of more than 20,000 words that faithfully recorded all of his activities from the time he left Philadelphia in 1776 to the present, including detailed descriptions of many of the purchases and shipments he made, at least to the extent he could reconstruct them in the absence of his account books. It was a confident and politic performance in which he was careful to understate his own contributions in deference to Franklin, Beaumarchais, and the French government. He avoided personal attacks against the Lee brothers, and he repeatedly praised Congress. At the conclusion, he answered the charges of public corruption head on:

> The settlement of the public accounts, which I am exceedingly anxious for, will shew, whether, during that time, I have applied one shilling of the public moneys to my own use. It is well known that my private fortune in America, which at the time I left my country was moderate, has not been augmented, but the contrary, by my absence; and I now assure Congress that, except [for] a few pieces of silk sent out to the care of my brother, the effects of which he left with me, and for which, I am accountable, and one hundred guineas or louis d'ors for pocket money, I brought nothing with me from France excepting my clothes.

If Congress reflected on the opportunities he had for amassing wealth from his position, he argued, it would realize that "I well knew I could have made a fortune equal to my wants or wishes. I never lost a moment on the subject."

The moderates in Congress were favorably impressed by Deane's narrative. This only enraged Lee's faction. Francis Lightfoot Lee wrote to his brother, Richard Henry, that "[a]lthough Deane had two Colleages, the word *We*, is never used in his Narrative, *I* did everything. *I* procured all the supplies, bro't about the Alliance, procured D'Estaings fleet, conducted them to America, discover'd the

designs of the Enemy & baffled them, in short I have establish'd the
Liberty and independance of America."

Tom Paine, who did not hesitate to invent facts to win arguments, disputed that Deane had anything to do with the delivery of
arms that had proved decisive at Saratoga. In a new series of articles, Paine claimed that the French had promised the arms as a gift
before Deane even arrived in France. This, of course, was the same
phony story that Arthur Lee had circulated. In fact, Paine, as the
secretary to the Committee on Foreign Affairs, had access to correspondence that proved that Lee was lying and that all of the arms
and supplies for 30,000 men arrived through the efforts of Deane
and Beaumarchais.

At this point, the French ambassador, Gérard, inserted himself
into the controversy in defense of Deane. Gérard told Congress that
Paine had contradicted the official account of the government of
France: namely, that France had not provided any arms prior to
the signing of the treaties. The Deane affair now threatened relations with France and the war with Britain. Rather than issuing a
public statement himself, Gérard demanded that Congress clarify
the record. Congress feared alienating America's first ally. Some delegates insisted that Paine must be censured to preserve the Franco-
American alliance. Deane's friend, Pennsylvania delegate Gouverneur
Morris, denounced Paine as a "meer Adventurer from England without Fortune, without Family or Connections ignorant even of
Grammar."

On January 12, 1779, Congress unanimously resolved to disavow
Paine's statements, and Paine was removed as secretary to the Committee on Foreign Affairs. More important, Congress unanimously
affirmed for the first time that "the supplies shipped in the *Amphitrite, Seine,* and *Mercury* were not a present," and that the French
king "did not preface his alliance with any supplies whatever sent to

America." In effect, Congress implied that Deane and Beaumarchais had told the truth and that Arthur Lee had lied about the nature of the arms shipments from France.

While Deane waited for Congress to clear his name and authorize his return to France, Gérard informed Jay in February that Spain was prepared to enter the war against Britain unless Britain agreed to a settlement mediated by Spain. This was great news, and Gérard wanted Congress to prepare for peace talks by clarifying the terms it would insist on in any peace treaty. For this purpose, a committee was appointed.

The committee recommended to Congress that at a minimum Britain should be required to recognize the independence of the States, withdraw its troops up to the Canadian border, respect the freedom to trade at New Orleans, and allow Americans to fish off the coast of Newfoundland. Of these terms, the only one that was highly contentious was the insistence on fishing rights. While fishing was a major industry in parts of New England, the mid-Atlantic and southern states had no economic interest in Canadian fisheries. Since Britain's defeat at Saratoga, the war was focused on the southern states. Why should they bear the burden of continuing the war solely to gain access to fishing rights for New England? Gérard, too, doubted that France and Spain would be willing to prolong the war for the sake of Boston fishermen. In the end, President Jay finessed a compromise: Congress would not insist on fishing rights, but it would affirm that in the event that the British prevented fishing off the coast of Newfoundland, the States were prepared to oppose Britain by force. At the end of February, Congress communicated its peace terms to Spain.

The Committee on Peace Terms then recommended to Congress that the commissioners Franklin, Arthur Lee, William Lee, and Ralph

Izard all be recalled from Europe and a new minister plenipotentiary be appointed to negotiate peace with Britain. Congress heatedly debated these recalls for five weeks, and ultimately agreed to recall William Lee and Ralph Izard. Only eight delegates voted to recall Franklin. Throughout the spring the recall of Arthur Lee became the most contentious issue. Although twenty-two delegates voted to recall him, and only fourteen delegates voted to retain him, the States were evenly divided so that Lee was spared a recall by a single vote.

This signaled that at least a majority of delegates in Congress no longer supported the Lee-Adams Junto. Deane's friends and those who favored a closer alliance with France were gaining strength. Partly, delegates were embarrassed by the public revelations that attended the skirmish between Deane, Paine, and Morris, and partly, delegates recognized that the French alliance was too important to the war effort. Arthur Lee was not a popular figure around whom to garner support. Even members of the junto privately voiced doubts about Lee's character. John Adams wrote to Massachusetts delegate James Lovell that Lee's "Countenance is disgusting, his Air is not pleasing, his Manners are not engaging, his Temper is harsh, sour and fierce, and his Judgment of Men and Things is often wrong." The junto was losing delegates, and some of the key leaders of the junto, including Samuel Adams and Richard Henry Lee, left Congress before the end of 1779. At the same time, moderates, like Jay, were in the ascendancy.

Yet the Deane affair remained impossible to resolve: the radicals were too weak to punish Deane, while the moderates were not yet strong enough to absolve him. For eight months after Deane had appeared in Congress and Congress had unanimously repudiated his chief accuser, he remained in limbo. Deane repeatedly asked permission to return to France, but to no avail. Although he was no longer a public servant, Congress refused to allow him to leave. Yet there was no reason for Deane to remain in Philadelphia except to give his enemies the pleasure of tormenting him further.

In June 1779, Spain joined the alliance against Britain. America's destiny would be determined by political events on the Continent, and the delegates supporting the Franco-American alliance gained strength from Spain's entry. It was hoped that Spain's declaration of war would push Britain to make peace. Now there was greater urgency to appoint a peace commissioner.

Gérard and Deane's friends favored appointing as the peace commissioner the popular new president, John Jay, who was considered pro-French and sympathetic to Deane. The Lee-Adams Junto supported John Adams as peace commissioner and wanted Arthur Lee appointed as a new minister plenipotentiary to Spain. This selection threatened once again to polarize Congress between the Lee-Adams Junto and the Deane-Franklin-Jay forces. In August, however, the delegates reached a compromise: Jay's friends agreed to appoint Adams as peace commissioner, and the junto agreed to abandon Lee and support Jay as minister to Spain. With that, Arthur Lee's tumultuous diplomatic career was ended. Lee received notice of his recall at Christmas, and by January 1780, he was on his way back to Philadelphia, seething with renewed rage toward Deane and Franklin.

With the removal of Lee and the appointment of a peace commission, Congress also finally agreed to give Deane leave to return to France. Deane requested that Congress appoint someone to conduct an audit of his accounts and reimburse him for the amount of his expenses over the last three years. The treasurer of the Congress sent him a draft in the amount of $10,500 for his time and expenses in Philadelphia over the last year. Given the rapid depreciation of the Continental currency, this amount was an insult, and Deane refused it.

———

IT WAS DEANE'S fourth sea voyage, and the dull routine of six weeks at sea was broken by the dramatic capture of two British vessels. One of the British ships fired at Deane's ship for more than an hour with its eighteen guns, but it caused no serious damage. Deane arrived safely at Rochefort in late July and reached Valentinois in early August of 1780. Franklin, who seemed younger, and even lighthearted, now that Lee was gone, welcomed Deane warmly and invited him to resume living at Valentinois. Chaumont and Beaumarchais were also glad to see Deane back from his trial by fire. It was surely an emotional reunion for Deane and his son Jesse, now fifteen, who was living with Franklin. Deane had not seen his only child in more than four years.

Even though Deane's supporters had ultimately triumphed over Lee's forces, Deane had reason to feel bitter. He tried to console himself that he had at least the confidence of knowing he was in the right. Yet the fact remained that Deane's life had been shattered. Deane had spent two years abroad waiting for Congress to act while neglecting his own business affairs and family. His finances were dissipated after years of uncompensated public service, during which he had been at risk of kidnapping, arrest, and assassination; for four years he had missed family, friends, and his beloved home in Wethersfield; his reputation was soiled by Lee's libels. And though he had returned to America with treaties of commerce and alliance, a French fleet, and the first foreign diplomat to recognize Congress, Deane had not received a word of recognition or thanks. Instead, he was offered only a token sum of worthless currency to pay for two years squandered in Philadelphia.

Franklin, recalling his own ordeal before Parliament in 1775 and believing that Deane, too, had been treated unfairly, offered Deane financial support while Deane struggled to rebuild his business. Deane painstakingly put together all of his financial records for Congress's auditor. He estimated Congress owed him more than 300,000 livres (about $2.3 million today) for his years of public service and uncompensated expenses. But he doubted that the men who had abused him in Congress would ever pay him.

Beaumarchais, too, was also having financial difficulties. Despite Congress's acknowledgment that the arms sales were not a gift, Congress made no effort to pay for them. Deane felt embarrassed that he could do nothing to compel his government to pay their debt to Beaumarchais. Moreover, even if Congress had the will to repay Beaumarchais, the economy was wrecked, and the currency was worthless. All that sustained the American military and government was France's largesse.

The Continental Army was again losing more battles than it was winning. While Congress had toyed with Deane's fate, the Americans had suffered a long succession of defeats, including major losses at Savannah, Augusta, and Charleston, where the Americans lost the entire southern army of 5,400 men. Contrary to expectations, d'Estaing's fleet had not won a single naval battle. The British had burned Portsmouth and Norfolk in Virginia, as well as Fairfield, Norwalk, and New Haven in Connecticut, and they had sent Indian tribes to terrorize settlements up and down the western frontier. Neither Congress nor most of the military command had proven effective in 1780. Once again, prospects for victory had dimmed.

Deane had told Congress that "whatever my fate may be, I can never be miserable, on the contrary I shall be essentially happy" knowing the part he had played in the Revolution. Yet after the public and private traumas of the last two years, he suffered from deep depression and anxiety. In this state of mind, Deane poured out his frustration, anger, and worry in his correspondence to friends and

family. His language was intemperate, but his concerns, especially
regarding the future of the United States, were understandable.
Deane's public trial by fire had brought out in his writing a more
reflective tone and a darker voice. Through the spring and summer
of 1781, Deane wrote numerous long, thoughtful letters questioning
the future of the war and the young republic.

To his brother Simeon he questioned whether "an independent
democratical government" could ever secure to posterity peace,
safety, and liberty. "[W]e ought to inquire if any country ever was,
for any time, even for one century, at peace, free, and happy, under
a democracy?" He could think of no historical precedent. Even if the
Revolution was won, what would be the condition of the country,
"ravaged and exhausted, our commerce destroyed, an immense in-
ternal and foreign debt contracted," and saddled with the expense
of establishing a new government? "Will the inhabitants of America,
taught to believe that they fought to exonerate themselves from
taxes" happily pay much greater taxes to a new government? To another friend he confessed that he had hoped independence could be
won with little difficulty or bloodshed, but "I need not tell you that
the hope proved abortive." Since independence, America had been
transformed by removing the "restraints of regular government," he
wrote. "Noisy and designing individuals had risen from the lowest
order, and displaced the best and most respectable members of society." The state governments were weak, and "even in Congress itself reason, patriotism, and justice were but too often vanquished
by faction, cabal, and views of private interest." Deane argued to
another delegate that Congress should negotiate a return to Britain.
France was "a great loser" on whom America could no longer rely.
If the war continued, all Americans could expect at the end was
unconditional surrender.

Perhaps most surprising, Deane had begun to question whether

the United States could negotiate with Britain separately, in violation of the treaty of alliance with France, which he had helped to
draft. He wrote to Jesse Root, a member of Congress, that France
had merely intended at the outset "to assist us just so far as might
be absolutely necessary to prevent an accommodation [with Brit-
ain]." Initially, while France violated its treaty obligations with
Britain, "it does not appear to have ever expected or desired that
we should become independent," and thus, France insisted on secrecy. France continued to harass and arrest American privateers
and slowed down the shipments of supplies. France "holds herself
at liberty to desert our alliance and independency at the end of an
unsuccessful war; and, as the present is not pretended to be a successful war, the inference is plain." Even after the French agreed
to the treaties, Deane argued, there was no reason to think that
the changes in policy "were the effect of a regard for our country,
any more than the preceding resolution to disown and abandon us
had been."

It was now clear to Deane that they had made a terrible
error in imagining that they could rely on support from abroad. The
Europeans only wanted to use them for their own purposes, but now
as Europe headed toward a general war, the Americans would be
abandoned. The Americans must find a way to restore relations with
the mother country as soon as possible. Deane expressed himself
even more bluntly to Major Tallmadge at Washington's headquarters. If Britain is defeated, Deane wondered, would France and Spain
"dictate the law to us also? They certainly will; it is not in the nature
of a despotic victorious power to do otherwise." America was
trapped between two great powers like "Scylla on the one hand and
Charybdis on the other, and our pilots drunk with the intoxicating

ideas of independent sovereignty, madly pushing us into that vortex in which our peace, liberty, and safety will be swallowed up and lost for ever."

THE SUN had barely set when Edward Bancroft headed into the Tuileries. Spring had indeed come to Paris, and the evening air was still warm and pungent with the scent of pollen. He found the familiar tree and pushed a thick roll of pages into the bottle. He thought of the smile these pages would bring to the British foreign secretary, Lord Weymouth, and he disappeared before the British agent arrived to retrieve them.

THIRTY–FIVE

THE SNUFFBOX

Paris and London,
October 1781–September 1789

The letters, which Deane had written to his friends and brother, somehow found their way into the ink-stained hands of James Rivington, a Loyalist New York publisher "ever ready to serve his King and Country." It would seem more than a coincidence that all of Deane's incriminating letters over a four-week period in May 1781 were intercepted at sea. More likely, the letters must have been turned over by someone who would have had access to all of Deane's correspondence over time—Bancroft.

In any event, Rivington now had eleven letters in Deane's handwriting. Rivington was a polished English gentleman whose journalistic standards were shaped entirely by self-interest and who had only an occasional relationship with the truth. On October 24, Rivington began publishing Deane's letters as a serial in his paper, *The Royal Gazette*. The series, which ran from October through December of 1781, proved so popular that he republished them as a separate pocket volume entitled *Paris Papers* for six shillings a copy. Not since d'Eon published some of Louis XV's diplomatic correspondence in 1764 had the world enjoyed such a candid look at the private letters of an important diplomat. All of New York and London were intrigued by the bathetic confessions of an American agent and emissary who gave credence to the claims that Britain was winning the war and who bluntly revealed the deep divisions both within the Congress and between France and America. George III was especially interested in Deane's call for a reconciliation with the mother country, and he was prepared to offer Deane a substantial bribe to encourage him to influence his friends in Congress.

Deane, who was in Ghent on personal business, only learned of the possible theft of his letters in late November, when Bancroft wrote to him that the vessel *L'Orient* had been seized by the British with important letters on board. It was not until late December that Deane heard that all of the incriminating letters he had written from May 10 until June 15 were now in the hands of the publisher. By the time Deane heard this, the letters had already appeared in New York.

What is curious is that Deane had a premonition that his letters might be intercepted and published. The very day that Rivington announced to the world his intention of publishing Deane's letters, Deane wrote from Ghent to his brother Barnabas, describing one of his letters:

> It is high time the curtain should be drawn up and that the actors behind the scene should be stripped of all disguise and false appearance, and the catastrophe of the piece should be placed in the full view of every one. I have attempted to do this. I expect to be abused for it, and am sure that I shall not be disappointed; . . . [S]hould that letter have been intercepted by the enemy, my sentiments will become more generally known than I wish for; but in

one word be assured that we shall, unless we make peace immediately, become eventually dependant, and that unconditionally, either on France or England.

Some people charged that Deane conspired to send the letters to Rivington, either directly or through a British agent, for the purposes of persuading the American public it was time to reconcile with Britain. The fact that Deane had already relocated himself in Ghent might support the idea that Deane expected letters to be published. Arguably, Deane tried to make the publication look accidental by writing in the form of letters to friends and family. And the fact that these letters are long and often eloquent suggest that Deane spent time crafting each of them.

Moreover, there is some evidence in the correspondence of George III that the British government had discussed using Deane to bring about reunion with the colonies. Months before Deane wrote the letters, George III wrote to Lord North, "I think it is perfectly right that Mr. Deane should so far be trusted as to have three thousand pounds in goods for America." Apparently, Britain was prepared to compensate Deane with trade in goods for his assistance. But the king recognized that Deane was not open to bribery. He added that "giving him particular instructions would be liable to much hazard." Instead, the king thought that if Deane, acting on his own, could bring "any of the provinces to offer to return to their allegiance on the former foot" that "would be much better" than trying to persuade Congress as a whole.

Historians have pointed to this letter as proof that Deane acted in concert with Britain in publishing the *Paris Papers*. But in fact, George III's letter suggests that whatever scheme the British government intended, Deane acted on his own, and their original plan was abandoned. First, there is no evidence that any compensation was ever provided to Deane. Three thousand pounds (worth more than $500,000 today) would have been an extraordinary sum, and the fact that he was reduced to living like a pauper is proof that if a bribe was ever offered, he refused it. Second, even if Deane had wanted to help the British, by 1781 he was in no position to influence any of the State governments, not even Connecticut's.

In July 1781, Lord North sent to the king "several letters which he has received from Mr. Deane, in order to be sent as intercepted letters to America." The prime minister noted that once the letters would be published Deane would not be able to return to America "without a re-union between Great Britain & the Colonies, & Mr. Deane seems in that respect, to have acted fairly, & to have put himself into his Majesty's power." However, Lord North feared that "the letters are written with so much zeal for a reconciliation" that they appeared to be written in concert with the British government.

The king acknowledged receiving "the intercepted letters from Mr. Deane for America." Why would the king in a private note to Lord North have referred to these letters as "intercepted" if Deane had intended to send them to Britain? In the same letter the king expressed his disappointment with the content of these letters. He agreed with Lord North that the letters had "too much appearance of being concerted with this country, and therefore not likely to have the effects as if they bore another aspect."

If Deane had been acting as a British agent, surely the British government would have given him some instructions as to what to say, or they would have returned them to Deane and asked him to try again. But clearly, Deane was not following instructions. A month later, George III approved the publication of the "intercepted letter from Mr. Deane," which he again criticized as "too strong in our favour" to be truly effective in influencing American public opinion. For these reasons, it seems clear that Deane acted for his own reasons and not for any benefits promised by the British government.

If Deane had intended for his opinions to be published, why not write another broadside to the American people, as he had done concerning his tenure as commissioner to France? Why would Deane have intentionally published his private letters and risked exposing his friends and family to embarrassment and guilt by association? And if he intended the letters to be read sequentially, the letters taken as a whole are largely redundant. Moreover, even after Rivington began publishing in late October, Deane continued writing more of the same for months until word reached him of the appearance of the *Paris Papers* at which point he stopped. If Deane knew the letters critical of France would be published, he would have known that he could not return to France. Yet, when he went to Ghent, he left behind clothes, papers, money, unpaid bills, and his son Jesse. He clearly planned on returning to Paris in a few weeks.

On balance, it seems more likely that the publication of these letters was not Deane's intention. He may have realized that someone in Valentinois had been stealing his mail for quite some time, and therefore it was only a matter of time before one of his letters was published. While many of Deane's friends were disappointed in him for losing faith in the Revolution, the letters show Deane was not afraid to advocate for peace talks without regard for the cost to himself. And it's equally clear that in spite of Deane's financial hardship, he never asked for nor received any payment from the British government or Rivington.

His friend Jeremiah Wadsworth from Hartford wrote Deane in early November, advising him that his letter of June 13 had come to him "in Mr. Rivington's paper" and expressing the wish that Deane would have "recovered your spirits" and renounced his mistaken opinions. Barnabas worried that his brother Silas would be destroyed by this publication, even if all he said was true. "He has given his enemies just the opportunity they wanted for to ruin him in, and I fear he will loose his friends in France by it." His brother Simeon, who would gladly have given his life for Silas, despaired that there was nothing he could do to spare his brother from the consequences of his act: "To oppose a torrent is madness."

Major Tallmadge wrote Deane from Wethersfield that some of Deane's "strongest advocates, have become your most inveterate enemies." He was being called a "traitor" and compared to his old friend Benedict Arnold, who had only recently been exposed as a British spy. Allies in Congress like Robert Morris and Gouverneur Morris felt they had been duped by Deane, while Thomas Paine crowed that his worst suspicions of Deane were proved justified.

Deane feared that he would be sent home from Europe to face charges for treason. The French government was insulted by Deane's characterization of their motives, regardless of their accuracy. Deane was now persona non grata and could not return to France. Only Beaumarchais showed some sympathy for his partner whose judgment had been colored by the abuses he had suffered, but who remained a hero for having forged the alliance with France. "I will always do him the justice to say that he is one of the men who have contributed the most to the alliance of France and the United States," Beaumarchais wrote.

Deane wrote a long letter to Franklin, defending his actions in sending the letters. All he was guilty of was expressing his view in private correspondence that "America previous to her dispute with Great Britain was the most free, & happy Country in the World," and that if America could return to that condition she would be far better off than in an alliance with a powerful French monarch. Deane pointed out that France was not acting from pure motives in supporting the Americans. It was, he wrote,

absurd, to suppose that the [French] Court was become convinced
of the Truth, of the doctrines advanced in Our declaration of
Independancy, and by an alliance with America, meant to subscribe
to those self evident Truths, of the natural equality of Men, of
their inherent, and unalienable rights, of the origin, and sole Object
of all civil Government, and to the rights of Subjects to refuse
Allegiance, or submission, to a Government, as soon as they judge
it to be oppressive.

France was merely acting "to humble an antient rival," whereas
America shared with Britain a system of justice and democracy.
Though the British government had become corrupt, if it could be
reformed, then the liberty of Americans would be safer under Parliament than in an alliance with a despotic French king. The British
Constitution was superior to independence for without limits on
self-government, experience showed "there cannot be found a single
instance of any Nation's enjoying Peace, Liberty, and safety, under a
Democracy."

In Deane's view, the burdens of the Revolution and the costs of
self-government had become oppressive for America, and Congress
had exceeded its power. "In my Letters," Deane wrote to Franklin, "I
censured with free & honest indignation the Arbitrary and unjust
proceedings of Congress, in forcing their depreciated, & depreciating
paper on honest Creditors, Widows, & Orphans in lieu of Silver, &
Gold." The treaty with France could not bind America to continue
the war if America were convinced that "her Peace, Liberty, and
safety will be secured by putting an End to the War." And Deane did
not consider himself personally bound to France by the generosity
shown him by the French government.

Deane acknowledged that he had been accused by his enemies
of acting as an agent in the employ of the British government. But

Franklin knew "how readily I undertook to procure Supplies, and to solicit foreign Aid, at a Time when both were become indispensible, when the Attempt was the most hazardous, and when few persons were more obnoxious to the British Government." Though Deane had never been compensated for his service, Franklin knew that Deane's conduct from his arrival in France to his recall was above reproach. In calling for reconciliation with Britain, Deane had said nothing that Franklin himself had not argued for during Franklin's time in London as the representative for Pennsylvania and Massachusetts. Indeed, even Congress had passed resolutions prior to the Declaration of Independence, expressing the hope that the colonies would remain loyal to the British Crown. Nothing that Deane had written in his intercepted correspondence could be regarded as treason. "If the British Parliament & Ministers are content to renounce forever all their unconstitutional claims" against the Americans and "are willing to Treat Us as Brethren as Friends and equals I confess that I can see no farther Cause for Contention with them." And "to continue the War to establish Our independent sovereignty on the ruins of the British Power," and at the risk of strengthening the French monarchy, "appears to Me to be to the last degree dangerous, and absurd."

Franklin, for once, was speechless. He did not know how to respond to Deane's lengthy defense, and he may have worried that his close association with Deane might now reflect poorly on him. Privately, he wrote to Morris, expressing sympathy: "Our former Friend Mr. Deane has lost himself entirely. He and his Letters are universally condemned." Franklin saw "no Place for him but England. He continues however to sit croaking at Ghent, chagrin'd, discontented, & dispirited." Yet, Franklin pushed Morris to help Deane obtain a final settlement of what was owed to him by Congress.

To Deane, Franklin wrote that he was not convinced by Deane's argument that the Revolution was futile and that America would be better off under the British Constitution than in an alliance with France. "[P]erhaps my answer would not convince you; but that I think Time will." And he cautioned Deane that "The Publication of those Letters has done great Prejudice to your Character there, and necessarily diminish'd much of the Regard your Friends had for you. You are now considered as having abandoned the cause of your Country, and as having with Arnold espoused that of its Enemies." Franklin did not think Deane was a traitor. But he did conclude that "your Resentments and Passions have overcome your Reason and Judgment; and tho' my ancient Esteem & Affection for you induce me to make all the Allowances possible," it was no longer possible "for me to say with the same Truth & Cordiality as formerly that I am, Your Affectionate Friend & humble Servant."

Deane replied to his old friend that

> I am free to join with you in an appeal to Time & Experience to determine whether independant Sovereignty, in the hands of a Democracy, ought to be preferred by the United States, to the British Constitution free'd from the Innovations, & corruptions which have in the course of Time crept into it. . . . You believe that the peace, Liberty & happiness of our Country, will be best secured, & supported, by a close alliance with France & the House of Bourbon, & under an independent Democracy; I have the misfortune to think differently.

Acknowledging their differences, Deane and Franklin parted company. The two friends who had together negotiated the Treaty of Alliance with France never exchanged another word. But Franklin would continue to insist publicly that he had "never known or suspected any cause to charge Silas Deane with any want of probity, in any purchase, or bargain, whatever, made by him for the use or account of the United States." Plainly, Franklin would not have risked his reputation to defend Deane's honor if he had any thought that Deane was a traitor.

Alone and depressed, Deane remained in Ghent, confined to bed for weeks with a persistent cold and dry cough, living on bran tea and honey, and despairing of his predicament: he was truly a man without a country. He wrote to Bancroft that "from the intolerant spirit which rages in America, I expect no charitable construction on either my words or actions." Unable to return to France, he asked Bancroft to pay off what he owed to Neff the tailor and Pascal the coach-maker. How would he survive in exile from France and the United States? He still held out some small hope of receiving compensation from Congress for his expenses, but that was unrealistic given the circumstances. And he had some money owed to him, including 2,000 pounds (about $370,000 today) he had lent to his brother Simeon to import French goods. If Deane had acted as a British agent, he had no reason now to remain stranded in Ghent and every reason to go to London where he could have resumed his business. But he remained in Ghent, grateful for his one true friend on whom he could rely—Bancroft.

SOON AFTER THE *PARIS PAPERS* appeared on the streets of New York, news arrived that Lord Cornwallis and his army had surrendered at Yorktown on October 19. It was almost exactly four years to the day after the surrender of Burgoyne at Saratoga. Nearly 9,000 American and 7,000 French troops had converged to lay siege on approximately 8,000 British troops behind the fortifications of Yorktown. The Americans were commanded by Generals Lafayette, Lincoln, and Steuben, and the French were led by General Rochambeau. In addition, Washington had another 2,900 men, plus 800 French marines, across the river, to prevent the British from escaping. The siege, orchestrated by General Steuben, was remarkably effective and the fighting was brief and relatively bloodless. Washington accepted the formal surrender, even though he had not taken part in the fighting. The final battle plan had been drawn up by Washington, Lafayette, and Rochambeau at a meeting in Wethersfield, Connecticut, at the former home of Silas Deane, where Washington had once stayed as a friend of the family.

The British withdrew from the south, and in April peace talks began in Paris, led by Franklin. Although over the next year some scattered fighting occurred between Indians and settlers, and there was a brief skirmish in South Carolina, the war had ended. The Treaty of Paris ending the Revolution and recognizing American independence was signed by Franklin in November 1782. The Americans had broken their commitment to France not to make a separate peace with Britain. The following January, Britain signed separate treaties with France and Spain. Deane's predictions of a catastrophic end to the war had proved wrong, while his prediction of his own undoing had proved remarkably prescient.

WITH THE WAR ENDED, Deane found himself still living in exile in Ghent. He feared that if he set foot on French territory he would be tossed into the Bastille for criticizing the king. In the mind of the American public, he was also guilty of treason. He had few friends left in Congress. He asked his brothers to sell off his personal and real property in Wethersfield, but the property was now tied up in a legal battle with his stepchildren. Deane had deposited a large sum of his own money with Monsieur Chaumont, the owner of Valentinois, who had advanced substantial sums to help the American commissioners, but Chaumont was now insolvent, and Deane lost everything. Meanwhile, Congress still had not considered whether to reimburse Deane for his expenses, which he claimed were 300,000 pounds (about $55 million). Deane was forced to borrow money from Bancroft to stay alive. Yet Deane was happy that the war was over and wished America a bright future. He had suffered greatly for expressing his convictions: "I must be that traitor to myself, which God knows I never was to my country." No fair-minded person could honestly accuse him of being in the pay of the British government considering "the distressed situation in which I have lingered out a wretched and obscure exile." He was living "in lodgings barely decent, without a servant," and dining in a manner in which he was "neither accustomed [n]or inclined to, and to which necessity alone could ever reduce me."

Deane decided to visit London in March 1783. His friend Jay cautioned him not to go, for fear that it would confirm the suspicions that Deane was in the employ of the British. Deane's son, Jesse, was ill in France with a tumor on his neck that would have to be removed surgically, but Bancroft advised Deane that he could not safely return to France. Deane arranged for a ship to take Jesse home. Deane hoped he might someday see his son again, but he did not know if that would ever be possible in America. Deane was also hoping to do some business in London. He had an ambitious plan to build a canal to connect Lake Champlain and the St. Lawrence River in which Lord Dorchester, the governor general of Canada, seemed interested. He also was looking into developing the Ohio River valley—the same land that Franklin and Lee had fought over in the 1770s. Now that the war had ended, Deane hoped to use his contacts in London to recruit English settlers for Ohio.

The day after Deane arrived in London he received a surprise visitor: Benedict Arnold. Since he had last seen General Arnold in

Philadelphia, Arnold had become a British spy. After Washington put him in command of the fortification at West Point overlooking the Hudson, Arnold plotted to surrender the post to the British. When Arnold's plot was revealed, he fled and joined the British Army as a general. At the war's end, he emigrated to London. Deane was inclined to slam the door in the face of America's most notorious traitor, but his loneliness and the memory of Arnold's generosity when Deane was living in Philadelphia prevented him. Arnold invited Deane to dinner with some British officers, but Deane refused. The next day Deane moved to a modest flat at 135 Fleet Street, hoping Arnold would not find him, but he continued to receive numerous written invitations to Arnold's home. In a few days, Arnold called again at Deane's new lodging. Deane pushed Arnold out to the stairwell and told him in front of witnesses never to return. The two men never spoke again.

Bancroft repeatedly discouraged Deane from returning to Paris and promised to visit Deane in London soon. So Deane remained in this unfamiliar city, and as the circle of his correspondence contracted and debts mounted, he slipped deeper into depression and poverty. Robert Morris turned his unopened letters over to Congress; his brother Simeon, who owed him thousands of pounds, did not respond to his pleas for help; his son Jesse never wrote Deane again, perhaps embarrassed by his father's infamy, or not forgiving his father for sending him home; and his stepson John Webb collected all the debts Deane was owed in Connecticut and squandered the money himself. Morris wrote to Deane to discourage him from returning to America, where he risked a hostile reception by the press and the Congress.

Deane's one hope was that he could persuade his friend John Jay to assist him in obtaining compensation from Congress, but even Jay refused to answer Deane's letters. When Jay, now minister to Spain, was in London on official business, Deane visited his lodging; he was turned away by a servant, and Jay left London without seeing him. Deane continued to write Jay until Jay could no longer restrain himself. Though it was "painful to say disagreeable things" to a friend, Jay wrote, "I love my country and my honor better than my friends." In Jay's view, Deane was either "exceedingly injured" or guilty of treason, and "while doubts remain on that point, all connection between us must be suspended." He had tried to keep an open mind to hear what he could say in his own defense, but he had received information that "you received visits from, and were on terms of intimacy with, General Arnold. Every American who gives his hand to that man, in my opinion, pollutes it." Jay would have nothing more to say to Deane in the future.

Deane could no longer expect to recover anything from Congress. He wanted to leave England, and he wrote to his brother Barnabas asking for fifty pounds (about $9,000 today) so that he might survive the winter and pay his passage in early spring to either Canada or possibly New England, if he were allowed to return. At the same time, his health rapidly deteriorated, beginning in the fall of 1787. He developed a cold that moved into his limbs and limited his ability to walk for many months, leaving him with permanent pain in his knees and ankles. Then during the summer of 1788 he began to suffer from a persistent dry cough and night sweats so severe that his linen was drenched every morning. He lost his appetite for days at a time and could hold down only fluids. He survived on eggs beaten in milk warm from the cow with sugar, nutmeg, and alcohol. He had hot and cold flashes and his whole body shook. In this condition his "constant and unfailing friend Dr. Bancroft" recommended he remain in London, and he prescribed laudanum, an opiate derivative, which Deane took. Deane may have developed an addiction to laudanum. His correspondence became less lucid and more sporadic. He seemed confused and forgetful. He became increasingly dependent on Bancroft, to whom Deane's mail was forwarded.

In his disoriented condition, Deane's flat at Fleet Street was robbed of all his clothing and other articles of value. Someone opened his trunk of papers and removed only the most valuable account books and letter books. Days later, a Monsieur Foullay approached Thomas Jefferson, now minister in Paris, to say that he had taken Deane's account books and letter books in satisfaction for an unspecified debt that Deane had refused to pay. Foullay had carried these books to Paris for the express purpose of offering them first to the United States in exchange for the amount owed by Deane, 120 pounds (roughly $22,000 today). If the United States would not pay for the books, Foullay threatened to sell them to the British government, which might be interested in knowing the sources of the arms that were sent to the Americans. Jefferson reviewed the books, which included all Deane's personal and official accounts from the time of his arriving in France to 1781 and his correspondence during the spring and summer of 1777, when he was serving with Franklin and Lee in Paris. Jefferson received authorization from Jay to buy the books and paid twenty-five pounds (roughly $4,600 today). Foullay had offered to obtain for Jefferson the remaining six to eight volumes of Deane's letter books, which Jefferson thought would be useful.

Rather than waiting for Foullay to "obtain" Deane's remaining books, by whatever means he employed, Jefferson wrote to Bancroft in London and asked Bancroft to get the books for him. Jefferson suggested that Bancroft could tempt Deane with money for the books, but that he should not say it was for Congress. He was prepared to pay as much as fifty pounds (roughly $9,200 today) for all the volumes. "What other way would best bring it about you know best," Jefferson added coyly, knowing that Bancroft could use the fifty pounds himself. However Bancroft did it, Jefferson was confident that his relationship to Deane would enable him to recover those books. Jefferson could justify to himself the theft of Deane's papers: it would be an act of patriotism to prevent the books from falling into the wrong hands. Bancroft did not refuse Jefferson, but wrote back that there were no other volumes in Deane's possession.

DEANE COULD NO LONGER manage on his own, and in November, he moved into a friend's home on Chapel Street. That winter was one of the worst to hit Britain in nearly fifty years. The Thames froze, carnival booths were erected on it, and pigs were spit-roasted over the ice. Deane could no longer go outside, and he desperately looked forward to the spring, when he hoped to return to America.

In 1789, a federal Constitution and a newly elected government led by President Washington replaced the Articles of Confederation and the Continental Congress. Deane had criticized the Revolution because he believed that democracy without a constitution and a strong national government like Britain's was untenable. His concerns were prescient. Time and experience had shown that without a strong constitution the states were ungovernable. The men who had served with Deane, including Adams, Franklin, and Jay, had drafted a constitution that addressed Deane's concerns and improved upon the British Constitution.

As Washington prepared to take the oath of office, Jay, who was about to be appointed the first chief justice of the United States, told Stephen Sayre that he wished Deane would now return. Jay was a close associate of President Washington, and it is likely that Jay spoke for Washington. Deane's brother Barnabas and his friends confirmed that it would be safe for Deane to come home, and a friend in Boston offered to pay Deane's passage. That June Deane wrote to his old friend Washington congratulating him on his presidency and asking him to again consider Deane's compensation claim. By the fall of 1789, Deane had recovered from his long illness and was ready to make the voyage.

On Monday, September 21, 1789, Deane left London with his friend Theodore Hopkins and Captain Davis of the *Boston Packet*. They rode along the Thames, sitting side by side in a small carriage. According to witnesses, Deane had "never looked better." He was animated and optimistic about starting his life over in North America. He was discussing his project to build a waterway along the St. Lawrence. He also had hopes of developing land in the Ohio River valley. At Gravesend, just southeast of London, near the mouth of the Thames, the men spent the night in the home of the captain's father-in-law. After a hearty breakfast they boarded the *Boston Packet*. As the ship departed down the Thames, Deane took Captain Davis's arm. He felt unsteady. He inhaled deeply the crisp autumn air. Suddenly, he turned to the captain and collapsed into his arms, gasping. After a few hours Deane slipped into a coma and died. Among Deane's possessions, the only property of any value was a gold snuffbox painted with a portrait of Louis XVI and surrounded by diamonds. It was sold for 90 guineas (about $17,000 today), and the money was sent to his brother for his son's support.

Deane was buried in an unmarked grave in a churchyard in Deal, England. Fate denied his last wish to return home to the nation he had helped found.

THIRTY–SIX

THE DECEITS OF
THE HUMAN HEART

Was Silas Deane really dead?

Only days before Deane left London, an acquaintance thought that Deane had "never looked better." He had recovered from his long illness, and he seemed optimistic about the future and looked forward to returning home. The suddenness of his death aboard ship left some people wondering whether he had faked his own death so that he could shed his old soiled identity and return with a new one. Others whispered that Deane had committed suicide. Few even suspected that Deane was murdered.

The circumstances of his demise—his sudden collapse, inability to speak, and quick death—all suggest that Deane might have died from a cerebral hemorrhage. Deane's undiagnosed illness could have weakened blood vessels, leading to a greater risk of a sudden rupture in the brain. Of course, anyone who drops dead without warning could be a victim of a cerebral hemorrhage, but it may be significant that Dr. Bancroft, who had been prescribing medicine for Deane and who knew Deane's condition best, did not think that Deane had died from natural causes.

A few months after Deane's death, Bancroft wrote to Joseph

Priestley, the renowned British scientist, that Deane had been depressed and had committed suicide. Although he was not present at the time of death and had no contact with anyone who was there, Bancroft described the details of Deane's passing based on Captain Davis's written account. During Deane's long illness, Bancroft had prescribed medicine, which was apparently laudanum, a highly addictive opiate derivative commonly prescribed for digestive ailments. Bancroft wrote that Deane had intentionally overdosed on the drug, but this explanation makes no sense. Laudanum, like morphine, causes a gradual lingering death, whereas Deane collapsed suddenly and remained unable to speak until his death four hours later. Bancroft, a well-respected medical authority, surely knew that Deane's symptoms did not point to an overdose of laudanum.

Moreover, Deane had not shown any signs of depression or an intention to kill himself. If he had meant to kill himself, why wait until he had borrowed the money from friends for his passage and boarded the ship? Deane was returning home with the acquiescence, if not quite the blessing, of Washington's administration. He had much to look forward to upon his arrival. In addition to being reunited with his son and siblings, Deane was contemplating two attractive business ventures: the royal governor of Canada had shown interest in Deane's bold proposal to build a canal from Lake Champlain to the St. Lawrence River, and Deane was negotiating with investors about developing land in the Ohio River valley. Nothing in Deane's letters or manner hinted at the possibility of suicide. This renders Bancroft's story not only puzzling but suspicious. But why would Bancroft have fabricated facts?

We know that Bancroft's love of money exceeded his love of country or friends. Bancroft had served the crown out of greed, not loyalty. He was disloyal even to his British spymasters. For example, he had never fully disclosed to the British that he had known in advance about James Aitken's plot to burn down the naval yards and had done nothing to stop it. If the British government knew that Bancroft had protected Aitken, it might be grounds for cutting off his generous thousand-pound pension (worth about $185,000 today). Moreover, as a stock speculator, Bancroft made his money by trading on the inside information he obtained through his rich network of social connections. If his British friends knew he had protected Aitken, his social position and his business would have suffered. And Bancroft had an application pending before Parliament for a valuable patent on chemical dyes derived from his research on tropical plants. Everything Bancroft had and hoped to gain depended upon Deane's silence.

Could he trust Deane to keep quiet? Bancroft knew that Deane had previously published embarrassing information about the American commissioners and Congress. What if Deane returned to the States and disclosed more information about Bancroft's role in the Revolution? Even if Deane promised not to disclose Bancroft's secret service to the American cause, Bancroft could not be sure that whatever was left of Deane's private papers did not contain some incriminating evidence. Those papers would likely end up in the hands of Congress if Deane pursued his claims for compensation from the U.S. government. After Bancroft failed to dissuade Deane from returning home, there was only one way to protect Bancroft's secrets.

Was Bancroft capable of murder? His duplicity was beyond doubt: he befriended Aitken in prison so he could extract information that was then used to hang him; he had put Deane's life at risk by disclosing his activities to the British government; he had stolen Deane's correspondence and sold it to the British ambassador; and he conspired to steal the rest of Deane's papers for sale to Jefferson, all the time lulling Deane into believing that he was Deane's loyal friend.

We do not need to speculate on the darkness of Bancroft's soul. In Bancroft's novel, *Charles Wentworth Esq.*, one of his characters observes that civilization has instructed men "how to perpetrate fraud and injustice with greater art, secrecy and success," and that law, rather than discouraging crime, "first created the temptation to evil." He adds that "no man, who is villain enough to meditate my murder, will be deterred by the punishment of laws, which by secrecy and art he either may, or at least will expect to elude." In these passages Bancroft reveals a distinct fascination for evil and murder.

But if Bancroft wanted to murder Deane, how could he have accomplished it at such a distance? Bancroft had prescribed medications for Deane from time to time, and he was an authority on indigenous South American plants and poisons. Bancroft possessed a collection of natural poisons begun during the time he lived on Paul Wentworth's plantation in Guiana. Bancroft left behind a tantalizing clue as to how he might have murdered Deane. In his *Essay on the Natural History of Guiana, in South America,* he specifically mentions how natives in that country used curare to kill an enemy stealthily. He notes that when a native intends to poison another, he will feign forgiveness for any past grievance and "even repay it with services and acts of friendship, until [he has] destroyed all distrust and apprehension of danger in the destined victim of the vengeance."

Before Deane left London, he may well have asked Bancroft to provide him with some medications for his trip. Bancroft would have had the opportunity to mix some poison into the laudanum or other medicine he supplied to Deane. Shortly after boarding the *Boston Packet*, Deane may have taken something like laudanum to prevent seasickness. That might explain his sudden collapse just as the voyage got under way. In sum, Bancroft had the motive, the opportunity, and the means to poison Deane and make it appear to be a suicide.

No one at that time would have suspected Bancroft, who was regarded by Franklin, Adams, and Jefferson as a devoted patriot. When Bancroft returned to America for a few months in 1783, he was regaled as a hero of the Revolution. In fact, even then he was working as a spy for the British government. He continued to receive payments as a British spy until his death in 1821. No one suspected Bancroft's treachery until 1888, when one historian, aptly named Benjamin Franklin Stevens, found Bancroft's secret correspondence in the files of Lord Auckland of the British Secret Service. Stevens discovered the British foreign minister's instructions to Bancroft to leave Deane's papers in a bottle under a certain tree in the Tuileries.

AFTER CONGRESS abruptly recalled Arthur Lee from Paris in 1779, he returned to Philadelphia to demand a hearing from Congress to clear his name. He found himself in the same awkward position as did Deane. He waited months before Congress would listen to him, and no reasons were given for his recall. Yet Congress would neither clear him of wrongdoing nor thank him for his service. Lee blamed "that old corrupt Serpent" Franklin and his allies in Congress for plotting against him, although there is no evidence that Franklin made any statements against Lee. Members of Congress already had sufficient evidence from Lee's erratic behavior that he was unfit for the diplomatic service.

Lee also submitted a claim for compensation for his time in Paris, but Congress was preoccupied with the war and the falling value of the Continental dollar. In the meantime, Lee needed a job. He sought an appointment as the first secretary of foreign af-

fairs, but the post went to Robert Livingston of New York. This
was enough for Lee to charge that New Yorkers were conspiring to
seize control of the national government. He had learned nothing
about how self-destructive his suspicions were. Lee returned to Virginia, feeling paranoid, dejected, and anxious about his financial
circumstances.

With the help of his family, Lee was elected to Congress at the
end of 1781, and he returned to Philadelphia determined to punish
his enemies, especially Robert Morris, whom he regarded as Deane's
partner in crime. Lee became the leading opponent of Morris, who
as the superintendent of finance was in effect the prime minister of
the national government. Lee had himself elected chairman of a
committee to oversee Morris's work as superintendent.

At the same time, Congress had appointed Thomas Barclay, a
partner in Morris's firm, to conduct an audit of Deane's claims. Lee
feared that Barclay would favor Deane, so Lee preempted Barclay
from recommending a generous settlement for Deane by issuing his
own report. In 1776, Deane had been promised that his expenses
would be covered by Congress and that he would receive a five-
percent sales commission on all goods he procured for Congress.
Lee's report denied Deane's expenses and any sales commissions
after he became a commissioner. This formula disallowed the bulk
of Deane's claim, but even Lee had to acknowledge that Deane was
owed a substantial amount by Congress. Nevertheless, Lee's report
recommended that Deane should receive less than Lee himself had
demanded as compensation for his service as a commissioner.

Since Congress had already appointed Thomas Barclay to audit
Deane's claims, it ignored Lee's report. In 1787, Barclay determined
that Deane was owed 6,117 pounds (about $918,000 today), far
more than Lee's report had determined. By the time Barclay issued
his report, Lee had joined the Board of the Treasury, and he ar-

ranged to bury the report without Congress taking action. Lee used his position on the Treasury Board to bully wealthy financiers and merchants from New York and Philadelphia whom he disdained. Like other proto-Jeffersonians, Lee sneered at their ostentatious tastes as evidence that they lacked civic virtue. Men like Deane, Franklin, and Morris were symptoms of a dangerous disease infecting the body politic. Lee's hostility to mercantile interests reflected a larger ideological struggle against centers of commercial power. He saw these same men seeking to strengthen the national government at the expense of states and agrarian interests.

Fearing the rise of this new class of men, Lee also opposed the adoption of the Constitution. The debate over the Constitution would divide the Lee-Adams axis. John Adams and his New England allies supported the Constitution and eventually formed the Federalist Party. By contrast, some of Lee's allies in Congress shared his animosity toward both commerce and national government, and years later, these men would coalesce around Jefferson's Republican Party. But unlike Lee, Jefferson and the Republicans were rabid Francophiles in the wake of the French Revolution. To the end of his life, Lee's sympathies remained with Britain and against France. Lee defended the idea of monarchy, looked forward to reestablishing an alliance with Britain, and warned that the French were untrustworthy. As a result of Lee's pro-British leanings, Congress considered a censure motion against him, and the Virginia Assembly tried to recall him from Congress. Both efforts were defeated by his politically powerful older brothers.

After Lee left Congress in 1784, Congress appointed him to settle land claims with the Iroquois. He used his position and his influence in Congress to acquire 8,500 acres of Indian land along the Ohio and another 10,000 acres in western Virginia. It must have seemed like poetic justice to Lee that at the end of his public career, he would finally achieve his father's dream of establishing a vast empire in the Ohio River valley. Ironically, having spent most of the prior sixteen years in public service, Lee died in 1792 with a substantial estate, while Deane, who had entered public service as a wealthy man, died a pauper.

THE BEINECKE RARE BOOK and Manuscript Library at Yale University still retains Deane's college essay quoting Cato. The wise man, Deane wrote, should beware of "the deceits of the human heart." Lee had succeeded in preventing Deane from obtaining any compensation for his public service during Deane's lifetime. It fell to Deane's granddaughter, Philura Deane Alden, to petition Congress for payment of the amount long due to Deane. In 1842, after a lengthy examination of all the documents, Congress paid Deane's heirs $37,000 (about $971,000 today, roughly the same amount originally recommended by Barclay). The congressional report found that "Mr. Deane performed highly important and valuable services for this country." The committee noted archly that despite Deane's efforts to settle his accounts, "from causes which it is not deemed necessary to further detail, he was unable to procure their adjustment." Specifically, Congress criticized Lee's attempts sixty years earlier to settle Deane's claims as "erroneous" and a "gross injustice to Mr. Deane."

More than a half-century after his death, Deane was at last vindicated.

THIRTY—SEVEN

THE CROSS

By the end of the American Revolution, Beaumarchais had bought and shipped arms and supplies to the Continental Army worth six million livres (about $46 million). Much of this was financed by the French government, expecting to be repaid by Congress, but about one-fifth of the total cost was borrowed by Beaumarchais's firm on his personal credit. Congress had specifically approved a contract with Beaumarchais's agent in 1778 for most of these supplies. In addition, both Franklin and Morris, as the superintendent of finance, had signed notes promising to pay Beaumarchais millions of livres. Indeed, Congress had already voted in 1779 to acknowledge its obligation to repay France for all the arms and supplies it had received. Yet, by the war's end, Congress, urged on by Lee, preferred to think of these arms as a gift from France. The conclusion that no payment was due flew in the face of the repeated assertions from the French government that it had never made such a gift.

In 1782, under pressure from the French ambassador and at the insistence of Morris, Congress sent Barclay to France to audit Beaumarchais's claims and reach a settlement. Beaumarchais objected that he had already submitted his claims to Deane, who had audited the account and determined in 1780 that Beaumarchais—on behalf of himself and the French government—was owed 3.6 million livres (about $28 million today). Beaumarchais reluctantly agreed to resubmit hundreds of receipts to Barclay. Yet, even then, no payment was made.

By this time Beaumarchais was supporting himself, his third wife, Marie-Thérèse, and his daughter, Eugénie, from his plays and his investments. He had recently established a company with the Pèrier brothers to provide water to the city of Paris by means of steam pumps. It was an ingenious and ambitious new venture. Still, Beaumarchais was being pursued relentlessly by the creditors of Rodriguez Hortalez and was forced to beg the French government for assistance to fend off his creditors.

As Beaumarchais teetered on the brink of insolvency, he was living far beyond his means. Anticipating great wealth from his Paris water company, he was constructing a second mansion in the Faubourg Saint-Antoine. For nearly two decades, he wrote to Jefferson, Franklin, Adams, Hamilton, and Jay at different times, imploring them to intervene on his behalf with Congress, but to no avail. A succession of congressional committees was appointed to investigate Beaumarchais's claims and then disbanded. Congress dawdled and delayed paying off its foreign creditors, and, until his death, Lee did his utmost to thwart any payments to Beaumarchais.

One of the issues that stymied any resolution of Beaumarchais's claim was that the French government had acknowledged giving the Americans three million livres in 1776 prior to recognizing the United States. Congress acknowledged that after ratifying the alliance with France it had received two million livres from France to purchase arms through Rodriguez Hortalez, but no one knew where the other million livres had gone. For years, France had not wanted to acknowledge publicly that it had violated its treaty commitments with England by giving a million livres to Beaumarchais to purchase arms for the Americans even before it had signed a treaty of alliance. Some members of Congress suspected that Beaumarchais had pocketed the million livres at the expense of the American war effort. That was not the case, but the government of Louis XVI refused to clarify what happened by admitting that France had lied to the British about its role in arming the Americans.

Alexander Hamilton, the first Treasury secretary, reported to Congress in 1789 that the United States owed Beaumarchais 2.28 million livres (roughly $18 million today), and the revolutionary French government disclosed to the Americans that the "missing million livres" had been paid to Beaumarchais to buy arms. The enemies of Deane and Franklin charged that Beaumarchais had lied by not disclosing earlier that he had received one million livres from the French government. This was a completely disingenuous argument to avoid paying Beaumarchais what he was owed. All the money that France had given Beaumarchais had gone to buy arms on the assumption that the Americans would pay it back to Beaumarchais. Beaumarchais could not disclose the secret payment by the French government precisely because it was contrary to France's stated neutrality at the time. Nevertheless, Beaumarchais's enemies argued that since the million livres was intended for the United States, Beaumarchais now owed the United States one million livres plus interest. Beaumarchais was denied justice from Congress. Nothing was ever paid to him for all his efforts and expenses.

To the end of his life Beaumarchais continued to insist that "I did more than any other Frenchmen, whoever they may be, for the freedom of America, that freedom that gave birth to ours, which I alone dared to conceive." But the world had moved on, and few people would recall his role in the American Revolution as the old order of France was toppled.

BEAUMARCHAIS HAD NEARLY completed the palatial mansion he had designed in the Faubourg Saint-Antoine in July 1789, when a mob stormed the Bastille Prison only blocks away. From the roof of his new home Beaumarchais watched the uprising and cheered the Revolution. Despite his loyal service to the king, he embraced the new democracy. At the request of the mayor of Paris, Beaumarchais took charge of removing the rubble left by the Bastille. It was the perfect metaphor for his contribution to clearing away the old order. But over the next several years, as terror gripped France, Beaumarchais came to doubt the revolutionary regime.

In 1792, France declared war on Austria and Prussia, and Austrian and Prussian troops streamed across the border, marching toward Paris. Wild crowds of Parisians frantically sought arms with which to defend their city from foreign invaders. A false rumor circulated that Beaumarchais was hoarding guns in his mansion, and the crowd stormed his home. Beaumarchais escaped just as tens of thousands of panicked citizens rushed inside the gates. The mob must have been amazed by what they found. There were no guns, of course, but the house and garden, which occupied about an acre of land in the center of Paris, was extravagant beyond imagination. Standing in front of the house was a statue of a gladiator surrounded by an immense courtyard. The façade of the house featured an arcade of columns forming a classical semicircle. There were at least two hundred windows gazing down on the excited masses pouring into the courtyard. The curious mob surged through the house, coursing up and down stairs, trampling the carpets, and tracking mud everywhere. The citizens searched vainly for weapons, all the while dazzled by the opulence. There was a tremendous circular salon with an intricate mosaic wood floor, exquisite murals, a cupola thirty feet high, mahogany doors, and a hulking mantelpiece made entirely of Carrara marble. Each room was lavishly furnished and decorated. Beaumarchais's desk alone cost 30,000 livres (about $231,000 today). Outside was a terraced garden planted with tall trees and rare flowers, a small rounded temple to Bacchus, an ice house, a Chinese bridge, and a pond large enough to float several boats. It was no wonder that Beaumarchais was deeply in debt. This house had cost him 1.6 million livres (roughly $12 million today), far more than he could ever have afforded. Remarkably, though the mob left everything in disarray, nothing was stolen or destroyed.

That night Beaumarchais returned home, but days later he was arrested with hundreds of aristocrats on suspicion of conspiring with France's enemies. They were tossed in l'Abbaye Saint-Germain, which had been transformed into a prison for the once high-and-mighty. On August 30, he was released for no apparent reason. He did not know that his young mistress, Amélie Houret, was sleeping with the procurator of the Paris Commune, Jacques Manuel. She had persuaded Manuel to intervene on Beaumarchais's behalf. Her timing was exceptionally fortunate for Beaumarchais: three days later, mobs stormed the prisons holding the "enemies of the Revolution" and murdered more than a thousand, including those unfortunate prisoners at l'Abbaye. Beaumarchais had escaped narrowly.

Beaumarchais returned home from l'Abbaye profoundly shaken by his arrest and the continuing violence of the mob. His age, sixty, was already catching up with him. He was almost completely deaf without the aid of his ear trumpet. But it was no longer safe for him to remain at his home. The Faubourg Saint-Antoine was at the center of the storm. Terrified that he would be killed, he fled Paris on foot at two in the morning.

In his comedies, Beaumarchais had depicted the common man, Figaro, as triumphing over the stupid and cynical aristocrats. Now, as the Revolution descended into chaos, the masses did not distinguish one rich man from another. Figaro was turning on him. Alone in the darkness, he hurried toward Versailles, ten miles away. He hoped to find refuge in the home of friends, but fearing he might be recognized on the highway, he stole across planted wheat fields like a hunted animal. He would not have been able to hear the voices or the footsteps of the approaching mob. As he darted breathlessly between trees from shadow to shadow, he prayed that the moonlight would not betray him.

THOUGH ONCE MORE Beaumarchais evaded his enemies, it was clear that his notoriety made him a target for the revolutionaries. Over the next several years, Beaumarchais suffered many indignities and injustices. He was exiled from France and thrown in debtors' prison in London. His business, home, personal property, and papers were ransacked, confiscated, or destroyed. His wife and daughter were imprisoned and sentenced to death until his wife agreed to renounce and divorce her husband. And when he finally returned to Paris in 1796, his beloved home had been ransacked and ruined, and he was utterly destitute. He spent the last three years of his life still trying to collect the debts that Congress owed to him while he was relentlessly pursued by his creditors.

Beaumarchais had exposed the foibles and corruption of the *ancien régime*. He had helped to unleash the revolutionary forces that destroyed the way of life he had enjoyed. His singular role in support of the American Revolution had fanned the flames of revolutionary spirit in France. French citizens were persuaded by the American Revolution that liberty and equality could be more than mere slogans. And by persuading Louis XVI to arm the Americans and fight Britain, Beaumarchais had unwittingly contributed to the insolvency of the French government. The American revolutionaries merely ignored Beaumarchais's contribution to their revolution, but the French revolutionaries threatened, abused, and destroyed him. At least he was spared the fate of many of his friends who faced the guillotine. He died of a heart attack in bed in 1799 at age 67. By then, he had lived long enough to appreciate what must have struck him as the final irony of his colorful life: he was an author pursued by the characters of his own invention.

MADAME DE BEAUMONT, the Chevalière d'Eon, kept her secrets as tightly as her corset. Like that of her nemesis, Beaumarchais, her life was dramatically altered by the French Revolution.

After her appearance at Versailles in 1777, she spent some time visiting various convents, but concluded that the contemplative life was not for her. Once France declared war on Britain in 1778, d'Eon pleaded with Vergennes to allow her to return to military service, but it was out of the question. When d'Eon tried to leave for America on her own, she was arrested and tossed into prison for disobeying her sovereign. She was released after agreeing to retire to her mother's home in Tonnerre. But the quiet provincial life made d'Eon restless, and when the war ended, in 1781, she returned to her home in London's Golden Square, where her precious library and most of her belongings were still being stored.

For a while, d'Eon lived comfortably on her pension from the French government. Old friends like John Wilkes were unaccustomed to seeing the captain of the dragoons in wigs and dresses, but they welcomed her back into their circle. D'Eon celebrated the fall of the Bastille and the old regime she had served. She volunteered to return to France and fight for the new republic against Austria and Prussia. She did not realize that the Revolution swept away the foundations of her own financial security; her pension soon stopped. Just as Beaumarchais was denounced as an émigré, so d'Eon was blacklisted and could no longer return to revolutionary France. Friends in London took up contributions for her, but over time she had to put all of her silver, jewelry, and china up for auction at Christie's. Nearly all she owned was eventually sold. At the age of sixty, d'Eon began to teach fencing to young men. Later, she performed in fencing competitions against men half her age. Her physical agility—despite wearing a dress and wig—so impressed English audiences that she was invited to perform at the Haymarket Theater in London before the Prince of Wales. The once dashing military hero had been reduced to a public attraction. She continued to fence publicly until age seventy, when she suffered a nearly fatal wound. She then sold off her swords and retired from her athletic career.

For a time d'Eon held on to her own flat, but when she could no longer afford it, she moved into the modest home of an elderly French widow, Mary Cole, who lived west of Grey's Inn in Bloomsbury. For more than a decade the two women were constant companions, supporting themselves as seamstresses. They were often in debt, and in her late seventies d'Eon was tossed into debtors' prison for several months.

After her release she suffered a series of maladies that left her confined to bed under the care of Mrs. Cole and a retired French doctor from the Fathers of Charity at Grenoble, Father Elysée. As she neared the end of her life in May 1810, d'Eon was forced to sell off her last treasure, the *Croix de Saint-Louis*, to feed herself. A few days later, age eighty-two, she passed away peacefully in her bed in the presence of the priest and Mrs. Cole.

As Mrs. Cole was preparing d'Eon's body for burial, she discovered something extraordinary and called to Father Elysée. The priest was so shocked he arranged an autopsy with several doctors and the Earl of Yarmouth attending. All the witnesses agreed that what Voltaire had called "a nice problem for history" was finally resolved: Madame d'Eon was, indeed, a man.

EPILOGUE

Thomas Copeland, a surgeon on Millman Street, was called to d'Eon's house. "I hereby certify," he wrote, "that I inspected and dissected the body of le chevalier d'Eon in the presence of M. Adair, M. Wilson, le père Elysée and found the male organs of generation in every respect perfectly formed." He signed the death certificate on May 23, 1810, and it was cosigned by eleven other men who viewed d'Eon's corpse—including the Earl of Yarmouth and two surgeons. D'Eon's landlord also wrote that "I declare that the chevalier Déon has lodged in my house about three years, and I knew her as a female, and I also declare that upon seeing the body after death, she proves to be a man." If there were any doubt that he knew what he was talking about, he added, "My wife makes the same declaration."

THE CHEVALIER D'EON was not the only "cross-dresser" involved in the secret diplomacy of the American Revolution. Deane, a shopkeeper, disguised himself as a businessman while secretly engaging in diplomacy and espionage; he was later denounced by the Lees for being what he pretended to be, a merchant in the pursuit of profit.

Beaumarchais, a playwright, masqueraded as a trader so he could smuggle arms for the Continental Congress; Congress, however, mistook him as Louis XVI's agent and never paid him. Bancroft, a British spy, assumed the role of secretary to the commissioners; yet history remembered him as an American patriot. Arthur Lee presented himself in the ill-fitting disguise of a diplomat, all the while secretly undermining his colleagues and the alliance with the French; Lee was motivated as much by revenge and real estate speculation as he was by genuine patriotism. Even Franklin used his celebrity as a mask for his secret diplomacy.

Eighteenth-century Americans regarded Europeans as intrinsically deceitful. The English and French aristocracies judged people based on birth and squandered the public treasury on their own patronage and nepotism. Aristocrats did not respect talent and hard work. Such societies naturally bred hypocrisy and corruption. Deane and Franklin would have expected Vergennes and Stormont to practice duplicity. And it was precisely because Americans feared that British corruption was infecting American society that Americans like Richard Henry Lee called for independence to insulate the colonies from this moral pestilence. American revolutionaries frequently used the language of moral virtue as a rallying cry. They believed it was possible to have self-government, but only if self-interest and factionalism were constrained by civic virtue and informed by a sense of the common good.

But the Americans were not free from sin. Centuries of European influence had already infected the body politic with land grants and royal patents, patronage, monopolies, the slave trade, and titles. The Lees, for example, modeled themselves after the British aristocracy. They bore the same obnoxious sense of entitlement, and they wielded the same sort of patrimonial authority over the Northern Neck of Tidewater Virginia. The Lees and the Franklins both competed over land grants and bent the instruments of government to pursue their own financial interest; both Arthur Lee and Ben Franklin dispensed government jobs to family members without any sense that they were committing precisely the same offense as the British aristocracy they were rebelling against.

Deane was relatively virtuous insofar as he neither sought nor received for himself or his family any direct benefits from public service. Though Deane was often portrayed as hypocritical and avaricious, there was little to support that. Deane's clandestine role was of a different nature. He fell from grace, after his return to Paris, when he could no longer tolerate the baseless charges of the Lees and their cronies. "Safety lies in silence," he had written as a young Yale student. But instead of pursuing a quiet life, he chose public service and suffered terribly as a result. He was too thin-skinned for the rough-and-tumble of American politics. Deane's loss of face led to his loss of faith in the Revolution; and once he became disillusioned, he was doomed.

When one considers all the duplicity and corruption that characterized the times, one might wonder whether this was the dawn of the Age of Enlightenment or the Age of Deception?

MUCH IS MADE of the fact that the revolutionary generation was singularly talented and comprised of so many brilliant men of great character. Were virtuous men like Washington and Adams truly indispensable to the Revolution? Or were the ideals of the Revolution just as often fought and won by men who were not as worthy as the principles they expounded? Principles of democracy, equality, and personal liberty were all realized by men who were far from perfect exemplars of their ideals. Should we denigrate their achievements merely because they were human and bound to err? The Calvinists thought that only bad people were made to suffer; the notion that only virtuous men could have won the Revolution is no more sophisticated.

By placing the founders of our nation on a pedestal, we risk setting up an impossible standard for future generations to follow. Perhaps we would be wiser to extract from our history the lesson that human frailty is part of our heritage. Just as virtuous men like Adams and Washington were capable of mean and spiteful acts, so too, hypocrites like Jefferson and the Lees were capable of statesmanship. Together, these men won a Revolution and built a nation.

The idea that history is not guided by great or virtuous individuals may be disconcerting, but our experience teaches us that sometimes history happens by accident. Chance casts people in extraordinary roles: a shopkeeper becomes a statesman; a playwright becomes a smuggler; a soldier-spy becomes a maiden. Gazing backward, we may think we discern some invisible hand that governs the outcome of wars and revolutions, but in the moment that history is being made, chance governs. A kingdom may be lost "for want of a nail"; Britain may have lost the American colonies in a wager over a dress.

There were good reasons for France to help the Americans, but Louis XVI thought there were better reasons for France to remain neutral. Beaumarchais helped to persuade Louis and to impress on Vergennes the urgency of acting quickly to safeguard the French sugar islands and weaken Britain. Why did the king and his minister care what a disgraced playwright thought about foreign affairs? Beaumarchais's pivotal role in resolving the Chevalier d'Eon affair won him their attention. D'Eon's threat to release Louis XV's secret correspondence would have risked a disastrous war with Britain, and Louis XVI and Vergennes were determined to avoid such a war at all costs. Beaumarchais permanently neutralized the threat the chevalier posed to the king by coaxing d'Eon to turn over the correspondence and declare that he was female. But, ironically, by agreeing to support Beaumarchais's arms smuggling, France was drawn into the very conflict that the king had employed Beaumarchais to avoid: war with Britain.

Beaumarchais's role was critical for the American Revolution. At the very least, Beaumarchais accelerated the decision to arm the Americans by a few months, if not years, and that time proved decisive. The arms arrived only weeks before the Battle of Saratoga. Without those arms, the Continental Army would have been crushed. Instead, the Battle of Saratoga changed the course of the war and persuaded France to ally itself with the Americans.

Why, then, aren't Deane and Beaumarchais remembered as heroes of the American Revolution? Deane and Beaumarchais risked their "lives, fortunes, and sacred honor" to secure the arms that Washington desperately needed. In the process, they challenged authority, provoked jealousy, greed, and animosity, and refused to stay silent when they disagreed with the policies of their governments. Politics rewards those who sail with the popular current—not those who ride against the tide.

It is left to history to correct the popular judgment. Reading history teaches us to doubt, to question, and, if we're lucky, to discover new heroes.

ACKNOWLEDGMENTS

This is not the book I intended to write. I was writing a different book about the history of international law in the United States when I discovered Silas Deane. All that I knew about him was that a shopkeeper from Wethersfield, Connecticut, had shown up in Versailles to negotiate an alliance long before Benjamin Franklin or John Adams arrived in France. I was curious as to how that happened, but I could not find any serious books about Deane. I tried to find Deane's personal papers, assuming they had survived. I had no idea how to find diaries or letters of an obscure figure from the eighteenth century, so I phoned a friend, David Kahn, who was then the executive director of the Connecticut Historical Society to ask his advice. To my surprise David replied: "We own his papers." He had only just discovered that fact a few weeks before when he came across some boxes left by Deane's descendants in the Connecticut Historical Society archives.

I flew to Hartford, Connecticut. The Connecticut Historical Society is located in a house adjacent to the University of Connecticut School of Law, where, coincidentally, I used to teach. The archivist showed me several boxes that looked as if they had not been opened in generations. I found letters to and from George Washington, Benjamin Franklin, John Adams, Thomas Jefferson, Louis XVI, John Jay, Robert Morris, Benedict Arnold, and many others. The story they revealed was an astonishing tale of innocence and intrigue—idealism, struggle, betrayal, and survival. I was hooked. I put my other manuscript aside and began six years of research in the United States, France, and England, and an enduring relationship with Deane, Beaumarchais, and d'Eon.

My research was greatly facilitated by the library staff at the U.C. Hastings College of the Law, especially Vince Moyer, who can find anything. My research assistants, Jean-Paul Buchannan, Stephen Miller, Ryan McCord, Chris Nolan, and Jakob Zollmann tolled many hours with microfiche and old manuscripts, helping me to uncover the full story. And Simona Angelucci, Jennifer Holly, Sophie Hubscher, Natacha Ivacheff-Kolb, Pauline Marcel, and Leo Spanos helped translate many of the documents from the archives of La ministère des Affaires étrangères in Paris.

Professors Robert Gross, Reuel Schiller, and William Taubman generously read drafts of my manuscript and helped me to sharpen my focus. I owe a special debt to Professor Gross, who first inspired my interest in the American Revolution in his class at Amherst College. Simon Burrows, Jonathan Conlin, Gary Kates, James Lander, Linda Meditz, Kenneth Minkema, Brian Morton, Donald Spinelli, and Douglas Winiarski were kind enough to share with me some of their historical expertise. Amber Cushing, Librarian at the New Hampshire State Archives; Lesley Whitelaw, Archivist of the Middle Temple; Jeff Collins, the archivist at the First Congregational Church of Wethersfield; Charles Lyle, the director of the Webb-Deane-Stevens Museum in Wethersfield; photographer Ruth Hanks; and Mathieu da Vinha, Coordinator of the Research Center at the Château de Versailles were also very helpful.

I am grateful to my literary agent, Doe Coover, and to my editor, Jake Morrissey, for giving an unknown writer a chance to tell an unfamiliar story. Sarah Bowlin, Ed Cohen, Claire McGinnis, and Kate Moreau were wonderful to work with at Riverhead. And I appreciate the generous support of my patient colleagues at the U.C. Hastings College of the Law, especially Deans Mary Kay Kane, Shauna Marshall, and Nell Newton.

I was blessed with great friends who thoughtfully commented on many drafts, pushed me to do better, and sustained me for six years, including Corky Ellis, Bob Graubard, David Friend, Mark Hager, Elise Kroeber, Peter Lee, Jane Shulman, James Sloan, Bertrand Vandeville, and Linden Wise. My friend and publicist Jan Saragoni Bradley and my consultant Roger Williams were invaluable. I am especially grateful to my friend and talented mentor Paul Aron, who spent countless hours advising, editing, and encouraging me through the whole process of this book, and to Rick Steele and Susan Nance, who helped me to find my voice.

I hope my effort is worthy of your confidence, friendship, and support.

NOTES

15   Britain prohibited merchants: Alden, *History of the American Revolution*, 35–42.

15   The other major: Wood, *The American Revolution*, 17–18

16   The nonimportation movement: Ferling, *A Leap in the Dark*, 30–43, 53–57, 85–86; Wood, *The American Revolution*, 32–35.

17   Following the enactment: Quoted in Clark, *Silas Deane*, 17.

17   In his elegant script: Silas Deane's Latin Dissertation, 1755, Beinecke Rare Book and Manuscript Library, Yale University Library.

CHAPTER 2

21   Despite a talented cast: Lemaître, *Beaumarchais*, 82; Grendel, *Beaumarchais*, 44–46.

22   From an early age: Dalsème, *Beaumarchais*, 3–4.

22   Possessing a sharp mind: Lever, *Beaumarchais* (trans. Emanuel), 4–6.

22   The young Caron: Quoted in Kite, *Beaumarchais and the War of American Independence*, vol. 1, 52.

23   Caron's defiance and brilliance: Grendel, *Beaumarchais*, 5–10.

23   Now tall and slender: Dalsème, *Beaumarchais*, 24–26.

24   Madame Francquet: Ibid., 27–28; Lever, *Beaumarchais* (trans. Emanuel), 10–12.

24   In the spring of 1760: Lever, *Beaumarchais* I, 118.

25   Pâris-Duverney, who was unmarried: Ibid., 120.

25   Pâris-Duverney gave him: Dalsème, *Beaumarchais*, 38–41; Lever, *Beaumarchais* (trans. Emanuel), 16–17, 43.

26   Beaumarchais teased Pâris-Duverney: Letter, Beaumarchais to Duverney, June 15, 1770, quoted in Dalsème, *Beaumarchais*, 79.

26   The plain language: Lever, *Beaumarchais* I, 120, 332.

27   While sodomy was officially: Blanc, "The 'Italian Taste' in the Time of Louis XVI," 69–84. Lever writes that some of his contemporaries thought that Pâris-Duverney was guilty of the "Socratic sin," and that Beaumarchais had "deployed charm and seductiveness in the old man's company." Moreover, their "strange letters" were characteristic of sodomites. Lever, *Beaumarchais* (trans. Emanuel), 48.

27   Pâris-Duverney introduced Beaumarchais: Lever, *Beaumarchais* I, 121–25.

27   On a poster: Dalsème, *Beaumarchais*, 70.

CHAPTER 3

31   Jonathan's was located: Straus, *Lloyd's*, 47–61, 81–89; Wright and Fayle, *A History of Lloyd's*, 6–19, 90–105.

32   There was always someone: Worsley and Griffith, *The Romance of Lloyd's*, 114–24.

32   On this particular Saturday: Kates, *Monsieur d'Eon Is a Woman*, 184.

32   In a thick accent: Homberg and Jousselin, *D'Eon de Beaumont*, 139–40; Cox, *The Enigma of the Age*, 84.

33   One of d'Eon's biographers: Homberg and Jousselin, *D'Eon de Beaumont*, 275.

33   Christened Charles-Geneviève-Louis-Auguste-André-Timothée d'Eon: Beaumont, *The Maiden of Tonnerre*, 3–4.

33   From an early age: Cox, *The Enigma of the Age*, 4–6.

34   Once, while serving: Quoted in Telfer, *The Strange Career*, 14.

34   Even in his middle years: Cox, *The Enigma of the Age*, 3–5; Nixon, *Royal Spy*, 160–61.

35   Louis XV had sent: Homberg and Jousselin, *D'Eon de Beaumont*, 26.

35   According to d'Eon's version: Kates, *Monsieur d'Eon Is a Woman*, 67.

35   According to d'Eon, Conti: Quoted in Kates, *Monsieur d'Eon Is a Woman*, 67–71.

36   Some scholars doubt: Kates, *Monsieur d'Eon Is a Woman*, 72–76.

36   A copy of a letter: Nixon, *Royal Spy*, 33–35.

37   What is indisputable: Kates, *Monsieur d'Eon Is a Woman*, 73.

37   When the British ambassador's: Cox, *The Enigma of the Age*, 16–23.

38   D'Eon later wrote: D'Eon, "The Great Historical Epistle by the Chevalière d'Eon, 1785," translated in Beaumont, *The Maiden of Tonnerre*, 14; Homberg and Jousselin, *D'Eon de Beaumont*, 31–40.

38   According to one version of d'Eon's story: Kates, *Monsieur d'Eon Is a Woman*, 74–76.

38   D'Eon later claimed: Cox, *The Enigma of the Age*, 20–22; Kates, *Monsieur d'Eon Is a Woman*, 70–76; Homberg and Jousselin, *D'Eon de Beaumont*, 30–31; Telfer, *The Strange Career*, 13–19.

38   Once the empress agreed: Homberg and Jousselin, *D'Eon de Beaumont*, 40–42.

39   He was wounded: According to a certificate of commendation signed by Marshall de Broglie on December 24, 1761; quoted in Homberg and Jousselin, *D'Eon de Beaumont*, 56–57.

40   Louis XV wrote to d'Eon: Letter, Louis XV to d'Eon, June 3, 1763, quoted in Kates, *Monsieur d'Eon Is a Woman*, 93.

41   He was, in fact: Gaillardet, *The Memoirs of Chevalier d'Eon*, xiv.

41   The French Foreign Ministry balked: Kates, *Monsieur d'Eon Is a Woman*, 97–98.

42   At that point, d'Eon claimed: Quoted in Homberg and Jousselin, *D'Eon de Beaumont*, 75–76.

42   The tone of d'Eon's letters: Letter, Duc de Praslin to d'Eon, 1763, quoted in Homberg and Jousselin, *D'Eon de Beaumont*, 77.

42   His correspondence with Praslin: Letter, d'Eon to Duc de Praslin, September 25, 1763, quoted in Homberg and Jousselin, *D'Eon de Beaumont*, 79.

42   D'Eon warned a friend: Letter, d'Eon to Claude Pierre de Sainte Foy, September 25 1763, quoted in Kates, *Monsieur d'Eon Is a Woman*, 100.

43   His extravagance quickly depleted: Cox, *The Enigma of the Age*, 34–35, 43–44.

43   To the Comte de Guerchy: Letter, d'Eon to Comte de Guerchy, September 25, 1763, quoted in Homberg and Jousselin, *D'Eon de Beaumont*, 79–80.

CHAPTER 4

45 **The Comte de Guerchy arrived:** Gaillardet, *Memoirs of Chevalier d'Eon*, xviii; Beaumont, *The Maiden of Tonnerre*, xiv; Cox, *The Enigma of the Age*, 62.

46 **Conscious of the growing threat:** Letter, d'Eon to Louis XV, November 18, 1763, quoted in Gaillardet, *Memoirs of Chevalier d'Eon*, 138–45; Homberg and Jousselin, *D'Eon de Beaumont*, 118-120.

47 **The British attorney-general:** Homberg and Jousselin, *D'Eon de Beaumont*, 102–12; Cox, *The Enigma of the Age*, 66–68.

47 **D'Eon responded to his guilty verdict:** Letter, d'Eon to Louis XV, November 18, 1763, quoted in Gaillardet, *Memoirs of Chevalier d'Eon*, 138–45; Homberg and Jousselin, *D'Eon de Beaumont*, 118–23; Kates, *Monsieur d'Eon Is a Woman*, 130–31; Cox, *The Enigma of the Age*, 57–58.

48 **Frightened for his life:** Homberg and Jousselin, *D'Eon de Beaumont*, 102–3; Cox, *The Enigma of the Age*, 59; Johnson, *The Ghost Map*, 16.

48 **Fearing imminent arrest:** Cox, *The Enigma of the Age*, 61.

49 **He wrote the king's secretary:** Letter, d'Eon to Jean-Pierre Tercier, March 23, 1764, Archives de ministère des Affaires étrangères (Paris), Correspondance politique, Angleterre, Supplement 13, 156–67, quoted in Kates, *Monsieur d'Eon Is a Woman*, 118.

49 **The king and Broglie knew:** Quoted in Cox, *The Enigma of the Age*, 77–78.

50 **One story was that a Russian:** Kates, *Monsieur d'Eon Is a Woman*, 191–92; Homberg and Jousselin, *D'Eon de Beaumont*, 136.

50 **A second possibility:** Homberg and Jousselin, *D'Eon de Beaumont*, 135; Cox, *The Enigma of the Age*, 63.

50 **A third is that d'Eon:** Kates, *Monsieur d'Eon Is a Woman*, 194.

50 **Louis XV, who could:** Letter, Louis XV to General Monet, October 28, 1770, *Correspondance secrète inédite de Louis XV, sur la politique étrangère*, ed. Edgar Boutaric (Paris, 1866), vol. 1, 411-412, quoted in Kates, *Monsieur d'Eon Is a Woman*, 182.

50 **The Marquise du Deffand:** Horace Walpole, *Memoirs*, vol. 4, 493.

50 **A London paper reported:** *London Evening Post*, March 9–12, 1771, quoted in Kates, *Monsieur d'Eon Is a Woman*, 183.

51 **A flattering poem:** Letter, Louis XV to General Monet, October 28, 1770, quoted in Kates, *Monsieur d'Eon Is a Woman*, 182–83.

51 **Reportedly, as much as 60,000 pounds:** Clark, *Betting on Lives*, 45–48; *Gazetteer and New Daily Advertiser*, March 11, 13, and 16, 1771, quoted in Kates, *Monsieur d'Eon Is a Woman*, 184.

51 **To Comte de Broglie:** Quoted in Homberg and Jousselin, *D'Eon de Beaumont*, 141.

CHAPTER 5

53 **Geneviève had lost:** Grendel, *Beaumarchais*, 47.

54 **Once he joked:** Quoted in Ibid., 49.

55 **The comte once exclaimed:** Quoted in Lemaître, *Beaumarchais*, 88.

56 **Beaumarchais wrote cryptically:** Quoted in Dalsème, *Beaumarchais*, 76.

56 **La Blache sent:** Lemaître, *Beaumarchais*, 88; Lever, *Beaumarchais* (trans. Emanuel), 48–50.

56 **Regretting the interference:** Quoted in Lever, *Beaumarchais* (trans. Emanuel), 45.

56 **Beaumarchais and Pâris-Duverney set up:** Lemaître, *Beaumarchais*, 89.

57 **Years later, in the sweet-scented:** Quoted in Lever, *Beaumarchais* I, 121.

57 **Beaumarchais's wife gave:** Lever, *Beaumarchais* (trans. Emanuel), 40–41.

57 **Vicious rumors circulated:** Lever, *Beaumarchais* (trans. Emanuel), 42.

58 **With Pâris-Duverney gone:** Dalsème, *Beaumarchais*, 81–87.

58 **He would later remark that La Blache:** Quoted in Grendel, *Beaumarchais*, 51.

58 **Madame Goëzman bluntly admitted:** Quoted in Lever, *Beaumarchais* (trans. Emanuel), 68.

58 **The judge's wife demanded:** Lemaître, *Beaumarchais*, 112–14; Lever, *Beaumarchais* (trans. Emanuel), 68–70.

59 **To make matters worse:** Lemaître, *Beaumarchais*, 98–108.

59 **After the court's judgment:** Lever, *Beaumarchais* (trans. Emanuel), 71.

60 **On the street, Parisians joked:** Quoted in Ruskin, *Spy for Liberty*, 56.

60 **Even Voltaire exclaimed:** Dalsème, *Beaumarchais*, 148.

60 **Though Beaumarchais felt vindicated:** Quoted in Lemaître, *Beaumarchais*, 129.

60 **Sartine advised Beaumarchais:** Grendel, *Beaumarchais*, 108.

61 **He wrote to the man:** Ibid., 110

61 **La Borde invited Beaumarchais:** Nixon, *Royal Spy*, 157–158; Telfer, *Strange Career*, 233; Loménie, *Beaumarchais and His Times*, 208; Dalsème, *Beaumarchais*, 166–167. The physical description here is based upon the location of the king's wardrobe and La Borde's apartments at that time according to the Research Center at the Château de Versailles.

62 **La Borde offered Beaumarchais:** Lemaître, *Beaumarchais*, 132–36.

62 **He left immediately for London:** Morton and Spinelli, *Beaumarchais and the American Revolution*, 7; Lemaître, *Beaumarchais*, 138.

63 **In May 1774, Beaumarchais returned:** Lever, *Beaumarchais* (trans. Emanuel), 71.

63 **As one of Louis XV's secret agents:** Dalsème, *Beaumarchais*, 174.

63 **A month later Beaumarchais:** Lever, *Beaumarchais* (trans. Emanuel), 88–89.

63 **Neither Sartine nor the king:** Loménie, *Beaumarchais and His Times*, 211; Lemaître, *Beaumarchais*, 141–42.

64 **Beaumarchais proceeded to London:** Loménie, *Beaumarchais and His Times*, 211–23; Lemaître, *Beaumarchais*, 141–52.

64 **When the crusading Beaumarchais:** Grendel, *Beaumarchais*, 119–33; Dalsème, *Beaumarchais*, 199–200.

64 **Whether anyone still believed:** Quoted in Lever, *Beaumarchais* (trans. Emanuel), 95.

65 **Once again, the king refused:** Lemaître, *Beaumarchais*, 156.

65 **Refusing to admit his own deceit:** Letter, Beaumarchais to Sartine, December 11, 1774, quoted in Dalsème, *Beaumarchais*, 205.

66 **Louis XVI thought d'Eon's demands:** Letter, Louis XVI to Vergennes, January 26, 1775, *Correspondance secrète inédite*, vol. 2, 445, quoted in Kates, *Monsieur d'Eon Is a Woman*, 219.

66 **Vergennes called d'Eon's letter:** Letter, Vergennes to Louis XVI, January 26, 1775, *Correspondance secrète inédite*, vol. 2, 444, quoted in Kates, *Monsieur d'Eon Is a Woman*, 219.

CHAPTER 6

68 **The delegates included John Adams:** McCullough, *John Adams*, 24.

70 **In his own words:** Quoted in McCullough, *John Adams*, 119, from Charles Francis Adams, ed., *The Works of John Adams*, vol. 2, 514.

70 **After their first meeting:** August 15, 1774, in Butterfield, ed., *The Adams Papers: Diary of John Adams*, vol. 2, 98.

71 **He marveled that:** Ibid., 99.

71 **In New Haven, Deane met:** Clark, *Silas Deane*, 21–23; Adams, *The Works of John Adams*, vol. 2, 345; Sabine, *Biographical Sketches of Loyalists of the American Revolution*, vol. 2, 533.

72 **That evening the three delegates:** Letter, Deane to Elizabeth Deane, August 26, 1774, *Deane Papers*, vol. 1, 6.

72 **The cramped conditions:** Letter, Deane to Elizabeth, September 6, 1774, *Deane Papers*, vol. 1, 10.

72 **Despite a lack of formal education:** Collier, *Roger Sherman's Connecticut*, 32–37.

73 **On Sunday evening:** Letter, Deane to Elizabeth, July 20, 1775, *Deane Papers*, vol. 1, 74.

73 **Deane began to regret:** Letter, Deane to Elizabeth, August 29, 1774, *Deane Papers*, vol. 1, 7.

73 **Though "Mr. Sherman is clever in private":** Letter, Deane to Elizabeth, August 28, 1774, *Deane Papers*, vol. 1, 5–8.

74 **Deane was exhilarated:** Letter, Deane to Elizabeth, September 6, 1774, *Deane Papers*, vol. 1, 15.

74 **At the opening session:** Letter, Deane to Elizabeth, August 29, 1774, *Deane Papers*, vol. 1, 7.

74 **He considered his fellow delegates:** Letter, Deane to Elizabeth, September 6, 1774, *Deane Papers*, vol. 1, 19–20.

74 **Deane gushed that:** Letter, Deane to Elizabeth, September 8, 1774, *Deane Papers*, vol. 1, 20.

74 **Though there was a large assortment:** Letter, Deane to Elizabeth, September 6, 1774, *Deane Papers*, vol. 1, 12–15.

76 **The Connecticut Assembly again chose:** November 3, 1774, Connecticut House of Representatives, *Journals of the Continental Congress*, vol. 2, 15.

76 **On Thursday, April 20, 1775:** Letter, Joseph Palmor to Deane, April 19, 1775, Knollenberg, *Growth of the American Revolution*, 234.

77 **Unable to manufacture or import guns:** Stephenson, "The Supply of Gunpowder in 1776," 271–72.

77 **"I beg leave to inform you":** Quoted in Jellison, *Ethan Allen*, 106.

78 **The ditches surrounding:** Ketchum, *Saratoga*, 28–30; Jellison, *Ethan Allen*, 104–7; Brands, *The First American*, 506–8; Srodes, *Franklin*, 276–77.

78 **On the road, he encountered:** Jellison, *Ethan Allen*, 108; Randall, *Benedict Arnold*, 84–85.

78 **That afternoon Parsons met:** Clark, *Silas Deane*, 28–29; Jellison, *Ethan Allen*, 109; Randall, *Benedict Arnold*, 87.

79 **With this financial backing:** Jellison, *Ethan Allen*, 103, 112.

79 **Ethan Allen and Benedict Arnold:** Randall, *Benedict Arnold*, 91–92, 99; Jellison, *Ethan Allen*, 105–18.

80 **As soon as the fort:** Randall, *Benedict Arnold*, 96–97.

80 **As they approached the city:** Letter, Deane to Elizabeth, May 12, 1775, *Deane Papers,* vol. 1, 47.

CHAPTER 7

82 **After his meeting with Foreign Minister:** Gudin, *Beaumarchais*, 163–64.

83 **D'Eon had read Beaumarchais's:** Quoted in Lever, *Beaumarchais*, (trans. Emanuel), 107.

83 **"Both of us probably felt drawn":** Quoted in Cox, *The Enigma of the Age*, 95.

83 **More to the point:** Homberg and Jousselin, *D'Eon de Beaumont*, 170.

83 **D'Eon arrived at Beaumarchais's:** Cox, *The Enigma of the Age*, 83.

83 **The chevalier's poise:** Letter, Beaumarchais to Louis XVI, April 27, 1775, Shewmake, *For the Good of Mankind*, 61; Dalsème, *Beaumarchais*, 223.

84 **Deserted by the king:** Quoted in Telfer, *The Strange Career*, 235; Cox, *The Enigma of the Age*, 94–95; Homberg and Jousselin, *D'Eon de Beaumont*, 170–71.

85 **Suddenly, he exclaimed:** Letter, Beaumarchais to Louis XVI, April 27, 1775, Shewmake, *For the Good of Mankind*, 60–61; Dalsème, *Beaumarchais*, 223.

85 **As d'Eon later explained in her** *Memoirs:* Beaumont, *The Maiden of Tonnerre,* 3–4; Cox, *The Enigma of the Age*, 4.

86 **From d'Eon's early years:** Cox, *The Enigma of the Age*, 4–6; quoted in Kates, *Monsieur d'Eon Is a Woman*, 71.

86 **The only hint:** Cox, *The Enigma of the Age*, 3–5; Nixon, *Royal Spy*, 160–61.

CHAPTER 8

87 **"I do assure you, Sire":** First Abstract for the King, Apr 27, 1775, in Donvez, *La politique de Beaumarchais*, 1599–1600; Gudin, *Histoire de Beaumarchais*, 168–69, as translated in Kite, *Beaumarchais and the War of Independence,* vol. 2, 18–19.

88 **In June, Beaumarchais returned to Versailles:** Lander, "A Tale of Two Hoaxes," 995, 1004.

88 **Vergennes agreed that if d'Eon:** Letter, Vergennes to Beaumarchais, June 21, 1775, Beaumarchais, *Correspondance*, vol. 2, 128.

88 **"If M. d'Eon is willing to adopt":** Letter, Vergennes to Louis XVI, August 7, 1775, quoted in Lemaître, *Beaumarchais*, 169.

88 **Vergennes worried that if d'Eon returned:** Letter, Vergennes to Beaumarchais, August 26, 1775, quoted in Lemaître, *Beaumarchais*, 169.

88   "If Mr. D'Eon wanted to wear women's clothes": Letter, Vergennes to Beaumar-
     chais, August 26, 1775, Shewmake, *For the Good of Mankind*, 66.

89   Years earlier, she had begun purchasing: Kimberly Chrisman-Campbell, unpub-
     lished manuscript; also discussed in Lander, "A Tale of Two Hoaxes," 1018.

89   And she may have started: Kates, *Monsieur d'Eon Is a Woman*, 191–95.

89   By July, Beaumarchais reported to Vergennes: Letter, Beaumarchais to Vergennes,
     July 14, 1775, Beaumarchais, *Correspondance*, vol. 2, 130.

91   After assuming command: Letter, George Washington to Lund Washington,
     August 20, 1775, Washington, *The Papers of George Washington*, vol. 1, 335–36.

91   Though Washington had been promised: Freeman, *George Washington*,
     vol. 3, 493.

91   The colonists were undisciplined: A survey of 27 out of 133 staff officers showed
     that 48 percent were merchants, 11 percent artisans, and 7 percent manufactur-
     ers. Carp, *To Starve the Army at Pleasure*, Appendix Table A.4, 225.

91   Supply shortages combined: Risch, *Supplying Washington's Army*, 282–83; W. J.
     Eccles, "The French Alliance and the American Victory," in Ferling, *The World
     Turned Upside Down*, 154.

91   Colonists without guns: Ferguson and Nuxoll, "Investigation of Government
     Corruption," 16–17; Freeman, *George Washington*, vol. 3, 509.

91   If the British attacked: Freeman, *George Washington*, vol. 3, 509.

91   Moreover, the colonies had no capacity: Ferguson and Nuxoll, "Investigation,"
     16–17; Risch, *Supplying Washington's Army*, 339–62.

92   He boasted to a friend: Letter, Beaumarchais to Sartine, November 17, 1774,
     quoted in Loménie, *Beaumarchais in His Time*, 211.

92   What she saw in her looking glass: Horace Walpole, quoted in Cox, *The Enigma
     of the Age*, 95.

92   She called him: Dalsème, *Beaumarchais*, 225; letter, d'Eon to Beaumarchais,
     December 1775, Beaumarchais, *Correspondance*, vol. 2, 157.

93   Beaumarchais was just three years: His first wife, Mme. Francquet, was thirty when
     he was twenty-four; his second wife, Mme. Lévêque, was in her early thirties.

93   If his wife were still alive: Letter, Beaumarchais to d'Eon, September 5, 1775,
     Brotherton Collection, Leeds University, quoted in Spinelli, "Beaumarchais and
     d'Eon," 7.

93   Minerva, the goddess: Letter, Beaumarchais to d'Eon, August 18, 1775, Beaumar-
     chais, *Correspondance*, vol. 2, 240.

93   For d'Eon, who all her life had: Gaillardet, *Memoirs of Chevalier D'Eon*
     (1866 ed.), 422.

93   She teased Beaumarchais: Ibid., 426.

93   She even quoted back: Quoted in Cox, *The Enigma of the Age*, 105–6.

93   Beaumarchais acknowledged to Vergennes: Letter, d'Eon to Beaumarchais, 1775,
     Beaumarchais, *Correspondance*, vol. 2, 158, note 1.

94   It stipulated that d'Eon: The text of "the Transaction" appears in Gaillardet, *The
     Memoirs of Chevalier D'Eon*, 252–58.

95   In a dramatic flourish: Quoted in Gaillardet, *The Memoirs of Chevalier D'Eon*,
     254–58.

CHAPTER 9

97   **His stout support for independence:** Butterfield, ed., *The Adams Papers: Diary of John Adam*, vol. 2, 96; Alsop, *Yankees at the Court*, 42.

97   **Among other assignments:** October 5, 1775, *Journals of the Continental Congress*, vol. 3, 1775, 277, note 1; September 19, 1775, *Journals of the Continental Congress*, vol. 2, 255.

97   **It soon became clear:** Letter, John Adams to Abigail Adams, October 19, 1775, Smith, *Letters of Delegates*, vol. 2, 202.

97   **Adams remarked:** John Adams to John Trumbull, November 5, 1775, Smith, *Letters of Delegates*, vol. 2, 304.

97   **On a typical day, Deane:** Letter, Deane to Elizabeth Deane, June 3, 1775, *Deane Papers*, vol. 1, 54.

98   **"People here, members of Congress":** Letter, Deane to Elizabeth, July 20, 1775, *Deane Papers*, vol. 1, 74–75.

99   **Sherman, in John Adams's words:** Quoted in McCullough, *John Adams*, 85.

99   **Sanctimonious and often rude:** Butterfield, ed., *The Adams Papers: Diary of John Adams*, vol. 2, September 15, 1775; Smith, *Letters of Delegates*, vol. 2, 13.

100   **For Sherman to succeed:** Collier, *Roger Sherman's Connecticut*, 92.

100   **A bitter division:** Boardman, *Roger Sherman*, 133; Collier, *Roger Sherman's Connecticut*, 112–113; Letter, Sherman to Wooster, June 23, 1775, as quoted in Fellows, *The Veil Removed*, 107; Freeman, *George Washington*, 474.

100   **He wrote to Elizabeth:** Letter, Deane to Elizabeth Deane, July 15, 1775, *Deane Papers*, vol. 1, 72–73.

100   **But Sherman and Wooster were furious:** Letter, Sherman to Wooster, June 23, 1775, as quoted in Fellows, *The Veil Removed*, 107; letter, Wooster to Sherman, July 7, 1775, quoted in Boutell, *The Life of Roger Sherman*, 88–89.

101   **Deane was "confoundedly Chagrined":** Letter, Eliphalet Dyer to Joseph Trumbull, quoted in Collier, *Roger Sherman's Connecticut*, 132.

101   **Ezra Stiles, a Congregationalist minister:** Stiles, *The Literary Diary of Ezra Stiles*, vol. 1, 654.

101   **Sherman most likely played:** Letter, John Trumbull to Silas Deane, October 20, 1775, *Deane Papers*, vol. 1, 86; Collier, *Roger Sherman's Connecticut*, 131–132.

101   **He wrote Elizabeth:** Letter, Deane to Elizabeth Deane, November 26, 1775, *Deane Papers*, vol. 1, 93–94.

102   **In private, Deane confided:** Letter, Deane to Elizabeth, January 21, 1776, *Deane Papers*, vol. 1, 100.

102   **In Deane's eyes, Sherman:** Ibid., 98.

102   **Once, Deane loaned Sherman his coach:** Letter, Deane to Elizabeth, July 23, 1775, *Deane Papers*, vol. 1, 73–77.

102   **With characteristic magnanimity:** Letter, Deane to Elizabeth, January 21, 1776, *Deane Papers*, vol. 1, 99.

CHAPTER 10

104   **"Beaumarchais was joined:** Gudin, *Histoire de Beaumarchais*, 175–76; Ruskin, *Spy for Liberty*, 93.

104 Once seated at the Lord Mayor's: Gudin, *Histoire de Beaumarchais*, 175–76.

104 Some London newspapers: Williamson, *Wilkes*, 146; Kronenberger, *The Extraordinary Mr. Wilkes*, 114; Homberg and Jousselin, *D'Eon de Beaumont*, 137–42; Kates, *Monsieur d'Eon Is a Woman*, 186.

105 In fact, Wilkes was as unsure: Quoted in Homberg and Jousselin, *D'Eon de Beaumont*,139.

105 Unperturbed by this news: Wilkes Papers, British Library, Additional Manuscripts 30866.

105 He was a radical: Postgate, *That Devil Wilkes*, 18–49; Cash, *John Wilkes*, 33–35.

105 The king called him: Kronenberger, *The Extraordinary Mr. Wilkes*, 114.

105 When John Montagu: Quoted in Cash, *John Wilkes*, 1–2.

105 The son of a malt distributor: Quoted in Trench, *Portrait of a Patriot*, 266.

106 When d'Eon feared: Kates, *Monsieur d'Eon Is a Woman*, 126.

106 In April 1763, Wilkes published: Postgate, *That Devil Wilkes*, 50–51, 111–31; Cash, *John Wilkes*, 68–72, 99–103.

107 There he inhabited a comfortable: Cash, *John Wilkes*, 218, 227–230; Telfer, *The Strange Career of Chevalier D'Eon*, 205.

107 Wilkes had begun his political career: Cash, *John Wilkes*, 49–50, 231–35.

107 Wilkes warned: *The Speeches of Mr. Wilkes in the House of Commons*, vol. 2 (1777), 12–31.

108 Wilkes declared that the American colonies: Wilkes, *The Speeches of Mr. Wilkes in the House of Commons* (1786), 296–315.

CHAPTER 11

109 At fifty-five, he looked: Price, *Preserving the Monarchy*, 18–19.

110 Six years before: Ibid., 8.

110 Vergennes questioned Choiseul's: Murphy, *Charles Gravier, Comte de Vergennes*, 97–101.

111 Privately, Louis XV: Van Tyne, "Influences Which Determined the French Government to Make the Treaty with America, 1778," 528–41; Van Tyne, "French Aid Before the Alliance of 1778," 20–30.

111 Choiseul's tenure as foreign minister: Murphy, *Charles Gravier, Comte de Vergennes*, 212–13; Dull, *A Diplomatic History of the American Revolution*, 36.

111 The twenty-two-year-old monarch felt: Quoted in Cronin, *Louis & Antoinette*, 68.

112 Vergennes's worldview: Dull, *A Diplomatic History*, 36; Murphy, *Charles Gravier, Comte de Vergennes*, 211–20.

113 Weaker states were: Quoted in Bemis, *The Diplomacy of the American Revolution*, 14.

113 Vergennes knew that: Murphy, *Charles Gravier*, 222–29.

113 Vergennes wrote to the Spanish ambassador Aranda: Letter, Vergennes to Aranda, November 25, 1775, quoted in Murphy, *Charles Gravier*, 228.

114 Vergennes warned: Letter, Vergennes to Count de Guines, June 23, 1775, Shewmake, *For the Good of Mankind*, 64; Bemis, *The Diplomacy of the American Revolution*, 19.

114 **Beaumarchais returned to Versailles:** Morton and Spinelli, *Beaumarchais and the American Revolution*, 24.

115 **Beaumarchais wrote:** Letter, Beaumarchais to Louis XVI, September 21, 1775, Shewmake, *For the Good of Mankind*, 70–71.

115 **Beaumarchais argued that France:** Ibid., 69–72.

116 **Beaumarchais cautioned:** Ibid., 72.

116 **At this point, Vergennes would not consider:** Dull, *A Diplomatic History of the American Revolution*, 48–49; Bemis, *The Diplomacy of the American Revolution*, 35; Murphy, *Charles Gravier*, 233.

117 **"All the sagacity":** Letter, Beaumarchais to Vergennes, September 21, 1775, Shewmake, *For the Good of Mankind*, 73.

CHAPTER 12

119 **These delegates included:** November 29, 1775, *Journals of the Continental Congres*, vol. 3, 392; Brands, *The First American*, 521; Van Doren, *Benjamin Franklin*, 538–539; Srodes, *Franklin*, 271.

120 **Just days before:** Hamon, *Le Chevalier de Bonvouloir*, 11–12, 26–27; Alsop, *Yankees at the Court*, 28–30; Morgan, *Benjamin Franklin*, 229–230.

121 **Vergennes thought Ambassador Guines:** Alsop, *Yankees at the Court*, 24–26.

121 **He instructed Bonvouloir:** Murphy, *Charles Gravier, Comte de Vergennes*, 232; Bendiner, *The Virgin Diplomats*, 50.

122 **The four men were perplexed:** Hamon, *Le Chevalier de Bonvouloir*, 28–29; Bonvouloir's Report, December 28, 1775, Wharton, *The Revolutionary Diplomatic Correspondence of the United States*, vol. 1, 334; Karsch, "The Unlikely Spy," Carpenter's Hall, at http://www.ushistory.org/carpentershall/history/french.htm.

123 **The five delegates asked:** Bonvouloir's Report, December 28, 1775, Wharton, *The Revolutionary Diplomatic Correspondence of the United States*, vol. 1, 334.

123 **But then Bonvouloir:** Ibid., 334–35.

123 **With growing frustration:** Ibid., 334.

124 **He wrote to Vergennes:** Ibid.

124 **In fact, at the time Bonvouloir:** Freeman, *George Washington*, vol. 4, 622.

125 **In case the report:** Alsop, *Yankees at the Court*, 31–32.

125 **Though the would-be diplomat:** Bonvouloir's Report, December 28, 1775, Wharton, *The Revolutionary Diplomatic Correspondence of the United States*, vol. 1, 334; Brands, *The First American*, 521; Isaacson, *Benjamin Franklin*, 321; Srodes, *Franklin*, 271–72; Morgan, "Ezra Stiles," 229–30; Alsop, *Yankees at the Court*, 26–35.

CHAPTER 13

127 **Washington's army was in desperate:** Risch, *Supplying Washington's Army*, 339–62; Freeman, *George Washington*, vol. 3, 509; Ferguson and Nuxoll, "Investigation of Government Corruption," 16–17.

127 **"Congress have left it":** Letter, Major J. Burnett to Jeremiah Wadsworth, March 18, 1780, as quoted in Carp, *To Starve the Army at Pleasure*, 69.

127   John Adams described: Quoted in Cook, *Dawn over Saratoga*, 13.

127   One soldier complained: Quoted in Nelson, "The American Soldier," in Ferling, *The World Turned Upside Down*, 47.

127   The men who had rushed off: Hatch, *The Administration of the American Revolutionary Army*, 93; Risch, *Supplying Washington's Army*, 282–83; W. J. Eccles, "The French Alliance and the American Victory," in Ferling, *The World Turned Upside Down*, 154.

128   Shortages were exacerbated: Carp, *To Starve the Army at Pleasure*, 67–68.

128   On March 2, 1776: Letter, Secret Committee to Deane, March 2, 1776, *Deane Papers*, vol. 1, 119.

129   It was roughly: Economic History Service, http://www.measuringworth.com/index.html.

129   It was essential to the success: Letter, Secret Committee to Deane, March 3, 1776, *Deane Papers*, vol. 1, 123; letter, Secret Committee to Deane, March 1, 1776, *Deane Papers*, vol. 1, 117.

129   Franklin instructed Deane: Ibid., 124–25.

130   Once Deane established: Ibid., 125.

130   Deane also knew Bancroft's: Anderson and Anderson, "Edward Bancroft, M.D.," 356.

130   Bancroft supported the American: Letter, Secret Committee to Deane, March 3, 1776, *Deane Papers,* vol. 1, 126.

131   Recognizing the need: Letter, Deane to Elizabeth Deane, March 2–3, 1776, *Deane Papers*, vol. 1, 119–21.

132   Only a few months earlier: Letter, Deane to Elizabeth, June 18, 1775, *Deane Papers*, vol. 1, 62.

132   It would be "criminal": Letter, Deane to Elizabeth, March 2–3, 1776, *Deane Papers*, vol. 1, 121.

132   In closing, Deane questioned: Ibid., 123.

CHAPTER 14

134   For months Wilkes: Quoted in Postgate, *That Devil Wilkes*, 208.

134   King George III and his government: One possibility is that Wilkes wanted to provoke the king to take excessive measures that would alienate Parliament and test the royal proclamation against treason in court. Lander, "A Tale of Two Hoaxes," 5–6.

135   Lord North had already arrested: Most historians believe that the alleged plot was fabricated, but the testimony against Wilkes had some corroboration, and at least one historian thinks that Sayre may have been involved in some conspiracy against the government (Sainsbury, "The Pro-Americans of London," 423, 437).

135   In addition to d'Eon and Beaumarchais: Wilkes, *Diary*, October 25, 1775.

135   The Lee brothers were frequent: Cash, *John Wilkes,* 249.

135   The Lees came from: Hendrick, *The Lees of Virginia*, 77–78.

136   Arthur Lee, the youngest: Potts, *Arthur Lee*, 10–14, 101.

137   While Arthur was still: Potts, *Arthur Lee*, 88-91.

137   During his years in London: Ibid., 35–36.

137 **Yet instead of being grateful:** Ibid., 81, 88-89,113. However, for a brief time after Franklin decided to support independence, Lee expressed admiration for him. Ibid., 114.

138 **Lee, like his brothers:** Lee, *An Essay in Vindication of the Continental Colonies of America, from a Censure of Mr. Adam Smith, in His Theory of Moral Sentiments. With Some Reflections on Slavery in General* (London, 1764), 11–16, 37–40; Potts, *Arthur Lee,* 28–30; Holton, *Forced Founders,* 67–70.

138 **Shortly after arriving in London:** Cash, *John Wilkes,* 234–35; Sainsbury, "The Pro-Americans of London, 1769 to 1782," 425–427.

139 **In fact, Wilkes's position:** Cash, *John Wilkes,* 231-235; quoted in Potts, *Arthur Lee,* 59.

139 **While Franklin excoriated Wilkes:** Potts, *Arthur Lee,* 60.

141 **Vergennes hoped that:** Ibid., 152; Stockdale and Holland, *Middle Temple Lawyers,* 148.

CHAPTER 15

142 **He would enter:** Williamson, *The History of the Temple,* 647–48; Home and Headlam, *The Inns of Court,* 64–75; Hendrick, "America's First Ambassador," 147.

145 **Wentworth had done very well:** Mayo, *John Wentworth,* 68, 165; Wentworth, *Wentworth Genealogy,* vol. 3, 11.

145 **Paul Wentworth was born:** Wentworth, *The Wentworth Genealogy,* vol. 3, 7–9; Wilderson, *Governor John Wentworth,* 152–53; Mayo, *John Wentworth,* 68, 82.

146 **Paul Wentworth returned:** Wentworth, *The Wentworth Genealogy,* vol. 3, 7–9, 12, 170–72; Cuthbertson, *The Loyalist Governor,* 48–50; Wilderson, *Governor John Wentworth,* 152–53; Mayo, *John Wentworth,* 68, 82.

146 **When Lee was a hungry law student:** Riggs, "Arthur Lee," 268, 273; May 27, 1775, Hutchinson, *The Diary and Letters,* vol. 1, 434–35; January 20, 1777, Hutchinson, *The Diary and Letters,* vol. 2, 129; Van Tyne, "French Aid Before the Alliance of 1778," 38–39; Potts, *Arthur Lee,* 133, 152; letter to Col. Worthington, March 6, 1775, Hutchinson, *The Diary and Letters,* vol. 1, 398; According to Potts, Wentworth lived in Lee's flat in 1774. More likely Wentworth was an occasional overnight visitor.

147 **Instead, while Lee secretly conspired:** Potts, *Arthur Lee,* 133, 135; Sosin, *Agents and Merchants,* 222.

147 **As one historian noted:** Trevelyan, *The American Revolution,* 337.

CHAPTER 16

148 **November brought miserable weather:** Morton and Spinelli, *Beaumarchais and the American Revolution,* 30; Homberg and Jousselin, *D'Eon de Beaumont,* 183.

148 **D'Eon celebrated the completion:** Lander, "A Tale of Two Hoaxes," 1017–18.

148 **Nursing a cough:** Cox, *The Enigma of the Age,* 101; Morton and Spinelli, *Beaumarchais,* 30; Kates, *Monsieur d'Eon Is a Woman,* 230.

149 **As he and Lee had agreed:** Letter, Beaumarchais to Louis XVI, October–November 1775, Shewmake, *For the Good of Mankind,* 75–81. Although this letter is dated

February 1776, in the *Deane Papers,* vol. 1, 100–15, Shewmake points out that it is referenced in another memorandum dated December 15, 1775, and so must have been completed before then. Shewmake also points out that this memorandum was found in the papers of the controversial French ambassador to the United States, Genet, who probably used it to try to solicit the support of the United States during the French Revolution (Shewmake, *For the Good of Mankind,* 38–39).

149 **Vergennes reacted coolly:** Murphy, *Charles Gravier, Comte de Vergennes,* 232–34.

149 **The king felt morally:** Kates, *Monsieur d'Eon Is a Woman,* 230–31.

150 **He begged Vergennes:** Letter, Beaumarchais to Vergennes, November 24, 1775, Shewmake, *For the Good of Mankind,* 81.

150 **The fact that Vergennes passed:** Price, *Preserving the Monarchy,* 22–23.

150 **In Beaumarchais's memorandum:** Letter, Beaumarchais to Louis XVI, December 7, 1775, Shewmake, *For the Good of Mankind,* 82–87.

151 **He warned the king:** Letter, Beaumarchais to Louis XVI, December 13, 1775, Shewmake, *For the Good of Mankind,* 88.

151 **A few days later he complained:** Letter, Beaumarchais to Louis XVI, December 15, 1775, Shewmake, *For the Good of Mankind,* 89.

151 **An Englishman once addressed:** Kite, *Beaumarchais and the War of American Independence,* vol. 2, 51.

151 **One London paper reported:** Kates, *Monsieur d'Eon Is a Woman,* 243, quoted in *Morning Post,* December 9, 1776; Cox, *The Enigma of the Age,* 103–4.

152 **D'Eon began to suspect:** Kates, *Monsieur d'Eon Is a Woman,* 231, citing d'Harvelay to Vergennes, November 14, 1775, Archives de ministère des Affaires étrangères, Correspondance, Angleterre, Supplement 16:446. By the spring of 1777, the *London Chronicle* (May 5) reported that the betting on d'Eon's gender totaled about 120,000 pounds. *London Chronicle,* as cited by James Oldham, "Judicial Activism in Eighteenth Century English Common Law in the Times of the Founders," *Green Bag* (Spring 2005): 269, 275. Thus, it seems unlikely that Beaumarchais and Morande alone would have invested as much as 100,000 pounds. Also Clark, *Betting on Lives,* 48.

152 **In a fit of pique:** Kates, *Monsieur d'Eon Is a Woman,* 232.

153 **"[As] to our approaching marriage":** Letter, d'Eon to Beaumarchais, December 1775, Beaumarchais, *Correspondance,* vol. 2, 157–58.

153 **Beaumarchais wrote to d'Eon:** Letter, Beaumarchais to d'Eon, January 18, 1776, Kates, *Monsieur d'Eon Is a Woman,* 235–36.

153 **Beaumarchais could not complain:** Letter, d'Eon to Beaumarchais, January 30, 1776, Kates, *Monsieur d'Eon Is a Woman,* 237–40; Spinelli, "Beaumarchais and d'Eon"; Lander, "A Tale of Two Hoaxes," 1019; Cox, *The Enigma of the Age,* 104–5.

155 **D'Eon's worst suspicions:** Kates, *Monsieur d'Eon Is a Woman,* 241–43.

CHAPTER 17

156 **That winter was one of the coldest:** Currie, *Frosts, Freezes and Fairs,* 11, 55.

157 **The Secret Committee in Philadelphia:** Letter, Secret Committee to Arthur Lee, November 30, 1776, Franklin, *The Papers of Benjamin Franklin,* vol. 22, 281.

157   **Lee and Beaumarchais discussed:** Letter, Beaumarchais to Louis XVI, February 29, 1776, Shewmake, *For the Good of Mankind*, 96–97.

157   **Beaumarchais laid out four possibilities:** Letter, Beaumarchais to Louis XVI, February 29, 1776, Shewmake, *For the Good of Mankind*, 97–99.

158   **In reality there was little evidence:** Dull, *A Diplomatic History of the American Revolution*, 57.

159   **Only six days later:** Letter, Deane to Elizabeth Deane, March 16, 1776, *Deane Papers*, vol. 1, 126–27.

159   **For several frustrating weeks:** Letter, Robert Morris to Deane, April 4, 1776, *Deane Papers*, vol. 1, 131.

159   **In the meantime, Congress sent:** Letter, John Hancock to Deane, April 3, 1776, *Deane Papers*, vol. 1, 131.

160   **From Canada, Deane's friend:** Letter, Benedict Arnold to Deane, March 30, 1776, *Deane Papers*, vol. 1, 128–31.

160   **To make matters worse:** Alden, *A History of the American Revolution*, 190.

161   **More than a month passed:** Letter, Deane to Robert Morris, April 27, 1776, *Deane Papers*, vol. 1, 134–35.

162   **The foreign minister prepared:** Dull, *Diplomatic History*, 57–59; Murphy, *Charles Gravier, Comte de Vergennes*, 234–35.

162   **On the one hand, he denounced:** Letter, Vergennes to Ministers, March 17, 1776, Stevens, *Facsimiles*, vol. 13, no. 1316; Wharton, *Revolutionary Diplomatic Correspondence*, vol. 1, 337–39.

163   **The French minister of war:** Wharton, vol. 1, 339; Price, *Preserving the Monarchy*, 49–51.

163   **Vergennes responded to Turgot's:** Wharton, *The Revolutionary Diplomatic Correspondence of the United States*, vol. 1, 335–36; Bemis, *The Diplomacy of the American Revolution*, 26–27. There is some dispute about the date of Vergennes's memorandum. Cornélis de Witt dated it to March 1776 in the appendix to his *Thomas Jefferson* (1860). Subsequently, Henri Doniol dated it to the end of 1775 in his *Histoire de la participation de la France à l'établissement des Etats Unis d'Amérique*. Subsequent scholarship by John J. Meng proved that it was written in April 1776. Meng showed that Vergennes was influenced by Beaumarchais's memoranda of February 1776 (Meng, "A Footnote to Secret Aid in the American Revolution," 791–95).

163   **Louis XVI had no sympathy:** Bemis, *The Diplomacy of the American Revolution*, 22, 27–28.

164   **After a few weeks:** Price, *Preserving the Monarchy*, 50–51.

CHAPTER 18

166   **Hunter wrote:** Letter, William Hunter to Deane, April 15, 1776, Collections of the Connecticut Historical Society 23, 19–20.

167   **After nearly four months:** Letter, Deane to Robert Morris, June 23, 1776, Franklin, *The Papers of Benjamin Franklin*, vol. 22, 487–90; James, *Silas Deane: Patriot or Traitor?* 11–12; Clark, *Silas Deane*, 43–44; Alsop, *Yankees at the Court*, 46.

168   He found a wine merchant: "Accounts of Silas Deane, 1776–1781," Silas Deane Papers, Library of Congress Manuscript Reading Room.

168   Deane found himself: "Refutation of the Calumny of Henry Laurens, 1784," *Deane Papers*, vol. 5, 331.

169   "I could not therefore solicit": Ibid.

169   Instead, he was compelled: Ibid., 332.

169   Though Franklin thought: Letter, Deane to Secret Committee, August 18, 1776, *Deane Papers*, vol. 1, 195; letter, Stormont to Weymouth, August 21, 1776, Stevens, *Facsimiles*, vol. 13, no. 1350.

169   Deane wrote that Paris: Letter, Deane to Secret Committee, August 16, 1776, *Deane Papers*, vol. 1, 212.

170   Marveling at Britain's: Letter, Vergennes to de Noailles, March 21, 1777, Stevens, *Facsimiles*, vol. 15, no. 1488.

170   Spying on foreigners: Letter, Vergennes to Beaumarchais, April 26, 1776, Stevens, *Facsimiles*, vol. 13, no. 1329.

CHAPTER 19

171   While originally the face value: Calculations based on McCusker, *How Much Is That in Real Money?* 73–75. In 1776, 200,000 Continental dollars spent in the United States might have purchased as much as $4.9 million today, according to the Economic History Resources available at www.eh.net/ehresources/howmuch/dollarq.php. That calculation, however, may not reflect the willingness of a French creditor to accept Continental dollars in 1776.

172   When Deane presented: Letter, Deane to Robert Morris, September 30, 1776, *Deane Papers*, vol. 1, 286.

172   On July 8: "Narrative of Edward Bancroft," August 14, 1776, *Deane Papers*, vol. 1, 179 (hereafter, Bancroft Narrative).

173   As charming as he was: Letter, Deane to Secret Committee, August 18, 1776, *Deane Papers*, vol. 1, 209–10; Stevens, *Facsimiles*, vol. 9, no. 890.

173   The following day Deane and Bancroft: Bancroft Narrative, *Deane Papers*, vol. 1, 181.

174   He told Deane that Vergennes: Morton and Spinelli, *Beaumarchais*, 54–55.

174   When Deane, Bancroft, and Dubourg arrived: Letter, Deane to Secret Committee, August 18, 1776, *Deane Papers*, vol. 1, 198; Bancroft Narrative, *Deane Papers*, vol. 1, 178–80.

174   Deane began by informing: Letter, Deane to Secret Committee, August 18, 1776, *Deane Papers*, vol. 1, 201.

175   Vergennes responded that an open: Ibid., 196–99.

175   Vergennes expressed his personal: Bancroft Narrative, *Deane Papers*, vol. 1, 177, 179–80.

175   The minister extended to Deane: Ibid., 180; "Our French Allies," *Harper's*, (April 1871), 753, 757.

175   Vergennes told Deane that he should maintain: Letter, Deane to Secret Committee, August 18, 1776, *Deane Papers*, vol. 1, 200–201.

175   First, Vergennes informed Deane: Ibid., 202; Morton and Spinelli, *Beaumarchais*, 54–56.
176   Dubourg was puzzled: Letter, Deane to Secret Committee, August 18, 1776, *Deane Papers*, vol. 1, 202.
176   Deane followed his meeting: Bancroft Narrative, August 14, 1776, *Deane Papers*, vol. 1, 180.
176   On the morning of July 20: Ibid., 182–83.
176   Deane asked if France: "Refutation of the Calumny of Henry Laurens, 1784," *Deane Papers*, vol. 5, 386–87.

CHAPTER 20

178   An envelope addressed: Letter, Beaumarchais to Deane, July 14, 1776, *Deane Papers*, vol. 1, 145–46.
179   They agreed that in exchange: Roderigue Hortalez & Co. to Secret Committee, August 18, 1776, Shewmake, *For the Good of Mankind*, 158.
179   Beaumarchais boasted to Deane: Ibid., 159.
180   Though he was virtually unknown: Ibid., 159; letter, Beaumarchais to Vergennes, October 14, 1776, Shewmake, *For the Good of Mankind*, 169.
180   In fact, Beaumarchais remained frustrated: Letter, Beaumarchais to Vergennes, September 25, 1776, Shewmake, *For the Good of Mankind*, 166.
180   He knew that he could offend: Letter, Beaumarchais to Vergennes, December 9, 1776, Shewmake, *For the Good of Mankind*, 178; letter, Beaumarchais to Vergennes, November 9, 1776, Shewmake, *For the Good of Mankind*, 173.
180   A week after Deane's first: Letter, Deane to Secret Committee, August 18, 1776, *Deane Papers*, vol. 1, 209–10.
181   Bancroft also contacted: Mayo, *John Wentworth*, 68, 165; Wentworth, *The Wentworth Genealogy*, vol. 3, 11. Bemis, "The British Secret Service and the French-American Alliance," 474, 475.
182   He had written: Bancroft Narrative, August 14, 1776, *Deane Papers*, vol. 1, 177–84.
182   While Deane had agreed to pay: Ibid., 474, 475–77; Edward Bancroft's memorial to the Marquis of Carmarthen, September 17, 1784, as quoted in Bemis, "The British Secret Service and the French-American Alliance," 492–94; Bessie Bies, "Edward Bancroft: A British Spy," Dissertation, University of Chicago, Department of History (1908); "Engagement of Dr. Edwards to correspond with P. Wentworth," December 1776, Stevens, *Facsimiles*, vol. 3, no. 235.
182   Charles Wentworth, vows: Bancroft, *The History of Charles Wentworth, Esq.* (1770), vol. 3, 93.

CHAPTER 21

184   Exasperated by French: Letter, Beaumarchais to Vergennes, November 12, 1776, Shewmake, *For the Good of Mankind*, 174; letter, Beaumarchais to Vergennes, July 26, 1776, Shewmake, *For the Good of Mankind*, 150.
184   By August, Rodriguez Hortalez: Letter, Beaumarchais to Deane, July 22, 1776,

Shewmake, *For the Good of Mankind*, 146; letter, Beaumarchais to Vergennes, July 25, 1776, Shewmake, *For the Good of Mankind*, 148–49; letter, Rodriguez Hortalez & Co. to Secret Committee, August 18, 1776, Shewmake, *For the Good of Mankind*, 157.

184 **Dr. Dubourg suggested that Deane:** Dubourg note, July 1776, Archives des Affaires étrangères, Angleterre, vol. 516, fol. 446, in Stevens, *Facsimiles*, vol. 13, no. 1343.

184 **Vergennes vigorously denied:** Letter, Stormont to Weymouth, August 21, 1776, Stevens, *Facsimiles*, vol. 13, no. 350; letter, Stormont to Weymouth, September 25, 1776, Stevens, *Facsimiles*, vol. 13, no. 1366.

185 **Beaumarchais went to great lengths:** Morton and Spinelli, *Beaumarchais*, 75.

186 **At one point the hapless comte:** Beaumarchais, *The Marriage of Figaro* (trans. John Wood), act 2, 146–57.

186 **Indeed, Ambassador Stormont:** Letter, Stormont to Weymouth, August 21, 1776, Stevens, *Facsimiles*, vol. 13, no. 1350.

186 **"[H]e is the most silent":** Letter, Beaumarchais to Vergennes, August 13, 1776, Stevens, *Facsimiles*, vol. 9, no. 889.

186 **Beaumarchais unburdened himself:** Letter, Beaumarchais to Deane, September 18, 1776, Shewmake, *For the Good of Mankind*, 164–65.

187 **Beaumarchais accused Dubourg:** Letter, Beaumarchais to Vergennes, August 2, 1776, Shewmake, *For the Good of Mankind*, 152–53.

187 **When Dubourg wrote to Vergennes:** Quoted in Grendel, *Beaumarchais*, 178.

188 **Vergennes's secretary, Gérard:** Letter, Deane to Secret Committee, August 18, 1776, Wharton, *Revolutionary Diplomatic Correspondence*, vol. 2, 116–18, 201.

188 **Arthur Lee was furious:** Letter, Lee to Deane, July 28, 1776, Stevens, *Facsimiles* vol. 5, no. 467.

189 **"The scale is coming":** Ibid.

189 **Deane informed Lee plainly:** Letter, Deane to Lee, August 19, 1776, *Deane Papers*, vol. 1, 226–27.

190 **Deane had little patience:** Letters, Deane to Delap, July 29 and 30, 1776, *Deane Papers*, vol. 1, 166–70.

CHAPTER 22

191 **Deane tried to focus:** Deane, "Memoir on the Commerce of America," August 15, 1776, *Deane Papers*, vol. 1, 184–95.

191 **On Saturday, August 17:** Morton and Spinelli, *Beaumarchais*, 65; letter, Deane to Charles W. F. Dumas, August 18, 1776, *Deane Papers*, vol. 1, 219.

192 **Almost immediately after signing:** Letter, Secret Committee to Deane, July 8, 1776, *Deane Papers*, vol. 1, 502–3.

192 **He quickly scribbled:** Letter, Deane to Vergennes, August 22, 1776, Wharton, *Revolutionary Diplomatic Correspondence*, vol. 2, 132–33.

193 **Deane was already predisposed:** Letter, Deane to Secret Committee, August 18, 1776, Wharton, *Revolutionary Diplomatic Correspondence*, vol. 2, 122.

193 **Neither Vergennes nor Beaumarchais:** Potts, *Arthur Lee*, 159–60.

193 **Lee returned to London:** Hendrick, "America's First Ambassador," 137, 147;

Franklin, Morris, et al., Memorandum, October 1, 1776, Wharton, *Revolutionary Diplomatic Correspondence,* vol. 2, 151.

193 **He knew that Beaumarchais expected:** In a letter to Robert Morris, Richard Henry Lee mentioned the plan to send the finest tobacco to France in exchange for arms. Richard Henry Lee to Robert Morris, December 24, 1776, *Correspondence of Robert Morris,* 59–60.

193 **Months earlier, Beaumarchais had written:** Letter, Beaumarchais to Lee, June 6, 1776, Wharton, *Revolutionary Diplomatic Correspondence,* vol. 2, 97.

193 **In his reply Lee:** Letter, Mary Johnson to Beaumarchais, June 14, 1776, ibid.

193 **After all, that was precisely what Lee:** Letter, R. Hortalez to Secret Committee, August 18, 1776, ibid., 129–31.

194 **Now Bancroft warned:** Letter, Edward Bancroft to Deane, September 13, 1776, *Deane Papers,* vol. 1, 237–40.

195 **Deane wrote Congress, warning:** Letter, Deane to Secret Committee, October 1, 1776, *Deane Papers,* vol. 1, 287–88.

195 **Vergennes warned Deane and Beaumarchais:** Letter, Beaumarchais to Vergennes, September 21, 1776, Stevens, *Facsimiles,* vol. 13, no. 1364.

196 **In response to this crisis:** "Memoire of Silas Deane to French Foreign Office," September 24, 1776, *Deane Papers,* vol. 1, 275.

196 **The revolution, he argued:** Ibid., 266.

196 **Deane's argument reviewed:** Ibid., 267.

196 **But Deane offered Louis XVI:** Ibid., 273.

196 **It was "impossible that":** Ibid., 281.

197 **In a postscript probably added:** Ibid., 283–84.

CHAPTER 23

199 **"For Heaven's sake":** Letter, Deane to Secret Committee, October 1, 1776, *Deane Papers,* vol. 1, 287–89.

199 **News of the Declaration:** Letter, Deane to Secret Committee, October 8, 1776, *Deane Papers,* 309.

200 **He knew that success:** Letter, Deane to Secret Committee, October 25, 1776, *Deane Papers,* vol. 1, 338.

200 **When Lee sent him:** Letter, Arthur Lee to Deane, October 4, 1776, *Deane Papers,* vol. 1, 304.

201 **Captain Lee had seized:** Letter, John Emerson to Deane, October 2, 1776, Stevens, *Facsimiles,* vol. 6, no. 587.

201 **Deane fretted:** Letter, Deane to Secret Committee, October 17, 1776, *Deane Papers,* vol. 1, 325–28.

201 **He moved to a spacious:** Letter, Deane to Edward Bancroft, undated, probably March 1777, *Deane Papers,* vol. 2, 8.

202 **Both Vergennes and Beaumarchais persuaded:** Letter, Beaumarchais to Deane, July 26, 1776, Shewmake, *For the Good of Mankind,* 151.

203 **It is unlikely that Deane:** "Le Stathoudérat du Comte de Broglie," in Doniol, *Histoire,* vol. 2, 50–97; "Agreement with Baron de Kalb"; *Deane Papers,* vol. 1, 344;

letter, Deane to Secret Committee, December 6, 1776, *Deane Papers*, vol. 1, 404; Unger, *Lafayette*, 19–20.

204 **As visitors in uniform:** Letter, Stormont to Weymouth, November 19, 1776, Stevens, *Facsimiles*, vol. 14, no. 1373.

204 **Among the men who found:** Unger, *Lafayette*, 8–15.

204 **When the three young men:** Letter, Deane to Secret Committee, December 6, 1776, *Deane Papers*, vol. 1, 404.

205 **The families of Lafayette:** Unger, *Lafayette*, 21–26.

205 **Vergennes feared that:** Letter, Vergennes to Superintendent of Police Lenoir, December 10, 1776, Shewmake, *For the Good of Mankind*, 179; Unger, *Lafayette*, 20–27.

205 **To complicate matters:** Unger, *Lafayette*, 23-26.

CHAPTER 24

207 **One day in early November:** Letter, Deane to Edward Bancroft, undated, probably March 1777, *Deane Papers*, vol. 2, 8–9; Warner, *John the Painter*, 109–10.

208 **Deane could see the man:** Letter, Deane to Edward Bancroft, undated, probably March 1777, *Deane Papers*, vol. 2, 9–10.

208 **Aitken said he had lived:** Ibid., 11.

209 **Aitken was actually an itinerant:** Aitken, *The Life of James Aitken*, 27–36; Warner, *John the Painter*, 78–90; Clark, "John the Painter," 1, 6–7.

209 **"[T]hough I may appear":** Letter, Deane to Edward Bancroft, undated, probably March 1777, *Deane Papers*, vol. 2, 9–11.

210 **Aitken's plan was to destroy:** Clark, "John the Painter," 4–5; Warner, *John the Painter*, 96.

210 **Deane was too shocked:** Letter, Deane to Edward Bancroft, probably March 1777, *Deane Papers*, vol. 2, 6–7.

211 **Deane made no effort to stop:** Aitken, *The Life of James Aitken*, 85; York, *Burning the Dockyard*, 2–5; Warner, *John the Painter*, 115.

211 **Aitken returned to England:** Clark, "John the Painter," 9.

212 **The next day Bancroft:** Aitken, *The Life of James Aitken*, 45–46; Warner, *John the Painter*, 135. Julian Boyd's study of Bancroft suggested that Bancroft had some prior knowledge of Aitken. Bancroft had carried back from London a cipher key that included Aitken's code number, zero (Boyd, "Silas Deane," 342).

212 **Bancroft was terrified:** Boyd, "Silas Deane," 338–42; Clark, "John the Painter," 14–16; Warner, *John the Painter*, 136.

213 **One month later, Aitken:** "Trial of James Hill alias John the Painter," in Howell, *Complete Collection of State Trials*, vol. 20 (1771–1777), 1335.

214 **When news of the trial spread:** March 14, 1777, *Diary of Hutchinson*, vol. 2, 143–44.

214 **Bancroft had visited:** Letter, Bancroft to the Marquis of Carmarthen, September 17, 1784, quoted in Bemis, "The British Secret Service and the French-American Alliance," 493.

214 **Deane looked to Bancroft:** Letter, Deane to John Jay, December 3, 1776, *Deane Papers*, vol. 1, 398.

215 **On the afternoon of March 10, 1777:** Warner, *John the Painter*, 220–225.

CHAPTER 25

216   **He dipped his pen:** Letter, Deane to Secret Committee, November 9, 1776, *Deane Papers*, vol. 1, 351.

217   **A copy of the Declaration:** Letter, Deane to Vergennes, November 20, 1776, *Deane Papers*, vol. 1, 358.

217   **Deane also conveyed:** Letter, Deane to Conde de Aranda, December 2, 1776, *Deane Papers*, vol. 1, 391.

217   **Painfully aware of Congress's:** "Memoire by Silas Deane," November 23, 1776, *Deane Papers*, vol. 1, 361.

217   **To Congress Deane expressed:** Letter, Deane to Secret Committee, November 28, 1776, *Deane Papers*, vol. 1, 372.

218   **Despite news that the British:** Letter, Deane to Charles W. F. Dumas, November, 1776, *Deane Papers*, vol. 1, 370.

218   **As Deane stepped:** Morton and Spinelli, *Beaumarchais and the American Revolution*, 80–81.

219   **In November the *Amphitrite*:** Letter, Beaumarchais to Vergennes, December 2, 1776, Shewmake, *For the Good of Mankind*, 177.

219   **When they were done:** "Invoices of *L'Amphitrite*, Accounts of Silas Deane, 1776–1781, Library of Congress Manuscript Collection.

219   **At that point the military officers:** Beaumarchais, *Correspondance*, 82; letter, Beaumarchais to Vergennes, December 16, 1776, Shewmake, *For the Good of Mankind*, 179–80; letter, Beaumarchais to Deane, December 17, 1776, Shewmake, 181.

220   **Stormont raced back:** Morton and Spinelli, *Beaumarchais*, 86; letter, Stormont to Weymouth, November 20, 1776, Stevens, *Facsimiles*, vol. 14, no. 1375.

221   **His messenger, however, was delayed:** Beaumarchais, *Correspondance*, 85–88.

221   **Congress had sent with Franklin:** Letter, Franklin to Deane, December 4, 1776, Franklin, *The Papers of Benjamin Franklin*, vol. 23, 26–27.

CHAPTER 26

223   **Franklin arrived at the dock:** Letter, Franklin to Benjamin Vaughan, September 18, 1777, Franklin, *The Papers of Benjamin Franklin*, vol. 24, 539; Blanc, "The 'Italian Taste' in the Time of Louis XVI," 79; Schiff, *A Great Improvisation*, 89–90.

224   **It was evident that Deane's hotel:** "Two Notes," December 30, 1776, Franklin, *Papers of Benjamin Franklin*, vol. 23, 100.

224   **On December 28:** Letter, Franklin to Secret Committee, January 4, 1777, Franklin, *Papers of Benjamin Franklin*, vol. 23, 113, n. 3.

225   **To make matters worse:** Morton and Spinelli, *Beaumarchais*, 55–56, 95–98.

225   **On the morning of Sunday, January 5:** Letter, American Commissioners to Vergennes, January 5, 1777, Franklin, *Papers of Benjamin Franklin*, vol. 23, 121.

226   **Thus the commissioners met:** Ibid., 122–23; Bemis, *The Diplomacy of the American Revolution*, 53.

226   **One of Franklin's friends in France:** Wood, *The Americanization of Benjamin Franklin*, 175–76; Schoenbrun, *Triumph in Paris*, 97–99; Van Doren, *Benjamin Franklin*, 576; Schiff, *A Great Improvisation*, 50–53; Bendiner, *The Virgin Diplomats*, 78; Isaacson, *Benjamin Franklin*, 329–30.

227 He carried a walking stick: Letter, Franklin to Emma Thompson, February 8, 1777, Franklin, *Papers of Benjamin Franklin*, vol. 23, 298.

228 Franklin could certainly afford: Van Doren, *Benjamin Franklin*, 569–72; Wood, *The Americanization of Benjamin Franklin*, 173–74, 180–81.

228 Even the British spies: Patton, *Patriot Pirates*, 159.

228 Franklin spent his days: Schiff, *A Great Improvisation*, 54.

229 Franklin confessed to her: Letter, Franklin to Madame Brillon, March 10, 1778, Franklin, *Papers of Benjamin Franklin*, vol. 26, 85–86.

229 "Do you know, my dear Papa": Letter, Madame Brillon to Franklin, December 20, 1778, Franklin, *Papers of Benjamin Franklin*, vol. 28, 253.

229 Franklin thought nothing: Isaacson, *Benjamin Franklin*, 356–62.

229 At thirty-six, Lee: Potts, *Arthur Lee*, 11; Hendrick, *The Lees of Virginia*, 367–68.

229 Lee left for Spain: Letter, Arthur Lee to Secret Committee, February 11, 1777, Wharton, *Revolutionary Diplomatic Correspondence*, vol. 2, 268.

230 During their meeting Morris: Potts, *Arthur Lee*, 169; letter, Arthur Lee to Richard Henry Lee, March 6, 1777, The Lee Family Papers, vol. 3, 120.

230 Deane and Franklin reported: Bendiner, *The Virgin Diplomats*, 70; letter, Deane to Robert Morris, September 23, 1777, *Deane Papers*, vol. 2, 146–50.

230 Morris wrote to Deane accusing: Quoted in Wagner, *Robert Morris*, 44-45.

231 Nonetheless, Lee met with Grimaldi: Letter, Lee to Grimaldi, March 5, 1777, Wharton, *Revolutionary Diplomatic Correspondence*, vol. 2, 279–80.

231 Lee told the foreign minister: Letter, Lee to the Court of Spain, March 8, 1777, Wharton, *Revolutionary Diplomatic Correspondence*, vol. 2, 282.

231 Grimaldi growled back: Letter, Grimaldi to Lee, March 8, 1777, Wharton, *Revolutionary Diplomatic Correspondence*, vol. 2, 282.

231 Grimaldi warned Lee: Letter, Lee to Floridablanca, March 17, 1777, Wharton, *Revolutionary Diplomatic Correspondence*, vol. 2, 290. Bemis calculated that Spain eventually loaned the Americans less than $400,000 between 1776 and 1779 (*The Diplomacy of the American Revolution*, 53, 91–92). Potts, however, reported that the Spanish lent the Americans as much as 400,000 livres (roughly $3 million today). The king of Spain was prepared to lend money to the Americans months before Lee's arrival (letter, Secret Committee to Commissioners, February 19, 1777, Wharton, *Revolutionary Diplomatic Correspondence*, vol. 2, 274).

231 Though Lee considered: Letter, Bancroft to Wentworth, May 1777, Stevens, *Facsimiles*, vol. 2, no. 151.

232 Franklin, who had more diplomatic experience: Letter, Franklin to Lee, March 21, 1777, Wharton, *Revolutionary Diplomatic Correspondence*, vol. 2, 298; Bemis, *The Diplomacy of the American Revolution*, 114.

232 Though he chastised Franklin: Potts, *Arthur Lee*, 166, 175–76; Schiff, *A Great Improvisation*, 73; Bemis, *The Diplomacy of the American Revolution*, 115.

233 Lee returned to Passy: Schiff, *A Great Improvisation*, 57.

233 In Lee's absence Deane negotiated: Commissioners and the Farmers General: Contract for Tobacco, March 24, 1777, Franklin, *Papers of Benjamin Franklin*, vol. 23, 514–17.

234 At the end of December, 1776: Letter, Lee to Secret Committee, December 31, 1776, Wharton, *Revolutionary Diplomatic Correspondence*, vol. 2, 242.

CHAPTER 27

235 **Lee wrote to a friend that the appointment:** Quoted in Hendrick, *The Lees of Virginia*, 266–67.

235 **By the early 1700s:** Maier, *The Old Revolutionaries*, 172.

235 **Tobacco prices were unstable:** Holton, *Forced Founders*, 52–53, 60–65; Maier, *The Old Revolutionaries*, 171–73; Breen, *The Marketplace of Revolution*, 121–22.

236 **Like many Tidewater growers:** Hendrick, *The Lees of Virginia*, 78.

236 **In 1747, Thomas Lee:** Royster, *The Fabulous History of the Dismal Swamp Company*, 40–42.

236 **John Robinson, the powerful Speaker:** Hendrick, *The Lees of Virginia*, 67–69; Royster, *Fabulous History*, 42.

237 **In 1753, Virginia governor:** Ellis, *His Excellency: George Washington*, 12–17; Flexner, *Washington*, 10–17; Royster, *Fabulous History*, 57.

238 **By then, Virginian planter John Mercer:** Potts, *Arthur Lee*, 40; McGaughy, *Richard Henry Lee of Virginia*, 34; James, *George Mercer of the Ohio Company*, 43.

239 **This was an opportunity for the Lees:** Letter, R. H. Lee, July 4, 1765, Lee, *The Letters of Richard Henry Lee*, 1:9, quoted in McGaughy, *Richard Henry Lee of Virginia*, 78.

239 **Richard Henry, untroubled:** Potts, *Arthur Lee*, 40–42; Hendrick, *The Lees of Virginia*, 132–33; McGaughy, *Richard Henry Lee*, 78–80; James, *George Mercer of the Ohio Company*, 51–53, 56; Maier, *The Old Revolutionaries*, 195–97.

240 **By now the Lee family:** McGaughy, *Richard Henry Lee*, 76–77.

240 **The Lee brothers appointed:** Hendrick, *The Lees of Virginia*, 118–20, 271–73; McGaughy, *Richard Henry Lee*, 73; Potts, *Arthur Lee*, 56–57.

241 **The most significant rival:** Royster, *Fabulous History*, 156–57.

241 **Though Franklin's reputation:** Ibid., 42–45, 156–57.

242 **The two competing bids:** Marshall, "Lord Hillsborough, Samuel Wharton and the Ohio Grant, 1769–1775," 717–39; Alvord, "Virginia and the West," 19–38; Lewis, *The Indiana Company*, 94–100.

242 **The Mississippi Company's loss:** Royster, *Fabulous History*, 234; Holton, *Forced Founders*, 95–98.

CHAPTER 28

243 **Lee went behind his colleagues:** Alsop, *Yankees at the Court*, 88–89; Potts, *Arthur Lee*, 179–83; Schiff, *A Great Improvisation*, 135–36, 146–47, 152–53.

244 **After a particularly nasty:** Letter, Deane to Lee, December 13, 1777, *Deane Papers*, vol. 2, 272–73.

244 **Beaumarchais resented Deane's insistence:** Letter, Beaumarchais to Deane, February 19, 1777, Shewmake, *For the Good of Mankind*, 200.

245 **Du Coudray accused Beaumarchais:** Morton and Spinelli, *Beaumarchais*, 99–103; letter, Beaumarchais to Vergennes, January 13, 1777, Shewmake, *For the Good of Mankind*, 188–89; letter, Deane to Beaumarchais, February 8, 1777, Shewmake, *For the Good of Mankind*, 195.

245 **Beaumarchais wrote to Vergennes:** Letter, Beaumarchais to Vergennes, January

30, 1777, Shewmake, *For the Good of Mankind*, 191; letter, Beaumarchais to Vergennes, January 27, 1777, Shewmake, *For the Good of Mankind*, 190.

246 **Soon after, the embargo was:** Morton and Spinelli, *Beaumarchais*, 110–12.

246 **Deane and Beaumarchais had labored:** Letter, Deane to Beaumarchais, February 24, 1777, Shewmake, *For the Good of Mankind*, 201.

247 **The Secret Committee, now:** Letter, Foreign Affairs Committee to Commissioners, May 30, 1777, Wharton, *Revolutionary Diplomatic Correspondence*, vol. 2, 327.

248 **"Congress have left it":** Letter, Major J. Burnett to Jeremiah Wadsworth, March 18, 1780, as quoted in Carp, *To Starve the Army at Pleasure*, 69.

248 **All Congress could do:** Ibid., 83.

248 **The value of the currency:** Alden, *A History of the American Revolution*, 255, 446.

248 **When merchants refused to accept:** Ibid., 68–69.

248 **War imposed severe economic hardships:** Letter, Greer to Davis, March 29, 1779, quoted in Carp, *To Starve the Army at Pleasure*, 72.

248 **"Great frugality and great industry":** Letter, Franklin to Joseph Priestley, July 7, 1775, Franklin, *The Papers of Benjamin Franklin*, vol. 22, 93.

249 **In July, Burgoyne chased the Americans:** Ketchum, *Saratoga*, 172–77, 217–18, 246, 248.

250 **"Our people knew not the hardships":** Letter, Robert Morris to Commissioners, December 21, 1776, Wharton, *Revolutionary Diplomatic Correspondence*, vol. 2, 236.

CHAPTER 29

252 **Franklin regularly attended:** Letter, Commissioners to Stormont, April 2, 1777, Franklin, *The Papers of Benjamin Franklin*, vol. 23, 548–549; Schiff, *Great Improvisation*, 86-87.

252 **Yet, the British Foreign Ministry:** Letter, Franklin to Benjamin Vaughan, September 18, 1777, Franklin, *Papers of Benjamin Franklin*, vol. 24, 539.

253 **Beaumarchais told Vergennes that unless France:** Letter, Beaumarchais to Vergennes, March 8, 1777, Shewmake, *For the Good of Mankind*, 206–8.

253 **One bright piece of news:** Letter, Samuel Cooper to Franklin, March 30, 1777, Franklin, *Papers of Benjamin Franklin*, vol. 23, 534; Morton and Spinelli, *Beaumarchais*, 106, citing Langdon's cargo list for the *Mercure*.

253 **The *Amphitrite* reached Portsmouth:** "Invoices of *L'Amphitrite*, Accounts of Silas Deane, 1776–1781," Library of Congress Manuscript Collection; Morton and Spinelli, *Beaumarchais*, 84, citing Langdon's cargo list for the *Amphitrite*. This list is illustrative of the kinds of supplies that were shipped, but it is not precise. The bill of lading and the cargo list for the *Amphitrite* were inconsistent. It appears that in the rush to deliver the arms, some of the cargo lists were confused, and cargo loaded on one ship may have appeared on another ship's bill of lading.

253 **Almost as soon as word reached the commissioners:** Einstein, *Divided Loyalties*, 45–46; Potts, *Arthur Lee*, 180–81, 189; letter, Deane to Bancroft, January 8, 1778, *Deane Papers*, vol. 2, 310; letter, Deane to Jonathan Williams, January 13, 1778, *Deane Papers*, vol. 2, 327.

254 **Bancroft walked purposefully:** "Engagement of Dr. Edwards," December 1776, Stevens, *Facsimiles,* vol. 3, no. 235; Bemis, "The British Secret Service and the French-American Alliance," 477. This location had been arranged by Paul Wentworth. The arrangement was made in December 1776, months before Bancroft's sudden departure for Paris, proving that Bancroft simply used the John the Painter affair as an excuse to obtain a job with the commissioners.

255 **Neither the British Foreign Ministry:** Einstein, *Divided Loyalties,* 23–24.

255 **One of the other British spies was Joseph Hynson:** Letter, Carmichael to Secret Committee, November 2, 1776, Wharton, *Revolutionary Diplomatic Correspondence,* vol. 2, 184–85; Lever, *Beaumarchais* (trans. Emanuel), 147; Bemis, "British Secret Service and the French-American Alliance," 478–81.

255 **Hynson and Carmichael were soon inseparable:** Bemis, "British Secret Service and the French-American Alliance," 481; letter, Deane to Hynson, October 26, 1777, Stevens, *Facsimiles,* vol. 2, no. 208.

256 **Lee blamed Deane:** Einstein, *Divided Loyalties,* 45–46; Schiff, *A Great Improvisation,* 147–48; Dull, *Diplomatic History,* 77.

256 **Lee himself regularly wrote:** Potts, *Arthur Lee,* 198.

256 **Franklin acknowledged it was impossible:** Letter, Franklin to Juliana Ritchie, January 19, 1777, Franklin, *Papers of Benjamin Franklin,* vol. 23, 211.

257 **In July, Ambassador Stormont confronted:** Letter, Vergennes to Commissioners, July 16, 1777, Wharton, *Revolutionary Diplomatic Correspondence,* vol. 2, 364–65; Dull, *Diplomatic History,* 80–81.

257 **Franklin and Deane wrote to Vergennes:** Letter, Franklin and Deane to Vergennes, July 17, 1777, Wharton, *Revolutionary Diplomatic Correspondence,* vol. 2, 365–66.

258 **As the London stock exchange roared:** Schiff, *A Great Improvisation,* 98.

258 **Privately, Vergennes wrote to Louis XVI:** Bemis, *The Diplomacy of the American Revolution,* 55–57; Dull, *Diplomatic History,* 90.

258 **Meanwhile, the commissioners, unaware:** "Commissioners' Memorandum for Vergennes and Aranda," September 25, 1777, Franklin, *Papers of Benjamin Franklin,* vol. 24, 556–63.

258 **"There is nothing better":** Letter, Lauraguais to Vergennes, September 20, 1777, quoted in Schiff, *A Great Improvisation,* 101.

259 **"[T]he situation of my Country":** Letter, Deane to Charles Dumas, October 1, 1777, *Deane Papers,* vol. 2, 164.

259 **He wrote to his brother:** Letter, Deane to Barnabas Deane, October 3, 1777, *Deane Papers,* vol. 2, 166.

CHAPTER 30

261 **The blackmailer Morande testified:** The case, *Hayes v. Jacques* (King's Bench, 1777), is unreported, but an abstract appears in "The Supplement," *The Universal Magazine* 60 (1777): 368–69.

261 **According to her account:** Cox, *The Enigma of the Age,* 114–15.

262 **D'Eon objected that she:** In Gaillardet, *Memoirs of Chevalier D'Eon,* 283.

262 **D'Eon later wrote:** Beaumont, *The Maiden of Tonnerre,* 36.

262 For this reason, Vergennes wanted: Homberg and Jousselin, *D'Eon de Beaumont*, 191–92.

262 In her memoir: Beaumont, *The Maiden of Tonnerre*, 24, from "The Great Historical Epistle by the Chevalière d'Eon, Written in 1785."

263 As d'Eon later recounted: Beaumont, *The Maiden of Tonnerre*, 57–59, 64-65; Kates, *Monsieur d'Eon Is a Woman*, 26.

263 In order to prepare her to be presented": Beaumont, *The Maiden of Tonnerre*, 68–69.

264 After a month of lessons: Schiff, *A Great Improvisation*, 109; Cox, *The Enigma of the Age*, 116–17; Gaillardet, *Memoirs*, 284–85; Homberg and Jousselin, *D'Eon de Beaumont*, 199–200.

264 D'Eon's miraculous conversion: Kates, *Monsieur d'Eon Is a Woman*, 260–61; Gaillardet, *Memoirs*, 284–90; Homberg and Jousselin, *D'Eon de Beaumont*, 214–16; quoted in Edna Nixon, *Royal Spy*, 207.

265 Madame d'Eon used her new prominence: Quoted in Gaillardet, *Memoirs*, 286–87.

CHAPTER 31

268 Beaumarchais arrived: Morton and Spinelli, *Beaumarchais*, 155–56.

268 Shortly before noon: The American Commissioners: A Public Announcement, December 4, 1777, Franklin, *The Papers of Benjamin Franklin*, vol. 25, 234; Austin, "Memoir of Jonathan Loring Austin," *Boston Monthly Magazine* (July, 1826), 59.

269 "Gentleman Johnny" Burgoyne's army: Hibbert, *Redcoats and Rebels*, 46–48, 94; Bobrick, *Angel in the Whirlwind*, 273.

269 The American rebels ahead: Quoted in Ketchum, *Saratoga*, 348.

270 Rather than abandon excess baggage: Ibid., 309–12, 331–32; Hibbert, *Redcoats and Rebels*, 175–78.

270 As the two armies began: Ketchum, *Saratoga*, 346, 355, 359–60, 380, 383.

271 Nearly all the general officers: Ibid., 346, 355, 359–60, 380, 383-404, 437; Middlekauff, *The Glorious Cause*, 383–85; Alden, *The American Revolution*, 322–27; Bobrick, *Angel in the Whirlwind*, 280.

271 When he returned to London: Quoted in Hibbert, *Redcoats and Rebels*, 340.

271 The stunned commissioners: Morton and Spinelli, *Beaumarchais*, 155–56; letter, Beaumarchais to Vergennes, December 5, 1777, Shewmake, *For the Good of Mankind*, 253–54.

272 He sent his secretary: Van Doren, *Benjamin Franklin*, 588.

273 The British agent Paul Wentworth reentered: Letter, Wentworth to Deane, December 12, 1777, *Deane Papers*, vol. 2, 271; letter, Deane to Wentworth, December 12, 1777, *Deane Papers*, vol. 2, 271.

273 Wentworth and Deane met at least twice: Einstein, *Divided Loyalties*, 30–32.

274 Franklin also agreed to talk: Van Doren, *Benjamin Franklin*, 589–92.

274 They knew that wherever they went: Brands, *The First American*, 543–44; Van Doren, *Benjamin Franklin*, 589–93.

274 Then, on the eve of the meeting: Trevelyan, *The American Revolution*, 358; Bemis, *The Diplomacy of American Revolution*, 70–74.

276   **Franklin put aside his customary brown jacket:** Letter, Commissioners to the
        Foreign Affairs Committee, December 18, 1777, Franklin, *The Papers of Benjamin
        Franklin,* vol. 25, 305–9; Schiff, *A Great Improvisation,* 130–32.

276   **Though the three commissioners signed:** Potts, *Arthur Lee,* 192–94; Hendrick, *The
        276 of Virginia,* 162–63, 321–22. Though Lee's biographer makes an argument that
        the letter may have been sent by Lee's secretary Thornton, who was a British spy,
        this makes no sense in light of the fact that Thornton reported to the foreign
        ministry and would not have risked exposing himself by writing to Lee's dearest
        friend in England, who was more sympathetic to the Americans. Shelburne never
        came forward to clear Lee's name, and Lee himself never disavowed the letter. The
        letter was consistent with Lee's systematic efforts to put Beaumarchais's smuggling
        operation out of business while claiming credit for the arms that France had pro-
        vided. Hendrick, *The Lees of Virginia,* 321–25.

277   **Deane realized that Lee:** Schiff, *A Great Improvisation,* 139; Dull, *Diplomatic His-
        tory,* 98.

277   **Stormont left so quickly:** Letter, Franklin to Lovell, July 22, 1788, Wharton,
        Revolutionary Diplomatic Correspondence, vol. 2, 559.

278   **On the first day of spring, 1778:** Van Doren, *Benjamin Franklin,* 595–96; Hen-
        drick, *The Lees of Virginia,* 294–95.

278   **For Silas Deane:** Letter, Deane to Jonathan Williams, March 21, 1778, *Deane
        Papers,* vol. 2, 420.

CHAPTER 32

279   **A fortnight before:** Letter, James Lovell to Deane, December 8, 1777, *Deane
        Papers,* vol. 2, 267.

279   **Ten days before:** Letter, Deane to Gerard, March 9, 1778, *Deane Papers,*
        vol. 2, 389.

280   **When Deane informed Beaumarchais:** Letter, Beaumarchais to Vergennes, March
        13, 1778, Shewmake, *For the Good of Mankind,* 290–96.

280   **Beaumarchais also wrote to Congress:** Letter, Beaumarchais to Congress, March
        23, 1778, Shewmake, *For the Good of Mankind,* 298–300.

281   **Once Deane received Congress's order:** Letter, Beaumarchais to Vergennes,
        March 9, 1778, Shewmake, *For the Good of Mankind,* 289; letter, Beaumarchais
        to Vergennes, March 13, 1778, Shewmake, *For the Good of Mankind,* 290–97;
        Journals of Congress, November 21, 1777, Wharton, *Revolutionary Diplomatic
        Correspondence,* vol. 2, 424; Journals of Congress, November 28, 1777, Wharton,
        Revolutionary Diplomatic Correspondence, vol. 2, 431.

281   **Lee blamed Franklin:** Letter, Arthur Lee to Franklin, April 2, 1778, Franklin, *The
        Papers of Benjamin Franklin,* vol. 26, 222.

281   **Franklin replied:** Letter, Franklin to Arthur Lee, April 3, 1778, Franklin, *Papers of
        Benjamin Franklin,* vol. 26, 223.

282   **He wrote to the president:** Letter, Franklin to Congress, March 31, 1778, *Deane
        Papers,* vol. 2, 445.

282   **As the day of Deane's departure:** Letter, Vergennes to Congress, March 1778,

Deane Papers, vol. 2, 435; letter, Vergennes to Deane, March 1778, *Deane Papers,* vol. 2, 436.

282 **Adams was accompanied:** Letter, William Temple Franklin to Deane, April 24, 1778, *Deane Papers,* vol. 2, 461.

283 **Deane traveled by coach:** Letter, D'Estaing to Deane, April 1, 1778, *Deane Papers,* vol. 2, 447; Hibbert, *Redcoats and Rebels,* 227; Bobrick, *Angel in the Whirlwind,* 356–57; Tuchman, *The First Salute,* 160; letter, Deane to the President of Congress, July 10, 1778, *Deane Papers,* vol. 2, 468.

283 **Still, he found comfort:** Letter, Deane to Beaumarchais, March 29, 1778, *Deane Papers,* vol. 2, 439.

283 **He was "happy":** Quoted in Clark, *Silas Deane,* 114–15.

CHAPTER 33

285 **The redcoats left the city:** Bobrick, *Angel in the Whirlwind,* 347.

285 **A week later a fleet:** Letters, Deane to the President of Congress, July 10 and July 11, 1778, *Deane Papers,* vol. 2, 468–71; Bobrick, *Angel in the Whirlwind,* 348.

286 **Gérard was received:** From *The Pennsylvania Packet,* July 14, 1778, reprinted in *Deane Papers,* vol. 2, 471–72.

286 **Over dinner that night Deane sat:** Randall, *Benedict Arnold,* 421, 435.

287 **Meanwhile, delegates in Congress:** Ibid., 435-437, 440–52.

288 **Samuel Adams objected that Deane:** Letter, Samuel Adams to James Warren, October 11, 1778, Smith, *Letters of Delegates,* vol. 11, 47–48.

288 **In truth, Deane's recall:** Wood, *The Creation of the American Republic,* 420.

289 **The Lee-Adams Junto saw:** Letter, Richard Henry Lee to Arthur Lee, October 27, 1778, Smith, *Letters of Delegates,* vol. 11, 132.

289 **Richard Henry Lee thought Franklin:** Letter, Richard Henry Lee to Arthur Lee, September 16, 1778, Smith, *Letters of Delegates,* vol. 10, 651–53.

289 **Similarly, Ralph Izard wrote Congress:** Letter, Izard to Henry Laurens, June 28, 1778, Wharton, *Revolutionary Diplomatic Correspondence,* vol. 2, 629.

289 **Eventually, the assault on Franklin's:** Observations on Lee's Letter of June 1, 1778, October 12, 1778, *Deane Papers,* vol. 3, 37.

290 **After being ordered:** Letter, Deane to the President of Congress, July 28, 1778, *Deane Papers,* vol. 2, 474–75; Proceedings for August 15–21, 1778, *Journals of the Continental Congress,* vol. 11, 799–802, 813, 826; letter, Deane to the President of Congress, September 8, 1778, *Deane Papers,* vol. 2, 480; letter, Deane to the President of Congress, September 11, 1778, *Deane Papers,* vol. 2, 480–81; letter, Laurens to Lowndes, August 18, 1778, Smith, *Letters of Delegates,* vol. 10, 473–75.

290 **In September 1778, Arthur Lee:** Proceedings of September 22, 26, 28, 30 and October 5, 1778, *Journals of the Continental Congress,* vol. 12, 942–43, 955, 984; *Deane Papers,* vol. 2, 483–86, 489–91; letter, Richard Henry Lee to Arthur Lee, September 16, 1778, Smith, *Letters of Delegates,* vol. 10, 653–54; Patton, *Patriot Pirates,* 76.

291 **Congress called Carmichael:** "Examination of William Carmichael, September 28 and 30, 1778," reprinted in *Deane Papers,* vol. 2, 491–99.

291   **James Lovell, a delegate:** Letter, James Lovell to John Adams, October 24, 1778, Smith, *Letters of Delegates*, vol. 11, 114.

291   **Richard Henry Lee suspected:** Letter, Richard Henry Lee to Arthur Lee, September 16, 1778, Smith, *Letters of Delegates*, vol. 10, 653–54.

291   **For Deane, defending himself:** Letter, Deane to the President of Congress, September 22, 1778, *Deane Papers*, vol. 2, 486–88.

292   **What made the allegations:** Letter, Deane to the President of Congress, October 12, 1778, *Deane Papers*, vol. 3, 13–33.

292   **He lived modestly:** "Silas Deane's Narrative," December 21, 1778, *Deane Papers*, vol. 3, 197–98.

293   **Some of Deane's contemporaries:** Patton, *Patriot Pirates*, 76-77.

293   **Deane thought that the public:** Letter, Deane to Barnabas Deane, November 30, 1778, *Deane Papers*, vol. 3, 61–62.

293   **In December, Deane published:** "Address of Silas Deane," *The Pennsylvania Packet*, December 5, 1778, reprinted in *Deane Papers*, vol. 3, 66–67.

294   **Deane described his relationship:** Ibid., 69–70.

294   **Deane explained how Lee's misrepresentations:** Ibid., 71–73. Samuel Adams also defended Dr. Berkenhout (letter, Samuel Adams to John Winthrop, December 21, 1778, Smith, *Letters of Delegates*, vol. 11, 363–64).

294   **In closing, Deane warned:** "Address of Silas Deane," *The Pennsylvania Packet*, December 5, 1778, reprinted in *Deane Papers*, vol. 3, 75.

CHAPTER 34

295   **Still in Paris, John Adams:** "John Adams' Diary," February 8, 1779, *Deane Papers*, vol. 3, 349.

295   **President Laurens accused:** "Henry Laurens' Speech to Congress," December 9, 1778, Smith, *Letters of Delegates*, vol. 11, 312–15; letter, Laurens to Samuel Huntington, December 11, 1778, Ibid., 330.

295   **Paine repeated the charges:** "Thomas Paine's Reply," December 15, 1778, *Deane Papers*, vol. 3, 86–100.

296   **He responded that in fact Deane:** "Robert Morris to the Public," January 7, 1779, Smith, *Letters of Delegates*, vol. 11, 430–31.

296   **The insults and counter insults:** Stahr, *John Jay*, 99.

297   **Samuel Adams charged:** Letter, Samuel Adams to John Winthrop, December 21, 1778, Smith, *Letters of Delegates*, vol. 11, 363.

297   **Years after the Revolution:** Rakove, *The Beginnings of National Politics*, 254; Stahr, *John Jay*, 92.

298   **At the conclusion, he answered:** "Silas Deane's Narrative," December 21, 1778, *Deane Papers*, vol. 3, 197–98.

299   **Tom Paine, who did not hesitate:** "Thomas Paine's Defence of the Lees," January 8, 1779, *Deane Papers*, vol. 3, 221–23.

299   **At this point, the French ambassador Gérard:** Letter, Gérard to President of Congress, January 5, 1779, *Deane Papers*, vol. 3, 246–47.

299   **Deane's friend, Pennsylvania delegate Gouverneur Morris:** "Gouverneur Morris's Speech in Congress," January 7, 1779, Smith, *Letters of Delegates*, vol. 11, 426.

299   On January 12, 1779, Congress unanimously: Proceedings in Congress, *Deane Papers,* vol. 3, 247–56; Potts, *Arthur Lee,* 215–16; Eric Foner, *Tom Paine and Revolutionary America,* 158–61.

300   The committee recommended to Congress: Stahr, *John Jay,* 99-101; Proceedings of Congress, February 23, 1779, Wharton, *Revolutionary Diplomatic Correspondence,* vol. 3, 58–61.

301   John Adams wrote to Massachusetts: Letter, Adams to Lovell, September 21, 1779, in *The Adams Papers: Adams Family Correspondence,* vol. 3, 231 note 1, quoted in Rakove, *The Beginnings of National Politics,* 260.

301   The junto was losing delegates: Potts, *Arthur Lee,* 239–40.

302   Gérard and Deane's friends: Rakove, *The Beginnings,* 249–74; Stahr, *John Jay,* 102–4.

302   Lee received notice: Potts, *Arthur Lee,* 240–41; Stahr, *John Jay,* 103–4.

303   One of the British ships: Letter, Deane to Simeon Deane, August 4, 1780, *Deane Papers,* vol. 4, 176–78; Clark, *Silas Deane,* 155–58.

303   He tried to console himself: Letter, Deane to James Wilson, May 13, 1780, *Deane Papers,* vol. 3, 151.

303   Franklin, recalling his own ordeal: Letter, Deane to Bancroft, November 23, 1781, *Deane Papers,* vol. 4, 537–40; letter, Deane to Samuel Parsons, October 21, 1782, *Deane Papers,* vol. 4, 517.

304   But he doubted that: Letter, Deane to Robert Morris, September 2, 1780, *Deane Papers,* vol. 4, 215.

304   Deane had told Congress: "Silas Deane's Narrative, December 21, 1778," *Deane Papers,* vol. 3, 203–4.

305   To his brother Simeon: Letter, Deane to Simeon Deane, May 16, 1781, *Deane Papers,* vol. 4, 340.

305   He could think of no historical: Ibid., 343–44.

305   To another friend: Letter, Deane to Jesse Root, May 20, 1781, *Deane Papers,* vol. 4, 349–50.

305   Deane argued to another delegate: Letter, Deane to James Wilson, May 10, 1781, *Deane Papers,* vol. 4, 312–13.

306   He wrote to Jesse Root: Letter, Deane to Jesse Root, May 20, 1781, *Deane Papers,* vol. 4, 360.

306   Even after the French agreed: Ibid., 373–75.

306   It was now clear to Deane: Ibid., 361–63.

306   Deane expressed himself even more bluntly: Letter, Deane to Benjamin Tallmadge, May 20, 1781, *Deane Papers,* vol. 4, 388–89.

CHAPTER 35

308   On October 24, Rivington began publishing: "The Intercepted Letters," October 20, 1781, *Deane Papers,* vol. 4, 500–501; letter, George III to Lord North, March 3, 1781, *Deane Papers,* vol. 4, 502.

309   The very day that Rivington announced: Letter, Deane to Barnabas Deane, October 21, 1781, *Deane Papers,* vol. 4, 507.

310   Arguably, Deane tried to make the publication: Letter, Deane to Charles Thom-

son, June 1, 1781, *Deane Papers,* vol. 4, 394–99. In this letter to the secretary of Congress, for example, Deane discusses a new edition of the Abbé Raynall's *Histoire Philosophique & Politique,* which was critical of France, rather than discussing his own views on the alliance.

310 **Months before Deane wrote the letters:** Letter, George III to Lord North, March 3, 1781, *Deane Papers,* vol. 4, 502.

310 **Historians have pointed:** e.g., Van Doren, *Secret History of the American Revolution,* 417–18.

311 **In July 1781, Lord North sent:** Letter, Lord North to the King, no. 3373, July 19, 1781, *Correspondence of King George III,* vol. 5, 255.

311 **The king acknowledged receiving:** Letter, George III to Lord North, July 19, 1781, *Deane Papers,* vol. 4, 503.

311 **A month later, George III approved:** Letter, George III to Lord North, August 7, 1781, *Deane Papers,* vol. 4, 503.

311 **For these reasons, it seems clear:** Hayden, "The Apostasy of Silas Deane," 95–103.

312 **His friend Jeremiah Wadsworth:** Letter, Jeremiah Wadsworth to Deane, November 1781, *Deane Papers,* vol. 4, 525–27.

312 **Barnabas worried that his brother:** Letter, Barnabas Deane to Jacob Sebor, November 11, 1781, *Deane Papers,* vol. 4, 531–33.

313 **His brother Simeon:** Letter, Simeon Deane to Deane, November 14, 1781, *Deane Papers,* vol. 4, 535.

313 **Major Tallmadge wrote Deane:** Letter, Benjamin Tallmadge to Deane, December 27, 1781, *Deane Papers,* vol. 4, 557–58.

313 **Allies in Congress:** Letter, Thomas Paine to Jonathan Williams, November 26, 1781, *Deane Papers,* vol. 4, 543–45.

313 **Deane feared that:** Letter, Deane to Barnabas Deane, January 31, 1782, *Deane Papers,* vol. 5, 22.

313 **Only Beaumarchais showed some sympathy:** Letter, Beaumarchais to Robert Morris, June 3, 1782, Shewmake, *For the Good of Mankind,* 401–402.

313 **Deane wrote a long letter to Franklin:** Letter, Deane to Franklin, February 1, 1782, Franklin, *The Papers of Benjamin Franklin,* vol. 36, 507–10.

314 **In Deane's view, the burdens:** Ibid., 511–14.

314 **Deane acknowledged that he had been accused:** Ibid., 517–24.

315 **Privately, he wrote to Morris:** Letter, Franklin to Robert Morris, March 30, 1782, Franklin, *Papers of Benjamin Franklin,* vol. 37, 74.

315 **To Deane, Franklin wrote:** Letter, Franklin to Deane, April 19, 1782, Franklin, *Papers of Benjamin Franklin,* vol. 37, 172–73.

316 **Deane replied to his old friend:** Letter, Deane to Franklin, May 13, 1782, Franklin, *Papers of Benjamin Franklin,* vol. 37, 365–66.

316 **But Franklin would continue to insist:** Certificate of Benjamin Franklin, December 18, 1782, *Deane Papers,* vol. 5, 117.

317 **Alone and depressed, Deane remained:** Letter, Deane to Bancroft, November 23, 1781, *Deane Papers,* vol. 4, 537–40; letter, Deane to Samuel Parsons, October 21, 1782, *Deane Papers,* vol. 4, 517.

318 The final battle plan had been drawn up: Ellis, *His Excellency: George Washington*, 131–32.

319 Yet Deane was happy: Letter, Deane to Barnabas Deane, July 25, 1783, *Deane Papers*, vol. 5, 173; letter, Deane to Jay, February 28, 1783, *Deane Papers*, vol. 5, 136–37, 140.

319 His friend Jay cautioned him: Letter, Jay to Deane, February 22, 1783, *Deane Papers*, vol. 5, 131.

319 Deane's son, Jesse, was ill: Letter, Deane to Simeon Deane, April 1, 1783, *Deane Papers*, vol. 5, 145–46.

319 He also was looking into developing: Letter, Deane to James Wilson, April 1, 1783, *Deane Papers*, vol. 5, 149–52; letter, Deane to Barnabas Deane, August 10, 1788, *Deane Papers*, vol. 5, 489–90.

319 The day after Deane arrived in London: Letter, Deane to Barnabas Deane, July 25, 1783, *Deane Papers*, vol. 5, 176; letter, Deane to Franklin, October 19, 1783, *Deane Papers*, vol. 5, 213.

320 So Deane remained in this unfamiliar city: Letter, Deane to Robert Morris, October 10, 1783, *Deane Papers*, vol. 5, 201–4.

320 When Jay, now minister to Spain: Letter, Deane to Jay, January 21, 1784, *Deane Papers*, vol. 5, 279–80; letter, Jay to Deane, February 23, 1784, *Deane Papers*, vol. 5, 280–81.

321 He wanted to leave England: Letter, Deane to Barnabas Deane, November 10, 1788, *Deane Papers*, vol. 5, 494–95; letter, Deane to Lord Sheffield, June 30, 1788, *Deane Papers*, vol. 5, 482–83; letter, Deane to Barnabas Deane, August 10, 1788, *Deane Papers*, vol. 5, 489–92: letter, Winthrop Saltonstall to Deane, November 19, 1788, *Deane Papers*, vol. 5, 502–3.

322 In his disoriented condition: Letter, Deane to Barnabas Deane, November 10, 1788, *Deane Papers*, vol. 5, 495; letter, Jefferson to Jay, August 3, 1788, *Deane Papers*, vol. 5, 485–86; letter, Jay to Jefferson, Office for Foreign Affairs, November 25, 1788, *Deane Papers*, vol. 5, 504–5; letter, Jefferson to Jay, March 15, 1789, *Deane Papers*, vol. 5, 514.

322 Rather than waiting for Foullay: Letter, Jefferson to Bancroft, March 2, 1789, *Deane Papers*, vol. 5, 512–13.

323 Deane could no longer manage: Letter, Deane to Barnabas Deane, February 1, 1789, *Deane Papers*, vol. 5, 511.

323 As Washington prepared: Letter, Barnabas Deane to Deane, December 6, 1788, *Deane Papers: Correspondence,* Collections of the Connecticut Historical Society 23 (1930), 235–36; letter, Deane to John Jay, June 25, 1789, *Deane Papers*, vol. 5, 526; letter, Deane to Barnabas Deane, April 7, 1789, *Deane Papers*, vol. 5, 514.

324 That June Deane wrote: Letter, Deane to Washington, June 25, 1789, *Deane Papers*, vol. 5, 526.

324 On Tuesday, September 22, 1789, Deane left: Boyd, "Silas Deane," 540; letter, John Brown Cutting to Thomas Jefferson, September 30, 1789, Jefferson, *Papers of Thomas Jefferson*, vol. 15, 500; letter, Edward Bancroft to Joseph Priestley, May 8, 1790, *Deane Papers*, vol. 5, 533–36.

324　**Among Deane's possessions:** Letter, Barnabas Deane to Theodore Hopkins, February 25, 1790, *Deane Papers,* vol. 5, 533.

CHAPTER 36

325　**Only days before Deane left:** Letter, John Brown Cutting to Thomas Jefferson, Sep. 30, 1789, Jefferson, *Papers of Thomas Jefferson,* 15, 500; Boyd, "Silas Deane," 173–74.

325　**He had recovered from his long illness:** Stinchcombe, "A Note on Silas Deane's Death," 619–24.

325　**The circumstances of his demise:** Anderson and Anderson, "The Death of Silas Deane: Another Opinion," 104.

325　**A few months after Deane's death:** Letter, Edward Bancroft to Joseph Priestley, May 8, 1790, *Deane Papers,* vol. 5, 533–36.

328　**In Bancroft's novel,** *Charles Wentworth Esq.***:** Bancroft, *Charles Wentworth,* 69–70.

328　**Bancroft had prescribed medication:** Quoted in Davidson and Lytle, *After the Fact: The Art of Historical Detection,* xxix.

328　**Before Deane left London:** Boyd, "Silas Deane," 165–87, 319–42, and 515–50.

329　**He continued to receive payments:** "Edward Bancroft's Memorial to the Marquis of Carmarthen," September 17, 1784, reprinted in Bemis, "The British Secret Service and the French-American Alliance," 493–95.

329　**No one suspected Bancroft's treachery:** Rumors that Bancroft was a spy first surfaced around 1884. George Bancroft, *History of the United States,* vol. 5, 17. But even Francis Wharton in his classic work in 1888 on early American diplomatic history dismissed the idea that Bancroft was a spy as manifestly absurd. See Wharton, *Revolutionary Diplomatic Correspondence,* vol. 1, 640–41.

329　**After Congress abruptly recalled Arthur Lee:** Letter, Arthur Lee to John Page, (June 4?, 1781), quoted in Potts, *Arthur Lee,* 251.

329　**Lee also submitted a claim:** Potts, *Arthur Lee,* 250.

330　**Lee became the leading opponent:** Rakove, *The Beginnings of National Politics,* 297–98.

330　**Lee's report denied:** Report of a Committee of Congress, November 4, 1783, reprinted in 27th 2d H.R. 952, p. 6.

330　**Since Congress had already appointed Thomas Barclay:** Ibid.

331　**Fearing the rise of this new class:** Potts, *Arthur Lee,* 254–60; Rakove, *The Beginnings,* 273–74.

331　**To the end of his life, Lee's:** Potts, *Arthur Lee,* 258–59; Hendrick, *The Lees of Virginia,* 369–70.

331　**As a result of Lee's pro-British leanings:** Potts, *Arthur Lee,* 258–59.

331　**After Lee left Congress in 1784:** Ibid., 267.

332　**The Beinecke Rare Book and Manuscript Library:** Silas Deane's Latin Dissertation, 1755, Beinecke Rare Book and Manuscript Library, Yale University Library.

332　**Lee had succeeded in preventing Deane:** An Act for the Settlement of the Accounts of Silas Deane, S.155, signed into law by President John Tyler on August 10, 1842 (27th 2d S., 155, July 27, 1842).

332 The congressional report found: Report of the Committee on Revolutionary Claims, 27th 2d H.R. 952, p. 4.

332 Specifically, Congress criticized Lee's: Ibid., 27th 2d S.R. 88, p. 3, 5.

CHAPTER 37

333 In 1782, under pressure from the French ambassador: Morton and Spinelli, *Beaumarchais*, 283–91; Lemaître, *Beaumarchais*, 264.

334 He had recently established a company: Lever, *Beaumarchais* (trans. Emanuel), 234.

335 To the end of his life Beaumarchais: Quoted in Grendel, *Beaumarchais*, 294.

336 Beaumarchais had nearly completed the palatial mansion: Lemaitre, *Beaumarchais*, 310–13; Loménie, *Beaumarchais and His Times*, 411–13.

337 That night Beaumarchais returned home: Lemaitre, *Beaumarchais*, 313–16.

337 Beaumarchais returned home from l'Abbaye: Ibid., 298, 313–14, 324–32.

339 After her appearance at Versailles: Cox, *The Enigma of the Age*, 120–22; Kates, *Monsieur d'Eon Is a Woman*, 262–63.

339 For a while, d'Eon lived comfortably: Cox, *The Enigma of the Age*, 125–33.

340 For a time d'Eon held on to her own flat: Ibid., 133–35.

EPILOGUE

342 Thomas Copeland, a surgeon on Millman Street: "Certificate of Thomas Copeland, surgeon, *Times* (London), May 25, 1810, and "Declaration of William Bowing," British Library, Add. MSS 27937, fo. 49.

343 American revolutionaries frequently used the language of moral virtue: Wood, *The Creation of the American Republic*, 65–70.

BIBLIOGRAPHY

I am grateful to the following institutions and libraries for allowing me access to their holdings:

Amherst College Library
Archive de la ministère des affaires étrangères, Quai d'Orsay
Bancroft Library, University of California at Berkeley
Beinecke Library of Yale University
Bibliothèque nationale de France
British Library Manuscript Reading Room
Connecticut Historical Society
Harvard University Library
Library of Congress Manuscript Reading Room
Lincoln's Inn Archives
Middle Temple Archives
New Hampshire State Archives
New York Public Library
San Francisco Public Library
State of Connecticut Archives

COLLECTED PAPERS

Adams, John. *The Works of John Adams.* Vol. 2. Edited with an introduction by Charles Francis Adams. Boston: Little, Brown, and Co., 1865.

———. The *Diary and Autobiography of John Adams.* Edited by Lyman Henry Butterfield. 4 vols. Cambridge, Mass.: Belknap Press of Harvard University, 1961.

Beaumarchais, Pierre-Augustin Caron de. *La politique de Beaumarchais.* Microform edited by Jacques Donvez, 1900.

———. *Correspondance.* 4 vols. Edited by Brian N. Morton and Donald Spinelli. Paris: A.-G. Nizet, 1969.

Beaumont, Charles d'Eon de. *The Maiden of Tonnerre: The Vicissitudes of the Chevalier and the Chevalière d'Eon.* Edited and translated by Roland A. Champagne, Nina Ekstein, and Gary Kates. Baltimore: Johns Hopkins University Press, 2001.

Colonial Connecticut Records, 1636–1776. The Colonial Connecticut Records Project. http://www.colonialct.uconn.edu.

Continental Congress. *Journals of the Continental Congress 1774–1789.* Washington, D.C.: Government Printing Office, 1905.

Cushing, Harry Alonzo, ed. *The Writings of Samuel Adams.* 4 vols. 1904–1908. Reprint, New York: Octagon Books, 1968.

Deane, Silas. *The Paris Papers; or, Mr. Silas Deane's Late Intercepted Letters to His Brothers, and Other Intimate Friends, in America.* Reprint by James Rivington, New York: Livingston, 1782.

———. The Silas Deane Papers, 1740–1782. Series 5: Memorials to Congress, 1835. Connecticut Historical Society.

———. *The Deane Papers, 1737–1789.* Edited and translated by Charles Isham. 5 vols. New York: New-York Historical Society Collections, 1886.

———. *The Deane Papers: Correspondence Between Silas Deane, His Brothers and Their Business and Political Associates, 1771–1795.* Collections of the Connecticut Historical Society 23. Hartford, Conn.: 1930.

Doniol, Henri. *Histoire de la participation de la France à l'établissement des Etats-Unis d'Amérique. Correspondance diplomatique et documents.* 6 vols. Paris: Imprimerie nationale, 1886–1889.

Franklin, Benjamin. *The Papers of Benjamin Franklin.* Edited by William B. Willcox, vols. 15, 17–26; edited by Claude A. Lopez, vol. 27. New Haven: Yale University Press, 1984.

Hutchinson, Thomas. *The Diary and Letters of His Excellency Thomas Hutchinson.* Edited by Peter Orlando Hutchinson. 2 vols. 1884–1886. Reprint, New York: Burt Franklin, 1971.

George III. *The Correspondence of King George III from 1760 to December 1783.* Edited by Sir John Fortescue. Vols. 1–6. London: Macmillan and Co., 1927–1928.

Jay, John. *The Correspondence and Public Papers of John Jay, 1763–1826.* Edited by Henry P. Johnson. New York: Da Capo Press, 1971.

Jefferson, Thomas. *The Papers of Thomas Jefferson.* Edited by Julian P. Boyd. 35 vols. Princeton, N.J.: Princeton University Press, 1958.

Lee, Richard Henry. *The Letters of Richard Henry Lee.* Edited by James Curtis Ballagh. 2 vols. New York: Macmillan Co., 1911–1914.

The Lee Family Papers. Rolls 1–8. Charlottesville, Va.: University of Virginia, 1966.

Louis XV. *Correspondance secrète inédite de Louis XV, sur la politique étrangère.* Edited by Edgar Boutaric. 2 vols. Paris: Plon, 1866.

Louis XVI. *Louis XVI and the Comte de Vergennes: Correspondence 1774–1787.* Edited by John Hardman and Munro Price. Oxford: Voltaire Foundation, 1998.

Robert Morris. *The Confidential Correspondence of Robert Morris: The Great Financier of the Revolution and the Signer of the Declaration of Independence.* Philadelphia: Stan V. Henkels, 1917.

Seventy-Six Society. *Papers in Relation to the Case of Silas Deane.* Printed by T. K. and P. G. Collins, 1855.

Shewmake, Antoinette, ed. and trans. *For the Good of Mankind: Pierre-Augustin Caron de Beaumarchais; Political Correspondence Relative to the American Revolution.* Lanham, Md.: University Press of America, 1987.

Smith, Paul H., ed. *Letters of Delegates to the Continental Congress, 1774 to 1789.* 26 vols. Washington, D.C.: Library of Congress, 1976–2000.

Stevens, B. F., ed. *Facsimiles of Manuscripts in European Archives Relating to America, 1773–1783.* 25 vols. London: 1889–1895, 1898. Reprint, New York: AMS Press, 1970.

Stiles, Ezra. *The Literary Diary of Ezra Stiles: President of Yale College.* Edited by Franklin Bowditch Dexter. 3 vols. New York: Charles Scribner's Sons, 1901.

Walpole, Horace. *Memoirs of the Reign of King George III.* Edited by Derek Jarrett. 4 vols. New Haven: Yale University Press, 2000.

Washington, George. *The Writings of George Washington from the Original Manuscript Sources, 1745–1799.* Edited by John C. Fitzpatrick. 39 vols. Washington, D.C.: Government Printing Office, 1931–1944.

———. *The Papers of George Washington: Revolutionary War Series.* Edited by Philander D. Chase. 18 vols. Charlottesville: University of Virginia Press, 1985.

———. *George Washington: Writings.* Edited by John H. Rhodehamel. New York: Library of America, 1997.

Wharton, Francis, ed. *The Revolutionary Diplomatic Correspondence of the United States.* 6 vols. Washington, D.C.: Government Printing Office, 1889.

Wilkes, John. *The Speeches of Mr. Wilkes in the House of Commons.* 8 vols. London, 1777 and 1786.

———. *The Correspondence of the Late John Wilkes with His Friends, etc.* Edited by John Almon. 5 vols. London: Printed for Richard Phillips, 1805.

———. *Diary.* British Library. Additional Manuscripts, 30, 866.

Wilkes, John, and Charles Churchill. *The Correspondence of John Wilkes and Charles Churchill.* Edited by Edward H. Weatherly. New York: Columbia University Press, 1954.

REFERENCE WORKS

Blanco, Richard L., ed. *The American Revolution, 1775–1783: An Encyclopedia.* New York: Garland, 1993.

Currie, Ian. *Frosts, Freezes and Fairs: Chronicles of the Frozen Thames and Harsh Winters in Britain Since 1000 A.D.* Surrey, U.K.: Frosted Earth, 1998.

Dexter, Franklin Bowditch. *Bibliographical Sketches of the Graduates of Yale College: With Annals of the College History.* 6 vols. New York: Henry Holt & Co., 1885–1912.

Greene, Jack P., and J. R. Pole, eds. *The Blackwell Encyclopedia of the American Revolution.* Cambridge, Mass.: Blackwell Reference, 1991.

Howell, T. B. *Complete Collection of State Trials and Proceedings for High Treason and*

Other Crimes and Misdeameanors. 21 vols. London: Longman, Hurts, Rees, Orme, & Brown, 1814.

Lesser, Charles H., ed. *The Sinews of Independence: Monthly Strength Reports of the Continental Army.* Chicago: University of Chicago Press, 1976.

McCusker, John J. *Money and Exchange in Europe and America, 1600–1775: A Handbook.* Chapel Hill: University of North Carolina Press, 1978.

———. *How Much Is That in Real Money? A Historical Commodity Price Index for Use as a Deflator of Money Values in the Economy of the United States,* 2d ed. Worcester, Mass.: American Antiquarian Society, 2001.

Peckham, Howard H., ed. *The Toll of Independence: Engagements and Battle Casualties of the American Revolution.* Chicago: University of Chicago Press, 1974.

Sabine, Lorenzo. *Biographical Sketches of Loyalists of the American Revolution.* 2 vols. Boston: Little, Brown, and Co., 1864.

Wentworth, John. *The Wentworth Genealogy: English and American.* 3 vols. Boston: Little, Brown and Co., 1878.

SELECTED BOOKS

Aitken, James. *The Life of James Aitken.* Winchester, Va.: Winton, printed by J. Wilkes, 1777.

Alden, John Richard. *The American Revolution, 1775–1783.* New York: Harper & Row, 1954.

———. *A History of the American Revolution,* New York: Da Capo Press, 1969.

———. *George Washington.* Baton Rouge: Louisiana State University Press, 1984.

Aldridge, Alfred Owen. *Franklin and His French Contemporaries.* New York: New York University Press, 1957.

Alsop, Susan Mary. *Yankees at the Court: The First Americans in Paris.* Garden City, N.Y.: Doubleday, 1982.

Augur, Helen. *The Secret War of Independence.* Boston: Little, Brown, 1955.

Baldwin, Ebenezer. *History of Yale College, from Its Foundation, A.D. 1700 to the Year 1838.* New Haven: Benjamin and William Noyes, 1841.

Bancroft, Edward. *The History of Charles Wentworth Esq.* 3 vols. London: T. Becket, 1770.

Bancroft, George. *History of the United States from the Discovery of the Continent.* 5 vols. New York: D. Appleton and Co., 1886.

Beaumarchais, Pierre-Augustin Caron de. *The Barber of Seville and The Marriage of Figaro.* Translated by John Wood. Baltimore: Penguin Books, 1964.

Belcher, Henry. *The First American Civil War: First Period 1775–1778.* 2 vols. London: MacMillan and Co., 1911.

Belknap, Jeremy. *The History of New-Hampshire.* Johnson Reprint Corporation, 1970.

Bemis, Samuel Flagg. *The Diplomacy of the American Revolution.* Bloomington: Indiana University Press, 1957.

Bendiner, Elmer. *The Virgin Diplomats.* New York: Knopf, 1976.

Bird, Harrison. *March to Saratoga: General Burgoyne and the American Campaign.* New York: Oxford University Press, 1963.

Bloomfield, Joseph. *Citizen Soldier: The Revolutionary War Journal of Joseph Bloomfield.*

Edited by Mark E. Lender and James Kirby Martin. Newark: New Jersey Historical Society, 1982.

Boardman, Roger Sherman. *Roger Sherman: Signer and Statesman*. New York: Da Capo Press, 1971.

Bobrick, Benson. *Angel in the Whirlwind: The Triumph of the American Revolution*. New York: Penguin Books, 1997.

Boutell, Lewis Henry. *The Life of Roger Sherman*. Chicago: A. C. McClurg and Co., 1896.

Bowen, Catherine Drinker. *John Adams and the American Revolution*. Boston: Little, Brown and Co., 1950.

Bowman, Allen. *The Morale of the American Revolution*. Washington, D.C.: American Council on Public Affairs, 1943.

Brands, H. W. *The First American: The Life and Times of Benjamin Franklin*. New York: Anchor Books, 2000.

Brecher, Frank W. *Securing American Independence: John Jay and the French Alliance*. Westport, Conn.: Praeger, 2003.

Breen, T. H. *The Marketplace of Revolution: How Consumer Politics Shaped American Independence*. New York: Oxford University Press, 2004.

Brookhiser, Richard. *Founding Father: Rediscovering George Washington*. New York: Free Press, 1996.

Carlyle, Thomas. *The French Revolution: A History*. 1906. Reprint, New York: Modern Library, 2002.

Carp, E. Wayne. *To Starve the Army at Pleasure: Continental Army Administration and American Political Culture 1775–1783*. Chapel Hill: University of North Carolina Press, 1984.

Cash, Arthur H. *John Wilkes: The Scandalous Father of Civil Liberty*. New Haven: Yale University Press, 2005.

Chernow, Ron. *Alexander Hamilton*. New York: Penguin Press, 2004.

Clark, Geoffrey. *Betting on Lives: The Culture of Life Insurance in England, 1695–1775*. Manchester, U.K.: Manchester University Press, 1999.

Clark, George L. *Silas Deane: A Connecticut Leader in the American Revolution*. New York: G. P. Putnam's Sons, 1913.

Clark, Ronald W. *Benjamin Franklin*. New York: Random House, 1983.

Collier, Christopher. *Roger Sherman's Connecticut: Yankee Politics and the American Revolution*. Middletown, Conn.: Wesleyan University Press, 1971.

Cook, Fred J. *Dawn over Saratoga: The Turning Point of the Revolutionary War*. Garden City, N.Y.: Doubleday, 1973.

Corwin, Edward S. *French Policy and the American Alliance of 1778*. Hamden, Conn.: Archon Books, 1962.

Coryn, Marjorie. *The Chevalier d'Eon, 1728–1810*. London: Frederick A. Stokes, 1932.

Cox, Cynthia. *The Enigma of the Age: The Strange Story of the Chevalier d'Eon*. London: Longmans, 1966.

Cronin, Vincent. *Louis and Antoinette*. New York: William Morrow, 1975.

Cuneo, John R. *The Battles of Saratoga: The Turning of the Tide*. New York: Macmillan, 1967.

Cuthbertson, Brian C. *The Loyalist Governor: Biography of Sir John Wentworth*. Halifax, Nova Scotia: Patheric Press, 1983.

Dalsème, René. *Beaumarchais, 1732–1799*. Translated by Hannaford Bennett. New York and London: G. P. Putnam's Sons, 1929.

Davidson, James West, and Mark Hamilton Lytle. *After the Fact: The Art of Historical Detection*. New York: Knopf, 1986.

Donvez, Jacques L. *La politique de Beaumarchais*. 6 vols. Thése pour le Doctorat d'Etat. Paris: J. Donvez, 1978.

Draper, Theodore. *A Struggle for Power: The American Revolution*. New York: Random House, 1996.

Dull, Jonathan R. *A Diplomatic History of the American Revolution*. New Haven: Yale University Press, 1985.

Durand, John. *New Materials for the History of the American Revolution*. New York: Henry Holt and Co., 1889.

Einstein, Lewis. *Divided Loyalties: Americans in England During the War of Independence*. Freeport, N.Y.: Books for Libraries Press, 1933.

Ellis, Joseph J. *His Excellency: George Washington*. New York: Knopf, 2004.

———. *American Creation: Triumphs and Tragedies at the Founding of the Republic*. New York: Knopf, 2007.

Fellows, John. *The Veil Removed; or Reflections on David Humphreys' Essay on the Life of Israel*. New York: J.D. Lockwood, 1843.

Ferguson, E. James. *The Power of the Purse: A History of American Public Finance, 1776–1790*. Chapel Hill: University of North Carolina Press, 1961.

Ferling, John. *John Adams: A Life*. New York: Henry Holt and Co., 1996.

———. *A Leap in the Dark: The Struggle to Create the American Republic*. New York: Oxford University Press, 2003.

———, ed. *The World Turned Upside Down: The American Victory in the War of Independence*. Westport, Conn.: Greenwood Press, 1988.

Flexner, James Thomas. *George Washington in the American Revolution, 1775–1783*. Boston: Little, Brown, 1967.

———. *Washington: The Indispensable Man*. Boston: Little, Brown, 1974.

Foner, Eric. *Tom Paine and Revolutionary America*. New York: Oxford University Press, 1976.

———. *The Story of American Freedom*. New York: Norton, 1998.

Ford, Thomas K., ed. *The Blacksmith in Eighteenth-Century Williamsburg*. Williamsburg, Va.: Colonial Williamsburg Foundation, 1971.

Freeman, Douglas Southall. *George Washington*. 7 vols. New York: Charles Scribner's Sons, 1951.

Furneaux, Rupert. *The Battle of Saratoga*. New York: Stein and Day, 1971.

Gaillardet, Frédéric. *The Memoirs of Chevalier d'Eon*. Translated by Antonia White. London: Anthony Blond Ltd., 1970.

Gaines, James R. *For Liberty and Glory: Washington, Lafayette, and Their Revolutions*. New York: Norton, 2007.

Gerlach, Don R. *Philip Schuyler and the American Revolution in New York, 1733–1777*. Lincoln: University of Nebraska Press, 1964.

Gerlach, Larry R. "The Connecticut Delegates and the Continental Congress:

From Confederation to Constitution, 1774–1789." Graduate thesis, University of Nebraska, 1965.

Gill, Harold B., Jr. *The Blacksmith in Colonial Virginia*. Williamsburg, Va.: Colonial Williamsburg Foundation, 1965.

Grendel, Frédéric. *Beaumarchais: The Man Who Was Figaro*. Translated by Roger Greaves. New York: Thomas Y. Crowell, 1973.

Gross, Robert A. *The Minutemen and Their World*. New York: Hill & Wang, 1976.

Gudin de La Brenellerie, Paul-Philippe. *Histoire de Beaumarchais*. Paris: E. Plon Nouritte, 1888.

Hamon, Joseph. *Le Chevalier de Bonvouloir: Premier émissaire secret de la France auprès du Congrès de Philadelphie avant l'indépendance américaine*. Paris: Jouve, 1953.

Hatch, Louis Clinton. *The Administration of the American Revolutionary Army*. New York: Longmans, Green, and Co., 1904.

Hazard, Blanche Evans. *Beaumarchais and the American Revolution*. Boston: Edwin L. Slocomb, 1910.

Hendrick, Burton J. *The Lees of Virginia: Biography of a Family*. Boston: Little, Brown and Co., 1935.

Hibbert, Christopher. *Redcoats and Rebels*. New York: Norton, 1990.

Higginbotham, Don. *The War of American Independence: Military Attitudes, Policies, and Practice, 1763–1789*. New York: Macmillan, 1971.

———, ed. *Reconsiderations on the Revolutionary War: Selected Essays*. Westport, Conn.: Greenwood, 1978.

Homberg, Octave, and Fernand Jousselin. *D'Eon de Beaumont: His Life and Times*. Translated by Alfred Rieu. London: Martin Secker, 1911.

Home, Gordon, and Cecil Headlam. *The Inns of Court*. London: Adam and Charles Black, 1909.

Horton, James Oliver, and Lois E. Horton. *In Hope of Liberty: Culture, Community, and Protest Among Northern Free Blacks, 1700–1860*. New York: Oxford University Press, 1997.

Ingpen, Arthur Robert, ed. *Master Worsley's Book on the History and Constitution of the Honourable Society of the Middle Temple*. 1910. Reprint, London: Gaunt, 2003.

Isaacson, Walter. *Benjamin Franklin*. New York: Simon & Schuster, 2003.

James, Alfred Proctor. *George Mercer of the Ohio Company: A Study in Frustration*. Pittsburgh: University of Pittsburgh Press, 1963.

James, Coy Hilton. *Silas Deane: Patriot or Traitor?* East Lansing: Michigan State University Press, 1975.

Jellison, Charles A. *Ethan Allen: Frontier Rebel*. Syracuse, N.Y.: Syracuse University Press, 1969.

Johnson, Steven. *The Ghost Map: The Story of London's Most Terrifying Epidemic—And How It Changed Science, Cities, and the Modern World*. New York: Riverhead Books, 2006.

Kates, Gary. *Monsieur d'Eon Is a Woman: A Tale of Political Intrigue and Sexual Masquerade*. Baltimore: Johns Hopkins University Press, 1995.

Ketchum, Richard M. *Saratoga: Turning Point of America's Revolutionary War*. New York: Henry Holt, 1997.

Kingsley, James Luce. *A Sketch of the History of Yale College, in Connecticut*. Boston: Perkins, Marvin & Co., 1835.

Kite, Elizabeth S. *Beaumarchais and the War of American Independence*. Vols. 1 and 2. Boston: R. G. Badger, 1918.

Knollenberg, Bernhard. *Growth of the American Revolution: 1766–1775*. New York: Free Press, 1975.

Kronenberger, Louis. *The Extraordinary Mr. Wilkes: His Life and Times*. Garden City, N.Y.: Doubleday, 1974.

Langguth, A. J. *Patriots: The Men Who Started the American Revolution*. New York: Simon & Schuster, 1988.

Lee, Richard Henry. *The Life of Arthur Lee*. Boston, 1829.

Lemaître, Georges. *Beaumarchais*. New York: Knopf, 1949.

Lever, Maurice. *Pierre-Augustin Caron de Beaumarchais*. Vol. 1, *L'irrésistible ascension (1732–1774)*. Paris: Fayard, 1999. (In Notes, cited as: *Beaumarchais I*.)

———. *Pierre-Augustin Caron de Beaumarchais*. Vol. 2, *Le Citoyen D'Amérique*. Paris: Fayard, 2003. (In Notes, cited as: *Beaumarchais II*.)

———. *Beaumarchais: A Biography*. Translated by Susan Emanuel. New York: Farrar, Straus, and Giroux, 2009. (In Notes, cited as: *Beaumarchais*.)

Lewis, George E. *The Indiana Company, 1763–1798: A Study in Eighteenth Century Frontier Land Speculation and Business Venture*. Glendale, Calif.: Arthur H. Clark, 1941.

Lewis, Paul. *The Grand Incendiary: A Biography of Samuel Adams*. New York: Dial Press, 1971.

Livingston, William Farrand. *Israel Putnam: Pioneer, Ranger, and Major-General, 1718–1790*. New York: G. P. Putnam's Sons, 1905.

Loménie, Louis de. *Beaumarchais and His Times*. Translated by Henry S. Edwards. New York: Harper & Brothers, 1857.

Lossing, Benson J. *The Life and Times of Philip Schuyler*. Vols. 1 and 2. New York: Henry Holt and Co., 1883.

McCullough, David. *John Adams*. New York: Simon & Schuster, 2001.

———. *1776*. New York: Simon & Schuster, 2005.

McGaughy, J. Kent. *Richard Henry Lee of Virginia: A Portrait of an American Revolutionary*. Lanham, Md.: Rowman & Littlefield, 2004.

Mackesy, Piers. *The War for America, 1775–1783*. Cambridge, Mass.: Harvard University Press, 1964.

Maier, Pauline. *The Old Revolutionaries: Political Lives in the Age of Samuel Adams*. New York: Norton, 1980.

Mayo, Lawrence Shaw. *John Wentworth: Governor of New Hampshire, 1767–1775*. Cambridge, Mass.: Harvard University Press, 1921.

———. *John Langdon of New Hampshire*. Port Washington, N.Y.: Kennikat Press, 1937.

Merrick, Jeffrey, and Michael Sibalis, eds. *Homosexuality in French History and Culture*. New York: Haworth Press, 2001.

Middlekauff, Robert. *The Glorious Cause: The American Revolution, 1763–1789*. Oxford: Oxford University Press, 1982.

———. *Benjamin Franklin and His Enemies*. Berkeley: University of California Press, 1996.

Miller, John C. *Sam Adams, Pioneer in Propaganda*. Stanford: Stanford University Press, 1960.

Millett, Allan R., and Peter Maslowski. *For the Common Defense: A Military History of the United States of America*. New York: Free Press, 1984.

Mitchell, Joseph. *Discipline and Bayonets*. New York: G. P. Putnam's Sons, 1967.

Monaghan, Frank. *John Jay: Defender of Liberty Against Kings and Peoples*. New York: Bobbs-Merrill Co., 1935.

Morison, Samuel Eliot. *John Paul Jones*. New York: Atlantic Monthly Press, 1959.

Morris, Richard B. *The Peacemakers: The Great Powers and American Independence*. New York: Harper & Row, 1965.

Morton, Brian N., and Donald C. Spinelli. *Beaumarchais and the American Revolution*. New York: Lexington Books, 2003.

Murphy, Orville T. *Charles Gravier, Comte de Vergennes: French Diplomacy in the Age of Revolution: 1719–1787*. Albany: State University of New York Press, 1982.

Nelson, Paul David. *General Horatio Gates*. Baton Rouge: Louisiana State University Press, 1976.

Nixon, Edna. *Royal Spy: The Strange Case of the Chevalier D'Eon*. New York: Reynal, 1965.

Palmer, David Richard. *The Way of the Fox: American Strategy in the War for America 1750–1783*. Westport, Conn.: Greenwood Press, 1975.

Patton, Robert H. *Patriot Pirates: The Privateer War for Freedom and Fortune in the American Revolution*. New York: Pantheon Books, 2008.

Pearce, Robert R. *A History of the Inns of Court and Chancery*. London: Richard Bentley, 1848.

Peckham, Howard H. *The War for Independence: A Military History*. Chicago: University of Chicago Press, 1958.

Petitfils, Jean-Christian. *Louis XVI*. Paris: Perrin, 2005.

Phillips, Paul Chrisler. *The West in the Diplomacy of the American Revolution*. 1913. Reprint, New York: Russell & Russell, 1967.

Postgate, Raymond. *That Devil Wilkes*. London: Penguin, 2001.

Potts, Louis W. *Arthur Lee: A Virtuous Revolutionary*. Baton Rouge: Louisiana State University Press, 1981.

Price, Munro. *Preserving the Monarchy: The Comte de Vergennes, 1774–1787*. Cambridge: Cambridge University Press, 1995.

Proschwitz, Gunnar von, and Mavis von Proschwitz. *Beaumarchais et le Courier de l'Europe: Documents inédits ou peu connus*, vols. 1–2. Oxford: Voltaire Foundation at the Taylor Institute, University of Oxford, 1990.

Quarles, Benjamin. *The Negro in the American Revolution*. New York: Norton Library, 1973.

Rakove, Jack N. *The Beginnings of National Politics: An Interpretative History of the Continental Congress*. New York: Alfred A. Knopf, 1979.

Randall, Willard Steme. *A Little Revenge: Benjamin Franklin & His Son*. Boston: Little, Brown, 1984.

———. *Benedict Arnold: Patriot and Traitor*. New York: William Morrow, 1990.

Risch, Erna. *Supplying Washington's Army*. Washington, D.C.: Center of Military History, U.S. Army, 1981.

Royster, Charles. *A Revolutionary People at War: The Continental Army and American Character, 1775–1783*. Chapel Hill: University of North Carolina Press, 1979.

———. *The Fabulous History of the Dismal Swamp Company: A Story of George Washington's Times*. New York: Knopf, 1999.

Rudé, George. *Wilkes and Liberty: A Social Study of 1763 to 1774*. Oxford: Clarendon Press, 1962.

Ruskin, Ariane. *Spy for Liberty: The Adventurous Life of Beaumarchais: Playwright and Secret Agent for the American Revolution*. New York: Pantheon Books, 1965.

Sainsbury, John. *Disaffected Patriots: London Supporters of Revolutionary America, 1769–1782*. Montreal: McGill-Queen's University Press, 1987.

Schama, Simon. *Citizens: A Chronicle of the French Revolution*. New York: Knopf, 1989.

Schiff, Stacy. *A Great Improvisation: Franklin, France, and the Birth of America*. New York: Henry Holt, 2005.

Schoenbrun, David. *Triumph in Paris: The Exploits of Benjamin Franklin*. New York: Harper & Row, 1976.

Sherrard, O. A. *A Life of John Wilkes*. London: George Allen & Unwin, 1930.

Sosin, Jack M. *Agents and Merchants: British Colonial Policy and the Origins of the American Revolution, 1763–1775*. Lincoln: University of Nebraska Press, 1965.

Srodes, James. *Franklin: The Essential Founding Father*. Washington, D.C.: Regnery Publishing, 2002.

Stahr, Walter. *John Jay: Founding Father*. New York: Hambledon and London, 2005.

Stinchcombe, William C. *The American Revolution and the French Alliance*. Syracuse, N.Y.: Syracuse University Press, 1969.

Stockdale, Eric, and Randy J. Holland. *Middle Temple Lawyers and the American Revolution*. Eagan, Minn.: Thomson, 2007.

Stourzh, Gerald. *Benjamin Franklin and American Foreign Policy*. 2d edition. Chicago: University of Chicago Press, 1969.

Straus, Ralph. *Lloyd's: The Gentlemen at the Coffee-House*. Whitefish, Mont.: Kessinger Publishing, 2008.

Tarbox, Increase N. *Life of Israel Putnam ("Old Put"), Major-General in the Continental Army*. Boston: Lockwood, Brooks, and Co., 1876.

Telfer, J. Buchan. *The Strange Career of the Chevalier D'Eon de Beaumont*. London: Longmans, Green and Co., 1885.

Thomas, Evan. *John Paul Jones: Sailor, Hero, Father of the American Navy*. New York: Simon & Schuster, 2003.

Thomas, Peter D. G. *John Wilkes: A Friend to Liberty*. Oxford: Clarendon Press, 1996.

Trench, Charles Chenevix. *Portrait of a Patriot: A Biography of John Wilkes*. London: William Blackwood & Sons, 1962.

Trevelyan, George Otto. *The American Revolution*. New York: David Mckay Co., 1966.

Tuchman, Barbara. *The First Salute*. New York: Knopf, 1988.

Tuckerman, Bayaerd. *Life of General Philip Schuyler: 1733–1804*. New York: Dodd, Mead & Co., 1903.

Unger, Harlow Giles. *Lafayette*. Hoboken, N.J: Wiley, 2002.

Van Doren, Carl. *Secret History of the American Revolution: An Account of the Conspiracies of Benedict Arnold and Numerous Others*. New York: Viking Press, 1941.

———. *Benjamin Franklin*. New York: Penguin, 1991.

Vizetelly, Ernest Alfred. *The True Story of the Chevalier D'Eon.* London: Tylston & Edwards, 1895.

Wagner, Frederick. *Robert Morris: Audacious Patriot.* New York: Dodd, Mead, 1976.

Warner, Jessica. *John the Painter: Terrorist of the American Revolution.* New York: Thunder Mouth Press, 2004.

Warren, Mercy Otis. *History of the Rise, Progress and Termination of the American Revolution.* Edited by Lester H. Cohen. 2 vols. Indianapolis: Liberty Fund, Inc., 1994.

Webber, Ronald. *The Village Blacksmith.* New York: Great Albion Books, 1971.

Wilderson, Paul W. *Governor John Wentworth and the American Revolution: The English Connection.* Hanover, N.H.: University of New England, 1994.

Williamson, Audrey. *Wilkes: A Friend to Liberty.* New York: E. P. Dutton & Co., 1974.

Williamson, J. Bruce. *The History of the Temple, London.* 1924. Reprint, London: Gaunt, Inc., 1998.

Wolf, Stephanie Grauman. *As Various As Their Land.* New York: HarperCollins, 1993.

Wood, Gordon S. *The Creation of the American Republic, 1776–1787.* New York: Norton, 1972.

———. *The American Revolution.* New York: Modern Library, 2002.

———. *The Americanization of Benjamin Franklin.* New York: Penguin, 2004.

Worsley, Frank Arthur, and Glynn Griffith. *The Romance of Lloyd's: From Coffee House to Palace.* London: Hillman-Curl, Inc., 1936.

Wright, Charles, and C. Ernest Fayle. *A History of Lloyd's from the Founding of Lloyd's Coffee House to the Present Day.* London: Macmillan and Co., 1928.

Wright, Robert K., Jr. *The Continental Army.* Washington, D.C.: Center of Military History, U.S. Army, 1983.

York, Neil L. *Burning the Dockyard: John the Painter and the American Revolution.* Portsmouth, U.K.: Portsmouth City Council, 2001.

SELECTED ARTICLES

Abernathy, T. P. "Commercial Activities of Silas Deane in France." *American Historical Review* 39, no. 3 (1934): 477–85.

Aldridge, Alfred Owen. "Thomas Paine and Comus." *Pennsylvania Magazine of History and Biography* 85, no. 1 (1961): 70–75.

Alvord, Clarence W. "Virginia and the West: An Interpretation." *The Mississippi Valley Historical Review* 3, no. 1 (1916): 19–38.

Anderson, Dennis Kent, and Godfrey Tryggve Anderson. "Edward Bancroft, M.D., F.R.S., Aberrant Practioner of Physick." *Medical History* 17, no. 4 (1973): 356–57.

———. "The Death of Silas Deane: Another Opinion." *New England Quarterly* 57 (1984): 98–105.

Bemis, Samuel Flagg. "The British Secret Service and the French-American Alliance." *American Historical Review* 29, no. 3 (1924): 474–95.

Blanc, Olivier. "The 'Italian Taste' in the Time of Louis XVI, 1774–1792." In *Homosexuality in French History and Culture,* edited by Jeffrey Merrick and Michael Sibalis. New York: Haworth Press, 2001.

Bloom, Richard. "Silas Deane: Patriot or Renegade?" *American History Illustrated* (November 1978): 33–42.

Boyd, Julian P. "Silas Deane: Death by a Kindly Teacher of Treason?" *The William and Mary Quarterly* 16, no. 2 (1959): 165–87; no. 3 (1959): 319–42; no. 4 (1959): 515–50.

Carter, Clarence E. "Documents Relating to the Mississippi Land Company, 1763–1769." *The American Historical Review* 16, no. 2 (1911): 311–19.

Cheney, Paul. "A False Dawn for Enlightenment Cosmopolitanism? Franco-American Trade During the American War of Independence." *The William and Mary Quarterly* 63, no. 3 (2006): 463–88.

Clark, Anna. "The Chevalier d'Eon and Wilkes: Masculinity and Politics in the Eighteenth Century." *Eighteenth-Century Studies* 32, no. 1 (1998): 19–49.

Clark, William Bell. "John the Painter." *The Pennsylvania Magazine of History and Biography* 63, no. 1 (1939): 1–23.

Conlin, Jonathan G. W. "High Art and Low Politics: A New Perspective on John Wilkes." *Huntington Library Quarterly* 64, nos. 3–4 (2001): 357–81.

———. "Wilkes, the Chevalier d'Eon and 'the Dregs of Liberty': An Anglo-French Perspective on Ministerial Despotism, 1762–1771." *English Historical Review* 120, no. 489 (2005): 1251–88.

Daniels, Christine. "Wanted: A Blacksmith Who Understands Plantation Work: Artisans in Maryland." *The William and Mary Quarterly* 50, no. 4 (1993): 743–67.

Destler, Chester McArthur. "Barnabas Deane and the Barnabas Deane & Company." *Bulletin of The Connecticut Historical Society* 35, no. 1 (1970): 7–19.

Ferguson, E. James, and Elizabeth Miles Nuxoll. "Investigation of Government Corruption During the American Revolution." *Congressional Studies* 8, no. 2 (1981): 13–35.

Fiske, John. "The French Alliance and the Conway Cabal." *Atlantic Monthly* 64 (1889): 220–39.

Fraser, John A., III. "The Use of Encrypted, Coded, and Secret Communications Is an 'Ancient Liberty' Protected by the United States Constitution." *Virginia Journal of Law & Technology* 2 (1997): 2–40.

Gerlach, Larry R. "Firmness and Prudence: Connecticut, the Continental Congress, and the National Domain, 1776–1786." *The Connecticut Historical Society Bulletin* 31, no. 3 (1966): 65–73.

———. "A Delegation of Steady Habits: The Connecticut Representatives to the Continental Congress, 1774–1789." *The Connecticut Historical Society Bulletin* 32, no. 2 (1967): 33–39.

Goldstein, Kalman. "Silas Deane: Preparation for Rascality." *The Historian* 43, no. 1 (1980): 75–97.

Hausmann, Albert. "Doctor of Duplicity." *Yankee Magazine* July (1975): 78–87.

Hayden, Ralston. "The Apostasy of Silas Deane." *The Magazine of History* 26, no. 3 (1913): 95–103.

Hendrick, Burton J. "America's First Ambassador." *The Atlantic Monthly* 156, no. 3 (1935): 137–48.

———. "Worse Than Arnold." *The Atlantic Monthly* 156, no. 4 (1935): 385–95.

Hoadley, Charles J. "Silas Deane." *The Pennsylvania Magazine of History and Biography* 1, no. 1 (1877): 96–100.

Holton, Woody. "The Ohio Indians and the Coming of the American Revolution in Virginia." *The Journal of Southern History* 60, no. 3 (1994): 453–78.

Kulikoff, Allan. "The Progress of Inequality in Revolutionary Boston." *The William and Mary Quarterly* 28, no. 3 (1971): 375–412.

Lander, James. "A Tale of Two Hoaxes in Britain and France in 1775." *The Historical Journal* 49, no. 4 (2006): 995–1024.

Marshall, Peter. "Lord Hillsborough, Samuel Wharton and the Ohio Grant, 1769–1775." *The English Historical Review* 80, no. 317 (1965): 717–39.

Meng, John J. "A Footnote to Secret Aid in the American Revolution." *The American Historical Review* 43, no. 4 (1938): 791–95.

Morgan, Edmund S. "Ezra Stiles: The Education of a Yale Man, 1742–1746." *The Huntington Library Quarterly* 18, no. 3 (1954): 251–68.

Nelson, Paul David. "Legacy of Controversy: Gates, Schuyler, and Arnold at Saratoga, 1777." *Military Affairs* 37, no. 2 (1973): 41–47.

Peabody, Oliver W. B. "Israel Putnam." In *American Biography*, vol. 3, edited by Jared Sparks. New York: Harper & Brothers, 1902.

Potofsky, Allan. "The Political Economy of the French-American Debt Debate: The Ideological Uses of Atlantic Commerce, 1787 to 1800." *The William and Mary Quarterly* 63, no. 3 (2006): 489–516.

Rakove, Jack N. "French Diplomacy and American Politics: The First Crisis, 1779." *Mid-America* 60 (1978): 27–35.

Redford, Phyllis H. "The Troubles of Silas Deane." *New England Galaxy* 13, no. 3 (1972): 12–20.

Riggs, A. R. "Arthur Lee: A Radical Virginian in London, 1768–1776." *The Virginia Magazine* 78, no. 3 (1970): 268–80.

Sainsbury, John. "The Pro-Americans of London, 1769–1782." *The William and Mary Quarterly* 35, no. 3 (1978): 423.

Sheridan, Richard B. "The British Credit Crisis of 1772 and the American Colonies." *The Journal of Economic History* 20, no. 2 (1960): 161–86.

Spinelli, Donald C. "Beaumarchais and d'Eon: What a Relationship." Unpublished paper presented at University of Leeds conference *The Chevalier d'Eon and His Worlds*, April 20, 2006.

Stearns, Raymond Phineas. "Colonial Fellows of the Royal Society of London, 1661–1788." *The William and Mary Quarterly* 3, no. 2 (1946): 208–68.

Stephenson, Orlando W. "The Supply of Gunpowder in 1776." *The American Historical Review* 30, no. 2 (1925): 271–81.

Stillé, Charles J. "Beaumarchais and the Lost Million." *Pennsylvania Magazine of History and Biography* 11 (1887): 1–36.

Stinchcombe, William. "A Note on Silas Deane's Death." *The William and Mary Quarterly* 32, no. 4 (1975): 619–24.

Trumbull, J. Hammond. "A Business Firm in the Revolution: Barnabas Deane & Co." *Magazine of American History* 12 (1884): 17–28.

Van Tyne, C. H. "Influences Which Determined the French Government to Make the Treaty with America, 1778." *The American Historical Review* 21, no. 3 (1916): 528–41.

———. "French Aid Before the Alliance of 1778." *The American Historical Review* 31, no. 1 (1925): 20–40.

Whitridge, Arnold. "Beaumarchais and the American Revolution." *History Today* 17, no. 2 (1967): 98–105.

INDEX